1994

TEXT

T E X T

Transactions of the Society for Textual Scholarship

6

Edited by

D. C. GREETHAM   *and*   W. SPEED HILL

PETER L. SHILLINGSBURG

Book Review Editor

AMS PRESS
NEW YORK

T E X T

Transactions of the Society
for Textual Scholarship

COPYRIGHT © 1994 by AMS PRESS, INC.

INTERNATIONAL STANDARD BOOK NUMBER

Set: 0-404-62550-9

Volume 6: 0-404-62556-8

INTERNATIONAL STANDARD SERIALS NUMBER
0736-3974

All AMS books are printed on acid-free paper that meets the guidelines for performance and durability of the Committee on Production Guidelines for Book Longevity of the Council on Library Resources.

AMS PRESS
56 East 13th Street
New York, N. Y. 10003, U.S.A.

Manufactured in the United States of America

In Memory

of

Fredson Bowers

President, Society for Textual Scholarship, 1985–87

Contents

Notes on Contributors

JOHN V. ANTUSH, Associate Professor of English at Fordham University, has edited three volumes of plays by Puerto Ricans living in New York. The most recent volume is scheduled to be published by Penguin USA in March, 1994. He has also published several critical articles about these plays. He is presently writing a book-length critical study of the New York Puerto Rican playwrights.

BETTY T. BENNETT is Dean of the College of Arts and Sciences and Professor of Literature at The American University. She is editor of *The Letters of Mary Wollstonecraft Shelley* (three volumes, 1980, 1983, 1988), co-editor of *The Mary Shelley Reader* (1990),and author of *Mary Diana Dods: A Gentleman and a Scholar* (1991).

FREDSON BOWERS was Linden Kent Professor of Literature Emeritus at the University of Virginia until his death in 1991.

JO ANN BOYDSTON, Distinguished Professor Emerita at Southern Illinois University, is editor of the thirty-seven volume edition, *The Collected Works of John Dewey*. From 1961 to 1993, she was Director of the Center for Dewey Studies; she was chair of the Modern Language Association,Committee on Scholarly Editions from 1989 to 1992.

ALAN C. DOOLEY is Professor of English and a Fellow of the Institute for Bibliography and Editing at Kent State University. He serves as Executive Editor of *The Complete Works of Robert Browning* and is the author of *Author and Printer in Victorian England*.

RICHARD J. FINNERAN, Hodges Chair of Excellence Professor at the University of Tennessee, Knoxville, is Series Editor for the Poems in the Cornell Yeats and co-General Editor of the Collected Edition of the Works of W.B. Yeats.

JOHN H. FISHER, student and editor of Chaucer's works, Chancery documents, and other Middle English literature, taught at New York University, Duke University, and Indiana University, and retired in 1988 from the University of Tennessee in Knoxville. For ten years he served as Executive Secretary of the Modern Language Association and for another ten as Executive Director of the New Chaucer Society.

MICHAEL GRODON,Professor of English at the University of Western Ontario, is co-editor of the *Johns Hopkins Guide to Literary Theory and Criticism* and author of books and articles on textual and literary theory and on James Joyce.

W. SPEED HILL teaches at Lehman College and The Graduate School of CUNY. Besides co-editing *TEXT*, he is general editor of *The Folger Library Edition of the Works of Richard Hooker*, volume 6 of which will appear in September 1993, and recently edited a collection of essays for RETS, *New Ways of Looking at Old Texts: Papers of the Renaissance English Text Society 1985–1991*.

CHRISTOPHER Z. HOBSON, a Ph.D. candidate at the City University of New York Graduate Center, teaches literature at Hunter College. He is the author of articles on Blake's *The Four Zoas* (*SEL*, 1993) and Shakespeare's *King John* (*Shakespeare Yearbook*, 1991), and co-author of a study in political science, *Trotskyism and the Dilemma of Socialism* (with Ronald D. Tabor; 1988).

MARY-JO KLINE is editor of the *Political Correspondence and Public Papers of Aaron Burr* (two volumes, 1983) and author of *A Guide to Documentary Editing* (1987).

RICHARD KNOWLES, Dickson-Bascom Professor in the Humanities at the University of Wisconsin—Madison, is co-general editor of the New Variorum Edition of Shakespeare and is completing the volume on *King Lear* in that series.

TIM WILLIAM MACHAN has edited works in Latin, Old French, Middle English, and Old Norse, and is the author of scholarly articles and books on textual criticism, including the anthology *Medieval Literature: Texts and Interpretation* (1991) and the critical study *Textual Criticism and Middle English Texts* (1994).

JOHN H. MIDDENDORF is Professor Emeritus of English at Columbia University, Editor Emeritus of the *Johnsonian News Letter*, and General Editor of the Yale Edition of the Works of Samuel Johnson.

JOEL MYERSON, Professor of English at the University of South Carolina, edits the annual *Studies in the American Renaissance* and is the author of the forthcoming book *Walt Whitman: A Descriptive Bibliography*.

DAVID J. NORDLOH, Professor of English and Director of the Graduate Program in American Studies, Indiana University, is also general editor and textual editor of "A Selected Edition of W.D. Howells."

MARIA GRAZIA PERNIS received a Ph.D. with distinction from Columbia University in 1990. Her interdisciplinary thesis "Ficino's Platonism and the Court of Urbino: The History of Ideas and the History of Art" reflects her interest in humanistic literature, Neoplatonic philosophy, and art history. She taught at CUNY Graduate School in the Fall 1992. She co-organized the Symposium "Facets of Piero della Francesca" held in

New York in February 1993. She has lectured, published articles, and is currently writing a book on Italian Renaissance art and patronage.

C. DEIRDRE PHELPS, who received her Ph.D. in English from Boston University in May 1993, has devoted the last twenty years to exploring every facet of American book and text history. After an A.B. in English and several years in textbook publishing design and project management, she became involved in printing history with the American Printing History Association, and acquired a degree in library science at Columbia University, concentrating in rare books and bibliography, and studying textual criticism with G. Thomas Tanselle. To expand the study of the physical book into cultural and critical areas, she then took master's degrees in history and English at Boston University, where she was a University Fellow. She has published various articles on American printing and publishing history, and is currently writing on authorship in New York in the 1830s.

DONALD H. REIMAN, Co-Editor of *Shelley and his Circle*, is also Editor-in-Chief of *The Bodleian Shelley Manuscripts* and *The Manuscripts of the Younger Romantics*. Among his recent books are *Romantic Texts and Contexts* (1987), *The Harvard Shelley Poetic Manuscripts* (1991), and *The Study of Modern Manuscripts: Public, Confidential, and Private* (1993), which derives from his James P. R. Lyell Lectures in Bibliography, delivered at Oxford in 1989. Johns Hopkins will also publish in four volumes *The Complete Poetry of Percy Bysshe Shelley*, of which Dr. Reiman is the Co-Editor.

RONALD SCHUCHARD, Professor of English at Emory University, is the editor of T.S. Eliot's Clark and Turnbull Lectures, to be published by Faber and Faber in 1993 as *The Varieties of Metaphysical Poetry*, and co-editor with John Kelly of three volumes of *The Collected Letters of W.B. Yeats*.

JAMES THORPE is a Senior Research Associate at the Huntington Library, of which he was Director from 1966 to 1983. His textual studies include *Principles of Textual Criticism* (1972).

KARL UITTI, John N. Woodhull Chair in Modern Languages at Princeton University, specializes in Romance Languages and in the literature of the Middle Ages, with an emphasis on French. In addition to publishing a number of books in other fields, he is the author of *Story, Myth, and Celebration in Old French Literature (1050–1200)* (1972) and editor of a scholarly edition with a modern French translation of *Le Chevalier de la Charrett (Lancelot)* (1989).

JOHN W. VELZ is editor of *Julius Caesar* in the MLA New Variorum Shakespeare, and author of a number of articles on Renaissance texts and on problems of editing. He is also at work on a monograph on Shakespeare's adaptations of medieval dramatic forms; he lectured in 1993 on this subject in nine universities in Poland, Latvia, The Czech Republic, Austria, and Germany.

JAMES L.W. WEST III is Distinguished Professor of English at The Pennsylvania State University, where he directs the Penn State Center for the History of the Book. His new edition of Dreiser's *Jennie Gerhardt* has recently been published by the University of Pennsylvania Press.

JAMES WILLIS, Professor of English at the University of Western Australia until his retirement, is the author of *Latin Textual Criticism*.

HUGH WITEMEYER is Professor of English at the University of New Mexico. He is the author of *The Poetry of Ezra Pound: Forms and Renewal, 1908–1920* and *George Eliot and the Visual Arts*. He is the editor of *William Carlos Williams and James Laughlin: Selected Letters* and co-editor of *The Letters of William Carlos Williams and Charles Tomlinson*.

DAVID YERKES is Professor of English and Comparative Literature at Columbia University.

Introduction

With this volume, *Text* expands its coverage to include a review section, and we welcome Peter L. Shillingsburg as book review editor. This new section will offer a broad range of subjects and treatments: short reviews of individual editions or books on textual scholarship, reviews of multiple-volume editions or of several different but related editions, and review-articles covering either editions or text-critical studies or collections. We also plan to include lengthy surveys of recent textual and editorial work in particular periods, disciplines, or genres. We trust that the addition of reviews to *Text* will confirm the journal's growing status as the publication of record for interdisciplinary textual scholarship, for the cumulative effect of the review section should be to offer a descriptive and critical analysis of textual work in all the disciplines covered by STS. Textual scholars wishing to contribute to this coverage (either by having their books reviewed or by writing reviews) should get in touch with Peter Shillingsburg at Department of English, Mississippi State University, Starkville, MS 39762.

This volume is also special for one other reason: it contains the last independent publication by Fredson Bowers—an article on apparatus that was read by G. Thomas Tanselle at the 1991 STS conference, on the very day that Professor Bowers died. We like to feel that he would have wanted it no other way: that his latest work was reaching an intended audience even as his long career in the forefront of textual scholarship drew to a close. Indeed, the transmission of the conference paper (and now the article) offers one of those complex documentary histories to which he brought so much illumination in his work. Professor Bowers wrote the essay on his typewriter, producing ribbon and carbon copy. Fearing that his health would not allow him to read the paper in person, he sent off the ribbon copy to David Greetham for safe keeping. Unfortunately, this copy did not arrive, and despite a post office search was never recovered. Very shortly before the conference, Bowers's associate David Vander Meulen did manage to discover a carbon copy of the essay in Bowers's papers, but it was not clear what stage of composition this carbon represented (Bowers often made further changes on either ribbon or carbon copies after a first draft). Nonetheless, since this was the only document to which we had access, Vander Meulen faxed the carbon to Tanselle, who make additional clarifications in those parts of the essay that had suffered in transmission (for example, some letters had been lost in marginal words). This single document bearing the marks of multiple stages of composition was used in preparing copy for the article as it is now published. While the circumstances of its preservation and transmission cannot assure us that this published version represents Bowers's *final* intentions in every detail (obviously he had no chance to check the copyediting or to confirm that the carbon was of his latest draft), we like to think that he would have been amused by the story of how the essay survived the various accidents and of how it is the product of several different technical means of production.

And it is for this humor and the marks of his friendship for, and involvement with, the concerns of STS and *Text*, as well as for his enormous contributions to twentieth-century textual scholarship, that we dedicate this volume of *Text* to his memory. Fredson Bowers was President of the Society for Textual Scholarship from 1985 to 1987, spoke at its inaugural conference in 1981 and at all but one of the subsequent conferences until his death in 1991, and published several essays in *Text*. The measure of his support can be told by the fact that of his last dozen published essays (since his first for *Text* in our first volume), seven were for STS in one form or other (conference, journal, or both). As representatives of the interdisciplinary group to which he contributed so liberally in his later years, we express our thanks in the form of this dedication.

As usual, *Text* and the Society for Textual Scholarship are dependent on the co-operation and assistance of various persons and institutions. We are grateful to the members of the *Text* Advisory Board who read submissions to the journal, and to the members of the STS Executive Committee; to New York University (Mervin R. Dilts), Fordham University (Robert Penella), the Pierpont Morgan Library (Fredric W. Wilson), and to several administrators at the City University of New York Graduate Center: President Frances Degen Horowitz; Provost and Vice President for Academic Affairs, Geoffrey Marshall; Vice President for Public Affairs and Publications, Nanette Shaw, together with Carol Rackmales, and Barry Disman (Graphic Design) and George Wittig (Graphic Arts); the Executive Officer of the English Ph.D. Program, Joseph Wittreich, the Deputy Officer Richard C. McCoy and Program Assistant Lynn

Kadison; Chief Librarian Susan Newman and her staff; Dining Commons Manager Steve Katz; Room Reservations Coordinator Barbara Burkett; research assistants Adam Goldberger, Patrick Curran, Thane Doss, and Bonnie Walker; and numerous friendly faculty who agreed to chair conference panels and otherwise participate in the conferences from which the bulk of *Text* articles are drawn. To all we extend our thanks for having made this volume of *Text* possible.

D. C. Greetham
W. Speed Hill
Peter L. Shillingsburg

The Society for Textual Scholarship
April 12, 1991
Reflections on Our Craft

JAMES THORPE

When I first entered the academic profession, right after World War II, at Princeton, one of the first things that struck me was the mystique about titles of talks and essays. I formed the impression that, with a good title, all you had to do was explain what the title meant or could be made to mean, and you were done.

My friend Richard Blackmur was a master of this craft. With such a title for a literary essay as "The Lion and the Honeycomb" or "Heresy Within Heresy," or "The Double Agent," you were halfway home before you started. Indeed, the subtitle of one of his books was "Essays in Craft and Elucidation."

When another Richard, Richard Finneran, told me that I had to give him a title for this talk, I responded (in desperation) with "Reflections on Our Craft"—not knowing what it meant, but imagining that it could be made to mean something or other. I knew that you had all had several kinds of "reflections," and that you had perhaps practised several kinds of "craft." And that if necessary you could fill in the gaps of my discourse. So I appeal to your generosity for fulfillment. My sources tell me that only one person in our assembly is truly practised in the craft of *guile*, however, and that *that* person alone will not have a smile on his or her face while I tell you my story. So, if you would like to reveal yourself by not smiling, please be my guest.

What I want to try to do this evening is offer some historical reflections—on the genesis, perhaps—of the noble aim of the Society for Textual Scholarship. We were established in 1979 as a group of scholars for the interdisciplinary discussion of textual theory and practice. Our company includes those who are concerned with any form of the transmission of communication by means of a text, and those who practise our craft in any of the great variety of fields of specialization. Our beginnings go a long way back. I would like to say a little about how our present aims are related to the earliest tradition of textual scholarship.

I'm sure that we have all been told over and over again that textual scholarship is the most fundamental and the most ancient form of literary scholarship. Perhaps we swell with pride upon hearing these remarks. Or maybe we are the nearest thing in academia to the Primal Scream. (If we ever need to rename our organization, perhaps we could think about "The Primal Scream Society" as a possibility.)

When the full history of textual scholarship comes to be written, it will include many famous names from earlier centuries, like St. Augustine of Hippo, St. Jerome of Dalmatia, and Erasmus of Rotterdam. It will also include a few famous names that we do not usually associate with textual scholarship, like Aristotle.

And it will prominently include, from early centuries, a good many people who are not household names at all. Like Demetrios of Phaleron. And Zenodotus of Ephesus. And Callimachus of Cyrene. And Aristophanes of Byzantium. And Aristarchus of Samothrace. These five were all associated with the Museum and Library of Alexandria in Egypt, during the third and second centuries before Christ. And it is about the textual work at that institution at that time that I wish to speak this evening, because of the bearing that it has on our ideals of textual scholarship.

The City of Alexandria was established, you remember, at the direction of Alexander the Great in 331 B.C. right after he had, at the age of twenty-five, conquered Egypt from the Persians. Alexander stood there on an island at one of the deltas of the Nile and ordered that his capital city should be located in that area. Seven years later—after conquering Persia, India, and all the rest— he died in Babylon, at the age of thirty-two. But one of his Greek generals, reputedly his half-brother, Ptolemy, took over Egypt, built Alexandria, and established a dynasty that lasted for three centuries, until the death of Cleopatra in 30 B.C. after her intricate—and intimate—encounters with Caesar and Antony.

Within fifty years of its foundation, Alexandria was the most populous city in the world, with some 300,000 inhabitants. The number grew to one million by the first century B.C. Within ten years of its establishment, the Museum and the Library had 200,000 books in it—by far the largest collection that there had ever been in the world—and by the first century B.C. the number was over 700,000.

Alexandria was the greatest center of culture in the world of classical antiquity. It was a magnet for poets, scientists, mathematicians, and learned men of all sorts. The Ptolemies were very rich, and they established a center for these people in and around the royal quarter of Alexandria; they invited learned men to come, and they gave them salaries. We say that they had a Museum (a home for the Muses, literally) and a Library, and Halls of Learning. But in fact all of these activities were actually integrated in an intellectual center of Hellenic culture. Like a University, in the pure sense of the word.

What was going on there during the third and second centuries B.C., the time on which I wish us to focus our attention? Here's a sample. Among the geometricians, Euclid was doing all of his important work on the theory of numbers—and he ventured to tell Ptolemy I that there was not, even for the King, a "royal road" to geometry. Among the poets, Theocritus was writing his most mature poems of nature and love, conveying a nostalgic affection for life. Among the astronomers, Aristarchus of Samos was developing the idea that the sun was the center of the solar system. Among the geographers, Eratosthenes was making a scientific map of the globe, calculating the circumference of the earth to within 200 miles of the actual figure, and devising the calendar that was later to be called the Julian Calendar. Among the mathematicians and engineers, Archimedes was inventing a new form of mathematics, calculating the value of Pi, and reducing to theory the five basic simple machines. In medicine, the practitioners were able for the first time to dissect dead bodies (which was strictly prohibited in Greece)—and cutting up some live bodies as well—and establishing the sciences of anatomy and physiology, developing anaesthesia, distinguishing veins from arteries and motor from sensory nerves.

There were colonnades, walks, and seats in and around the Museum where (according to Vitruvius) scholars "who take delight in studies can engage in disputation." There was a dining hall for them in the Museum, and rooms and studies for the scholars.

It was in this kind of interdisciplinary context that the textual scholars of whom I wish to speak were carrying on their work. But before talking about their endeavors, let me first say a little about the collections they worked on and how those collections came to be so enormous.

The building up of the institution and its collections was the work of a series of scholars. First, Demetrios of Phaleron, a philosopher who had been for ten years the administrator of the city of Athens. Ptolemy got him to come to Alexandria in 307 B.C., and Demetrios planned the physical and intellectual structure of the Museum, the Library, the Halls of Learning, and the collections of books. Ptolemy told Demetrios to get, if possible, all the books in the world.

Demetrios started about his task as if it were the most perfectly natural thing in the world to do. He had Ptolemy write to his fellow rulers everywhere and ask them all to send him their books. At the instigation of Demetrios, dozens of agents were sent out all over the Mediterranean and Near Eastern world to buy books for the Royal Library at Alexandria. They were supplied with silver talents from the Egyptian treasury, and they bought everything they could lay their hands on, from private owners, from dealers, and from towns and cities that were willing to sell. The books were, of course, manuscripts on papyrus rolls. They were not easy to identify. If a title was given at all, it was at the end of the text, and only sometimes was a label stuck into one end of the roll. The agents bought without regard to subject, whatever they could get. No matter. They were carrying out their directions: get all the books in the world. Since the Ptolemies were rich and most of the rest of the world was poor, it is easy to see why the accumulation was so large, especially since the buying continued for a couple of centuries. Greek texts were their main desiderata, but they also acquired Babylonian, Hebrew, Egyptian, and Indian texts as well.

Those other books were often turned into Greek so that they could be made easily useful to the scholars at Alexandria. There is a very early tradition that Demetrios was responsible for the Septuagint, the translation into Greek of what we call the Old Testament. He got Ptolemy to ask the High Priest in Jerusalem to send scholars to Alexandria in about 285 B.C. with copies of their holy book. Seventy-two Rabbis were sent—six from each of the twelve tribes of Israel—with the Hebrew text. Hence the Septuagint, the work of the seventy (or seventy-two). (Some of these details are doubtless wrong, but the conclusion is right.) This translation has been the crucial text in the transmission of the Old Testament in western culture: it was the source of quotations by the writers of the New Testament, it was the basic Old Testament text for the early Christian church, and it is still the text of the Greek Orthodox Church.

When the agents went searching for books to buy for the Library at Alexandria, it mostly had to be a roll here and a roll there. There were relatively few books anywhere. One large collection was purchased, however, reputedly the most important early collection and perhaps the largest anywhere—Aristotle's library. When Aristotle died, he left his collection to his pupil Theophrastus, who was Demetrios's teacher. After Theophrastus's death, Demetrios got Ptolemy to buy the library from Theophrastus's heir and incorporate it into the Library at Alexandria.

Another notable acquisition was that of the official texts of the Greek tragedy writers, Aeschylus, Sophocles, and Euripides. In the middle of the fourth century B.C., Lycurgus had issued a decree in Athens to prepare an official copy of their works for deposit in the state archives. It was said that this copy was made with care on the basis of the earliest known copies; according to Galen, "probably from the manuscripts of the authors." Athenian actors were required to compare their performance texts with this official copy. Ptolemy borrowed this archival copy to be copied for the Library at Alexandria and left a deposit of silver talents (the current equivalent of perhaps $150,000) to guarantee its return. The manuscript was copied in Alexandria, all right, but Ptolemy returned the copy, keeping the original for his library and forfeiting the deposit.

The Ptolemies had other clever ways to increase the size of the Library. One was an embargo on all books in ships that entered the harbor at Alexandria. All vessels were searched, and all books were confiscated. Copies were made and given back to the owners, but the originals were retained for the Library.

When Demetrios died, early in the third century, his role as a collector and head scholar was taken over by a series of men who continued to expand the collection. And they began to use the collection, too. It is about their use of the collection, as textual scholars, that I now want to speak.

After Demetrios, Zenodotus of Ephesus became the head of the Library, in the early part of the third century. Zenodotus stands at the front of our mystery as the first real textual scholar and editor. He chose Homer as his subject. He was the first serious editor of Homer (or of any other writer) in that he tried to restore and present what he thought to be the genuine, original *Iliad* and *Odyssey*. To that end, he examined the various sources that had been assembled in Alexandria. Using these texts as his basis, he practised both recension and emendation: he selected, after reviewing all the evidence, what he took to be the most trustworthy basis for a text, and then he went through and tried to eliminate what he took to be errors of transmission. He marked lines that he thought spurious with a symbolic pointed obelus in the margin. And it was Zenodotus who first divided the *Iliad* and the *Odyssey* into twenty-four books, naming them after the letters of the Greek alphabet. And he also wrote an Homeric Glossary.

It is, of course, significant that the first Greek textual scholar should work on Homer. It would have been like a medieval Christian working on the Bible. Because Homer was central to Greek culture: Homer was the common text for students, the source for ceremonies and rituals, the noblest form of language, the font of knowledge and beauty and wisdom. You remember that when Alexander finished his three years as a pupil of Aristotle, the master gave him (according to the legend) a copy of Homer that Alexander carried with him on all of his military campaigns.

Come back to all those books collected at the Library at Alexandria—several hundred thousand after half a century and getting bigger all the time. Heaps of rolls, all stacked up in large halls, helter skelter. Every sort of thing, in duplicates, quintuplicates, no order, no catalog. As a textual scholar, what would you have done if you had wanted to use books of interest to you?

Callimachus of Cyrene did just that, in the middle of the third century. He began to sort them out and prepare lists of what was there. He was by profession a poet and epigram writer, and sixty-four of his epigrams are still extant, like this one: "They told me, Heraclitus, they told me you were dead." But he was also a member of the center at Alexandria, and he tried to put the books into some sort of usable order. He began drawing up what he called a "List of writers who have won fame in every branch of learning, and the books they wrote." This catalog—which is now lost and known only from references to it—ultimately (under his successors) ran to 120 volumes and included biographies and commentaries. The books were arranged by genre, in eight classes (drama, poetry, legislation, history, and so forth), and by order of merit within each genre. These lists, or canons, were to be the basis for editions and for further study. And the books were indeed studied and edited.

Let me speak briefly of the work of two other textual scholars at Alexandria in the second century B.C., both of them librarians there. Aristophanes of Byzantium—no known relation to the writer of comedies, any more than I am to the star athlete—and his pupil and successor, Aristarchus of Samothrace.

Aristophanes came to the Library when he was a young student, and he distinguished himself by the width and depth of his reading. Vitruvius tells us of his first public note. At the games in celebration of Apollo, contestants read their poems in competition for the Prize of Letters before an assembly that included the public, seven judges, and Ptolemy. One year there were only six judges, and Ptolemy asked for a suggestion for a seventh. The learned men at the Museum suggested the young man who spent so much time reading, Aristophanes, and Ptolemy appointed him. At the end of the contest, the other six judges agreed with the choices suggested by the applause of the people and of Ptolemy. But Aristophanes denounced the favorite pieces as pure plagiarism. He took Ptolemy and his fellow judges to the Library and showed them the originals of the works that had been copied. The favored contestants confessed and were sent away in disgrace. Aristophanes was given a high office and ultimately made librarian.

He used his learning and his energy to good effect. He edited many writers, including the first collected edition of Pindar, in seventeen books. As well as Anacreon, Hesiod, and Homer. He invented the Greek accents, and devised textual signs to indicate words and passages that were suspect. He was the father of lexicography and prepared the Greek Lexicon. He continued work on the lists of material in the Library, and in his spare time wrote a good many essays, as "On Courtesans," "On Comic Roles," and "Masks." (If you think *he* was industrious, however, don't forget Didymus of

Alexandria of the first century B.C., who was said to have written
3,500 books—enough to get him promoted almost anywhere—and
he was nicknamed "brazen-guts" or "iron bowels" for his efforts.)

The fame of Aristophanes as a textual scholar spread around the
world. The King of Pergamum heard of Aristophanes and invited
him to come to his court as Librarian. Ptolemy responded in a way
that some of you who are responsible for departments or colleges
might like to use in countering offers for your stars. He put Aristophanes in prison. But Aristophanes survived, and lived to do
more textual work.

My last example, and perhaps the supreme critic of antiquity, is
Aristarchus of Samothrace, a pupil of Aristophanes and his successor as Librarian. He edited various poets and prose writers, including Herodotus, and he wrote textual commentaries on many writers. His major effort was the edition of Homer, which brought
together all the work that had been done up to that time. Aristarchus's writings were said to fill 800 rolls. He was venerated
because he brought two kinds of knowledge to bear on his textual
work. First, a very exact knowledge of the language that was used
by the writer he was editing. And second, his deep knowledge of
the historical setting of the works he edited, and his effort to be
sure that the text was true to its original historical environment.

Aristarchus was said to have had, in all, forty pupils who looked
to him as their principal master. We might say supervisees, but the
relationship was then more exclusive than ours. They included the
son and heir of the ruling Ptolemy, as well as the uncle of that
young man. When the uncle had his nephew murdered in a palace
revolution, Aristarchus had to go to Cyprus (either voluntarily or
involuntarily). He was then an old man of about 75, suffering from
the dropsy, and it was said that he starved himself to death. Not a
fate likely to be suffered soon by anyone here for the dinner this
evening.

André Bonnard, in his immense study of Greek Civilization, calls
Zenodotus, Aristophanes, and Aristarchus the founders of textual
criticism. Notice, first, what a profound effect all the textual scholars of Alexandria had on our knowledge of the culture of Greece.
Much of what we know about that culture—and we know precious
little, actually—derives ultimately from the material brought together and studied and edited at Alexandria. And yet very little of

what was assembled there has survived, and apparently almost nothing of what they did not include on the Lists. Even the work of the Alexandrian scholars themselves exists mainly in references by later writers or in later editions which preserve their commentaries in the scholia. For example, it is only from two tenth- and eleventh-century manuscripts of Homer, now in Venice, that we know of the readings introduced by Zenodotus, Aristophanes, and Aristarchus.

Rather than lament these losses, however, we can rejoice with a classical scholar of this century, Thomas E. Page, the editor-in-chief of the Loeb Classical Library, who said that "But for the patronage of the Ptolemies and the labours of devoted students in the Museum, Homer, for instance, might have wholly perished, and we might know nothing of Aeschylus. We still owe Alexandria a great debt."

Saving the text may be the most important thing we can do. Beyond that, it is good to observe their basic principle, which was to respect the manuscript tradition, even if they couldn't exactly understand it. We might say: try to trace the text back to its original form, and respect what you are led to. Their basic procedures, after getting back to the original form of the text, all depended on using a comprehensive knowledge of the language and the historical setting of the original text to detect and remove errors, to introduce their own conjectures where necessary, and to write systematic commentaries on the text from a literary, historical, and textual point of view. They considered historical scholarship to be an essential part of their equipment as textual scholars.

Moreover, their work was certainly interdisciplinary in nature, working with all the kinds of texts there were in all the fields that existed. And they carried on their textual work in close converse with the greatest and most imaginative specialists in all the other known fields, in science and mathematics, and geography, and all the rest.

I hope that our textual scholarship will continue to build on the model of the Library at Alexandria. And that it will continue to come always closer, in spirit, to the harmonious reunion of human learning.

Why Apparatus?

FREDSON BOWERS

The purpose of the apparatus of a scholarly edition is to enable a reader to identify the variant readings in the different documents that have gone into the making of the contrived edition he is holding in his hand. By means of this apparatus the essential features of each of the utilized documents can be reconstructed, and occasionally certain features of documents that have merely been consulted. One problem of apparatus is the extent to which an editor is bound to provide all the evidence for the reconstruction of documents whether or not they have been substantively utilized. A good many years ago a young scholar accosted me at a learned meeting to show me page after page of every spelling and punctuational variant between the first edition of a lengthy Robert Greene romance and several quite unauthoritative early reprints. My stunned reaction was simply—"Whatever for?" Except for some distorted idea of tradition I do not know what had caused this young man to visualize to what possible use the record of such meaningless minutiae of printer's variants without authority could possibly be put. But I do know that the edition has not yet appeared.

"Whatever for?" strikes me as a pertinent question when we come to consider the purpose and the use of apparatus. I take it as a given that authors of note should have standard edited texts of maximum use to the widest variety of readers. We must have critically and historically surveyed textual standards to which we can go. Usually this means that a scholar must survey all available textual evidence and reconstruct what he takes to have been the author's ultimate intention in a form as close to the ideal as is possible according to the nature of the preserved materials. This survey may involve little more than a relatively faithful reproduction of

11

the first edition of Hawthorne's *Scarlet Letter* once it has been established that no subsequent edition was touched by the author. Or it may involve more complex cases like his *Blithedale Romance* where the printer's-copy authorial manuscript is preserved and the problems center on the kinds and particularly the specific cases of authorial changes during the proofreading as reflected in first-edition variation, in this example also containing three instances of authorial self-censorship. Or as is true for certain of William James's works we may have a manuscript, a journal publication, and finally a revised book version.

Whatever the nature of the textual materials, scholars need editions that are more authoritative than any of the original documents may prove to be. For instance, if one reads Fielding's *Tom Jones*, the first edition will be unsatisfactory since it was subsequently revised. The second and third editions are mere reprints of the first, each corrupt. Unfortunately, when Fielding revised the fourth edition he was given as printer's copy the volumes of the third edition to annotate, and since he did not engage himself to any collation, he unwittingly passed through most of the third-edition errors in the midst of his fourth-edition revisions. Only a critically edited text can separate the sheep from the goats and provide Fielding's revised intentions freed from the taint of the transmissional error passed on from his third-edition printer's copy.

But any defence of a critically edited text and its apparatus is imprecise if it does not refer back to the audience addressed and the resulting form of the edition so produced. I take it that for general purposes the most broadly useful text is the one we should aim at, not a tunnel-vision edition aimed only at specialist scholars. To some extent the definition of broad usefulness will differ according to the period. A scholar of the Elizabethan drama, for instance, can scarcely be satisfied by a modernized text except for general acquaintance with the main outlines of plot and character. Thus some popularity may need to be sacrificed if we are to produce what may properly be called a standard edition,[1] which must necessarily be in the "old-spelling" or original text even though this is readily adjustable for the ease of a larger than usual group of students.

The problem of old spelling diminishes as the centuries wear on until at the present day it vanishes into the mystique of attacking the difficulties of distinguishing house-styling from authorial characteristics that are worth preserving. Also, the earlier need to remove extensive textual corruption may sometimes be replaced by a study, with the pertinent material presented, of the very process of initial composition as represented by pre-copy-text manuscripts, as most usefully pointed out by our colleague Don L. Cook's essay in TEXT 4 (1988), pp. 77–91. It is certainly true that no critic can truly understand a work of art if he has not studied its process of composition, the way in which the final version was built up. (On the contrary, post-publication authorial revision can usually be dealt with without too many problems.) Yet even though the presentation of pre-copy-text variants is not always easy, it is rather horrifying to contemplate their substantives being barred from the apparatus and the reader left in ignorance.

To my way of thinking, the ideal form of a present-day edition corresponds closely to that of the Center for (Committee on) Scholarly Editions, which requires a reading text accompanied by an apparatus that enables a careful student to reconstruct the various stages of the work's composition whenever such a record is practicable. I suggest that for scholarship it is not enough to offer no matter how carefully edited a text without the evidence on which it has been constructed, an absence that puts the reader exclusively at the editor's mercy—and competence. For general reading purposes, it is true, the plot of Fitzgerald's *Great Gatsby* is not altered no matter what edition one reads. But a careful reader will appreciate the very different overall effect produced by an editor's choice of the meaningful light punctuation of the manuscript as against the heavy-handed Scribner housestyling. And to go one step further, a knowledgeable reader would be happy to be confirmed in his belief that the Queensborough bridge connects Manhattan with Long Island City and not, as Fitzgerald has it, with Astoria, and to know that it must have been the iris of the billboard face in the Valley of the Ashes that was a yard across and not Fitzgerald's impossible *retina*, which is invisible. Changes of this nature, even down to the punctuation system, must be recorded as part of the evidence that turns the first-edition copy-text into a scholarly edition as well.

The recording apparatus may be roughly divided into two parts, which may be thought of as *active* and as *passive*, or as *editorial* and as *historical*. Of these the record of the active or editorial intervention is the more important: a reader must be informed each time the editor has altered the base-text on which the edition has been founded. The casual reader may not care; but the text of a standard edition serves more than the casual reader (even if he were in the majority) and there are many users who *do* care whether they are reading what the preserved documents contain or what some editor rightly or wrongly thinks should have been printed. For some purposes, of course, a scholarly reader may on occasion be no more than a general reader. Nevertheless he should like to be using a trustworthy document.[2] However, the moment any specificity enters, the situation changes radically. When a question of meaning is involved in difficult language or syntax, or when a scholar must use the edition as the copy for a quotation, the authority of the full-fig edition is required, and it is an essential part of that authority that the facts be provided.

The record of emendation, then, is of supreme importance, and except when a clear text is required is best placed for immediate reference at the foot of the page. But the matter becomes complex when the question arises as to just what categories of emendation should be recorded, the more especially if awarded the prominence of so immediately accompanying the text. I fancy that a reader does not want to be constantly interrupted by having to consult an undigested mass of relative trivia mixed with the important substance that he is after. Thus a distinction has grown up between separately placed records of what are called substantive emendations—that is, of the words themselves—and of what are known as the "accidentals" or incidentals of a text, such as its spelling, punctuation, word division, and the like. Especially when the record of the accidentals variants is extensive, experience suggests the advisability of segregating the two classes into different lists that can be consulted according to the degree of interest, or the necessity, of the various readers.

To take a practical example, which I choose merely because I happen to be working on the text at the moment. A play called *The Fair Maid of the Inn* was written about 1625 by Massinger, Webster, and Ford, with some possible sort of assistance from John Fletcher. Its only substantive text is that of the first edition in the 1647 Beaumont and Fletcher Folio; but in the second edition in 1679 some unknown editor made a number of shrewd but unauthoritative guesses to correct a number of the faulty substantives while at the same time scarcely touching the accidentals, if at all, but leaving them to the 1679 printer.

The text of the play is a mess. The 1647 compositor was careless not only in typographical matters but in memorial word substitutions, such as *order* for *ardor*, *times* for *vines*, or *wish* for *miss*. He set much prose as ragged impossible verse, and a few verse passages as prose. He often joined a linking part-line to form a full line with its preceding or succeeding verse, so that his idea of verse lining was eccentric. To use the play at all properly an intelligent reader needs the presence of a thorough editorial housecleaning. But how much of this housecleaning to record? The repair of some sixty or seventy verbal errors needs special attention. Obviously, this attention to the sense comes first, in a separate list, and then if a student wishes to check the discretion of the editor in relining the verse, say, he can consult a separate list of the accidentals, which also contains emendations of the spelling and punctuation, these of some magnitude. Can this second list be spared? Only at the expense of leaving the reader completely at the editor's discretion in respect to the metrics and the punctuation meanings, often of importance. No edition could be called standard that adopted such a policy of exclusion.[3]

The passive or historical part of the usual collation may itself consist of two parts. The standard apparatus is called the Historical Collation, which records the substantive variant readings in early editions up to some established significant date, and preferably also the variants culled from the work of preceding editors, thus giving the reader a conspectus of the history of the text's transmission and the scholarly attempts at its repair. To record here even more than the most egregious accidentals that go beyond normality into the special area of semi-substantive meaning is to invite the question "Whatever for?" On the other hand, the record of verbal variation in early editions not only provides information about the degeneration of the text but also of the form of the text that various generations read and criticized. Whether a generation read Shakespeare's *Romeo and Juliet* in its first or second quarto or in the 1685 Folio edition, or a text based on this latter, has something to do with its evaluation of the play. The record of the variant substantives of preceding editors not only shows what early edition they used as base-text but also offers the reader a choice of alternative readings, some of them certainly of merit, to those that the editor has selected in the standard text he is trying to construct. For a reader concerned with the details of a text's meaning, the historical account of its transmission has a considerable importance. If space is a major

consideration this Historical Collation can sometimes be spared if it
shows no particular significance, as in *The Scarlet Letter,* but such a
loss I suggest would seriously inhibit that reference usefulness of
what purports to be a standard edition.[4]

A second form of historical collation records the variants in the
documents that precede—not follow—the one chosen as copy-text.
Here we enter upon a more disputed territory, for the argument
can be, and has been, made that the scholar so concerned with the
pre-copy-text form of the work should be required to do his own
private research from the original documents or their facsimiles or
photo-reproductions. This argument is sometimes flawed. Pre-
copy-text matter may constitute some approach to a different version of a work that should be presented in immediate connection to
the standard text. Sometimes deletions and substitutions are important enough to be reproduced. Not only the specialist but anyone
seriously interested in Fitzgerald's *Great Gatsby* should be made
aware in a standard edition of the serious cuts and substituted passages that went into the final composition in print of this significant
book. It is true that for this book a facsimile of the manuscript is in
print, but this does not cover all of the pre-copy-text material.
Moreover, collation is a time-consuming process for which an editor deserves gratitude for substance as well as for accuracy. Finally,
not all important works are available in facsimile. Especially for the
radically altered passages not only the specialist but many a teacher
and student can use this part of the apparatus.

Some discretion is needed, of course. To be full scholarship,
every difference between a manuscript in the course of its composition and the eventual print is of concern for a study of authorial
style as well as substance. But if practical considerations intervene
it may still be possible to assist a reader to reconstruct pre-copy-
text versions if the listing is confined to the substantive variants in
the final form of the manuscript, the alterations that produced
these final forms being omitted as well as the accidental variations.[5]

Over-scrupulousness can be an editorial disease, nevertheless. In
part because certain essays in William James's *Pragmatism* volume
were substantively revised in the book from their journal form, the
book becomes the superior copy-text. This means that the Historical Collation lists all the substantive variants in the early version as
against the final, thus reversing the usual process of noting later
revisions to the copy-text. But although it is more than highly prob-

able that for the book James at least partially revised various of the journal accidentals, as well as accepting in proof a certain amount of book house-styling inferior in authority to the journal forms, the question then arises as to whether all accidentals as well as substantive variants of book from journal should be listed. In the James edition this was done since the number was not so great as to prove unmanageable; but one can readily imagine other examples where such scrupulousness would have piled up such a mass of material as to chew up page after page of expensive typesetting to less than commensurate value. Thus even though accidentals may be emended in the text from some pre-copy-text forms, it seems to me that an editor is not bound—as he is with substantives—to print the whole body of evidence on which he drew in selecting the accidentals readings of his edited text so long as he records every emendation to the copy-text itself but not the rejected accidentals.[6]

It follows that one cannot lay down hard and fast rules about apparatus. However, there are certain essentials that must govern the form and content of the apparatus of any standard edition that aspires to even temporary definitiveness. A full record of editorial intervention is a positive necessity. In all cases of revision, real or suspected, an Historical Collation that provides the evidence for the evaluation of authority versus non-authority of such substantive editions is a desideratum up to some point where the author or documents deriving from him could no longer affect the text. In cases where no authority can be established, this list might be omitted if the reader were prepared to take an editor's statement on trust and if he were prepared to lose the record of preceding editors' emendations rejected by the standard edition.

As Don Cook has pointed out, serious problems may exist about the presentation of pre-copy-text documents. Sometimes this problem can be ameliorated by simply reprinting the pertinent passages so that comparison may be made by the reader with comparative ease. Other lists may be so manageable that an apparatus reconstruction of the substantive variants of the earlier documents is possible by listing.

The real problem of pre-copy-text reconstruction rests on an attempt to list all accidentals changes, as well as substantive alteration, made by an author in the process of writing out his manuscript, and possibly working over a typescript. Ideally every such fact enables a reader to reconstruct the original form of the work in its entirety without reference to reproductions and individual collation. Such a list can be of intense interest to the specialist concerned with the compositional development of an author. But when the result is so lengthy that the total value, or the ease of useability, is seriously in question, some thought may be given to the forced and regrettable omission of this part of the apparatus that lists the process of alteration even though facsimiles or other photographic reproductions of the originals are not available. Even so, the provision remains that no photographic reproduction can equal in authority the apparatus made up by a careful editor working from the originals. Examples multiply of the scholarly errors that result from secondary use of xeroxes, and these not only of manuscript texts. And I do find the concept of every man his own collator questionable when an edition that purports to be standard should provide him with every scrap of evidence about the work he is consulting.

NOTES

1. The purpose of the apparatus of a scholarly edition is to enable a reader to identify the variant readings in the different documents that have been collated by the editor since they have gone into the making of the work being edited. By means of this apparatus the essential features of each of the documents can thereby be reconstructed. One problem of apparatus is the extent to which an editor is bound to provide the evidence for collateral documents that he has not directly utilized.

2. The text of the standard edition can always serve as the basis for popular reprints in various forms, as is encouraged by the Center for (Committee on) Scholarly Editions and put into practice in the Library of America.

3. Both lists are required for any attempt to reconstruct the details of the copy-text.

4. To suggest that specialized scholars can construct their own lists is to make exorbitant demands on their time in order to secure occasional information that should be readily available for their use. The notion of every man his own collator is not an attractive one.

5. This reverses the process of recording substantive variants from the copy-text found in later editions. True variants constitute not merely differences between the final form of documents, but also alterations of original differences that may have produced the similar final form or else a different one. Somewhere, one supposes, a line must be drawn between this desirable com-

pleteness for the whole range of composition and the question of the useability of such information in list form. On a theoretical basis, for example, it would be possible to contrive a complete apparatus for reconstructing the manuscript, the two revised typescripts, the serial publication, and the revised serial publication tear sheets that served as printer's copy for the book of Fitzgerald's *Tender is the Night*. But the difficulty of using such a complex apparatus for even more complex alterations might well outweigh the wish to be complete.

6. Of course, if in the James edition the journals had provided the copy-texts, it would have been ridiculous to record all of the rejected accidentals variants in a revised book version, even though such an Historical Collation of substantives would be mandatory.

Standards for Scholarly Editing: The CEAA and the CSE

JO ANN BOYDSTON

Fredson Bowers said in 1980, "When the history of scholarship in the twentieth century comes to be written, a case can be made that it will be known as the age of editing."[1] One might also make a strong case that the "age of editing" in this country began just after mid-century and that the growth of scholarly editing here has been both encouraged and influenced by the two agencies that have provided federal funds to editions—the National Historical Publications Commission (now the National Historical Publications and Records Commission), and the National Endowment for the Humanities, which has made substantial grants directly to editions as well as to the Modern Language Association's Center for Editions of American Authors.

These two agencies have supported editions in different fields and established different requirements for editions that apply for funding.[2] Since 1964 the NHPC/NHPRC has provided financial support for editions of historical papers; when it was reactivated in 1950, its mandate was to cooperate with and encourage "Federal, State, and local agencies and nongovernmental institutions, societies, and individuals 'in collecting and preserving, and, when it deems such action to be desirable, in editing and publishing the papers of outstanding citizens of the United States, and such other documents as may be important for an understanding and appreciation of the history of the United States.'"[3] Grants are made on the basis of editor's qualifications, general description of nature of project, and the organization's evaluation of the importance of the material to be edited.[4]

Soon after it was established in 1965, the NEH began making

small grants for editorial research through its Research Division; its program on Editions continues to support a variety of editorial activities. Since the creation of the Editions program, decisions about NEH grants have been based on a combination of readers' reviews, panel decisions, and staff recommendations; applications require statements of editorial method, sample pages, plan of volumes, and detailed work plans.[5]

However, from 1966 to 1976, the NEH supported an editing program with more specific direction and detailed requirements—the MLA's Center for Editions of American Authors. As the first organization that published editorial standards and reviewed completed volumes to certify that they met those standards, the CEAA strongly influenced editing in the United States.[6] G. Thomas Tanselle has said, with ample justification, that "the existence and the accomplishment of the CEAA as an institution constitute a phenomenon unique in the history of literary scholarship in English."[7]

In 1967, the CEAA published its first *Statement of Editorial Principles*, indicating that the CEAA was "concerned primarily with American literary documents of the nineteenth century," and that its principles were "chiefly based on the theory and practice of W. W. Greg, Fredson Bowers, and other textual scholars." Five years later, the CEAA revised this *Statement* to encourage editors not seeking NEH/CEAA grants, "who have or wish to have the . . . approval of the Center . . . to prepare editions and apparatus which meet the Center's standards and to submit them for the award of the seal [of approval]." The CEAA also slightly modified some of its standards in 1972; for example, the phrase "potentially relevant forms of the text" was substituted for "authentic forms of the text," and "examining the printer's copy and reading the proofs" took the place of "proofreading and preserving the purity of the text."[8] In addition to establishing editorial standards, the CEAA required that editions published under its auspices include a statement of editorial principles and procedures used, and that printer's copy of the editions undergo peer review and receive committee approval.

In 1976, the CEAA was succeeded by the Center (later Committee) for Scholarly Editions. Although the NEH has not funded the CSE, the Endowment has continued to provide funds directly to editions; a number of NEH-supported editions that had been affiliated with the CEAA have continued to follow CEAA/CSE standards, seeking review and approval by the CSE.

The CSE's first statement explains the transition from the CEAA to the CSE:

> The Center for Scholarly Editions (CSE), administered by a Committee on Scholarly Editions, was suggested by an ad hoc committee of the Modern Language Association in the spring of 1975 and [was] officially established . . . as an entity within the MLA on 1 September 1976. . . .The . . . impending expiration of the grant from the National Endowment for the Humanities [to] the MLA Center for Editions of American Authors (CEAA) . . . offered an appropriate moment for the MLA to rethink its role in promoting editorial scholarship. The CEAA not only had fostered the production of a large number of editions of American authors but had increased the awareness of editorial problems among members of the profession generally. It seemed natural, therefore, that the next step should be a broadening of the scope of the MLA's committee on editions to encompass more than American literature. Accordingly, no restrictions were placed on the content of the editions with which the CSE could concern itself: editors of any kind of work or document—whether literary or not—from any country can feel free to seek the services of the CSE.[9]

The CSE has followed the CEAA practice of publishing editorial standards; in this respect, the CEAA and the CSE are unique among organizations that have promoted scholarly editing in this country. As successor to the CEAA, the CSE inherited and benefited from the CEAA's contributions to scholarly editing, from the momentum the CEAA gave to large reliable editions (some of them still in progress), and from the stimulus the CEAA provided for all scholarly editors to learn from their own experience and that of others. Certainly a major legacy of CEAA, carried on by the CSE, is this tradition of establishing and publishing standards for editing along with a process of peer review that tries to ensure adherence to those standards. As W. Speed Hill, former chair of the CSE, has pointed out, the "CSE is the only organization *exclusively* devoted to setting and maintaining standards of performance in scholarly editing. Unlike the CEAA or the NEH, it has no funds to grant; unlike O[xford] U[niversity] P[ress] or MLA, it does not decide whether to publish or not. Because less is at stake, its standards can be more disinterested."[10]

The standards enunciated by the CSE in 1976 were in fact little different from the standards first announced by the CEAA in 1967 and revised in 1972; what clearly did change, as the CSE *Statement* quoted above shows, was the scope and purview of the CSE.

In establishing editorial standards, both the CEAA and the CSE have been guided by the belief that, as Tanselle has said, "All textual scholarship is related, for the same activities are involved, regardless of the diversity of the materials. One must decide whether to produce a diplomatic—that is, unaltered—text of a single document or a critical text, which is a new text that incorporates the results of editorial judgment regarding variant readings and errors. One must assemble the relevant or potentially relevant documents (handwritten, typed, or printed), then find out in what ways their texts differ by collating them, then attempt to determine the relationships among the texts, and finally, if the edition is to be critical, construct a new text by choosing among variant readings and by making conjectures where errors seem to be present in all texts."[11]

The 1991 CSE statement of "Aims and Services" reflects this orientation in language only slightly revised from the 1977 CSE *Introductory Statement*:

> Varying editorial projects require varying editorial policies and procedures. Clearly a nineteenth-century Spanish novel and an English diplomat's papers require different treatments, as do a twentieth-century poem and a medieval romance, or a scientific treatise and a Renaissance play. Editing a work that survives in variant texts is different from editing the only extant text of another. The committee believes, however, that some issues are common to almost all scholarly editing (the choice and/or treatment of the basic text to be edited, for example, and for most kinds of projects the presentation of variant readings from other authoritative forms of the text) and that these issues—both theoretical and practical—can be clarified and focused through communication among persons from widely varying fields.[12]

The CSE has from the start been hospitable to a wide range of editions; the latest document, "Aims and Services of the Committee on Scholarly Editions," simply tries to make more explicit the CSE's ecumenical position with respect to the content, period, genre, language, and editorial approach of editions it would like to help.

Perhaps the most noticeable change in this "Aims and Services" statement is the CSE's effort to deal with the issue of copy-text, or what some call "copy-text editing," the matter in both the CEAA and CSE standards that has been most frequently and most heatedly discussed. In its first statement, the CSE clearly defined "copy-text" as "the text that the editor is following as the basic text."[13] This definition of copy-text includes texts existing only in a unique document, as in letters, or in a single version of an unpublished text, *as well as* texts into which other textual witnesses are incorporated. The CSE statements have always said that scholarly editors must scrutinize critically "every word of the text," and that the editor may decide, after carefully assessing the evidence, to alter certain readings in the copy text "or to suggest alternative readings."[14] However, some editors equate the Greg/Bowers theory of copy-text with "eclectic editing" that incorporates other textual witnesses into a basic text. To avoid misunderstanding, the new CSE statement uses, when appropriate, the terms "copy-text" or "base text," and, more frequently, simply "basic text," recognizing that regardless of editorial approach and regardless of the product and the way it is presented, most editing starts with a basic, or primary, text.

Greg's rational of copy-text—as extended and applied by Fredson Bowers—was of course the foundation of the CEAA principles and procedures. It continues to be most useful and appropriate for many editions; we found it so in editing thirty-seven volumes of the writings of John Dewey. However, the committee fully agrees with Bowers, who said to the Society for Textual Scholarship several years ago that it really is fruitless to argue "whether a single methodology (like copy-text) can be developed to deal with" all textual problems, because "a considerable flexibility is required in matching methodology to the particular textual situation."[15] David Nordloh, a former chair of the CSE, captured the CSE's position when he said: "I think that Greg's rationale . . . is a marvelous theoretical instrument. But I wouldn't insist anyone else blindly follow it; it is after all, only one of a number of available constructs."[16] For example, although many CEAA/CSE approved editions have followed Greg's rationale, the CEAA and the CSE have also approved editions that present unique documents, such as letters and manuscripts. The CSE emphasizes that editors using a variety of editorial approaches are welcome to seek consultation, review, and approval by the committee.

When the CSE said in 1977 that it was concerned with all scholarly editions "whether literary or not," it formally recognized that the CEAA, despite its declared interest in literary works, had in fact placed no restrictions on the content or genre of editions it would consider. When the CEAA began awarding its seal of approval in 1967, one of the volumes so approved was John Dewey's *Psychology*, the first volume published in *The Early Works of John Dewey*, and the thirty-seven volumes of the Dewey

Works now constitute the largest edition approved by the CEAA and the CSE. By 1976, when the CSE was formed, eight volumes in the Dewey *Collected Works* and three in *The Works of William James* had been approved by the CEAA, and nine of those eleven had been published. Now, volumes of philosophical works make up one-quarter of the volumes approved by the CEAA and the CSE. But the CEAA's focus on literary works has led to identification of both the CEAA and the CSE with literary works only; reviewers and essayists ordinarily refer to the CSE's standards as principles and procedures for editing literary materials, and editions other than philosophical and literary have been slow to understand that the CSE standards do apply to their work. The CSE is therefore continuing its efforts to make clear that its work encompasses inter-disciplinary *textual* scholarship, not just literary or philosophical scholarship.

Whereas the CEAA had been, by name and by purpose, limited to considering "American Authors," the CSE's *Introductory Statement* noted its interest in working with editions "from any country." Even though editors of non-English materials have served several terms as members of the CSE, only English-language editors had up to 1991 formally sought committee consideration. The CSE continues to try to reach editors of materials in other languages, in the belief that, as Daniel Eisenberg, an editor of Cervantes, says: "textual criticism . . . is, like linguistics, international in its fundamentals, however national its application. While the myriad small decisions in editing—treatment of spelling details, accidentals, emendations based on knowledge of the language or of the author—are unique to each language's literature, the basic procedures and the major steps in the editorial process are universal."[17] Eisenberg has recommended "to the Cervantes Society editors that they seek [the CSE emblem]."[18] The CSE scheduled a 1991 MLA convention presentation on the critical editing of Spanish materials and a discussion of editing libretti in German and Italian; an old French edition of the *Fables* of Marie de France is following the CSE standards; and a recent consultation with the editors of Paul Tillich's *Systematic Theology* led to appropriate principles for a critical edition based on Tillich's texts in both German and English.

The CEAA favored presentation of previously published material in "clear text," or on pages unencumbered by symbols, apparatus, or footnotes, so that approved texts could be easily reprinted for classroom use. As John H. Fisher pointed out in 1969, "[b]y the time the Center was founded, . . . the Emerson edition had already published three volumes and committed itself to three more of diplomatic text"; however, he added, "[t]he Emerson is the only MLA edition which is not now producing a clear text."[19] Although the CSE also encourages reprinting of approved texts for general and classroom use, the 1977 CSE *Statement* pointed out that ". . . different forms of presenting textual information may be appropriate in different circumstances. Some documents, such as private journals, may justifiably be edited with a record of canceled and inserted words and passages incorporated into the main text and identified by certain symbols."[20] The committee continues to encourage submission for review of diplomatic texts, genetic texts, parallel texts, and facsimile editions. An outstanding example of volumes not in clear text is found in the three volumes of the Mark Twain Letters, presented in what the editor Robert Hirst has named "plain text," with all Clemens's alterations shown on line so that readers see what the recipients of Clemens's letters saw.

Albert J. von Frank, editor of the four-volume series of *The Sermons of Ralph Waldo Emerson*, describes another approach made possible by computer technology: "Given my sense of the value of genetic-text transcription on the one hand, and, on the other, my sense that the audience nevertheless *required* a clear text, I really did not want to choose. And I am rather pleased now that work is done on the first volume to be able to say that we never did." The editors of the *Sermons* first produced the edition's texts in genetic form and read that form against the manuscript to perfect it, "then from that produced the clear text and textual notes in a single operation, copying from one window on the computer screen to another. . . . The computer has both altered and demystified the fundamental question facing editors of manuscript materials: 'Should I produce a genetic text or a clear text?' The new and more appropriate form of the question is simply 'Which of the two should I publish?'—and the answer to that question is to be found . . . in a consideration for the largest audience, a consideration which need no longer disenfranchise scholarly readers for whom genetic texts are treasuries of insight."[21]

Because the CSE in its 1977 *Statement* did not refer specifically to the periods of writings it hoped to consider, it has sometimes been seen as interested primarily, if not exclusively, in nineteenth-

and twentieth-century writings and in multi-volume collected editions. The committee has in fact approved a number of single volumes, and, whereas the CEAA's original emphasis was on nineteenth-century American literature, the CSE wants also to work
with editors of earlier periods and actively seeks their involvement.
Editors of medieval, Renaissance, and eighteenth-century materials
have started to request consultation and approval by the CSE: for
example, a reviewer has been assigned to the first volume of the
Independent Works of William Tyndale (*Answer to Sir Thomas
More's* Dialogue, 1531); in 1990, the CSE approved the first volume
(Volume 6, Funeral Poems, 1600-1615) of *The Variorum Edition of
the Poetry of John Donne*; also in 1990, Ernest W. Sullivan's consultation for the CSE with the editor of Hector St. John de Crève-
coeur's 1780 *Letters from an American Farmer* led to a revised editorial approach and acceptance of the volume by the University of
Georgia Press; and in 1991, the committee approved Valerie
Wayne's edition of Edmund Tilney's *The Flower of Friendship*
(1568), to be published by Cornell University Press.

As the basis for approving volumes, the CEAA wisely established in 1966 a process of peer review. The first CEAA *Statement*
said plainly: "Editors know that they must search out every possibly relevant form of a text and that in editing the work they must
submit their evidence as well as their conclusions to others."[22]
Following CEAA's lead, the CSE has continued to require peer
review of completed volumes; it has distinguished its *emblem* of
approval from the CEAA *seal* of approval with a new design and a
new name.[23] The CSE is thus the only organization formally and
publicly concerned with what Hill has called "issues of accuracy of
detail"—which it tries to ensure through the mechanism of review
—and "quality control of the product"—which it tries to ensure
through its standards for proofreading. Inasmuch as editors and
consultants or reviewers have a common goal—that of maintaining
high standards of accuracy, consistency, utility, and quality not only
in the editing but throughout the process of publication—the CSE
considers the review process to be another form of consultation
designed to help an editor improve the product. The committee
appoints consultants and reviewers who are experienced editors
thoroughly acquainted with the period of works under consideration, in order that the complete edition—text as well as historical or
interpretive introductions, and explanatory and historical notes—is

reviewed by those who are true peers, fellow editors who are fully informed about the period, the language, and predominant editorial practice relevant to the volume under review.

Peer review of completed volumes is based on the "Guidelines for Reviewing Editions," a revised version of the CSE "Guiding Questions," which in turn grew out of a similar document used by the CEAA "inspectors." These reviews were in the beginning usually conducted on site and have gradually come to be done more frequently by mail.[24] The CSE Guidelines are intended to present the whole range of editorial possibilities that would meet high standards. These guidelines, currently being revised once more, state clearly that:

> The CSE does not prescribe a particular method of editing; the committee's position is that different approaches are appropriate in different situations. Editors who are thoroughly acquainted with editorial options applicable to their materials and with the relevant documentary texts and who are sensitive to the circumstances attending the composition and production of all forms of the text can choose editorial procedures appropriate to their materials, carry out those procedures accurately and consistently, and explain exactly what they have done and why.
>
> The guidelines . . . suggest some considerations that the CSE regards as fundamental to the preparation and publication of useful, reliable scholarly editions. They include the kinds of inquiries that an editor, reviewer, publisher, or informed critic needs to make in order to form a judgment about the accuracy and completeness of a scholarly edition, and they can therefore serve as a working checklist of matters that may demand attention in producing scholarly editions.
>
> Just as no list of general guidelines can anticipate all of the special problems encountered in editing a particular edition, so also many of the questions posed below will not be applicable to every edition; they are intended only to provide a framework for identifying issues and for dealing with them reasonably.

The CSE "Guidelines" repeat the simple statement of standards from the "Aims and Services of the CSE":

Standards for the "Approved Edition" and "Approved Text" Emblems

> The editorial standards that form the criteria for the award of the CSE "Approved Edition" emblem can be stated here in only the most general terms, as the range of editorial work that comes within the committee's purview makes it impossible to set forth a detailed, step-by-step editorial procedure. Rather, the CSE emphasizes that editors who are thoroughly acquainted with the scholarship on editorial approaches applicable to their

materials, who are fully knowledgeable about the relevant documentary texts, and who are sensitive to the circumstances attending the composition and production of all forms of the text can judge what editorial procedures are appropriate to their materials, carry out those procedures accurately and consistently, and explain exactly what they have done and why.

Whatever specific editorial theory and procedures may be used, the editor's basic task is to establish a reliable text. Many, indeed most, scholarly editions include a general introduction—either historical or interpretive—as well as explanatory annotations to various words, passages, events, and historical figures. Although neither is essential to the editor's primary responsibility of establishing a text, both can add to the value and usefulness of the edition. Whatever additional materials are included, however, the CSE considers the following essential for a scholarly edition:

1. A *textual essay*, which sets forth the history of the text and its physical forms, describes or reports the authoritative or significant texts (both manuscript and printed), explains how the text of the edition has been constructed or represented, gives the rationale for all decisions affecting its construction or representation, and discusses the verbal composition of the text as well as its punctuation, capitalization, and spelling.

2. An appropriate *textual apparatus*, which (1) records alterations or emendations in the basic text(s), (2) discusses problematical readings (if not treated in the textual essay), (3) reports variant substantive readings from all versions of the text that might carry authority, and (4), indicates how the new edition treats ambiguously divided compounds (if any) in the basic text as well as which line-end hyphens in the new edition should be retained in quoting from the text. These four kinds of information need not be presented in any specific arrangement, and not all obtain in every situation, but the CSE requires that, when applicable, they should be available within or together with each volume bearing the "Approved Edition" emblem.

3. A *proofreading plan* that provides for meticulous proofreading at every stage of production so that the work of constructing the text, the textual essay, and the textual apparatus is not compromised in the printed volume.

The revised CSE "Guidelines for Reviewing Editions" also reflect the committee's response to editing and distribution possibilities offered by the new technology, for example: computer collation; production of both clear and genetic texts, as well as simultaneous production of various versions of a text; optical scanning to produce electronic texts (with integral search-and-retrieval programs); encoding of printer's copy files; storage of electronic files; and nonprint editions.

Although the CSE differs in scope from its predecessor, the CEAA, the two organizations have always had a common dedication to promoting the highest standards of scholarly editing and to helping editors and publishers produce reliable texts in well-prepared editions. To this end, the CSE continues to encourage editors to seek the committee's services in editing any kind of work or document, in any language, from any period, and it welcomes suggestions, criticisms, and comments in its efforts to extend and improve its services to *all* scholarly editors.

NOTES

1. Bowers, "Editing a Philosopher: *The Works of William James,*" *Analytical and Enumerative Bibliography* 4 (1980): 3–36, p.1.

2. W. Speed Hill compares the standards of the major funding organizations with those of the Committee on Scholarly Editions in "The Case for Standards in Scholarly Editing," *Literary Research* 13 (Winter 1988): 203–11.

3. Quoted in "National Documentary Sources: A Program for Their Preservation and Presentation," National Historical Publications Commission, General Services Administration, [mimeo, n.d.] The guidelines for NHPC/NHPRC grant applications first set up in 1964 have continued to obtain; see "Foreword," in "National Documentary Sources," p.[ii], which says that the document "is intended to assist prospective grantees in preparing project proposals for grants under this program", "General Information," p.2, refers to "recent legislation . . . approved July 28, 1964." The section entitled "Description and Explanation of Proposed Project" reads: "The project proposal should begin with a summary description of the project. This summary should be followed by a more detailed statement of work to be undertaken and should include (a) a careful estimate of the quantity of material involved, (b) an indication of the status of literary property rights in such material, (c) relationship of this project to previous work done with the material, (d) relationship of the project to related projects previously undertaken or currently proposed elsewhere, and (e) relevance of the project to the stated objectives and purposes of the grant program. A general plan of the work should be outlined. Evaluation of the project proposal depends to a large degree upon the adequacy and accuracy of this information. Therefore, the project proposal should be a carefully prepared document." The NHPRC policy of regrants to successful ongoing projects led to an even less formal application process after the grant program was fully established.

4. Although the NHPC/NHPRC does not publish standards or requirements for editions published under its auspices, various approaches used by these editions are described by Mary-Jo Kline in a volume sponsored by the Association for Documentary Editing, *A Guide to Documentary Editing* (Baltimore: Johns Hopkins University Press, 1987).

G. Thomas Tanselle has made a thorough, rigorous analysis of the editorial methods of "historical" editions in his classic essay, "The Editing of Historical Documents," *Studies in Bibliography* 31 (1978): 1–56 (reprinted in *Selected Studies in Bibliography* [Charlottesville: Bibliographical Society of Virginia, 1979], pp. 451–506).

5. According to Richard Ekman, former Director of the NEH Division of Research Programs, the first time the word "editing" appeared in a budget line item was in 1970, when an allocation was made to "Editing and Publications." These allocations appeared under various titles up to 1978, when a separate program called "Editions" was formed. Between 1970 and the end of FY 89, the NEH allocated $50,285,216 to editing projects; for FY 90, the amount was approximately $3.5 million, the average provided for editorial projects during the last few years.

6. The most complete list of references on CEAA editions and discussions about those editions, as well as on scholarly editing in general, is G. Thomas Tanselle's bibliographical essay in *The Center for Scholarly Editions: An Introductory Statement* (New York: Modern Language Association of America, 1977), pp. 4–15. Tanselle has also generously made available for CSE distribution "An Interim Supplement" to that essay (extracted from his most recent Columbia University course syllabus); he is preparing an expanded and updated bibliographical essay, accompanied by a comprehensive checklist, for publication by the MLA.

7. "Greg's Theory of Copy-Text and the Editing of American Literature," *Studies in Bibliography* 28 (1975): 167–229; reprinted in *Textual Criticism Since Greg: A Chronicle 1950–1985* (Charlottesville: University Press of Virginia, 1987), pp. 1–63, p. 3. I would extend Tanselle's appraisal to include more than "literary scholarship"; the CEAA through its editorial standards has had a marked influence on textual scholarship in general.

8. Center for Editions of American Authors, *Statement of Editorial Principles and Procedures* (New York: Modern Language Association, 1967; rev. ed. 1972), p. iv.

9. "The Center for Scholarly Editions: An Introductory Statement," *PMLA* 92 (September 1977): 583–597, p. 583; also published separately as a pamphlet (New York: Modern Language Association, 1977). This statement, issued in the name of the CSE, was written by G. Thomas Tanselle.

10. W. Speed Hill, "The Case for Standards," p. 209.

11. G. Thomas Tanselle, "Classical, Biblical, and Medieval Textual Criticism and Modern Editing," *Studies in Bibliography* 36 (1982): 21–68, p. 23.

12. The CSE *Introductory Statement* was later revised and reprinted in *PMLA* as "The Committee on Scholarly Editions: Aims and Policies," annually (except

1990 when it appeared as a "Report" of the CSE, and 1991). The statement of the "Aims and Services of the Committee on Scholarly Editions" is being published by MLA as a brochure in 1991.

13. CSE, *Introductory Statement*, (1977 MLA pamphlet), p. 2.

14. Ibid.

15. Fredson Bowers, "Unfinished Business," *TEXT 4* (1988): 1–11, p. 2.

16. David Nordloh, "Theory, Funding, and Coincidence in the Editing of American Literature," in *Editing and Editors: A Retrospect* (New York: AMS Press, 1988), pp. 137–55. p. 152.

17. Daniel Eisenberg, "On Editing *Don Quixote*," *Bulletin of the Cervantes Society of America* 3 (Spring 1983): 3–34, p. 3.

18. Ibid. p. 19.

19. John H. Fisher, "The MLA Editions of Major American Authors," *Professional Standards and American Editions* (New York: MLA, 1969), p. 22.

20. CSE, *Introductory Statement*, p. 3.

21. Albert J. von Frank, "Genetic Versus Clear Texts: Reading and Writing Emerson," *Documentary Editing* 9 (December 1987): 5–9. pp. 8–9.

22. Center for Editions of American Authors, *Statement of Editorial Principles and Procedures* (New York: MLA, 1967; rev. 1972).

23. A number of volumes in large editions that were inspected and approved by CSE continued—for the sake of continuity and consistency, and with the encouragement of CSE—to use the CEAA seal, a practice that makes it difficult now to fix precisely the number of volumes actually approved by each organization. A case in point is *The Collected Works of John Dewey*, which has the CEAA seal through five volumes of *The Early Works* and ten volumes of *The Middle Works*; the first CSE emblem appears in Volume 11 of *The Middle Works*, published in 1980.

24. In 1966, for example, the reviewer of the first Dewey volume based his report on a duplicated draft document entitled "Guiding Questions for CEAA Textual Experts" (dated 24 October 1966). This review, requested—and subsidized—by the Southern Illinois University Press after printer's copy for the volume had been submitted, was conducted at the Center for Dewey Studies.

Variorum Commentary

RICHARD KNOWLES

In one way I am here under false pretenses, since the New Variorum Shakespeare is not a critical edition and so is unlike all the others being discussed in these two sessions.* When he began the series in 1871, Horace Howard Furness followed the lead of Steevens, Malone, and Boswell in attaching his commentary to a critically edited text, but after his first four editions he chose instead to use a simple unedited reprint of his copy-text, for a good reason. In a Shakespeare variorum, all of the textual notes, recording the collation of a hundred or more editions, and a large part of the commentary notes, elucidating particular words, lines, and passages, are concerned with textual problems in the original Quarto or Folio copy-text. Furness apparently discovered that it was a very inefficient procedure to remove the difficulties from the text by critical editing, only to have to reconstruct them in both ranks of notes in order to make comprehensible what the history of editing and commentary had been trying to clear up. For that reason the New Variorum text is now a modified diplomatic reprint, cleaning up a few meaningless typographical blemishes and relining the prose but otherwise leaving the copy-text untouched, so that the textual obscurities are displayed plainly and in their original context. That system seems to be most convenient for reader and editor both.[1] Nonetheless, even though its text is not of the critical kind, the Shakespeare Variorum edition offers nothing if not commentary, and so its principles and practices, though different in important respects from those in all other kinds of edition, may at least provide one perspective on the writing of commentary.

There are two kinds of commentary in the New Variorum, both of them encyclopedic: the notes, and the lengthy appendices on text, date, sources, criticism, music, and staging. I shall be talking mainly about the notes.[2] The guidelines, such as they are, for the line-by-line commentary are spelled out in the *Shakespeare Variorum Handbook* (New York: MLA, 1971). The general advice is contained in one meager paragraph, which I quote:

> The commentary notes will provide, as in previous New Variorum editions, a condensed historical survey of significant attempts (including those of the present editor) to establish, elucidate, and interpret particular words, phrases, lines, and passages. Like the surveys of opinion in the appendices, the commentary should provide a comprehensive, historical perspective. This means that much commentary that seems to the editor mistaken will be included along with that which seems to him correct (mere nonsense of course to be excluded), and that wherever possible, credit will be given to the first editor, scholar, or critic to provide each explanation.[3]

In two further paragraphs elucidation is explained as including definitions; explanations of syntax; and identifications of allusions, analogues, and sources, including proverbs and biblical passages. Interpretation is explained as explications of the sense of the lines; inferences about tones of voice, state of mind, or intent of speaker; identification of metrical or stylistic features; relation of lines or passages to a larger context; comparison of lines with other lines in the play or its sources; and discussion of stage business;—in short, pretty much everything except appreciative criticism of the lines, which is mostly ignored, and criticisms of the play's structure, characters, style, meaning, and literary value, which are treated at length in a separate appendix. Decisions about which words, lines, and passages need commentary are in large part, but hardly exclusively, determined by what has been commented on in the past.

When I wrote that advice in 1971, I congratulated myself that I had wisely left enough latitude to accommodate the taste and predilections of individual editors but had otherwise given sufficient guidelines. Sheer fatuity! At later meetings of Variorum editors the subject of commentary kept coming up. Soon after the Handbook was published, Mark Eccles gave a paper recommending more original lexical commentary through the use of English dictionaries from the 16th century through Johnson. In 1975 Marvin Spevack read another such paper urging that commentary notes on Shakespeare's language not simply translate it into modern idiom but comment on it from an Elizabethan perspective as an idiolect in some degree normal, in others unique. Two or three years later Cyrus Hoy offered further guidelines, stressing the need to combine both an unbiased report and an authoritative assessment of extant work. And in Berlin in 1986 I presented a paper recommending that the growing mass of material on theatrical practice be confined to the appendices on staging except when it is needed in a commentary note to elucidate a passage or situation whose meaning is disputed or genuinely unclear.[4]

Albeit this collective general advice may be of considerable use, it is still inadequate when an editor is dealing with textual particulars. Though I am in the middle of writing my commentary on *Lear*, I still find myself consulting Hyder Rollins or Shaaber or Black or Eccles to see how they handled a problem—a time-consuming process. Moreover, for the sake of economy of space alone, my co-general-editor Robert Kean Turner and I have had to develop rules of thumb for paring down over-long notes in manuscripts submitted to us for review. For instance, we exclude most discussion of conjectural emendations that no editor has ever found worth adopting. For the record we list these conjectures in an appendix, but since they are non-starters we don't waste precious space in the notes in discussing them. For another instance, we try to reduce to a minimum unnecessary references to other works by Shakespeare or his contemporaries. If Schmidt's *Lexicon* or Abbott's *Grammar* cite examples of a usage from several Shakespearean plays, that fact is noted and neither these examples nor others provided by various editors are duplicated in the Variorum note. A reader wanting a list of such parallels need only consult Schmidt or Abbott. Similarly if a definition is well established in the *OED*, or a proverb in Tilley, or an idea or a theatrical or literary convention is discussed and documented exhaustively in some standard secondary work, there is no need in the Variorum to duplicate or augment the wealth of citation from contemporary literature that has been adduced in those standard works; a cross reference to them is enough. A splendid display of editorial learning is not an important purpose of the notes. Also for economy, words, constructions, facts, ideas, etc. are annotated only once, and all recurrences in the text receive only a cross-reference to the original note; similarly anything discussed in an appendix gets only a cross-reference, not duplicate treatment. And so on; the aim is to give the maximum information in the most efficient, least tedious way.

In the paragraph quoted above from the Handbook, the phrases "historical survey" and "historical perspective" point to the main difference between a variorum commentary and all others. The name "variorum" comes from the Latin phrase *editio cum notis variorum*, meaning "edition with the notes of various" editors and commentators. Though the tradition of the Shakespeare variorum begins with Theobald, who collected in his footnotes the comments of Pope, Warburton, himself, and a handful of others, this form of edition is much older than Theobald. It derives most directly from classical studies. Late classical commentaries on ancient authors, such as Servius's on Vergil or Porphyrion's on Horace, expanded in later manuscripts by the scholia of other commentators, provide the remote model; Renaissance editions of ancient authors, especially of Ovid and Vergil, included such commentaries, augmented by still later additions, in their margins or appendices or ultimately notes, and thus established the form of the modern variorum. The usefulness of the form is suggested by many non-literary analogues, such as the biblical *Glossa ordinaria*, Renaissance encyclopedias, Talmudic commentary, or the *Digest* for the *Codex Justinianus*; indeed, modern case law relies on a kind of continuing variorum of precedents. That is to say, the variorum is a time-tested scholarly method of accreting, comparing, and synthesizing interpretations,[5] like such other traditional reference works as dictionaries and encyclopedias, with which variorums have much in common.

In most critical editions, commentary limits itself to the one interpretation that latest scholarship and the best judgment of the editor accept as right. A variorum, on the other hand, tries to give the whole range of interpretation that has ever been thought by serious scholars to be possible. This is the crucial difference between a variorum and critical editions, even such richly illuminating ones as the California Dryden, the Yale Pope, Harold Williams's *Poems of Jonathan Swift*, and the individual-play volumes of the Arden, Oxford, and Cambridge Shakespeares. Though these have many of the features of variorums—textual collations, generous commentary, appendices (or introductions) on particular topics—they represent mainly the individual editor's best judgment of the most probable reading, the most satisfactory range of interpretation—which often means the readings and interpretations currently most acceptable. The Variorum, on the other hand, attempts to represent the whole history and range of knowledge, explication, interpretation, and theatrical practice.

There are many reasons for doing so. One is to provide a reader with all the information he needs to make up his own mind; another is to provide critical and cultural history. As to the first, a variorum is a detailed and comprehensive map of a territory, allowing a scholar, critic, or director to know as efficiently as possible what has already been discovered, what range of fact and interpretation is already known to exist, and what further exploration might remain to be done. As the editors of the recently inaugurated Chaucer Variorum say in their preface, "The complete justification for a variorum edition is the record it presents of the history of scholarship, in short, the commentary," which will serve as "a starting point for future scholarship." The completeness of a variorum guarantees that future scholarship will not proceed unaware of what has already been done. According to a recent study, scholars in the humanities read—have time to read—at most one or two percent of what is published in their fields. If this is true, much of modern scholarship, to say nothing of the four hundred years of work preceding it, is "alms for oblivion, . . . good deeds past, which are devoured / As fast as they are made, forgot as soon as done." A variorum tries to guard against oblivion, lest something valuable be overlooked or forgotten. As to a variorum's purely historical value, Cyrus Hoy compares a New Variorum editor to the curator of a museum, having in his care not only the Shakespearean text of a play but also a critical and scholarly heritage of secondary material—vast, unwieldy, contradictory, and of varying value—that has come to attach to that text. The variorum editor must both help to explain the text and, by discriminating selection, illustrate the critical response to it over the years.

Such an approach is not always in critical favor, of course, especially in periods that place a premium on novelty, modernity, or theoretical abstraction. But the continuing usefulness of variorums to scholarship is suggested by the recent inception of at least two major new ones, for Chaucer and Donne, by the continuing support for them by such agencies as the Guggenheim Foundation and NEH, by the willingness of scholars of the first rank to undertake the years of labor that they require, and (to my mind not least) by the strong early sales of Marvin Spevack's new *Antony and Cleopatra*. I have no doubt that the latest generation of graduate students and young scholars, preoccupied as they have been taught to be with the latest theoretical and political approaches to literature, have resorted to variorums less often than previous generations.

But there are encouraging signs of change, among them the emerging interest in the cultural construction of an author—in how his perceived identity and reputation are artifacts of the culture that receives him. To a Variorum editor, the discovery that every critical and cultural age reinvents Shakespeare in its image is equivalent to discovering that the sun rises in the east. All criticism is autobiography, and a Variorum edition is nothing if not a detailed record of how the mirror that Shakespeare held up to nature has reflected every generation that has looked into it. To the culturally-minded critic a variorum offers instantly to hand a full and detailed history of the changing tides of opinion and taste concerning a literary work. Moreover, I have lately discovered, variorums may now even be considered "politically correct"! Recently, in a national news magazine, Professor Stanley Fish (who has several times written about variorums) defined the essence of PC as "the ideology of difference."[6] Difference, the whole known possible range of it—in textual variants, spectrum of meanings, critical approaches, historical and cultural changes of taste—is exactly what a variorum tries to represent.

Professor Hill has asked all of us in this conference to speak about both the theoretical and practical sides of the commentary we write. Insofar as I have been distinguishing the basis and intent of a variorum from that of other editions, I have done something of the first. At one time I toyed with the idea of discussing here some of the relevance to editors of the modern controversy between semiotics and pragmatics: the challenges of Barthes and Foucault to the idea of authorial intention; the Saussurian emphasis on word as sign; Ricoeur on surplus meaning; Derrida on floating meaning and pure intertextuality; and the opposed ideas of Wittgenstein, Ogden, Richards, Austin, Searle, and Quentin Skinner on words or speeches as acts, whose meanings may be fixed by convention or context. The latter kind of approach is of course especially relevant not only to drama but also to critical editing, which must attempt to recover the historical identity of a text, not create freely a variety of new ones. I quickly abandoned this ambitious notion, partly in the expectation that others in this session would probably discuss such ideas much better than I could, but mainly because such issues, so important to recent fashions of interpretation, have very little to do with variorum editing. The variorum enterprise is so thoroughly an exercise in historical reconstruction—of the author's intention, of contexts of language and ideas, of modes of interpretation—that recent "deconstructionist" or "post-modern" theories, largely ahistorical in practice, seem to have little help to offer except as a healthy reminder of the uncertainty of all knowledge. I decided to limit myself to something much simpler and more immediately relevant; an exemplification of some basic practical rules that help to realize a variorum commentary's basic theoretical ideal of historical comprehensiveness. One is R. P. Blackmur's advice, "Use everything"; another could be Pyrrho the Skeptic's, "Trust nothing"; and a third might seem congenial to that skeptical pragmatist Richard Rorty: "Decide how well it works." Let me illustrate with a few examples from *King Lear*.

The first rule, Use everything, is basic. Variorum editors must instinctively agree with Wittgenstein's *mot*, "Only the exhaustive is interesting." More importantly, the scholarly world expects that in a variorum (if anywhere) all known options are accounted for—that the commentary will afford the kind of exhaustive coverage that, given the overwhelming mass of past and current scholarship on Shakespeare, would take a scholar and his research assistants, starting from scratch, months or years to achieve. We know that for hundreds, probably thousands of words and lines in Shakespeare there can be no certain interpretation, but only a range of possibilities. A variorum tries to present that whole range. When Goneril, fulsomely flattering Lear, declares herself "an enemy to all other joys / Which the most precious square of sense possesses" (Q) or "professes" (F), one is confronted with several problems, including the alternative readings in Q and F and the several possible meanings of "precious." But the word "square" is the real puzzler. Four classes or general kinds of meaning for that word have been proposed by commentators, as have all of the following specific terms in each class: 1) square=extent or area—e.g., full complement, compass, comprehension, area, domain, fulness, wealth, part, piece, sphere, province, position on a chess board, region, segment, summit, acme, square on a map; 2) square=measure—estimate, the carpenter's square, rule, or other measuring instrument, standard, test, canon, criterion, pattern, example, or guiding principle; 3) square= perfection, highest degree—the Pythagorean tenet that the square is the most perfect figure, the symmetry, regularity, and harmony of proportion represented by the square, absolute perfection; and 4) square=a scheme of four parts or sides—the four nobler senses (excluding touch), Regan's previously named quartet of "grace, health, beauty, and honor," the astrological square of the twelve houses of the zodiac, and the psychological diagram of the four mental powers of sense, appetite, motion, and judgment. Though most commentators today accept some version of 2), square=measure, practically any of these meanings makes a kind of sense (though frequently so forced, and all sufficiently doubtful, that many textual emendations have been suggested).

I expect that we shall never know with any certainty which is the true or intended meaning; that being the case, I would hate to ignore any possibility by choosing and thus seeming to insist on only one or two of them, and so I must, and gladly do, present them all. This is a luxury most critical editions cannot afford. A variorum editor knows from his experience how often interpretations get lost and forgotten, only to reappear as new discoveries decades or centuries later. Correspondents occasionally ask me if their bright new interpretation concerning some part of a play I am working on has ever been anticipated; so far, it always has been, often by centuries. As the memories of the profession, variorums help prevent both oblivion and redundancy.

As for the advice to trust nothing (or nobody), one might hope that it was a truism adhered to by all scholars, and yet every variorum editor finds many instances of reports and opinions universally received as truth which have no basis in fact whatsoever. In working on *As You Like It* I found that a quotation long and widely accepted as dating the play was itself misdated (no one had ever checked); that the theory that Touchstone was a role written for Robert Armin collapsed in the face of new evidence that in 1599–1600 Armin was working for some other master than the Lord Chamberlain; and so on. Users of reference works rightfully expect complete reliability as well as thoroughness, and that is why a variorum editor must scrupulously attempt to verify every fact and quotation cited by previous commentators. When Lear first presents Cordelia to the court, he calls her, in lines unique to the Folio, "our joy . . . to whose young love / The vines of France and milk of Burgundy / Strive to be interest." There are several things that need commentary here, not least why milk seems to be the drink of choice in Burgundy! But the most interesting word here is "interest." Theobald, sensing an obscurity, first changed the Folio spelling to make the word the past participle of the verb "interess," and a great herd of editors and commentators have followed; only a few mavericks try to make "interest" a noun or a shortened form of "interested." But what does it mean to say that milk and wine strive to be interest or interessed to Cordelia's love? The verb "interess," which does not occur elsewhere in Shakespeare, might mean here "to be invested with, to have a right or share in," or "to be concerned or involved with." These meanings makes a kind of sense, but a highly convoluted and figurative sense: The King of France, as represented by his land's vines, and the Duke of Burgundy, as represented by his land's milk, strive (contend) to be invested with or involved in the love of Cordelia.

The difficulty is that neither the *OED* nor any other dictionary attests to the idiom "be interested *to*"; the preposition is always *in* or *with*, but Shakespeare says clearly "interest to." I have no doubt that what has happened here is that Theobald's emendation from "interest" to "interested" is wrong, and has been followed too meekly and trustingly by centuries of editors. Most commentary on Shakespeare is derivative and repetitive.[7] If one looks in the *OED* under the Folio's original word, "interest," one finds a sense of the word common in Shakespeare: "advantage, benefit." That makes a simple, straightforward sense here: the riches of the suitors, their lands rich in vines or milk, compete with each other to enrich, to be a benefit to, Cordelia in marriage. This reading does not entail a combination of emendation, *and* a usage unique in Shakespeare, *and* an unattested idiom, *and* a tortuous figurative reading. But no one has ever proposed it; editors have not been skeptical enough of the received interpretation.

Let me give one other example, one with much more serious consequences for the play as a whole. When Lear abdicates, he retains one hundred knights, for many possible reasons which I do not intend to discuss. He makes one other proviso: that he retain "the name and all the additions [F: addition] to a king." Everything else of his kingship—land, sway, revenue, execution—he gives to his sons-in-law. I asked several of my colleagues what they thought Lear meant by "additions" to a king; the gist of what they answered was unanimously—"perks." That in fact is what I had always thought, because that is how all editors have glossed the term, to wit (and these are all actual glosses): Lear wishes to keep the privileges of kingship, state and ceremonies, outward honor, pomp, external observance, perquisites, precedence, marks of distinction—

and so on. Many critics have waxed eloquent on Lear's unwisdom in defying a law of nature, attempting to keep the "attributes" of kingship without its responsibilities. Clearly they accept at face value Goneril's convenient rationalization, that Lear's attempts to protect his friends and servants from mistreatment—to protect his Fool from Oswald's harassment, and Kent from the indignity of the stocks—are "gross crimes," showing that Lear is trying to "manage those authorities that he hath given away."

But wait a bit. "The name and all the additions to a king" does not mean anything like the perquisites or attributes of kingship. It means one thing only: a form of address, a name. Shakespeare uses the term "addition" (in a non-mathematical or non-quantitative sense) many times, and in every case it means a name, almost always the name *added to* the proper name in order to show rank, occupation, or other distinction. Lear wants to keep as a mark of courtesy the titles he has been used to during all of his life, just as a retired colonel or judge today keeps *his* honorific. Lear simply wants to keep the name—"king"—and all his customary forms of address—"royal Lear," "your majesty," "your grace"—as marks of respect. In fact everyone automatically uses these titles for Lear throughout the rest of the play. The one exception is instructive. When Lear demands of Oswald, "Who am I, sir?", the steward puts on the "weary negligence" urged by Goneril and answers not "the King" or "royal Lear" but only "my lady's father," a bit of insolence that earns him a beating and a tongue-lashing on "differences" of rank. An exact understanding of the term "addition" is crucial to our understanding of Lear. To make it mean more than his accustomed forms of address is to misunderstand and exaggerate Lear's demand, making him seem more vain, arbitrary, and unrealistic than he is. Some salutary doubt of the received opinion is called for.

Doing a variorum edition tends to make one a skeptic. Having seen how over the centuries critics have advanced quite contradictory interpretations with passionate assurance, one begins to approach all interpretations including the latest and most modish with, to be sure, sympathetic interest and often fascination, but also with an attempt at cool appraisal—with one auspicious and one doubting eye. And here I come to the third of my rules for commentary: Judge and evaluate; see and say how well an idea works. The variorum commentator, having tried to be an exemplary reader of the text, and having surveyed with such thoroughness all of its textual, linguistic, and critical problems, and its scholarly, critical, and theatrical heritage,—that editor ought to be in a uniquely favorable position to comment authoritatively on the issues. All variorum editors have tried to do this; had they not, they would have abdicated a crucial part of their editorial responsibility. The last thing a reader wants is a boneyard of dead opinions, arbitrarily excerpted or paraphrased, and assembled together as if they were all equally useful or useless. I shall end by quoting again from Cyrus Hoy: "Without the commentator's appraising voice, bizarre views jostle side by side with sober ones, and arguments grounded in fact risk being cancelled out or compromised by arguments spun out of conjecture. Bad money drives out good money, and it is very much the commentator's responsibility to guide the reader so that he can distinguish between what is plausible and what is dubious. . . . What is needed is the force of a controlling intelligence which only the commentator can supply: an intelligence that is not simply content to catalogue opinions, but is prepared to arbitrate among them, and may even be prepared to advance views that supplement or correct prevailing opinions." That ideal of the variorum editor, like Imlac's ideal of the poet, is probably impossible to achieve; but I invite you all to see for yourselves how nearly Marvin Spevack has realized it in his new New Variorum *Antony and Cleopatra*.

NOTES

*A version of this paper was first presented at a session on "Constructing a Commentary for a Critical Edition," sponsored by the Division on Methods of Literary Research at the MLA Convention, December, 1990.

1. Other variorums find other kinds of text, including critical texts, most convenient. The Chaucer Variorum commentary, because Chaucer's text is based on a complex manuscript tradition, is attached to both an edited text and a companion facsimile of one of the manuscripts. The Spenser Variorum, not greatly concerned with textual matters because the original text is so clean, provides a conservatively edited old-spelling text. The Milton Variorum, consisting of commentary only, is keyed to the pre-existing critical text of the standard Columbia edition, with which it must be used.

2. In large measure the appendices are continuations of the notes, gathering in one place related material that would otherwise be dispersed among many notes, or material that is too bulky for the notes. The Spenser Variorum's preface states simply, "The general plan is followed of including the briefer

expository material in the commentary [notes], and of reproducing or summa-
rizing the longer studies in the appendices." The Milton Variorum uses introductory essays rather than appendices, as the preface explains: "In the head-
notes to the shorter poems and in the introductions to the longer ones we
have treated matters of dating and the circumstances of composition as far as
sound evidence permits. And in the introductions to the longer poems we
have tried to present the continuing and active discussion of the major problems of theme and artistry in conjunction with our notes on the relevant passages."

3. Similarly the preface to the Milton Variorum: "While the chief end is interpretive criticism, the larger part of a variorum commentary must necessarily
be given to supplying information of all kinds, from the history and meaning
of words to the history and meaning of ideas. Our object in this work is to furnish a body of variorum notes and discussions uniting all available scholarly
illumination of the texts on all levels from the semantic and syntactical to
those of deliberate or unconscious echoes of other works in all the languages
known to Milton. In notes on the longer passages we have considered their
inner rhetorical organization and involvements in the design of the poem as a
whole, in the backgrounds of the literary traditions of which they themselves
are outstanding developments, and in the many aspects of Milton's interests—
theological, cosmological, hexameral, historical, psychological, and so on."
Incidentally, the so-called "Yeats Variorum" is not a variorum at all, since it
records no commentary, only textual variants.

4. All but the first of these papers were circulated to Variorum editors, but to
my knowledge none was published.

5. I am indebted to my colleague John B. Dillon for information about variorum
precedents and analogues.

6. *Newsweek*, 24 Dec. 1990, p. 50.

7. As is most criticism. The fact needs emphasis. It is sometimes suggested that
variorums will soon be rendered obsolete by the computer's ability to do
rapid searches through vast bodies of material. All recent Shakespeare
Variorum volumes have been printed from computer tapes, which might be
published as ROM discs subject to computer searches; it is altogether probable that in the future, variorums will be published as both books and discs.
But the alternative that is often proposed, that a considerable fraction if not
all of the extant scholarship on Shakespeare will someday be transferred from
printed to machine-readable form, subject to rapid searches, no more offers
an alternative to a variorum than comparable data banks would offer to dictionaries or encyclopedias. Even if such a plan were economically and practically feasible, its fruits would generally be useless except for very limited purposes. A search for all interpretations of a word or passage or whatever in all
the editions and commentaries and critical studies of *Hamlet* would yield an

overwhelming mass of material, much of it erroneous or loony, a great deal of it flatly contradictory, and at the best, most of it endlessly, uselessly redundant. Such a search needs to be made only once, as it is by a variorum editor, who selects whatever is usable once and for all and ignores the remaining enormous mass of the useless and the continually repeated. For most purposes, no researcher will prefer hundreds or thousands of pages of undigested data to a syncretic statement—selected, assimilated, digested, organized, when necessary evaluative—by a competent authority. Variorums may be published by and read on computers, but they cannot be made or replaced by them.

Public and Private in the Study of Manuscripts

DONALD H. REIMAN

Three of my 1989 Lyell lectures on "The Study of Modern Manuscripts" focused on differences among three distinct categories of post-Medieval manuscripts—*public*, *confidential*, and *private* manuscripts. *Modern manuscripts* were defined as those produced in times and cultural contexts where printing had begun to replace scribal copies as the primary medium of disseminating information; the era of modern manuscripts is now ending, as various electronic media have begun to usurp that role. The golden age of modern manuscripts in England lasted approximately from the execution of King Charles I until the end of World War I—that is, between the ascendancy of the middle classes, with their passion for record-keeping and introspection, and the impact of the telephone and typewriter on their writing habits.

If instead of attending the STS Conference in New York in 1991, you were in Philadelphia as a delegate to the Continental Congress of 1776, you—like John Adams—would be taking copious notes on these proceedings and soon afterwards would write *personal* letters to your spouse and intimate friends and *confidential* letters to your political allies and professional colleagues. You also would engage in *public* writing stimulated by the interchanges at the gathering: whether or not you intended to publish your memoranda immediately, you would draw up notes on what people said and did, together with your reactions to their ideas. You might choose either the form of a quasi-public journal-of-record, or formal memoranda that might suitably find their way to newspapers. Some of these records you would keep only for *private* consultation. Other drafts, originally aimed at the *public*, you would reject and reclassify as *private*, as you replaced them with revised documents that better expressed your sentiments or that seemed to represent your *public* position more effectively. While working out your arguments, you and like-minded delegates might pass *confidential* drafts of your ideas back and forth among yourselves to get one another's reactions and to test the impact of various ideas and rhetorical strategies. Accompanying these drafts might be also be *confidential* letters, keyed to the prejudices of the individuals to whom they were addressed, giving the reasons behind your arguments. While this process was in train, you might send a brief—possibly anonymous—account of your ideas to a newspaper in Boston, while you worked to prepare another, longer and more rhetorical version for publication as a pamphlet in Philadelphia, where your colleagues remained assembled. And all this time, in *private* letters to your absent spouse, besides expressing affection and longing and discussing finances and family problems, you might give a quite different account of public events—confiding your fears and doubts about your public ideas, problems with your health, anger about personal slights, distress relating to your own mistakes, and other matters that might bear on the public proceedings but that were never intended for the eyes of either your confidential political allies or the larger public.

Documents of these disparate types have often been classified simply as the manuscripts of John Adams, or Edmund Burke, or William Wordsworth. Insofar as they survive, all three kinds of manuscripts have provided scholars with copy-texts—or at least with partial authority—for critical editions of such figures. Sometimes the official or professional correspondence of political figures has been issued separately, and often the letters of literary figures are collected and edited apart from their creative writings. But as I demonstrate in the Lyell Lectures, not only have the editors of letters (and, consequently, biographers who rely on their editions) often caused confusion by failing to distinguish among public, confidential, and private documents, but editors of poetry and literary prose have sometimes wronged their subjects by applying the same editorial methods and standards to writings that their authors had both completed and *released* as public writings and to documents that the authors had rejected as public expressions of their ideas, sentiments, or art; some editors have even given primary authority to those that survive only in a fragmentary, imperfect state, or that are clearly rough or intermediate drafts.

Textual theoreticians who insist that the intentions of the author should be the final authority in determining the text of the work often advocate using the author's surviving press-copy as copy-text in order to approach that intention more closely, but this practice raises another question basic to the nature of modern manuscripts. Editors have sometimes carried their quest for holograph or authorially sanctioned documents so far that where part of a work survives in press-copy manuscript and the rest does not, they have used the surviving manuscript fragments as copy-text for those portions of an edition and based other parts of the same text on the author's intermediate fair-copy holographs, corrected proofs, or the published text of the first edition. In my opinion, such Byzantine maneuvers contravene a central fact of authorial intention during the eighteenth and nineteenth centuries: Authors who prepared works for *public* dissemination clearly expected, willed, and intended certain changes to take place between the time the manuscript left their hands and the work appeared in its public dress. Some authors—Shelley among them—wished to limit and control the number and nature of the changes during the publishing process and to approve alterations of any feature of the text by printer or publisher, while others—Byron, Keats, and Dr. Johnson among them—encouraged friends, editors, and publishers to correct their orthography, punctuation, and consistency of style, just as they usually left to the publisher, or to the printer, such matters as the typography, the layout of pages, and the arrangement of the volumes.[1]

The issue of whether the intention of an individual author or the socializing process should be the final determinant in choosing a copy-text often disappears when we consider the true nature of *modern manuscripts*. Unlike earlier scribal manuscripts (which were themselves the published texts), modern holographs or transcriptions by amanuenses working under the supervision of the author that served as press-copy were intended merely as way-stations to the printed text.[2] Consequently, the later editor, in the absence of specific evidence to the contrary, must assume that the author's intentions include such features of the socializing process as the format of the pages, the use of spaces between cantos, stanzas, acts, or chapters, the introduction of some uniformity or conventionality in orthography and basic punctuation—for example, that full stops will appear at the ends of sentences and that paragraphs will begin on a new line.

The consequences of this point for editorial theory may not be immediately apparent. Hitherto, pseudo-Marxist textual theorists have based their attacks on the Greg-Bowers-Tanselle method of editing on assumptions that ignore the individual author's own intentions in favor of an ideological theory of the relations between writers, the means of production, and readers whose interactions produce "socialized" texts. My quarrel with Greg and Bowers has nothing to do with the absurd view that the unitary author does not exist: Not only do individuals exist, but the greatest geniuses among them discover ideas and create works of art that thousands of average persons, even under the same social conditions, could not achieve in millennia. (If this were not the case, we would have the works of five Shakespeares from Elizabethan England and Salieri's compositions would equal Mozart's.) I argue, instead, that the very nature of the transmission process—the way manuscripts have been used and viewed by authors attempting to reach the public since at least the eighteenth century—shows that Bowers, when insisting that modern editors follow press-copy manuscripts (even when uncensored) in preference to the printed texts that were set from them, simply misreads the author's very voluntary *intentions* that Bowers declares are the editor's polestar.

If, as I think can be demonstrated in a large majority of the cases hitherto debated, the author *intended* to have the publisher and/or the printer prepare the text for the public according to the conventions of the day, leaving regulation of what Greg called "accidentals" largely to the printer, then editors have far less need to distinguish between "accidentals" and "substantives" in textual analysis, and, except for identifiable typographical errors and other errata, the printed edition represents the best surviving evidence of the author's final intention at the time the work was released for publication. Later changes in the both verbal and the formal elements of the texts of authorized editions of the work (i.e., texts released with the author's explicit approval) should thus be judged on the same basis as readings in the first edition: What evidence is there, or how likely is it, that the author specifically initiated or approved of this specific change? Lacking such evidence or likelihood, the editor will choose to follow the selected copy-text both in its verbal text and its orthography and pointing, on the grounds that it is better to represent consistently one version that the author is known to have approved than to meld two or more such versions into an original pattern never sanctioned as a coherent, authorized text of the work.

To support this view of press-copy manuscripts as way-stations, rather than final intentions, the Lyell Lectures provide examples showing that such nineteenth-century authors as Jane Austen, Percy Bysshe Shelley, and W. M. Thackeray devoted more care in preparing presentation copies of manuscripts they intended for private perusal (and which were, therefore, the final texts of those works) than they gave to manuscripts they intended for the press. Using as examples *private* manuscripts that these three authors gave to friends, I show that they perfected these presentation copies of their stories and poems as they did not feel compelled to do when readying works for the public, because they then expected the publisher, printer, and they themselves (while reading proofs) would cooperate in bringing the text to a level of perfection similar to that they achieved in their presentation transcripts.

To see how manuscripts of *public* works differ from their authors' final intentions, I discuss Shelley's *Laon and Cythna; or, The Revolution of the Golden City*, the twelve-book romance-epic that is Shelley's longest poem. The manuscript of *Laon and Cythna* that went to press was a holograph that Shelley delivered to Buchanan McMillan, a printer whom Shelley had selected to set at least part of the poem in type before he had secured a bookseller to distribute it. McMillan's compositors presumably followed Shelley's explicit instructions not to emend anomalies.[3] Yet even in this case, collation of the surviving setting copy with the first edition indicates clearly that Shelley expected the compositors to make a number of changes in order to present his work to the public.

For one thing, the orthography of the press-copy manuscript contains ampersands and other standard abbreviations ("w^{d}." for "would," "sh^{d}," for "should") that Shelley intended the printers to spell out in full. Similarly, the compositors corrected Shelley's misspellings to the conventional orthography—especially words containing the combination *ie* or *ei* (such as the possessive adjective "their," which Shelley often, but not invariably spelled "*thier*"). Either the compositors or Shelley when reading proofs added initial capital letters to the beginnings of some nouns (less often they removed such capitals) and modified the pointing in a number of places—adding commas, changing dashes to semicolons and other marks of punctuation, and adding or subtracting apostrophes to conform to current typographical practice. Shelley, like Coleridge, often included an apostrophe in the possessive adjective "its" ("it's")—a usage sanctioned by grammar books of the eighteenth century but fallen from favor by 1817.

Lastly, McMillan's print shop regularized the pattern of the poem's Spenserian stanzas: Shelley's arabic numbering was changed to small roman numerals for the stanzas of each canto; the compositor regularized the indentations that Shelley's holograph employs (sporadically) to mark the rhyme scheme, leaving only the ninth line of each stanza—the Alexandrine—extended to the left of the other eight lines. The pages were arranged in the standard pattern for poems with eight- or nine-line stanzas, with two stanzas on each page. The heading of each canto was printed in Gothic type. These and other matters of format and typography, not indicated in Shelley's holograph, helped produce the bibliographic codes that identified Shelley's poem as a typical exotic romance of the period in *ottava rima* or Spenserian stanzas, the best known of which was Byron's *Childe Harold's Pilgrimage*.[4] The page layout, like Shelley's deceptive title, was clearly part of his plan to follow up the success of such romances—including pre-eminently Scott's and Byron's poems and Thomas Moore's *Lalla Rookh* (1817)—by disguising his revolutionary poem as one of the exotic adventure narratives currently popular with British readers. Yet these patterns appear only sporadically, if at all, in the setting-copy holograph. Shelley's intention was that the printer and (for the title page) his publisher would add elements to his manuscript version that would enable his private vision to circulate successfully in the public marketplace. Whether Shelley verbally instructed the printer in the forms he desired, or McMillan's compositors added them according to the rules of their craft, the first printing provides a more authoritative copy-text than does the setting manuscript, which survives only in fragments anyway.

But what of cases where the text is censored or otherwise changed *against* the author's will? In exploring this question, I compare two celebrated cases of pre-publication censorship: The first is Shakespeare's attempt to name the comic lead in his first play on *Henry IV* Sir John Oldcastle before he was (apparently) forced by pressure from Lord Cobham, a descendant of Oldcastle, to change the name to Sir John Falstaff. The second instance is the censorship of Shelley's *Laon and Cythna* by its printer Buchanan McMillan and its publisher Charles Ollier, who forced Shelley to rename his poem *The Revolt of Islam* and to cancel twenty-eight leaves, eliminating most of the derogatory references to Christianity and changing the relationship of the hero and heroine, who are lovers, from blood brother and sister in the original text to an orphan girl (Cythna) raised in Laon's home. In Shelley's case, we know exactly how the text was changed and in what spirit the author accepted these alterations. An eye-witness to the proceedings, Thomas Love Peacock, testifies that Shelley resisted all revisions at every step:

> Mr. Ollier positively refused to publish the poem as it was, and Shelley had no hope of another publisher. He for a long time refused to alter a line: but his friends finally prevailed upon him to submit. Still he could not, or would not, sit down by himself to alter it, and the whole of the alterations were actually made in successive sittings of what I may call a literary committee. He contested the proposed alterations step by step: in the end, sometimes adopting, more frequently modifying, never originating, and always insisting that his poem was spoiled.[5]

Based on this and other evidence, a number of editors and textual critics have argued that Shelley's intention for *Laon and Cythna* was so thwarted by the censorship of printer and publisher that the modern editor should restore the original text that Shelley fought so hard to maintain. In a note written in a copy of *The Revolt of Islam* that he gave to friends in Italy, Shelley continued to express unhappiness at the censorship of *his* poem, indicating that he was dissatisfied with the changes forced on the published version.[6] Clearly, the refusal of others to publish his text unless he altered it was the sole reason he had finally acquiesced to the changes. Further relevant facts also support an editor's decision to turn back the clock and undo the surgery performed at birth: The original text of *Laon and Cythna* had neither been lost nor totally sidetracked from literary history. A few copies of the original version had been distributed before the mutilation, including one that fell into the hands of the *Quarterly Review*, where it was attacked in one of the few widely-read reviews of the poem. That review of his repressed and withdrawn poem, in turn, provoked Shelley to start an epistolary quarrel with Robert Southey (whom he believed to be the reviewer), to satirize the Lake Poets in *Peter Bell the Third*, and to attack the *Quarterly* reviewers in both the Preface and the text of *Adonais*.[7] Moreover, because no cancel leaves had been supplied for the large stock of unbound sheets remaining in the

overstock of unsold copies of *The Revolt of Islam*, a new issue of
the poem sold in 1829, bound up with a new title page listing John
Brooks as the publisher and *The Revolt of Islam* as the title, that
actually consisted of the uncanceled sheets of the original printing
of *Laon and Cythna*. Robert Browning (for one) later noted the
differences between the received text and the copy that he as a boy
had bought from John Brooks.[8] Thus, Shelley's preferred but suppressed text played an active part in the history of the poem's
reception and reputation from the very first and had figured importantly in literary history even before Harry Buxton Forman restored
that text in his critically edited Library Edition of 1876.

The case of "Oldcastle" vs. Falstaff is not nearly as clear in its
circumstances. We have no documentary evidence, for example,
and no eye-witness testimony about Shakespeare's intentions. Was
Shakespeare equally reluctant to rename his comic character in
Henry IV, Part 1, when the censor came to him or to his acting company to ask that Oldcastle, a Lollard martyr, not be slandered by
having his name associated with a charming but self-indulgent
hedonist? Gary Taylor has argued—in a provocative and cleverly
sustained paper entitled "The Fortunes of Oldcastle"—that for
Henry IV, Part 1 the editor should restore Shakespeare's original,
uncensored version of the text by replacing the name Falstaff with
the name Oldcastle in this play, though not in the succeeding
plays—*Henry IV, Part 2*, *Henry V*, and *The Merry Wives of Windsor*—in which the name Falstaff was used from the start.[9] If one
judges the evidence of this censorship to be convincing and then
follows the rule of adhering strictly to authorial intention, trying to
undo all interference of outside social constraints by recognizing as
authoritative the last stage of creation in which the author wrote entirely according to his own, untrammeled creative freedom, one may
well judge "Falstaff" vs. "Oldcastle" by the rule in Shelley's case.

Some problems arise, however, with the story of the censorship
of Shakespeare's drama that are not present in that of Shelley's
poem. First, most of the evidence for the existence of the earlier
version and all the evidence on the reasons for change would be
classified as hearsay and deemed inadmissible in a court of law.[10]
There is no sixteenth- or seventeenth-century manuscript or printed text, extant or reported, that contains the putative "uncensored"
version of the play. Indeed, Shakespeare seems to have taken the
name of Sir John Oldcastle, Lord Cobham, from an anonymous

play entitled *The Famous Victories of Henry the Fifth* (ca. 1588), and in making this change, he seems also to have changed the names of two other companions of King Henry V in that play from Harvey and Russell to Bardolph and Peto. Thus with or without the imposition of censorship from Sir William Brooke, the Lord Cobham of Shakespeare's day (who as Lord Chamberlain held a life-and-death grip on a playwright's future), Shakespeare seems to have opted for less prominent or nonhistorical names for the disreputable companions of Prince Hal. Whatever Shakespeare's intentions may have been when he originally wrote the First Part of *Henry IV*—by the time he wrote the *Henry the Fourth, Part 2* and, by royal request, *The Merry Wives of Windsor*, the playwright had clearly ratified the use of the name Sir John Falstaff for the character, because neither he nor his company made any attempt to revive it even after the Cobhams fell out of favor in court.[11]

The traditional arguments in support of retaining "Falstaff," rather than substituting "Oldcastle," are these: We know that Shakespeare accepted the name Falstaff, because he used this name in three subsequent plays. There is ample documentary evidence—including at least six quarto texts of *Henry IV, Part 1* published between 1597 and 1623 and the folio of that year—that the publicly approved name of the character was Falstaff. Not only have four centuries of subsequent theatrical and publishing history established the name Falstaff in the three plays by Shakespeare, but the same period of historical study has established that the character of Sir John Oldcastle is not a model appropriate to the character of Falstaff as he evolved in that first play—a discrepancy that Shakespeare himself might have accepted, once it had been pointed out to him, even without the threat of censorship. Approaching the editorial questions raised by the censorship of *Henry IV, Part 1*, from the study of modern manuscripts, we can add two points. First, since the circulation of manuscripts among a small circle was still a normal mode of "publication" in the 1590s (*vide* Donne's poetry), had Shakespeare felt the need to establish a text of *Henry IV, Part 1* using the name Oldcastle, he had only to have friends copy and circulate such a text (e.g., from a prompt copy). Second, in the absence of such contrary evidence, the printing of "good" quartos in 1597/8 that not only use the name Falstaff in the text, but feature it on the title page, is sufficient to establish this version as the authorial one. Even the surfacing of a prompt copy of the play with Oldcastle's name would not show that this was Shakespeare's preference for his final *public* text, in the face of the whole of theatrical and publication history from 1598 to 1623.

On the more general issue of when an editor should try to undo contemporary censorship of the author's intentions, I would say that an editor should return to the readings of manuscripts or other authorially approved documents at those places where a previously accepted text can definitely be shown (from other contemporary evidence) to have been censored in a way that the author continued to reject. But there is a serious danger in altering a text on the basis of a few fragments of contemporary evidence, linked by a web of conjecture. To do so violates the organic integrity of the living work of literature.

In my fifth and final Lyell lecture, "Toward a Personalist Poetics," I evoke from the earlier analysis of public and private elements in the modern manuscript tradition a theory of criticism that emphasizes the human and personal at the expense of the abstract and desiccated side of literary analysis. Without reducing great literature to what C. S. Lewis slightingly characterized as the "expression of personality,"[12] I view literary works as themselves being living organisms that we may call "persons." A literary work is produced by a fruitful union of an author and an age, each of which also implicates a cultural heritage from the past. Under this perspective, a literary creation is more than a pattern of plus signs and zeros, presences and absences, just as we and those people we love are more than mere sequences of biochemical reactions.

When the literary work is conceived as a "person," the editor plays the role of *family physician*, sometimes helping to bring the work into the world and ultimately attempting to repair surgically the ravages of "Fate, Time, Occasion, Chance, and Change." The *literary historian* is seen as *biographer* of the poem, play, or novel, identifying and analyzing both hereditary and environmental factors that influenced its nature and nurture, but treating the work, not as a lifeless pattern of signs, but as a vital organism that continues to develop as it interacts with readers reared in different times and places. Finally, the *literary critic*, whose function it must always be to mediate between the literary work and the strangers it meets in its stages along life's way, plays the role of *family friend*, sympathetically introducing the living creation to new circles of acquaintances, pointing out its virtues and exculpating its faults, whenever it is misunderstood or gives offense.

To understand the distinctions among *private, confidential,* and *public* manuscripts helps the scholar and critic to see how individual authors are able, with the help, not of sociological concepts, but of other *people*—friends, amanuenses, readers for the press, printers, and publishers—to bring forth works of art that eschew *merely* personal and private considerations. For we can see clearly how human personality and character transcend merely material influences (such dehumanized abstractions as "the means of production") as soon as we realize that we are more likely to become what we theorize than what we eat.

In drawing a more humane portrait of the literary creation, I am trying to counteract recent attempts to turn into mere phonemes and tropes, or units of production and consumption, what Milton characterized as "the precious life-blood of a master spirit" and what Gerard Manley Hopkins in his sonnet "To R. B." depicted as a child begat upon his mind, "the mother of immortal song," by "[t]he fine delight that fathers thought." Humanists have too often surrendered their birthright in vain attempts to win the blessing of the physical and social sciences. Perhaps the generation of critics who denied that poems have authors will force us to reaffirm our rightful heritage—a faith that human nature and the intellectual creations that embody its highest aspirations are, if lower than the angels, still well above than the muck and mechanism of nonliving nature. The uniqueness of the generative writers of the Romantic era can be traced in the individuality of their holograph manuscripts as they struggled to transform their privates woes or visions into living creations that could carry their experience and wisdom to a public beyond their own private circles. Awareness of the individuality of each of those artists and respect for the peculiar vitalities of their creations are among the rewards of those who devote themselves intensively to the study of modern manuscripts.

NOTES

1. See Donald H. Reiman, "Gentlemen Authors and Professional Writers: Notes on the History of Editing Texts of the 18th and 19th Centuries," in Richard Landon, ed., *Editing and Editors: A Retrospect,* Papers given at the twenty-first annual Conference on Editorial Problems, University of Toronto, 1–2 November 1985 (New York: AMS Press, 1988), pp. 99–136.

2. Exceptions to this generalization would include a relatively few manuscripts prepared by authors when they sent their work to simple job printers who would take no responsibility for correcting the text and when the authors themselves would be unable to read proofs. I can think of no actual instances, but I can imagine that such might have been the case with small groups of poems sent home by soldiers in the trenches during World War I or on isolated islands in World War II.

3. See Harry Buxton Forman, *The Shelley Library: An Essay in Bibliography* (London: Reeves and Turner, for the Shelley Society, 1886), pp. 71–87; Donald H. Reiman, ed., *Shelley and his Circle*, (Cambridge, MA.: Harvard University Press, 1973), V, 141–89; and Tatsuo Tokoo, *Bodleian MS. Shelley d. 3: A Facsimile Edition with Full Transcription and Textual Notes* (*The Bodleian Shelley Manuscripts*, VIII) (New York and London: Garland Publishing, 1988), pp. xi–xxi.

4. Other volumes featuring long stanzaic poems that either were or pretended to be such escapist romances include *Richard the First* by Sir James Bland Burges (1801; Spenserian stanzas); *Gertrude of Wyoming* by Thomas Campbell (1809; Spenserian); *The Four Slaves of Cythera* by Robert Bland (1809; within a poem in couplets Bland introduces a 68-stanza poem in what a note calls "the octave stanza, and the manner of the Italian school"); *Sir Edgar; A Tale in Two Cantos* by Francis Hodgson (1810; eight-line stanza ending in an Alexandrine); *Psyche* by Mary Tighe (1811; Spenserian); *Hermilda in Palestine* by Edward, Lord Thurlow (1812; *ottava rima*); and *Orlando in Roncesvalles* by John Herman Merivale (1814; *ottava rima*). All of the men named were friends or acquaintances of Byron.

5. Forman, *A Shelley Library*, p. 75; from *Fraser's Magazine* (March 1862).

6. This annotated copy is now in the Harry Ransom Humanities Research Center, University of Texas at Austin. By February 1821, Shelley also found aesthetic flaws in the text; in a letter to Ollier, he asked whether "there is any expectation of a second edition of the 'Revolt of Islam'? I have many corrections to make in it, and one part will be wholly remodelled" (*The Letters of Percy Bysshe Shelley*, ed. Frederick L. Jones [Oxford: Clarendon Press, 1964], II, 263).

7. See *Shelley and his Circle*, ed. Donald H. Reiman (Cambridge, MA: Harvard University Press, 1973), VI, 926–27, 931–34.

8. See Forman, *The Shelley Library*, pp. 77–80; Frederick A. Pottle explored the question further in his Yale dissertation, published as *Shelley and Browning: A Myth and Some Facts*, with Foreword by William Lyon Phelps (Chicago: The Pembroke Press, 1923).

9. Taylor, "The Fortunes of Falstaff," *Shakespeare Survey*, 38 (1985), 85–100. In

"William Shakespeare, Richard James, and the House of Cobham," *RES*, N.S. 38 (August 1987), 334–54, Taylor provides additional information about Dr. Richard James (1592–1638), the historian whose dedicatory epistle to Sir Henry Bourchier of ca. 1634 is the chief source of our information on the circumstances of the censorship of *Henry IV, Part 1*.

10. Or in scholarship on nineteenth-century figures. Taylor cites as "the most explicit deposition" on the change and the reasons for it the autograph letter from Dr. Richard James (see note 9); James, "a friend of Ben Jonson and librarian to Sir Robert Cotton," probably (Taylor argues convincingly in *RES*—see note 9) wrote this letter "c. 1634" (Taylor, "Fortunes of Oldcastle," p. 86). James could have had no first-hand knowledge of Shakespeare's supposed troubles with the authorities in 1597, because he was five years old at the time. From the passages quoted, it is clear that James is a Puritan hostile to Shakespeare's treatment of the character, whether named for Sir John Oldcastle or Sir John "Falstaffe" or "Fastolff," who, James declares, was "a man not inferior [of] Vertue though not so famous in pietie as the other" and also a Lollard stalwart. Thus even if James had access to the basic story he tells directly from the mouths of Shakespeare's contemporaries and friends, he cannot be assumed to have transmitted it reliably. Having a quarrel with Shakespeare's portrayal of Sir John, James (like Shelley's detractors John Taylor Coleridge and Robert Southey) was a person likely to retail—and embroider—any gossip about how Shakespeare was rebuked and disciplined for it.

Scholars of nineteenth-century literature have learned to discount all stories based on such hearsay by younger members of the Shelley circle (such as Thornton Hunt) or by those who never knew the poet (such as Jane, Lady Shelley), unless these stories can be corroborated by reliable contemporary documentary evidence. Renaissance scholars, with less evidence available to support (or disprove) their theories, may—like cosmologists—be tempted to invent more than they can discover.

11. Though Taylor develops an elaborate scenario in "William Shakespeare, Richard James, and the House of Cobham" (note 9) to prove that Shakespeare was still smarting from the censorship of the name "Oldcastle" by the time he wrote *Merry Wives*, this second argument weakens the case in "The Fortunes of Oldcastle."

Taylor notes that by the spring of 1596/97, "Sir William [Brooke] was dead; his son Henry, though now Lord Cobham, was not Lord Chamberlain, or a member of the Privy Council, or an old friend of any influential courtier. As [David] McKeen says [in "'A Memory of Honour': A Study of the house of Cobham in Kent in the Reign of Elizabeth I"—unpublished Ph.D. thesis, University of Birmingham, 1966, pp. 997–98], 'The new lord was fighting for his political life' in March and April of 1596/97"—the date that Taylor would prefer for the court performance of *The Merry Wives of Windsor* ("William Shakespeare . . . and the House of Cobham," p. 349). If, as Taylor argues, Shakespeare felt free to retaliate against the Brookes through his use of the name Brooke in *Merry Wives*, he certainly had ample opportunity to revive the name Oldcastle in his plays during the reign of James I, had he felt moved to do so. And if he had done so, the evidence would appear in the folio text of 1623.

12. See C. S. Lewis's debate with E. M. W. Tillyard, published as *The Personalist Heresy: A Controversy* (London: Oxford University Press, 1939).

The Science of Blunders:
Confessions of a Textual Critic

JAMES WILLIS

Some apology is sure to be demanded for a life largely devoted to what has been often called "mere verbal criticism" and regarded as no more than fiddling with letters and words which are of no importance in the wider horizon of the historian or the literary critic. Now while it would be useless to attempt to apologize for the lack of success with which I personally have practised the trade of a critic, for the trade itself much may be said in its defence. That textual criticism is a waste of time will be always believed by those who accept the texts of Greek and Latin authors as coming from heaven above by permission of the Syndics of the Oxford University Press, and therefore I will preach only to the convertible—to those who are willing to ask the simple question, "How do we have any knowledge of the Greek and Roman world?"

We know of the Greeks and Romans through concrete objects and through the witness of words. Temples, bridges, houses, statues, and the like have physically survived the centuries, and from them we can learn much; inscriptions on durable material have survived, and the diligent collecting and examining of these have made immeasurable additions to our knowledge: yet if we want to know what Greeks and Romans thought and said about the world and about each other, we depend overwhelmingly on written materials— "the literary sources", as professional historians call them often with a somewhat depreciating tone. Here we are not dealing with physical survivals. Sophocles and Plato and Cicero and Virgil did not carve their works in imperishable bronze or stone; they wrote them, or caused them to be written, on highly perishable papyrus. Before that substance crumbled, the text would be copied (or so the author

63

hoped) onto new papyrus; when that in turn crumbled, onto new, and so forth: the material passed away, but the text lived on, so that nothing of the original thought and language was lost.

Oh that it were so indeed! But the real world is not like that. At every copying there is the possibility of human error. I say "the possibility", but it is nearer to certainty. Copying is usually a boring task; boredom breeds inattention; inattention breeds mistakes. Therefore the manuscripts of classical authors contain mistakes. The detection and correction of mistakes in texts is the function of textual criticism. Therefore textual criticism is necessary, Q.E.D.

But, you will say, with that instinctive distrust of deductive reasoning which is the salvation of the English-speaking world, that is a mere train of thought. "Where are they, these supposedly inevitable errors? We read Caesar at school, and the text seemed alright." Yes: a school text seems pretty good, but precisely because textual critics have worked upon it. Consult anything that claims to be a scholarly edition, and you will find at the bottom of the page an apparatus criticus, which most people, including some dictionary-makers, prefer to disregard. That apparatus is essentially a record of the mistakes which various copyists have made in various manuscripts, and in some difficult texts the critical apparatus can fill half of the page. Now if there are several rival readings, only one can be right. They may be all wrong, and then we can recover what the author wrote only by conjectural emendation, which is a polysyllabic way of saying by guess or by God. Now to tell which, if any, of a number of variant readings is the original, we have to assess two kinds of probability. One is commonly called intrinsic probability: we ask, "How likely is it that Virgil or Ovid or Juvenal wrote these words? Are they Latin? Are they sense?" The other has been named transcriptional probability; we ask, "How likely is it that this reading should have arisen from that by a mistake in copying?"

Now some mistakes in copying betray themselves at once by giving a ludicrously inappropriate sense. The *Times of Allahabad* once wrote of India as "the cradle of civilization and nursery of rats"; the *Manchester Guardian*, which was at one time noted for the quaintness of its misprints, had to correct a line of poetry in which the words "and would his duty shirk" had been misprinted as "and mould his dirty shirt"; I observed recently in reading a trivial science-fiction story that, while the author had wanted to speak of that well-known astronomical object the Crab Nebula, the monotype operator had unfortunately confused the letters *b* and *p*. We have all heard of such absurd blunders, the most hackneyed involving the confusion of *battle* and *bottle*, *winch* and *wench*, *live* and *love*, and so forth.

Unfortunately not all copying-mistakes are ludicrous, and (which is more troublesome) not all are obvious to the general reader. There is a scene in the novel *Jane Eyre* in which the housekeeper Mrs Fairfax takes the heroine up to the roof of Thornfield Hall to show her the view over the park and surrounding countryside. As they descend, Jane goes first, while Mrs Fairfax stays to secure the trapdoor. A moment later Jane hears Mrs Fairfax's step on the "great stair". The immediate context, together with the general topography of Thornfield Hall as given in the book, makes it impossible that Miss Brontë should have written "the great stair". It was the garret stair that was supporting the respectable weight of Mrs Fairfax, yet "great stair" appears in every edition. Likewise, in one of the quoted fragments of Menander's *Dyscolus*, one of the personages addresses another as *daer* "brother-in law". No one looked on this reading with suspicion, particularly (I suppose) since a play of Terence's, based on a Greek New-Comedy original, is called *Hecyra* or *The Mother-in Law*. But when the full text of the *Dyscolos* was recovered, the Terentian title proved to have given us what is vulgarly called a bum steer, for one of the personages in Menander's play is a slave called Daos, and it is he who is being addressed in the vocative case *Dae*.

Here there might have been some reason to question the reading, for *daer* is a remarkably old-fashioned and poetic word to find in the colloquial language of New Comedy. In other instances there is nothing at all to raise suspicion. In Shelley's *Stanzas Written in Dejection near Naples* we find in some editions the words, "the breath of the moist air is light," but in the better texts which follow the first edition we find, "The breath of the moist earth is light." The latter is better certainly, but who would have dreamed of suspecting *air* if we had no other witness to the text? Again, in a fragment of Archilochus, long known from its being cited by Macrobius, the poet calls upon Apollo to point out (*sémaine*) the guilty; a papyrus fragment now has instead *pémaine*, 'afflict', which seems to me better and worthier of the vindictive Archilochus. There could have been, however, no reason whatever to suspect *sémaine* of being a false reading.

Here are two important points. First, there is no such thing as certainty in textual criticism. A word or phrase may be quite unobjectionable; it may give excellent sense and perfect grammar, but it may be wrong for all that. You will hear from time to time a classical scholar gravely declaring that a conjectural emendation may be ingenious and attractive, but that it can never be certain. True, but the same holds good of the transmitted text. Of a very few Latin authors we have manuscripts which go back to classical antiquity, which even so is much as if our best authority for the text of Shakespeare were a hand-written copy dating from the nineteen-thirties. With reasonable luck we may have manuscripts going back to the tenth or ninth century, which by careful comparison one with another will let us reconstruct the readings of a single manuscript which survived the chaos of the seventh and eighth centuries to reach the Carolingian age. Of many authors the textual fortunes have been much worse. For the poems of Catullus we can go no further back than a manuscript which existed at Verona in the fourteenth century, but which exists no longer. For the historical work of Velleius Paterculus we have no better authority than the earliest printed edition. If certainty is what we are looking for, the texts of classical authors are an ill-chosen hunting-ground.

The second point is equally to be borne in mind. If the witnesses to our text do not agree among themselves, it is not enough to choose a reading which is satisfactory in itself: we must choose that reading which best explains how the others could have arisen through faulty copying. Thus we may note the *pémaino* is a fairly rare verb, virtually confined to poetry (Liddell and Scott give about thirty occurrences), while *sémaino* is common in all periods and types of literature (L. & S. give some 140 occurrences); consequently *pémaino* is more likely to have been corrupted into *sémaino* than vice versa. The problem may be made clearer by an example fabricated for the purpose in English. Let us suppose that someone has written a melodramatic story of love and virtue triumphant while lust and villainy are discomfited, and that the vile Sir Jasper is riding as fast as he can in pursuit of his fair prey:

Sir Jasper lashed his horse furiously,

says one manuscript copy;

Sir Jasper lashed his beast furiously,

says another, while a third has

Sir Jasper lashed his breast furiously.

Which is the true reading? there is nothing wrong with *horse* in itself, but if the author wrote *horse*, how came it to be corrupted into *beast*, and *breast*? *Breast* of course is nonsense. Now if the author wrote *beast*, a dreaming copyist might have written *breast*, especially if he was thinking of the wedding guest who beat his breast when he heard the loud bassoon. An intelligent scribe, confronted with the absurd reading *breast*, might see that Sir Jasper must be whipping his horse and mend the text accordingly.

A rather similar problem, except that the true reading needs to be supplied conjecturally, is found in *Northanger Abbey*, Chap. 26: "By ten o'clock, the chaise-and-four conveyed the two from the Abbey. . . ." Who were the two occupants of the chaise? They were General Tilney, his daughter Eleanor, and the heroine of the romance, Miss Catherine Morland. Therefore Miss Austen could not have written *the two*. What did she write? In a copy possessed by her sister Cassandra the word *two* has been corrected to *three*, but there are not many people who would misread *three* as *two*. There can be little doubt that we must read *conveyed the trio from the Abbey*, as several critics have proposed independently. To ask whether Miss Austen elsewhere speaks of a group of three people as a trio is a legitimate question. She does indeed: *Mansfield Park*, Chap. 11: "They were now a miserable trio. . . ."

Such situations as this occur very often in texts of the Greek and Latin classics, and it is the duty of any responsible editor to regard as the most authentic reading the one which best explains the genesis of the others. Hence arises the dictum "Difficilior lectio potior" —"The more difficult reading is to be preferred." With the truth of this principle no one can disagree, provided that we remember that by "difficult" we mean "difficult to the copyist", not "difficult to the modern scholar". As a general rule, the men who copied manuscripts in the Latin middle ages knew a little Latin, but not much, and this is perhaps the state of affairs most productive of mistakes. If we know nothing of a language, we copy the text letter by letter, and our mistakes are confined to letters. If we understand a language perfectly, our grasp of its meaning helps us to do our job of copying, because we will not write anything that is senseless. But if we are perched on the isthmus of a middle state, we will tend to replace unusual words and constructions by others that we know better, turning *correption* into *corruption* or *correction, contusion* into *confusion, ingenuous* into *ingenious* and so forth.

In the eighteenth century the common way of producing a new edition of a classic was to reprint the text of the most esteemed previous edition, making changes only where something seemed to be wrong with the reading accepted by one's predecessor. The next step was to look in any manuscripts that came to hand until one of them yielded a reading that gave a tolerable sense. This reading would then be adopted into the text, the editor proudly claiming that he had restored the true reading from an excellent manuscript reposing in the library of that munificent patron of the arts, the Palsgrave of Pumpernickel, to whose mightiness he dedicated his humble work. In other places neither the editor nor his readers had any idea on what manuscript authority the text was based.

If this is the wrong way to use manuscripts, what is the right way? When the gods have so driven a man out of his wits that he decides to produce a critical edition of a classical Latin author, what does he do? Obviously he must find out what the manuscripts of that author are. For the modern scholar this is usually a straightforward task. Several standard works will tell him what the most important manuscripts are; after that he betakes himself to the published catalogues of manuscript collections. There may be in these some errors and omissions, for the cataloguing of manuscripts is slow work and badly paid work, and it is not easy to find men and women to do it well. Yet we owe a great debt of gratitude to those obscure researchers, for without their guidance we should be wandering in darkness. Within a few months we should know of all the manuscripts which contain our author's work. Now we have to examine them all and record all their variant readings.

Here a difficulty can arise. When I began work on the text of Martianus Capella, I soon learned that there were nearly 250 manuscripts of this author, whose text ran to a little over 530 pages in the previous printed edition. A few calculations of the time needed to report the variant readings of a single page, with the assumption that I should work on it for three hours every day, excluding Saturdays and Sundays, revealed that the task would take me roughly thirty years, after which I should still have to select the readings which seemed to me best, reduce my collations to the form of a critical apparatus, type the whole thing out together with prolegomena and index, and correct the proofs. Since I was already thirty-eight years old, I had obviously started too late. I felt like the old lag who, when sentenced to fifteen years' penal servitude, cried out, "But, My Lord, I shall never live to finish such a sentence." The judge, you will remember, kindly replied, "Never mind: just serve as much of it as you can." But in sober truth this is a difficult problem. If there is not time to examine all the manuscripts, which of them do we exclude? It would seem reasonable to omit the later manuscripts and take a stand on the early ones; yet there may be a fifteenth-century manuscript copied directly and carefully from one of the ninth century, which is no longer extant. I am ashamed of the advice which I should give to a young scholar in such a case, for I should say, "If you have ten or a dozen from the ninth and tenth centuries, stick to those and neglect the others. As for the hypothetical manuscript of late date which is a copy of a lost manuscript better than any which survive, forget it. Probably there isn't such a manuscript; if there is, maybe no one will find it, and if someone does find it and makes a great fuss about it, with a little bit of luck you'll be able to argue that all its good readings are conjectural." Strict scientific method could be followed only if one had a team of devoted students who would each examine a few manuscripts and hope to get Ph.D.s or published articles out of it as their cut. In the heyday of the German universities this farming-out of learned labour was a regular part of the system.

Well, setting this problem aside, let us suppose that the collation of manuscripts is completed. We have now all the readings of all the manuscripts. What do we do with them? We examine them in the hope of doing two things: first of working out in individual passages by what historical process the different readings in different manuscripts arose; secondly of establishing in consequence what relationships there are between the various manuscripts—whether manuscript B is a copy of manuscript A, or whether A and B are copies of an original which is not one of those known to us and therefore presumably is no longer extant. The first of these inquiries involves what I have called the science of blunders—the name *sphalmatology*, jokingly invented by the late J. B. S. Haldane, has not achieved circulation, but the study deserves to be an-ology in its own right, and to endow a readership in it would be less waste of money than many things which I have seen done in the academic world.

Of course to the average classical scholar, who is no more exempt than the rest of mankind from a distaste for thought, the whole thing is very simple. Mistakes of one letter occur from time to time; mistakes of two letters are rare; mistakes of three or more letters hardly ever happen. This view arises from a wrong approach—from that approach which tries to find out things about the real world by thinking about them without observing them. If I wanted to know what are the most common causes of breakdowns in motorcars, I should not try to work it out by deductive inference from first principles: I should instead write to the R.A.C. and ask whether they kept records of all the occasions on which their breakdown service was summoned and of the cause of the breakdown on each occasion: if they did, and if they were willing to impart that information to me, I should be in a fair way to gain the knowledge I wanted by inductive reasoning from observed phaenomena, which I take to be the only way of finding out what happens in the real world. We can know what mistakes are likely, therefore, only by seeing and noting what mistakes are actually made. Most copyists do not copy letter by letter; their unit of recognition is the word or small group of words. A single proof of this fact will suffice. No two words are more often confused in Latin manuscripts that *voluntas* 'will' and *voluptas* 'pleasure'. This can hardly represent a confusion between *n* and *p*, for the two letters are quite unlike each other. On the other hand, in most manuscripts of the middle ages an *n* can look very like *u*, and *c* can look very much like a *t*; yet we never find *noluntas* or *voluncas* as misreadings of *voluntas* because these are not Latin words.

We may reinforce this lesson as to confusion of single letters by considering the trouble sometimes given by the old-fashioned long *s*, which lingered in English printing until the end of the eighteenth century. The form of the letter may mislead us into thinking that we see *fight* or *fought* or *flew* when in truth we have *sight* or *sought* or *slew*, but we never think that we see *fparrow* or *fpinfter* or *faufage*, because those are not English words. In a man who writes a book about the eighteenth century one does not expect to find such confusions, but here is a quotation from a poem of Bath and its waters as it appears in John Walters's book on Beau Nash:

> Here beauteous females in conception flow,
> By genial waters soon more fertile grow.
> Here barren ladies may their wants relieve,
> But by the waters only they conceive.
> Here balls and plays and all diversions reign,
> No pleasures fully, and no freedoms stain.

Only a moderate degree of attention was needed in order to see that the rhymester wrote *slow* in the first line and *sully* in the sixth. *Soon* in the second line escaped corruption because there is no English word *foon*.

I am not saying, of course, that difficult hands with badly formed letters do not make mistakes more likely: they certainly do. That busy publicist Horace Greeley wrote one of the worst hands ever known. An American typesetter once said of it that if Belshazzar had seen that writing on the wall, he would have been a heap more frightened than he was. In one article Greeley quoted Polonius's words, "'Tis true 'tis pity, and pity 'tis, 'tis true." The baffled compositor produced the following strange arithmetic: "'Tis two, 'tis fifty, and fifty 'tis, 'tis five." Another famous Yankee, the Reverend Henry Ward Beecher, had a scarcely less atrocious hand; it was said that only his daughter could read it, and that she worked on three fundamental principles—that if a letter was dotted, it was not an *i*, if it was crossed, it was not a *t*, while if a word was spelt with a capital letter, it did not begin a sentence. Yet even the realm of typesetting is subject to Murphy's Law. Edward Lane, the Victorian translator of the *Arabian Nights*, wrote a clear and elegant copper-plate hand, and yet he found his proofs abounding with errors. When he sought an explanation, the printer told him that his writing was so good that the setting of it was entrusted to apprentices: the time of an experienced man would be wasted on such easy work. For many decades now, of course, printing-houses have demanded that all copy be typewritten: whether this practice has made printing more accurate I cannot say.

The most common kind of mistake then is the replacement of a word by another of similar shape, usually a more common word. The horse-hoe recommended by Jethro Tull becomes a horse-shoe; the fossil plants called calamites become *calamities*; *immortality* becomes *immorality*, and so forth. F. W. Hall in his *Companion to Classical Texts* cites two beautiful examples from the *Times* newspaper: "One doctor described his case as that of miniature development" (for *immature*); and, "The Crown makes no claim to lumbago found in lands sold by it prior to 1901" (the mineral *plumbago* being intended). An edition of the bible printed in 1717 by the Clarendon Press gave the heading to Luke chap. 20 as "Parable of the Vinegar" (for *vineyard*). Sometimes the mistake seems to have arisen from a mis-hearing of dictation, as when the *Daily Telegraph* at some time in the nineteen-fifties assured the British people in regard to one of their recurrent financial crises that "We have shot the rabbits and are now in clear water again."

This last error leads us to another curious cause of copying-mistakes, which could be called preoccupation. The notion of shooting, no doubt, brought rabbits and such small deer into the compositor's mind. Similarly a familiarity with the routine of the printing-house may have produced the famous blunder, "Printers have persecuted me without a cause," and Freudian psychologists will have no difficulty in explaining why the printer of the bible in 1621 omitted the word *not* in the seventh commandment. A striking example of this kind occurs in the text of Horace (Carm. 3, 18, 12): the poet describes a country village on holiday, and says that the community on holiday lies in the fields together with the oxen who also are at ease—*festus in pratis iacet otioso cum bove pagus*. A copyist who must have been familiar with Isaiah 11.6, "The wolf also shall dwell with the lamb, and the leopard shall lie down with the kid," has written *pardus* "leopard" for *pagus* "village". In the passage where Tibullus says to his girl-friend, "I should love to live with you" (*tecum vivere amem*), some dreaming monk has written *tecum vivere amen*.

The substitution of words not of the same shape but of the same meaning is less frequent, but more troublesome. This fault is the fault of memory rather than of vision, and it occurs often in quotations made from memory. Thus Milton's "Tomorrow to fresh woods and pastures new" is often misquoted as "Tomorrow to fresh fields and pastures new"; we often hear that a little knowledge is a dangerous thing, but Pope wrote "a little learning"; Quintilian quotes the second line of Virgil's first eclogue from memory and gives us a rustic muse (*agrestem Musam*) where the manuscripts of Virgil have a woodland Muse (*silvestrem Musam*). In Latin manuscripts the substitution of a synonym, where it occurs, more often than not arises from the misunderstanding of an explanatory note. *Tepor*, for example, means warmth, and so does *calor*, but the later is a much more commonplace word, as is shown by its survival in the romance languages (Sp. *calor*, Fr. *chaleur*); hence someone who thinks that other readers may stand in need of his expert guidance (a type of human personality that is always with us) writes *calor* between the lines or in the margin to tell lesser mortals that that is what *tepor* means. The next numbskull to copy out the text supposes that *calor* is a correction and writes it in place of *tepor*. Or of course he may suppose that the marginal reading is something that has been left out and ought to be restored, and so he writes *tepor calor*.

There is of course one area in which the mistaking of individual written characters is the predominant type of error—that is in the copying of numerals. To mistake one numeral for another—a 1 for a 7, a 3 for a 5, etc.—is too common to need remark. Some interest attaches, however, to the mistaking of figures for letters or vice versa. A printer once described an old country house as having "219-209 passages", where the author had written *zig-zag*. The title of a book on F. Scott Fitzgerald appeared in a bookseller's catalogue as "Scott Fitzgerald—Chronicler of the 1933 Age" (for *Jazz* Age), and that great navigator James Cook was oddly transformed by a French typesetter into "M. le capitaine 600 kilomètres." Several years ago, when numerical postcodes were a new thing, my friend, Dr Melville Jones, received a letter addressed to him in Dalkeith, Waboog.

More troublesome than substitution is omission. Few things are easier in copying than to leave out several words because the same word occurs twice, especially if it should occur the second time immediately under the place where it occured first. In looking through the typescript of this paper I found that I had typed "from time", where I meant "from time to time". A striking example in Greek comes from Euripides' Helen. Menelaus meets that heroine in Egypt, and asks her (since he does not recognize her at once),

> Ἑλληνὶς εἶ τις, ἢ 'πιχωρία γυνή;
> Greek art thou, or a native of this land?

She replies

> Ἑλληνίς· ἀλλὰ καὶ τὸ σὸν μαθεῖν θέλω
> Greek; and thy nation too I fain would know.

In the text of Euripides, through the repetition of the first word, the verse has entirely vanished. By a remarkable stroke of luck Aristophanes puts the verses into the mouths of Euripides and the disguised Mnesilochus in the *Thesmophoriazusae*, and so the loss can be repaired. For the most part, however, what is lost is lost, and nothing but the discovery of new manuscripts independent of those which we have (a prospect most unlikely in the case of Latin authors) holds out any hope of restoration.

Loss can of course be occasioned by purely mechanical misfortunes. No bookbinding lasts for ever: the stitching goes, and leaves can fall out, sometimes to be lost, sometimes to be replaced in the wrong order. Sometimes a single leaf that has become detached is the only part to survive. In 1772 a single leaf was found from the ninety-first book of Livy in the Vatican Library; what happened to the rest is anybody's guess. When Aldus Manutius was editing the letters of the younger Pliny, he used a manuscript of the early sixth century from a monastery near Paris. What happened to it after he had used it we do not know; the monastery certainly never got it back. Shortly before the First World War, however, Pierpont Morgan bought six leaves of an ancient manuscript which had been owned by some Neapolitan nobleman: they are part of that missing manuscript, but no-one knows when they became detached or where the rest of it is, if it still exists.

Thus far we have considered mostly mistakes which arise at a single blow. It is, of course, possible that an error committed by one scribe may engender a second error by another, and that in turn a third, and so forth. From that rich storehouse of blunders and lies, the transmission of Martianus Capella, I draw an example. Taking his material from Pliny the Elder, Martianus writes that the province of Hispania Baetica has four seats of the administration of justice, and he gives their names. Unfortunately there are only two names in his list; two have been lost through similarity of ending— *Cordubensem . . . Hispalensem*. The manuscripts of Pliny have all the four names, and thus we can see that the omission of two was a blunder made by a copyist—not by Martianus Capella himself, for he would not then have put the numeral *quattuor*. Now of the manuscripts of Martianus Capella a few faithfully retain the original mistake; the rest have either altered *quattuor* to *duo* or left out the number altogether. There is a remarkable corruption in the same author's book on geometry, where it can be shown that the reading printed in the Teubner edition of 1925 was the last of five stages of corruption, the first having been the omission of ten or eleven words caused by the similarity of ending of two Greek words.

Now here I think that textual critics have to keep their imagination under control. The five-stage corruption which I have just mentioned is attested in the manuscripts—the simple omission which began it, the various attempts of copyists to fill the gap, and the conjectures of editors who did not realize that the manuscripts which they were using were falsified. But beware the flashing eyes and floating hair of him who postulates such a chain of successive corruptions when none of the intermediate stages is attested, who tells you that *skull* was corrupted to *skill*, then *skill* to *still*, *still* to *stall*, *stall* to *stalk*, *stalk* to *stack* and so forth. With enough ingenuity one can devise a number of stages through which almost anything could be corrupted into anything else, but these schemes bear as much relation to real events in copying as the designs of Heath Robinson bear to real engineering.

With any luck, by the time we have analysed the mutual relations of the variant readings, we should be able to work out the mutual relations of the manuscripts. Then, if we can show that manuscript Q was directly copied from manuscript P, we can forget about Q, for it has no independent authority. Now we can argue that Q is copied from P if it has every one of P's mistakes plus some of its own. There is one abatement of the severity of this condition: If Q has a few readings right where P has them wrong, it may be that the man who wrote Q was a clever guesser. Now the idea of being able to discard some of the manuscripts as being mere copies of others is very attractive, and editors have often been seduced by its charms so far as to discard manuscripts which could not possibly be mere copies of certain known others. Struck by a few agreements in error, they have overlooked true readings which could not plausibly be assigned to conjecture. One editor of Euripides went so far as to discard one manuscript as being a copy of another when the supposed copy contained two plays which were not in the supposed original. My own experience leads me to suspect that direct copies of extant manuscripts are rather rare birds, because so many manuscripts which formerly existed now exist no longer. If we had now every manuscript that there ever had been of the classical text in which we were interested, it would be possible to work out exactly how they were related each to each; with at least three quarters of them missing, the task is enormously difficult, but it would still be theoretically possible except for one thing which I have not mentioned: the variant readings of one manuscript often find their way into a manuscript that is not related to it by direct copying.

There were textual critics in the middle ages too (it is a curse from which no period of history has been wholly exempt), and they would sometimes try to improve the text of their own manuscript of Juvenal, for example, by consulting another manuscript and noting its variants in the margin. When the manuscript thus supplied with variants was next copied out, the copyist would adopt some or all of the variants, and the manuscript thus produced would give a text which is mixed and comes effectively from two sources, not one. For this reason it is not very often possible to say, "This manuscript is a copy of that," while on the other hand we can often say, "This manuscript is more recent than that and has many of its characteristic errors." The family-trees of manuscripts which you will often find in the prolegomena to critical editions are not comparable with the family-trees of noble families: they deal with general resemblances rather than with precise questions of fatherhood and motherhood. Again we are in a position where, with the sensible Mrs Dashwood, we may say, "Are no probabilities to be accepted, merely because they are not certainties?"

Let us suppose then that our editor has surveyed the manuscript evidence, classified the manuscripts, and decided what readings, on the basis of that manuscript evidence, are best attested, is he ready to sit down at his typewriter or his word-processor and start typing up the copy for the printer? No, he is not; there is other evidence that he has not yet examined. Simply by examining the manuscripts of Euripides, however well you did that job, you would not be able to restore that missing line in the *Helen*, of which we spoke earlier. Sometimes earlier writers are quoted or imitated or parodied by later writers, and if those sources survive, they may cast light on passages imperfectly transmitted in our manuscripts. We have seen how the text of a source, Pliny the Elder, revealed to us exactly what had gone wrong in the text of Martianus Capella, and indeed in that author, since most of the sources are extant and since the manuscripts of Martianus himself are very corrupt, the careful comparison of the sources and the borrowings pays considerable dividends.

Here I may make one of those confessions promised by my subtitle. In 1968 I produced what was meant to be a critical edition of Macrobius. I will refresh your memories: he was an author of the fifth century and a rank plagiarist by modern standards. He throws around the names of old republican Roman writers and of little-known Greek writers, but we have good reason to believe that they are all at second hand, for in many cases the books from which he took his material survive, and we see that he suppressed the name of the immediate source, leading us to believe that he had personally read those writers whom he parades before us. Thus much of his material comes from the second-century Aulus Gellius: roughly speaking, all Macrobius' knowledge of Roman republican literature is borrowed from Gellius. Hence the editor of Gellius cannot neglect the evidence of Macrobius, and Mr Peter Marshall made exemplary use of that evidence in producing his Oxford Classical Text of Gellius. The editor of Macrobius, on the other hand, rushed into print without carefully examining the evidence of Gellius, and not only did he receive unfavorable reviews—that does not matter—but he left the text unimproved where it could have been made better. For example, Macrobius speaks of the notorious Egyptian king Busiris, who was accustomed, he says, to sacrifice on his altars men of all nations—*homines omnium gentium*. Now the corresponding passage of Gellius has *hospites omnium gentium*, "foreigners of all nations". This is obviously the true reading: Busiris did not sacrifice his fellow-Egyptians, he sacrificed only foreigners who came to Egypt from outside. This is evidence of a kind which no editor can afford to dis-regard if he wants to do his job in a workmanlike manner.

So much then for the way in which the textual critic approaches and performs his task. If he does it well, what does he gain there-by? For himself, very little beyond the satisfaction of a job well done. He will not receive rave reviews, because those who are not textual critics cannot judge his work, and those who are include among their ranks some of the most quarrelsome of mankind. Further, the critic becomes (unless he is of most unusual character) emotionally involved with his work. The pangs of a lover whose addresses are scorned are less severe than those of the emendator whose darling conjecture is accepted by no one. His attitude tends to be, as Miss Tallulah Bankhead so well expressed it, "To hell with criticism: praise is good enough for me." Extravagant expectations of this kind are, in the normal course of human affairs, doomed to disappointment, and the man of philosophic mind may draw much consolation from the reflexion that his reviewers and his employers are two different sets of men. But for the world of literate men and women, what is gained by the successful performance of the textual critic's task?

Here I shall, with your permission, invoke the privilege accorded to old age ever since Homer drew the character of Nestor, of talking of oneself. I have produced critical editions of two Latin authors, Macrobius and Martianus Capella. Neither is an author of the first rank, yet both will find readers for different reasons. Macrobius, as we have seen, preserves a great deal of material from Greek and Latin literature; he chose well the authors whom he decided to plagiarize, and where his sources have perished he may be thanked for his choice, if not for his methods. Martianus Capella also preserved here and there pieces of ancient learning which otherwise would never have been known to the Latin middle ages, during which his encyclopaedic work enjoyed an enormous vogue. I will try to say what I think was achieved by those two undertakings.

The text of Macrobius was not improved very much. A few better readings appeared here and there, but in the main the text remained as readers were accustomed to see it. The progress made was that the manuscript basis for the text was now put before the reader. Of the two preceding editors, one had examined a large number of manuscripts and editions, but the people who collated manuscripts for him were incredibly negligent and missed two-thirds of the variant readings; the other, although his manuscript collation was of admirable accuracy, used only two manuscripts and took no account of any others. Hence what was needed was a survey of the manuscript evidence. Because the text was (apart from several lacunae) very well preserved, this work did not make us believe new things about the text of Macrobius, but it provided us with observational grounds for believing what we already did believe.

With Martianus Capella the state of affairs was different. A good edition had been produced, after forty years of devoted work, by Dr Adolf Dick, who was headmaster of the Cantonschule of St Gall in Switzerland. He used nine early manuscripts, and he recorded all their variants accurately. His one shortcoming was that he did not understand how full of lies those manuscripts were. Since the work of Martianus was used from the ninth century on for instruction in schools, and since the text of the sole manuscript in which it had reached the Carolingian renaissance was deplorably corrupt, the schoolmasters at once began to correct the mistakes so as to provide their boys with a readable text. In doing so they filled the manuscripts, even very early ones, with conjectural readings which were in some cases very clever but which covered up the original damage to the text. The task of the critic was here to find, if possible, manuscripts which had not been tampered with and in which the faults of the archetype could still be clearly seen. There are in fact some six or seven among the 250 manuscripts which are free in this way from deliberate alteration. With the assistance of the catalogue of manuscripts drawn up by Claudio Leonardi and the penetrating study of the earliest among them by Jean Préaux in Brussels, it was possible to find what those manuscripts were and to use their testimony, together with the collateral evidence of those writers whom Martianus had used as sources, to purge the text of mediaeval fabrications which had persevered through every printed edition.

Something, I think, was gained for our understanding of Martianus Capella himself. He had traditionally been written off as one of the greatest asses ever to have set pen to paper, but upon careful examination it appeared that corruption in his text or in the texts of his sources accounted for many of his most remarkable blunders. It was unfair, for example, to blame him for assigning to Alexander a victory in *Arabia* instead of *Arbela* when it is obvious that *Arabia* was the reading of the manuscripts of his source Pliny the Elder, or to blame him for misunderstanding the text of Pliny as it stood in nineteenth-century editions, when those editions were following a conjectural supplement proposed by the renaissance humanist Ermolao Barbaro. I have been led to the opinion that he was not a fool and that he was making an intelligent and serious attempt to compress a liberal education into four or five hundred pages.

This is what I think I have done: it is fair to say that other views have been expressed in print and that they are less favourable. But whether or not my work has been successful, I have enjoyed doing it, and the attitude of mind engendered in studying the transmission of Latin texts has been a source of great pleasure in looking for and sometimes stumbling over mistakes made by modern typists and compositors which throw light on the blunders of ancient and mediaeval copyists. Also—though this has not much directly to do with the trade of textual criticism—I have enjoyed being surrounded by those whom I may call in plain English, not in the jargon of the lawcourts, my learned friends. From them, and often from my students, I have often learned to correct my opinions and to stock my head with as much wisdom as Providence had ever ordained that it should possess. If any of those benefits have ever been to the slightest degree returned, I am very happy, and I can wish nothing better to the young among us than that they may spend forty years as interestingly and instructively and happily as I have spent my working life.[1]

NOTE

1. Books used: F.W. Hall, *Companion to Classical Texts* (Oxford, 1913), J. A. Willis, *Latin Textual Criticism* (Urbana: Illinois University Press, 1972), R. T. Gould, *"Mistakes and Misprints" in The Stargazer Talks* (London, 1943), and Falconer Madan, *Books in Manuscript*, 2nd ed. (London, 1927).

Fair Copy, Authorial Intention, and "Versioning"

JAMES L. W. WEST III

In this paper I should like to discuss further one or two concepts touched upon in an earlier article entitled "Editorial Theory and the Act of Submission" (*PBSA*, 83 [1989], 169–85). I want to examine the term "fair copy" and to deal with its relation to authorial intention; I also wish to consider how an author's preparation of fair copy can affect the editorial technique called "versioning."

The words "fair copy" are reassuring to a scholarly editor. The existence of a fair copy somewhere along the line of textual transmission for a particular literary work gives the editor great moral authority. He can know that there once did exist, in space and time, a copy of the text to which (for that moment) the author had applied the finishing touches. Even if this fair copy no longer survives, its one-time existence suggests that there is a tangible goal toward which an editor can strive, or, alternately, a hypothetical point from which he can commence. The editor knows that the author, at a point when the text was still fully under his control and physically in his possession, directed his attention to a single document and got "just right." Then and only then was the work submitted to something called the "publication process."

Perhaps the mental image of a fair copy, conveyed to a publisher in a kind of ceremonial act, has been attractive to scholarly editors because most of them are teachers, and all of them have at some point been students. Submitting a fair copy of a poem or a novel to a publisher is rather like turning in the final, corrected copy of a term paper to a professor near the end of a semester. The pedagogue's assumption is that this embodiment of the student's work is the best that he or she can do. The student has worked hard on the document and finally, in the wee hours of the morning, has said: "There! I'm done! This copy is just the way I want it." Authors (most of whom have also been students) presumably think in the same fashion. They prepare a copy of the literary work which suits them in all details; they place this single copy on the desk and say with satisfaction: "There! Finished!" Of course even the most inexperienced author knows that he is not really finished, but, paradoxically, this fact gives added authority to the fair copy. Its creation, one imagines, must have been a private act about which the author could say, "At least for now, this once, without interference, I have created a copy of this text to suit myself and only myself." The fair copy represents the best that the author can do; it is what he intends for the literary work at that time and in that place. It is the final copy of his term paper, and he means to submit it, not to a professor, but to an authority figure with much greater power—a publisher.

For some literary works, this description of fair copy is correct. The author did apply the final touches to a single copy of the text and then conveyed it to the publisher with the implied or stated message: "This is the way I want it." Normally, behavior such as this occurs early in the author's career. One commonly finds it in the compositional history of first novels, for example. The author has no publisher or contract and must shop his manuscript about. He must put his best foot forward—must dot his i's, cross his t's, and "submit clean copy." Years later, when this first novel has attained the status of a classic, a scholarly editor can plan his entire strategy around this fair copy, especially if it still survives. Its existence clarifies immensely the question of intention.

What I wish to examine here, however, are cases in which this scenario was not played out. These are instances in which there was never a fair copy and never a formal act or ceremony of submission. For such works, fair copy existed only in some blurry, in-between region of intention, somewhere midway between the submission of a manifestly unfinished form of the text to the publisher and the emergence of that text, some months later, as a published artifact. This changes things considerably for the scholarly editor. It makes it much more difficult to create an ideal text—if that is one's goal—and it requires a different way of thinking about intention and the compositional process.

I want to discuss several of the fair copies prepared by two modern American novelists, Theodore Dreiser and Ernest Hemingway. We shall see that early in their careers both of these writers prepared fair copies very carefully for their novels. Later, when they were settled in more-or-less comfortable relationships with publishers and had some leverage in the literary marketplace, they were much less apt to prepare fair copies, submitting instead largely finished documents that would be brought to completion and publication in collaboration with publishers.

Dreiser prepared fair copies of his first two novels—*Sister Carrie* (1900) and *Jennie Gerhardt* (1911). He had a typescript made of *Sister Carrie*, polished it, submitted it to Harper and Brothers in the spring of 1900, had it rejected, revised and polished it further, and submitted it to Doubleday, Page and Company—where it eventually served as setting copy for the first edition. But Dreiser learned that the text of *Sister Carrie* was far from being fixed or stable in his fair copy. The text was bowdlerized and altered in numerous ways on the fair copy itself and was changed further in proof. To the publisher, Dreiser learned, his carefully revised fair copy was simply a point from which to begin making alterations.[1]

For a variety of reasons Dreiser was unable to finish his second novel, *Jennie Gerhardt*, until the spring of 1911. He prepared a fair-copy typescript, submitted it to Macmillan, had it rejected, submitted it to Harper and Brothers, and had it accepted. But this time the fair copy proved to be even less sacrosanct. Harper's editor Ripley Hitchcock and several subeditors under his direction almost completely rewrote *Jennie Gerhardt* for print, covering Dreiser's fair copy with so many alterations that they had to have a fresh typescript made for the compositor. Indeed, Dreiser's fair copy was so covered with editorial changes that Hitchcock was reluctant to let him see it and had to be prodded, by Dreiser's literary agent, to allow him to examine it. Dreiser fought against much of the cutting and alteration of *Jennie Gerhardt* and succeeded in having some material restored before publication, but he was still unhappy about what had been done to his novel and was worried that the Harper editors had cut too deeply.[2]

For all his irritation, Dreiser had at least learned a lesson about fair copy. A fair copy took much time, energy, and emotion to prepare. Much of that effort, however, was likely to be wasted. At this point in his career Dreiser had set himself the hellishly difficult task of turning out a new novel every six months. He seems to have realized—perhaps with a sigh of relief—that at least he would not have to prepare fair copies for these projected novels. If the publisher were going to cut, rewrite, and repunctuate the text in any case, then why not *allow* him to do this work, and other scut-work as well, especially if it were "part of the service"? For Dreiser it now became a question of how much labor he could shift from his own shoulders (or those of his assistants and amanuenses) to those of the publisher.

One can see the results of Dreiser's thinking in the preparation of the text of his next novel, *The Financier* (1912). Dreiser produced a holograph manuscript which was not a first draft but was not exactly a fair copy either. Evidences of several layers of work survive in this document: there are numbering sequences on the leaves which indicate additions and cuts after initial inscription, and there are bridge passages and leaves on which the writing ends mid-folio and mid-sentence—as if to indicate revision and splicing. Dreiser appears to have invested a good deal of labor in this draft, but it is not a true fair copy. Punctuation is haphazard and spelling erroneous, some passages are in need of clarification, and there are inconsistencies in chronology and characterization. This is the document which Dreiser gave, in batches, to Ripley Hitchcock at Harper. His implied message could not have been: "This is precisely the way I want it." The message must have been more nearly: "You take it from here for a while; I'll come back later, and we'll work toward the printed text together." This is in fact how *The Financier* was produced. Hitchcock had a typescript made at the Harper offices, and he and his subeditors cut and revised it. Dreiser then re-entered the compositional process, and together he and the Harper editors brought the first edition into being. Dreiser had learned to co-opt the publisher's energy and resources; he had spared himself the effort of preparing a fair copy and the irritation that he knew would come when the text of his fair copy was not respected.[3]

How does this change the way one would prepare a critical edition of *The Financier*? Without a true fair copy, a text brought by Dreiser to a point of stasis, how should one proceed? I would suggest that an editor would still be able to use Dreiser's holograph as copy-text, but that the editor's attitude toward emendations accepted from later forms of the text would probably need to change. With both *Sister Carrie* and *Jennie Gerhardt*, one could view variants between fair copy and first print quite circumspectly. Dreiser created fair copies of these works; he brought their texts to points of stability, so far as he was concerned, at particular moments in their making. His fair copies can therefore be treated as beginning points in the editorial process, and their authority is strong enough that an intentionalist editor can see himself as guarding their readings against later corruption. With *The Financier*, by contrast, the holograph does not possess quite this same authority, and one would probably have to be rather more liberal in one's attitude toward the publisher's (and the author's) alterations between holograph and print. The dials on the "intention machine" would have to be adjusted to allow more revisions and cuts from the first printing to be emended back into the copy-text—or at least so it appears from this vantage point.

For Hemingway my remarks will be more general and tentative, since I have not produced a scholarly edition of one of his works and have spent only one extended period studying his literary papers at the Kennedy Library, where they are housed. That introductory look suggests, however, that Hemingway's attitude toward fair copy follows a progression quite similar to the one described above for Dreiser. Hemingway appears to have invested much time and energy in the preparation of fair copies for his first two novels, *The Sun Also Rises* (1926) and *A Farewell to Arms* (1929). His method is of some interest: in both cases he had a ribbon and at least one carbon copy made of the text, then submitted one of the carbons to his publisher, Charles Scribner's Sons, to serve as setting copy. Meanwhile Hemingway retained the ribbon copy and entered final revisions on it, as he re-read it from time to time. This ribbon copy was, in effect, his fair copy, though he never submitted it to his publisher. When galleys arrived, Hemingway transferred most of his late revising and polishing from the ribbon typescripts to the proofs. To judge from his markings on the galleys for both novels, he apparently decided against some of his ribbon-copy revisions, once the typeset text was in front of him, or he decided to execute different revisions of passages which had dissatisfied him. And of course he made other, independent alterations while reading through the galleys.

This was a fairly elaborate process, and it suggests that Hemingway cared a great deal about the form in which his texts would be published. One can therefore understand his frustration when he found out that the editors at Scribner's were going to take many liberties, large and small, with his texts. These texts were going to be cut, bowdlerized, and thoroughly restyled in accidentals.[4] Hemingway also learned that Maxwell Perkins, his chief editor at Scribner's, often would not turn his full attention to a book until its text had been set in type. Perkins could afford this luxury because Scribner's operated its own printing plant, which was more responsive (and less expensive) than jobbers would have been. If, therefore, Perkins were going to treat the setting copy as no more than an intermediate stage and were not going to examine it carefully, then Hemingway might as well do the same, withholding his full attention from the text until it was set in type.

One sees evidence of this shift in Hemingway's thinking with his next book, *Death in the Afternoon* (1932).[5] He assembled a first draft of this book that is a composite of holograph and typescript leaves. He did have this draft typed, but he was far from finished with the text. He revised this typescript heavily in his own hand and then, without having it retyped, sent it on to Scribner's. Type was set from this revised typescript. Only then did Hemingway and Perkins get down to real work—in the galleys. Fortunately all of these stages of the text are extant, so it will be possible for an editor to identify who did what to *Death in the Afternoon* at every stage of its development. But the ideal text toward which a critical editor should strive never came close to existing as a fair copy. It existed only in the abstract, somewhere between the typescript Hemingway sent to Scribner's and the published book that he and Perkins put out.

As with *The Financier*, this should affect quite significantly a scholarly editor's thinking and procedures. Copy-text for a critical edition of *Death in the Afternoon* should probably be the revised typescript which Hemingway sent to Scribner's, but—in line with Hemingway's own attitude—this text should not be treated with quite the same respect that one would accord a true fair copy. The text aimed for in a critical edition would instead exist somewhere between that typescript and the text of the first edition.

Situations such as these will create problems for an editor committed to a technique which Donald H. Reiman, in an intelligent and practical-minded book chapter, has called "versioning."[6] The essence of versioning, if I understand the approach correctly, is to publish incarnations of a work of literature from various points in its textual history. No synthesis is attempted, no ideal text aimed for. Each version of the text is considered to possess some authority, and the entire literary work exists as a kind of continuum, from early through intermediate to late versions. Together these versions possess a collective final authority.

This is an attractive approach for anyone who has ever suffered through the preparation of a critical edition, but I do not believe that it is flexible enough to be applied usefully to all textual situations. It seems to me that inherent in versioning is an assumption that each embodiment of the text chosen for reproduction possess some measure of finality, that it be a text to which either the author, or the author plus the publisher, has at some point applied a final "Voila!" (This can happen, of course, at more than one moment in the history of the text.) If this is so, then versioning will work satisfactorily, in theory, for such novels as *Sister Carrie* and *Jennie Gerhardt*, or for *The Sun Also Rises* and *A Farewell to Arms*, but it will not work especially well for books like *The Financier* and *Death in the Afternoon*. The versions of these two works that survive are not sufficiently final, or "fair," to be of very wide use or interest if reproduced. And the same problem crops up in subsequent books by both Dreiser and Hemingway—Dreiser's *The Titan* (1914) and *The "Genius"* (1915), for example, and Hemingway's *To Have and Have Not* (1937).

The technique of versioning looks as if it would be much easier to apply to lyric poems than to novels. Lyrics can be published or facsimiled in numerous versions and can be compared and discussed at length. And there are often numerous successive *published* versions of lyric poems—periodical, first book, collected edition, revised and enlarged collected edition, deathbed edition. But the same technique would not be realistic for *The Financier*, at 780 pages in its first edition, or for *Death in the Afternoon*, at 517. Nor is photo-facsimile really a workable approach. The holograph of *The Financier* is fully 1663 pages in length—much too long for reproduction in anything other than microform. The relevant materials for *Death in the Afternoon* occupy over five hundred leaves of archival material, rather too many to be facsimiled for this "less-than-major" work by Hemingway.

Versioning appears to be a workable editorial technique for

short writings that survive in multiple published forms, each of which can be thought to possess some measure of finality, but it is not an attractive alternative for long works which exist only in intermediate, "un-fair" copies or in published texts which were produced in (often vexed) collaboration with trade editors. Opportunities to edit these lengthy works of prose, in fully funded editions, do not arise with great frequency. If publisher and financing are in place, it seems to me that one cannot lose one's nerve, abdicate one's responsibility to the author and the text, and opt for versioning as an editorial technique. Rather, one is obliged to seize the chance to apply one's critical intelligence to the surviving drafts, with or without an existing fair copy, and attempt to create an eclectic ideal.

NOTES

1. For an extended account of the composition and publication of Dreiser's first novel, see the historical commentary of the Pennsylvania Edition of *Sister Carrie* (Philadelphia: University of Pennsylvania Press, 1981), pp. 503–41.

2. A brief account of the composition of Dreiser's second novel is included in James L. W. West III, "Double Quotes and Double Meanings in *Jennie Gerhardt*," *Dreiser Studies*, 18 (Spring 1987), 1–11. A longer account is included in the Pennsylvania Edition of *Jennie Gerhardt* (Philadelphia: University of Pennsylvania Press, 1992), pp.421–60.

3. For a much fuller account of the complexities of composition, see James M. Hutchisson, "The Creation (and Reduction) of *The Financier*," *Papers on Language and Literature*, 27 (Spring 1991), 243–59. I am not addressing here a separate set of questions relating to Dreiser's revised edition of *The Financier*, published by Boni and Liveright in 1927.

4. See Frederic Joseph Svoboda, *Hemingway and* The Sun Also Rises (Lawrence: University of Kansas Press, 1983); Michael S. Reynolds, *Hemingway's First War: The Making of* A Farewell to Arms (Princeton: Princeton University Press, 1976); Reynolds, "Words Killed, Wounded, Missing in Action," *Hemingway Notes*, 6 (Spring 1981), 2–9; Scott Donaldson, "Censorship and *A Farewell to Arms*," *Studies in American Fiction*, 19 (Spring 1991), 85–93.

5. See the excellent study by Robert W. Lewis, "The Making of *Death in the Afternoon,* " in *Ernest Hemingway: The Writer in Context*, ed. James Nagel (Madison: University of Wisconsin Press, 1984), pp. 31–52.

6. Reiman, "'Versioning': The Presentation of Multiple Texts," in *Romantic Texts and Contexts* (Columbia: University of Missouri Press, 1987), pp. 167–80.

The Politics of Editing

The Politics of Funding

W. SPEED HILL

In a professional milieu in which to be (or not to be) politically correct is national news, surely, we may say, scholarly editing is not so much *a*political as *pre*-political: the laying of a foundation for subsequent critical or interpretative work, in the service of whatever view of cultural history, of whatever degree of political correctness, seems relevant. Alas, such does not seem to be the case. As each of the essays within this group insists, every choice is a political choice: it will favor one person or one group over another in the allocation of limited resources. The decision to fund A necessarily means that B will *not* be funded. The question, then, is how to decide between A and B on a basis that is politically impartial, if not nonpolitical; and, if it is editing that we are talking about, on a basis relative to the putative importance of the text itself and the adequacy of the proposal, not on such "extraneous" matters as the race, nationality, ethnicity, gender, sexual preference, ideology, and/or political affiliation of the editor or the author of the work to be edited. It is to operate at this level of political neutrality that the Editions Program at the National Endowment for the Humanities (NEH), together with the National Historical Publications and Records Commission (NHPRC) the principal funding agencies for scholarly editing in the United States, was originally designed and has since conducted itself.

In my experience as a panelist for the NEH, I was unable to detect any attempt, overt or covert, to decide funding on grounds other than the merit of the proposals before us. Two elements went into a successful application: (1) the virtually unanimous enthusiasm of the profession, as evidenced by the specialist reviews solicited by the staff, and (2) the unequivocal endorsement of the panelists. As ten or twelve specialist reviews were solicited for some

93

applications (the number is now limited to seven), and as the six (now five) panelists were each from different disciplines, periods, or even professions, the two screens together assured that only the faultless and blameless would pass scrutiny.

I should say, however, that my experience was limited. Each panel is reconstituted each year; occasionally, in the past, one was asked to serve on successive panels, but this is not now done. As a result, the only continuity from year to year is that supplied by the staff members who shepherd the applications to the panel. Thus the chemistry of each individual panel is an unknown—like being on a holiday cruise aboard ship: six highly energized professionals interacting intensively for one or two days, never to meet—as such—again. Anything could happen—and did. Moreover, two aspects of the panel review process are wholly outside the purview of the panelists themselves: (1) how they themselves are chosen, and (2) how funding is to be allotted once the applications have been ranked, for each panel judges only a portion of the total. One can make few valid inferences from what one does not know, but my sense is that the NEH staff are scrupulous in seeking a variety of qualified specialist reviewers and in constituting a panel representative of scholarly editors, scholarly end-users, and—at my last panel—publishers of scholarly editions. The models for such peer-review panels were developed by the National Science Foundation, the National Institutes of Health, and the National Institues of Mental Health and were in place before the NEH. Thus the presumptively apolitical character of scientific research became the model for guaranteeing apoliticality in the award of NEH funds to editors and editions. On the other hand, if these activities have been guided by a subtle political hand of which I am not aware, I would by definition be the last to hear of it.

So far, so good: applications solicited from all interested scholars, applicants assisted by a highly professional and competent staff, applications reviewed by a wide range of expert reviewers, applications ranked by a panel of astute (and politically neutral) generalists. Ergo, core professional criteria remain salient and issues of political correctness peripheral. But perhaps my point of view is too narrow; perhaps it has been deliberately limited so that I would function as an efficient reviewer (unpaid) and panelist (underpaid) and not rock the boat by asking too many questions. For it is perfectly clear that some funding of editing *is* political. Two examples are well known. The CEAA project to edit *American* authors was funded first by grants from the Department of Education and sub-sequently by the NEH. True, there existed no editorial tradition for American authors prior to the CEAA; nonetheless, the promoters of that project invoked various patriotic reasons for the *political* necessity of such editions, just as the NDEA (*National Defense* Education Act) supplied graduate fellowships to an entire genera-tion of humanists on the grounds that Russia was out-stripping us in military technology, largely on the basis of the relative size of Sput-nik, which dwarfed the grapefruit-sized satellite (the French called it "le pamplemousse") earlier hoisted into orbit by the United States. One ought not argue with success, for within a generation, the corpus of nineteenth-century American authors has been im-maculately edited in editions that are literally monumental. Edmund Wilson, however, did so argue, specifically with respect to early examples of "The Fruits of the MLA" (1968), and after pro-tracted negotiations between Wilson, the NEH, the Ford Found-ation, and many others, the initial volumes of the Library of Amer-ica appeared in 1982, to rival the CEAA volumes and, in select instances, to reprint them. The Library of America has been an ob-vious success. To be sure, no commercial publisher was willing to risk its capital on the patriotic demand for an American Pléiade, but once the taxpayers supplied the start-up funds—and they con-tinue to subsidize the publication of less popular volumes, as well as the keeping in print of the entire series—a commercial publisher (Time-Life) was happy to assume mail-order marketing responsibil-ity (this is now handled in-house).

No one would begrudge the success of either project, but both elided—at least initially—the process of peer-review that has become routine for applications nowadays to the NEH. To be sure, no such mechanism was in place when the CEAA's initial applica-tion was made to the Department of Education; and the NEH stopped funding the CEAA as such in 1976 and subsequently required each edition individually to show cause why its funding should be continued. The Library of America tapped a market for American literature that the CEAA (and its successor, the CSE) were quite unable to reach. While some CEAA texts were not made available to it (but now are, like Thoreau), others have been (like Melville). Evidently, then, it's all right to be political in one's editing as long as one is editing out-of-copyright "classic" American texts.

But perhaps stepping back further will reveal the truly political character of the editorial establishment's (alleged) hegemony. Let us pose the question: what does it take to get edited? Answer: Well, you have to be canonical. But how do you get canonical? Well, you have to be printed, reprinted, anthologized, and yes, edited (preferably badly) before. But how to do all these good things? Well, you have to be really good, or important (mere popularity will not cut it, otherwise we would have a scholarly edition of *Gone With the Wind* instead of the Gabler edition of *Ulysses*)—and dead. (As Gary Taylor has said, the author is *always* dead.) Does it help if as an author you are (or were) white, male, and heterosexual? Well, yes it does, *but these are not the real issues.* But if these are *not* real issues, why do the panels at the national conference of our principal professional organization, the MLA, pay such attention to them? Because, comes the reply, such voices have been historically suppressed, and it is our professional obligation as teachers of literature to empower and enfranchise the heretofore silenced. As editors our responsibility is, analogously, to make available what has hitherto been suppressed.

Let me illustrate. In 1983 I organized an MLA panel entitled "The Ideology of Editing." George F. Farr, then the Assistant Director for the Division of Research Materials, of which the Program for Editions was a sub-division, spoke for the NEH. Paul Lautner, associated with the Feminist Press, spoke for the editorially disfranchised. The two might just as well have been speaking on different panels. Paul asked what it took for an edition of a non-canonical woman author to get funded? George said, "Simply apply." Paul said, "We have, and we were turned down." George said, "Apply again, our staff is there to help you." Paul said, "We did, and we were still turned down." The very process of peer-review, which to George guaranteed the necessary professionalism of the funding process, was to Paul and Paul's Press an equally efficient guarantor that reprints of works of important but neglected women writers would *not* be funded. Why? Because they were (as yet) uncanonical, or because the applicants were insufficiently skilled in the preparation of complex, institutionally-based grant applications, or because the applicants were frankly not interested in the niceties of copy-text, historical collations, emendations, substantives and accidentals, and all the other minutiae dear to the Greg-Bowers-Tanselle-trained textual critic. An inescapable consequence of the structure of the review process at the NEH is its focus on method:

methodology we all have in common, even if we edit different texts. Therefore, an application to edit a "lesser" writer that displayed faultless methodological expertise or even novelty will be more favorably viewed (in my experience) that an application to edit a "greater" writer in a proposal that was methodologically flawed or otherwise deemed wanting. All the more cause to lament the fate of writers demonstrably *un*canonical whose would-be editors simply wanted to make available texts that have been allowed to go out of print—allowed, that is, by publishers who were themselves white, male, presumably heterosexual or in the closet, and certainly dead.

Had we time, we could continue backing up, in search of a perspective that would bring the whole cultural-literary-editorial enterprise within a single, comprehensive, and finally non-political point of view. But (a) we do not, and (b) such a perspective would only minimize the very internal conflicts and ideological contradictions that advocates of "political correctness" are attempting to foreground. Rather, let me propose two alternatives.

First, one can edit. That is what many of us enjoy doing and do best. But *scholarly* editions are typically the *end-products* of an entire history of publication, re-publication, reprinting, anthologizing, analysis, commentary, and consequent canon-formation. This does not mean that one cannot have a scholarly edition of newly collected materials, materials heretofore suppressed or fugitive or private; but there will first have to be created a demonstrable demand—academic if not commercial—for them. Furthermore, in a free market economy, scholarly editions will *always* require some form of subsidy; no conceivable market exists (with the exception of the student market for editions, say, of Shakespeare) that would warrant the editorial and production costs of *any* scholarly edition were it to be marketed on its own. In such capital- and labor-intensive enterprises, the anticipated market returns will never justify the investment of the necessary capital. But subsidies are like water: they flow from above, and they follow lines of least social, political, and institutional resistance. Moreover, there are subsidies of all sorts, direct and indirect, apart from the formal grants approved by the NEH or NHPRC: the individual research time of the editor, its support funded directly as well as implicit in one's job description—by his or her institution, the willingness of the publisher to publish the edition so long as more profitable volumes elsewhere on its list cover the cost of the edition. Given the structure of the decision-making process governing these subsidies, within and without the NEH and the NHPRC, within university administrations, and at scholarly publishers, it should come as no surprise that the decisions that emerge do not seriously challenge existing professional and cultural orthodoxies. No institution, academic, governmental, or nonprofit (such as a university press), can be expected routinely to fund projects bent on its own subversion or displacement. The recent debate over NEA grants illustrates a relevant exception, for the expectation that contemporary art will directly challenge the host society is, paradoxically, an accepted aesthetic orthodoxy, for which there is no parallel in scholarly editing. An insurrectionary *edition* is a professional oxymoron. This is not to say that *within* the editorial establishment, there are not revolutionary editions, such as the Kane-Donaldson *Piers Plowman*, Bédier's *Lai de L'Ombre*, and Bowers's *Dekker*, but they are revolutionary in their methodology, not in their choice of text to be edited. Of course, there are exceptions, such as the recent, self-consciously iconoclastic Oxford Shakespeare. And NEH officials are quick to list the women and the blacks whose papers the Endowment has funded. But the Endowment peer-review structure itself remains intact, however adroitly it has accommodated itself to a less canonically-based program of subventions in certain exceptional cases.

Alternatively, recognizing that the scholarly editor must necessarily *accept* the history of his or her text as a *donnée*, to be analyzed, charted, rationalized, explained, and so encoded within the text as editorially established, you can simply decline the honor. If you feel history has been unfair to you, if it has suppressed or marginalized you, muffled your voice and co-opted your autonomy, denied you and people like you their rightful identity, you are not likely to become a scholarly editor. You will *not* accept history; you will be outraged by it, and *that* will be your strength. You will not edit tracts, you will *write* them. To the retrospective view of the editor you will oppose the prospective view of the revolutionary. To validation by reference to past origins you will oppose self-authentication proceeding from present protest and rebellion. You will refuse to be patriarchially incorporated into an existing cultural tradition; instead, you will insist on your own autonomy as distinct, separate, *un*incorporated—and valuable precisely because of that separateness. But because scholarly editing has customarily attached itself to a larger socio-political institution or cultural tradition, your calling is likely to be a solitary one. Like Carlyle's Diogenes Teufelsdröckh, you must become your own editor, adept in self-construction and self-presentation, not an acolyte reverently attending on your memory of your forebears in a posture of filial piety within a hierarchically constituted institution. It is an heroic role, assumed against formidable odds—truly Blakean. Had Thomas Carlyle (unaffiliated) applied for the NEH, *Sartor Resartus* would *not* have been funded.

Historian-Editors and "Real Politics," or "If you don't have a good sense of humor, you're in a hell of a fix"

Mary-Jo Kline

Six years ago, I reported to the STS on my experiences as author of *A Guide to Documentary Editing* under the alert eyes of successive committees, executive subcommittees, and other watchdogs of the Association for Documentary Editing. Any of you present then know that I am painfully familiar with scholarly politics among members of the ADE in general, and historian-editors in that association in particular. Today, I shall ignore the internal political structure of editing to discuss, instead, some ways in which the work of editors with historical training has been affected by "real politics," the considerations of the political process by which public office and power are won in America.

I will apologize in advance to those who decry any distinctions between "literary" and "historical" editors. I do not pretend that any or all of these practices have merit, only that they exist. Like the *Guide to Documentary Editing*, this paper will be "descriptive" rather than "prescriptive" or "proscriptive."

Political realities intrude upon lives of historian-editors in two ways. As most will edit the papers of men and women who hoped to influence American public policy, the politics of the eras in which their subjects flourished will mold their editorial policies. Second, unlike most projects in purely literary textual scholarship, the "papers projects" of American history have been, from the beginning, peculiarly sensitive to the political climate of the times in which these projects have been created—and, more important, in which they have been *funded*.

The modern era of historical "papers projects" began in 1950 when President Truman revived a moribund federal agency, the National Historical Publications Commission, "to make available to our people the public and private writings of men [yes, "*men*"] whose contributions to our history are now inadequately represented by published works."[1] The Commission realized that its resurrection at the height of the Cold War was no coincidence, and early NHPC reports were filled with reminders that "publication of the papers of the Nation's leaders, even in a critical period of international crisis, would be evidence both at home and abroad of an abiding faith in the future of the Nation. . . ."[2]

Supporters of the traditional "Founding Fathers" in the 1950s and 1960s missed no opportunities to point out how the ideas of these statesmen might serve the nation in the new international crisis. Appeals to patriotism had very practical value. Funding generally relied on grants from the federal government, with supplementary aid from state agencies and quasi-public organizations like the Mount Vernon Ladies Association. At every turn, such funding agencies extracted promises (usually cheerfully given) that the editions would make documents more "accessible" to a wide public.

Most of these editorial projects had their offices on university campuses, but few senior staff members had faculty status or tenure. Thus the historian-editors were exquisitely vulnerable to review by public agencies and public officials whose disfavor could affect the very continued existence of their projects.

For historian-editors, as for textual scholars involved in editions under CEAA sponsorship, political demands accelerated and modified in the late 1960s. Not long after Lewis Mumford and Edmund Wilson attacked the CEAA for perceived elitism in textual apparatus, historian-editors were challenged by Jesse Lemisch for an equally pernicious elitism inherent in the limitation of federally funded projects to those of a few "great White Fathers."[3] Lemisch's attack struck home. By the late 1970s, the NHPC (now the NHP*R*C) sponsored projects focussing on the papers of well known women and prominent black leaders as well as an increasing number of projects aimed at reconstructing the records of organizations rather than of famous individuals. As the focus of these papers projects changed, so did their methods.

Selection

The "politicization" of historical editing becomes apparent as soon as editors, be their subjects traditional or "radical," select the documents to be published in their volumes. Here they are only maintaining a long tradition in the editions of the papers of American statesmen.

In the late 1820s, Jared Sparks reviewed the manuscripts of George Washington for publication and came across a seventy-three-page manuscript in Washington's hand, the fair copy of an address proposed for presentation at Washington's inaugural in 1789. Once Sparks determined that the words laboriously copied out by Washington were the brainchild of his aide, David Humphreys, and that Washington had vetoed the text, his interest vanished. Sparks was concerned with Washington the politician, not Washington the literary critic. Not only did he omit the text of the Humphreys message from his edition of Washington's works, but he did not even bother to include the manuscript in the bundles that he returned to Mount Vernon after his editorial work was done. Instead, he retained the manuscript and cut it into snippets of various sizes for autograph seekers.[4] A quarter century later, Henry A. Washington, editor of the nine-volume "Congress Edition" of Jefferson's papers made editorial selection policies a vehicle for his own pro-slavery views: he deliberately suppressed passages—or whole documents—in which Jefferson confided reservations on the subject of slavery.

Modern historian-editors have not, of course, destroyed documents that they deemed politically inconsequential, nor have they allowed their own preferences in the voting booth to affect their choice of documents to be published. But "real politics" have molded their selection of materials in a subtler way.

Historian-editors assume that readers of their editions are interested in the public life of the edition's subject. Thus, a select edition will almost certainly focus on this area, with editors automatically jettisoning correspondence and papers relating to such obviously "uninteresting" matters as private land speculations and other business records.[5] Even in "comprehensive" editions, selection of a less obvious form can take place when editors economize on space by consigning certain "less important" documents to footnotes. And reviewers have already remarked on the potential for bias inherent in such decisions in editions like the *Papers of Ulysses S. Grant*.[6]

Thus, even at the rudimentary step of selection, the historian-
editor risks perpetuating shaky assumptions of "significance" or
"importance" by applying conventional, political standards to the
choice of documents.

Organization of Editions

But assumptions about political significance (and the basic
assumption that what is political is significant) only *begin* when historian-editors decide what to include or emphasize in their volumes. The very organization of editions can reflect similar biases.

The Adams Papers edition best demonstrates this danger. As
this project publishes the papers of several generations of a single
family, some organizational scheme was clearly needed. Three separate series of volumes were decreed: one of diaries and journals;
one of "family correspondence"; one of "public" papers and "general" correspondence for each major Adams statesman.

The drawbacks became clear when the first two volumes of John
Adams's *Papers* finally appeared in 1977, more than 15 years after
the appearance of the 4-volume edition of his *Diaries* and almost a
decade after the publication of the fourth volume of the Adamses'
Family Correspondence. James Hutson pointed to the flaw inherent
in the system: "The predominantly political writings in these volumes give the impression of disembodied intellectualism, of ideas
wrenched from their social context. Our comprehension of these
writings would have been improved had they been chronologically
integrated with Adams's letters to his wife and family. . . ."[7]

The editors of Washington's and Madison's papers have adopted
another variety of politically-determined "series" organization for
their volumes: their subjects' papers are divided into *chronological*
series, the period divisions corresponding to the major terms of
public service of each man's life. For Madison, this means that one
team of editors is at work completing the volumes for his Congres-
sional career while another works ahead on the records of his
tenure as Secretary of State and still another does preliminary work
on his Presidency. For Washington, work is almost complete on the
"colonial" series, while three volumes of "Revolutionary" papers
have already been published. And although none of the volumes
for the Confederation period have gone to press, three volumes of
"Presidential" papers have already appeared.

This chronological leapfrogging has been justified by the assumption that readers should not have to "wait" to see the records of any statesman's Presidency, records the editors assume are of greater significance than those of Washington's semi-retirement in the 1780s or Madison's brief withdrawal from public life in the late 1790s.

Such organizational assumptions are peculiar to historian-editors with a bias toward *political* history. The editors of the Thomas A. Edison *Papers*, all historians of science, deliberately rejected the division of the Edison edition into separate "scientific" and non-technical series so that their edition would place Edison's contributions to science and technology within the broader context of his personal life and intellectual development.

Textual Methods

Decisions on textual policies have their elements of "real politics" as well. (And here I recognize that some present argue that historian-editors have no textual policies.) The highly-emended volumes of the traditional "Founding Fathers" series of the 1950s and 1960s were defended, in part, by the argument that readers would find diplomatic transcriptions less "accessible." If the average level of editorial intrusion in "historical" editions is now lower, this process began even before the publication of G. Thomas Tanselle's 1978 essay "The Editing of Historical Documents."[8] Conservative emendation found advocates among historian-editors as soon as they moved beyond the papers of the Great White Fathers: it was impossible to justify tinkering with the spelling and punctuation of the ill-educated by claiming devotion to the final intentions of an author who did not understand the uses of a comma or had never heard of a dictionary.

And in general, historian-editors show more respect for the textual integrity of public and politically influential documents than in private correspondence. Even editors of "Founding Fathers" editions left inviolate texts whose sources were the public press. And the editors of the *Ratification of the Constitution* series employed elaborate synoptic texts to trace the evolution of the articles of the American Constitution through the debates of the Philadelphia Convention of 1787.[9]

Contextual Annotation

The "political" aspects of historical editing are nowhere more apparent than in the area of non-textual annotation, a pastime which historian-editors consider part of their editorial mandate but which textual editors regard as collateral window-dressing for their texts. The demand that historical editions be "accessible" and somehow democratic goes far to account for the inclusion of such annotation as part of the very process of "editing" among historians, and this field offers peculiar opportunities for politicization.

Politically minded editors, like any others, can distort their own standards of annotation simply by failing to recognize the limits of his or her own interests and expertise. One reviewer of volumes 16 and 17 of *The Papers of Benjamin Franklin* found that the editors, all experts in the field of British colonial politics, had neglected Franklin's role in science and culture, where documents were published with notes "less reliable than in the annotation of political papers."[10]

But the gravest risk an historian-editor runs is that he or she will become so thoroughly immersed in the public career of the edition's subject that contextual annotation becomes a platform for after-the-fact political partisanship, making the editorial notes a reenactment of old political battles.

The most notorious offender in this area was doubtless Julian Boyd, founder of modern historical "papers projects." The last three volumes of *Papers of Thomas Jefferson* to appear under Boyd's editorship showed the depth to which he had committed himself to Jefferson's political ideals. The form Boyd's political advocacy took was the presentation of substantial numbers of documents as part of related groups, out of any chronological sequence, the clusters prefaced by lengthy editorial introductions. When these documents were written by or addressed to Jefferson and when the editorial notes analyzed significant aspects of Jefferson's career, few chided Boyd for producing volumes with increasingly topical organizations.

But with volume 17 of the edition, published in 1965, Boyd overstepped acceptable bounds. More and more of these topical groupings were mere excuses for lengthy defenses of Jefferson against the machinations, real or imagined, of Hamilton and the Federalists. By the time that volume 19 appeared in 1975, one weary reviewer counted eleven such lengthy editorial notes, totaling 287 pages (almost half of the volume's text) and remarked sadly that most had no bearing on the documents in the volume but, instead were ". . . more chapters in Boyd's remarkable history of the United States under President Washington."[11]

While the considerations of modern "real politics" (such as the "political correctness" of verbiage in notes and even in index entries) can be annoying or inconvenient, they pale beside the larger sin of annotating a statesman's papers as though one were Thomas Jefferson or Andrew Jackson or Woodrow Wilson.

Historian-Editors as Politicians

If the textual and annotational policies of historian-editors are sometimes distorted by their exposure to "real politics," that exposure served them well in some of the more practical aspects of maintaining an editorial project in modern America.

In 1981, the new Reagan administration targeted the National Historical Publications and Records Commission as an appropriate area for cost-cutting. Historian-editors were exposed to the "real politics" of their own time in a way few anticipated: the budget presented to Congress that year eliminated the NHPRC without further ado, and NHPRC-funded projects and the scholars who formed their audience faced an immediate challenge.

Appropriately, the editor who orchestrated the response was one whose scholarly career had schooled her in the most mundane workings of the American political system: as director of the Documentary History of the First Congress, Charlene Bickford was present at the creation of the legislative system that she now manipulated. Until the principal players in this remarkable lobbying effort choose to tell their story, I can offer only the general outlines of the incident.

At first, the lobbying campaign seemed doomed. The Democratic House, terrified of charges of "budget busting," voted down the NHPRC appropriations bill. Undaunted, the historians turned their attention to the Republican-controlled Senate, where, providentially, the new Senate Majority Leader was Howard Baker, a son of Tennessee, a state which boasted *three* Presidential papers projects dependent on NHPRC funds: the Andrew Jackson, James K. Polk, and Andrew Johnson projects. As Wayne Cutler, editor of the Polk edition, remarks, battles for funds for the NHPRC projects are always eased by the fact that "Politicians believe in the Presidency," in large part because most of them aspire to that office. Legend persists that Baker himself, shortly after his elevation to the Majority Leadership, attempted to transfer to his office those volumes from Thomas Jefferson's personal collection that had been part of the Library of Congress since 1815.

In any event Baker was sympathetic to the needs of the NHPRC, especially when an aide pointed out that a state like Tennessee, with its complement of nineteenth-century Presidents, was shortchanged in comparison with those whose native sons had won the Presidency in the mid-twentieth century and thus qualified their home states for the creation of full-fledged patronage-rich, tourist-attracting Presidential libraries. If the NHPRC died, Tennessee would have nothing to show for sending Jackson, Polk, and Johnson to the White House. Tennessee was not to be denied. The NHPRC was rescued, continuing to fund projects to this day, albeit at a somewhat reduced level.

The reduction of NHPRC funding levels brought more historically-oriented projects into a new world of scholarly and "real" politics, that of the National Endowment for the Humanities. When the NEH decreed drastic cuts for a broad variety of editorial projects in 1986, historian-editors had an advantage over literary scholars: veteran arm-twisters, project directors reactivated, on a reduced scale, the armies of influential supporters who had served them well in 1981. In short order, NEH "chairman's grants" restored the funds cut from the various presidential projects.

Historian-Editors and Literary Textual Specialists

Understanding the ways in which "real politics" past and present affect the behavior of historian-editors may make it a bit easier for editors with literary backgrounds to deal with us. Among your colleagues in the Association for Documentary Editing, promoting such understanding is almost an obsession. Thirteen years after G. Thomas Tanselle's essay on the "Editing of Historical Documents" forced the two groups to acknowledge each others' existence, serious problems of communication still exist. Three years ago, Joseph McElrath offered useful hints to historian-editors of the ADE on how to understand the "lits" in his excellent "Tradition and Innovation: Recent Developments in Literary Editing."[12] McElrath patiently explained that firmly constructive criticism of the kind Tanselle had generously offered was routine "[i]n the LIT tradition, [where] feathers have often been ruffled and sent flying; indeed, dippings and pluckings have frequently occurred with both passionate and passionless dispatch."

Let me return this favor by pointing out that, to the politically-oriented historian-editors, papers like Tanselle's read like scurrilous flyers in an especially nasty campaign, slipped by dark of night into the mailboxes of constituents [scholar-readers] and even prospective campaign contributors [the NHPRC and the NEH]. In this light, the historian-editors' reaction may seem less irrational and paranoid. Harry Truman, whose executive order began the tradition of modern "historical" editing with all its faults, admirably described the attitude that makes it difficult for the partisan-minded to accept such criticism lightly. Politically-oriented editors, like the Presidents whom Truman characterized forty years ago, "may dismiss the abuse of scoundrels, but to be denounced by honest men, honestly outraged, is a test of greatness that none but the strongest men can survive."

And recognition of another attitude necessary for survival in the world of American politics may make more forgivable another trait of historian-editors that annoys our colleagues among textual specialists. Here I refer to our regrettable tendency to crack bad jokes about ourselves, to trade irreverent gossip about the figures whose papers we edit, even to coin such vulgar terms as "hits" and "lits" to describe wings of the ADE. If we are sometimes guilty of apparently inappropriate levity, it is because we have learned another important lesson from Harry Truman. In editing the records of American political history, as in being one of that nation's leaders, "If you don't have a good sense of humor, you're in a hell of a fix. . . ."

NOTES

1. *Public Papers of Presidents of the United States: Harry S. Truman, 1950,* Washington: 1965, p. 417.

2. NHPC, *A National Program for the Publication of Historical Documents,* Washington, D.C., 1954, p. 14.

3. American Historical Association *Newsletter*, vol. 9, #5 (November 1971): 7–27.

4. The reconstruction of those bits and pieces of the Humphreys inaugural message that have been located can be seen in *The Papers of George Washington: Presidential Series*, ed. Dorothy A. Twohig, vol. 2 (1987): 152–73.

5. I confess to embracing this assumption myself, and I here refer you to the introduction to the *Political Correspondence and Public Papers of Aaron Burr*, edited by myself and Joanne Wood Ryan, 2 vols., Princeton University Press, 1983.

6. See Brook Simpson's review of vols. 15 and 16 of the Grant edition, *Documentary Editing*, vol. 12, #1 (March 1990): 5–8.

7. *William and Mary Quarterly*, 3rd series, vol. 35 (October 1978): 751–53.

8. *Studies in Bibliography*, 31 (1978): 1–56.

9. See *Documentary History of the Ratification of the Constitution*, vol. 1: 271–96.

10. *Journal of American History*, vol. 60 (March 1974): 1071–72.

11. Robert McColley, *William and Mary Quarterly*, 3rd series, vol. 41 (May 1975): 256–58. The editor as a political partisan of his subject commits sins closely related to the editor-as-would-be biographer. In this pattern, everything relating to that subject begins to seem important. The modern edition most frequently criticized for this trait from the outset (as contrasted to Jefferson, where critics spotted the trait only as time went on), was that of the papers of Jefferson Davis. In reviewing the second volume of this series, David Herbert Donald pointed out: "The editor has chosen to include any or all materials that some future biographer of Jefferson Davis might want to consult. . . . For instance, a five-line newspaper announcement of a meeting to organize the Vicksburg Jockey Club followed by seven closely printed, double-column pages of biographies of the fifteen other Warren County residents who, along with Davis, signed the notice; for the most part these men had no other connection with Davis and most of their names do not appear elsewhere in his *Papers*" (*American Historical Review*, vol. 82 [December 1977]: 1329–30).

12. *Documentary Editing*, December 1988.

Editing and Politics

Joel Myerson

Let me make a proposal that may seem ungentlemanly, unscholarly, and unlikely: that virtually everything we do as editors is in some way political. I would like to suggest that political thinking enters into our plans and decisions as editors with much greater force than we would like it to—or, perhaps, believe it has. To put it another way, when we choose the subjects for our editions and the editorial policies we will use in preparing these editions, we usually base our decisions as much on politics as on sound scholarly principles.

Take, for example, the ways in which we select the people to whom we devote our editions. The earliest editors took as their subjects white males because the choice was obvious: had not white males made the most visible early contributions to the history, literature, and culture of our country? Historians called them "The Founding Fathers" (a phrase that Herman Melville most definitely would have approved of for its "spermatic" qualities), while scholars in my own field called them "The Major Writers of American Literature." Politically, though, these choices did little more than to reinforce the cultural assumptions that predominated during the period when these men lived—times when non-whites and females were denied access to the mainstream of American life. There were no black presidents, no female generals, and—even worse—no female authors who were considered worth studying.

This latter point is an especially sensitive one to me because I am a scholar of nineteenth-century American literature who has published a number of books on Margaret Fuller and Louisa May Alcott. I well remember how hard it was to publish on these figures when I began my work in the early 1970s. My bibliography of Fuller's writings was turned down by a university press because she was not considered important enough to have a volume devoted solely to her, and besides, the reviewer commented, "Perry Miller was already doing it." Naturally, I took it as clear evidence of Fuller's importance that Professor Miller would rise from the dead to continue his work on her, but the press remained unconvinced. But I can understand how the press's reader came to his conclusion, given the history of how American literature, and particularly my own period in it, was studied, defined, and categorized.

The story of nineteenth-century American literature seems to have gone through two phases. In the first phase, the greatest American author was the composite Bryant-Longfellow-Holmes-Emerson-Whittier-Lowell; in the second phase, he was Poe-Hawthorne-Melville-Emerson-Thoreau-Whitman. In both phases, the greatest American author was defined by mirror images of himself—white males. Kermit Vanderbilt's *American Literature and the Academy* (1986) traces the history of the discipline in the twentieth century and among the thirty-nine illustrations of the participants provided, only one of them is of a woman.

I do not mean to suggest that the first subjects of documentary and critical editions were undeserving of being chosen. But the evidence does suggest that the process of selecting the subjects for the earliest modern editions was often subtly and not-so-subtly informed by issues unrelated to the importance of an historical figure or the quality of a writer's works. In a real way, these choices reflected contemporary values and the people who made them.

In this context, we cannot ignore the important political influence that textbooks have had upon editing. One reason we edit texts is to have people use them: we make new texts available, and we provide more accurate versions of texts that are already in use. From the nineteenth century on, textbooks were compiled by white males and reflected their patriarchal perspective. Ironically, such nineteenth-century anthologies as *The American Common-Place Book of Poetry*, edited by George Cheever in 1831, and Rufus Griswold's 1842 *The Poets and Poetry of America* presented women writers in relative proportions to male writers not matched until the 1980s. Only after the Civil War, when the male New England authors of Ticknor and Fields's firm began to dominate the anthologies, did women see the place devoted to their works begin rapidly to disappear.

By the mid-twentieth century, women had become officially marginalized in anthologies. *Major Writers of America*, edited by Perry

Miller and others in two volumes in 1962, declares Emily Dickinson the only female who was also a major author. The famous *American Tradition in Literature*, edited by Sculley Bradley and others for Norton, includes only Anne Bradstreet, Dickinson, and nine twentieth-century female authors in its third edition of 1967. Those anthologies that deal with discrete periods of American literature show little improvement in the representation of female authors. The *Anthology of American Literature*, edited by George McMichael and others in 1974, saw only Bradstreet, Mary Rowlandson, and Phyllis Wheatley as the female writers worth including in the volume covering the colonial through the romantic periods. The volume dealing with Ralph Waldo Emerson through Stephen Crane in *American Literature: Tradition and Innovation*, edited by Harrison Meserole and others in 1969, includes only Dickinson, Sarah Orne Jewett, Kate Chopin, and Mary E. Wilkins Freeman. And the influential *American Literature: The Makers and the Making*, edited in 1974 by the powerful triumvirate of Cleanth Brooks, R.W.B. Lewis, and Robert Penn Warren, publishes only Harriet Beecher Stowe and Julia Ward Howe in the volume covering the years 1826 to 1861.

From all of this, it is hard to escape the conclusion that textbook publishers wanted works by white male writers to include in their volumes, which were quite often read by predominantly or even exclusively white male audiences (many of whom were attending college on the GI Bill). The all-white male editors were more than willing to meet that demand, while making few demands of their own for enlarging non-white male representation.

All of these points touch upon the larger battle over canonicity now being waged. As blacks and women became less marginalized, as they were seen as contributors to the growth of American literature rather than as hindrances to it or ciphers in its development, there has been a call for their writings to be made accessible. The politics of meeting the needs of textbook arbiters and cultural critics has remained constant over time—today, however, the pendulum is swinging in a different direction.

As I move on now to the politics of funding, I am struck by the redundancy of the phrase. Funding is by nature political, and politics, as well as logic, dictates certain relationships between funders and fundees. In many cases, though, politics alone has become the most crucial aspect of funding for editions.

Large-scale federal funding for scholarly editions is a force that has entered academe at a rather late date. Although the National Historical Publications Commission was created by Congress in 1934, it did not directly offer money to historical projects until 1964. Literary editions were first funded by NEH in 1966, although a few projects had earlier received monies from the Office of Education of the Department of Health, Education, and Welfare. And every edition funded at the beginning was of a white male's writings.

The impact that real money had on the world of literary editing was immediate and highly visible. No longer did editors need to teach correspondence courses and summer school, and their garages often sported new-model cars and even boats. There was no doubt about it: "Cadillac" editions had replaced the "Studebaker" editions of old. The timing could not have been better: money began flowing generously just as New Criticism placed an emphasis on the importance of reading individual works for the intrinsic value of what those works themselves contained, rather than on the external biographical or historical forces working upon them. The New Critics needed reliable texts upon which to base their readings, and a generation of editors suddenly sprang up to supply these wants.

The serpent in this otherwise luxurious garden was of course money. No longer was the importance of an edition the prime consideration for undertaking it; rather, some people needed a positive answer to the question "Is it fundable?" before even beginning a project. The idealistic pursuit of truth was replaced by a rapacious gallop for gold. But at its best, the influx of federal funds opened up editing to those who had previously been disenfranchised. Women and blacks paid taxes; just as they were seen as a source for federal funding, so too did they now become a beneficiary of it. Editions of writings by women and blacks were funded, and because of this action, their writings were made available in ways that would have been impossible before. And as these new texts became accessible, new interpretations of American literature, history, and culture were made possible. The old cycle repeated itself but for the better: new interpretations demanded even more new texts, and the people who had been excluded from anthologies were now included by both critical and popular demand.

At its best, then, the rise of editing as a respectable and fundable profession paralleled the establishment of federal funding for editorial projects to result in a synergetic relationship from which everyone was a winner—funding agencies, scholars, and readers alike. Unfortunately, this relationship is now under serious attack from people like the senior senator from North Carolina, who was brilliantly portrayed in a recent "Kudzu" cartoon as saying (*vide* the United Negro College Fund's motto), "A mind is a terrible thing. Period." I think it fair to say that in the present political climate neither NEA nor NEH will soon fund a *catalogue raisonné* of the works of Robert Mapplethorpe. We should all be concerned when political considerations become not *one* of the considerations for funding decisions but *the* consideration.

Another political concern of editors is their choice of editorial methods—the politics, if you will, of editorial theory. Whether intended or not, there are certain political implications behind today's editorial theories, and I would like to suggest them here in a somewhat generalized form and without any critical hierarchy intended.

The Greg-Bowers theory proposes, in the least complex situation, the potential reconstruction of a particular form of a text at a particular point in time. The text is in a sense the property of the author, and we, as editors, protect the author and the author's work from being sullied. We are, therefore, the guardians of tradition, a role not very popular today and considered by some to be elitist. In a parallel example, Jerome J. McGann suggests an almost Marxist, collective ownership of the text among the author and other participants in its creation: the "workers" of the text have indeed united. Peter Shillingsburg has proposed an egalitarian opening up of textual editions, so that all versions of the work are accessible to everyone. No longer are editors posing as guardians of texts, but, rather, as disseminators of them. All these textual policies have political ramifications, ranging from hierarchical assumptions about the relations between author, editor, and reader, to ones in which barriers are destroyed. I would continue on with these speculations if I were a psychohistorian, but I am not, so I will not.

Politics also plays a role in how people use our editions. Too few books carry an acknowledgment to the effect that the completion of it would have been impossible without the publication of the primary documents upon which its researches are based. It is almost as if some authors feel that in giving editors credit for our editions they are somehow diminishing their own achievement as a biographer or their acumen as a literary critic. Editors are too often portrayed as harmless drones who perform the uncreative drudgework that is nevertheless necessary before more creative minds can make something substantial out of it. This depiction of the editor as scribe, transmitting the great words of the past for use by the great minds of the present, with nary a thought contributed by the scribe during the entire process, is sadly all too common.

This brings me to my final point, a brief discussion of the worst kind of politics—academic politics. Too few schools are like the Universities of Virginia and South Carolina, which recognize the contributions that editors make. More often the attitude is that editing is easy and unintellectual, and, therefore, not deserving of the monetary rewards and high status given to critics, who, unlike editors, are required to think. Part of the problem is that the by-line "edited by" appears not just upon CSE-quality editions, but on textbooks and cheap paperback reprintings as well. The result is that good editors get tarred by people who do little or nothing to create lasting scholarship, as all are subsumed under the title "editor." But a large part of this is political—the "us versus them" syndrome. Since there are more critics than editors, the majority has chosen to demonstrate their might. A decision that one type of good scholarship is better than another type of good scholarship has always been a political decision, the winner inevitably being the party with the greatest numbers. Fortunately for editors, critics are now debating among themselves the question of who is "politically correct," and we editors just might, after all, rise phoenix-like from the ashes of this fracas.

Creating a National Agenda—and Abandoning It

DAVID J. NORDLOH

At the risk of being labeled politically incorrect even as I open my mouth, I'll begin by venturing to complain that politics is the structuralist vocabulary of the present age. Since the essence of any structuralism is a polarity, fit by definition to encompass every- thing, conscious or unconscious, relevant or irrelevant, into its terms, then every action I take—and particularly every intellectual action—has its potential for political interpretation; every action I don't take—even the most innocent—is equally susceptible. Teach- ing the canon is as provocative as not teaching it. I used to imagine that speaking out at a faculty meeting could cause me problems; now not attending one causes even more. The whole matter—and I hope I'm not alone in feeling so trapped in the newest Puritanism— is tiring and finally unproductive. It makes me nostalgic for the old days, when we were either inner-directed or outer-directed, for example, or when everything was sex: unlike the most energetic of the participants in the current political/intellectual discussion, David Riesman was at least kind enough to suggest that, whatever my "directedness," it wasn't my fault; and phallic symbolism was at least worth a few laughs.

It is politics in this pervasive, overly reflexive sense that I em- phatically don't want to talk about. If everything is political, then nothing is effectively political. If editing is a political act, it is hardly distinguishable from literary theory or bibliography in being so. And since even my remarks here are, in a structuralist light, politi- cally construable, they form part of the problem, not part of the solution—another contribution to the reflexive dilemma: even if I stop to ask myself what motive I have for doing what I'm doing, my characterization of my action nonetheless remains my own, and I'm as likely to be as misguided in my assessment as I am in the activity whose motive I'm assessing.

I want to step out of that noose and into a more immediate, more limited, more pragmatic circle about which I feel a little better informed: politics as the identifiable, participatory process by which public policy is formed and public resources are allocated. More specifically, I want to talk about the relationship between editing and federal support for editing in the United States. From my perspective, which in avoiding the pitfalls of reflexivity may lead me into the trap of pragmatism, the crucial issue about politics and editing—the question which makes a difference to our decisions about whether and what to edit, about the availability of resources for editing activities—is whether the effort we expend to achieve support for editing ought to be directed to the political environment or not. What value, if any, lies in hoping for or depending upon a favorable political climate for that support? "Political climate," of course, means both inclusion in the dominant political agenda and access to the money that follows from that status; in American politics in this age, after all, money is the surest indication that the agenda means business.

My position on the matter, as you'll see soon enough, is that we ought mostly to abandon our efforts to influence the political environment in the support of editing, that we should turn—as we are already turning—elsewhere. We've tried the public-agenda route, and we've failed.

But let me focus this discussion on several observations, whose validity I'll try to establish:

> *One*, the efforts of the editorial segment of the historical and literary communities to incorporate editing into the national humanities agenda have mostly failed;
> *Two*, the initiative in securing the resources essential to the support of editing as nonetheless a significant and demanding intellectual activity ought to be directed elsewhere—toward institutional and private patronage.

Those are the headlines. Here is the news.

Let me supply some history to accompany my first observation, that "the efforts of the editorial segment of the historical and literary communities to incorporate editing into the national humanities agenda have mostly failed." No doubt many in this audience could supply additional, more personal facts to substantiate it. I'll take the longer view. The two major American federal agencies involved in the support of editing are the National Historic Publications and Records Commission and the National Endowment for the Humanities. The histories of these agencies do not reflect a compelling national mandate in support of editing. Rather, they suggest that support for editing has been both the creation of the editorial community and a coincidence.

I couldn't begin to recount the history of the first of these agencies with the thoroughness that my colleagues among the historians, particularly members of the Association for Documentary Editing and particularly Raymond W. Smock, historian of the U. S. Congress, have already done. In fact, in a session on "The Future of Federal Funding of Editing" at a meeting of the ADE this past fall in Charleston, South Carolina, Ray Smock skillfully described the founding and foundering of NHPRC.[1] The effective heroes of his story, quite tellingly, are not politicians and national leaders or even the American public but historians, and particularly J. Franklin Jameson, who fought from the 1880s through the 1920s for the creation of a federal commission to preserve and publish the documents of the nation's history effectively; and Julian Boyd, whose publication of the first volume of *The Papers of Thomas Jefferson* in 1950 finally brought the work of editors among the historians to the attention of President Truman, who in turn called upon the long-extant but mostly ineffectual NHPC (I'll supply the "R" in just a moment) to look into the matter. Through the 1950s and early 1960s NHPC concentrated on making lists of documentary priorities, people to be honored with editing projects, mostly presidents and founding fathers and assorted others, without regard to whether there were even documents to edit. (Revealing a newer historical—and political—consciousness than the members of the commission could have imagined, Ray Smock notes that a preliminary "short list" in 1951 of sixty-six figures included only three women—Jane Addams, Susan B. Anthony, and Clara Barton—and one black—Booker T. Washington; and that a later, longer list of 361 didn't improve the proportions: about two dozen women and two blacks.) Coincidentally, after all that effort the historians got their greatest boast—i. e., real money—as a coincidence of the same brief Camelot impulse that produced the National Endowment for the Humanities: in 1964 Congress appropriated $350,000 for NHPC projects. Following that came a ten-year period of grad-

ual increases, to $750,000 by 1974. In 1975, suddenly, the appropria-
tion was $2 million—but only because what was NHPC now
became NHPRC, with the "publications" division and the newly
added "records" division dividing the funds equally. The "R" story
by itself only supports my argument: the records division, focussing
on archival preservation and control as opposed to publication, sig-
nalled the success of the archivists in at last enacting *their* mandate.
And the current story of NHPRC is an inventory of disputes
between editors and archivists about allocation of funds and of the
lobbying of Congress by their representative organizations. The
goal: to get *someone* in the Congress to take up the cause. How
many people in your precinct know about the matter—or care?

The history of the National Endowment for the Humanities is
equally instructive, and a little more encouraging. I don't particularly own this story, but I *was* one of the first people to benefit from
NEH funding, as a graduate student employed on an hourly basis
at the W. D. Howells project in Indiana in 1966, the first year NEH
money was allocated—and I *have*, secure in my editorial dotage,
told several versions of it in recent years.[2] In contrast to the NHPC/
NHPRC story of significant direct political effort, the relation of literary editors to NEH is mostly coincidence. In the late 1950s, a
group of Americanists associated with the Modern Language
Association had organized informally to urge some means of better
preserving and transmitting the American literary heritage, represented by the—fairly innocuous word that has recently become
politicized—"canon" of major authors. The group began to develop
detailed plans, even to parcel out projects among the scholars who
made up the group (which explains Howells at Indiana, for instance—nothing else seems to). Several projects even antedated
NEH, utilizing institutional funds and general programs of other
federal agencies. And then, to quote myself from my presentation
on the NEH at last fall's ADE meeting—

> when the NEH opened shop, the MLA was ready. And the NEH, on its
> side, seems to me to have seen opportunity in the MLA affiliation, not prin-
> ciple. Here [in the Center for Editions of American Authors, MLA's orga-
> nizing committee in that editorial initiative] was an immediate, fully devel-
> oped funding venture, a way to prove that, despite doubts to the contrary,
> money could be spent reputably and substantially on the humanities.[3]

My reading of the relation of NEH to the MLA editions and to
editing generally is that national priority was at best a variable in an

equation, not a principle. Evidence: the period of greatest support for editing of any kind was the second year of NEH's funding activity, 1968, when the $350,000 devoted to that purpose represented 7.3% of total available funds of $4.7 million—but that was also the period when the CEAA constituted one of the few significant institutional activities prepared to take what NEH was prepared to give. Evidence: emphasis on editing as crucial to NEH's mission dropped even more quickly than NEH funding of editions did. The NEH's first annual report, for fiscal year 1966, gives the CEAA program prominent place, and stresses the international cultural value of the American writers being edited: "Emerson is the most revered non-Asiatic philosopher-writer in Asia; . . . Twain and Melville are counted among the world's greatest novelists. . . . Their works are monuments; yet the monuments are defaced and eroded. Both staff and Council thought it desirable to support restoration through a program for editions of pure texts."[4] The third annual report, for 1968, also gives the editions program prominent place, but what seems to me an increasingly defensive one: texts are corrupt, Endowment support emphasizes the availability of "unencumbered" reading texts to the general public, 139 scholars are employed (was I included in the head count?), and the published volumes are stacking up—the report even features a photograph of a staff member admiring part of the stack.[5] More prominent in the same report, however, is the NEH's very dramatic discovery of a more timely agenda: "What of such problems, brought to us daily in the newspapers, as race, war and peace, and the pressures of population? . . . When we say race, we mean Negro. It is difficult to find anything but the most trivial generalizations about Negroes in most general books on American history."[6] Throughout the 1968 report appear versions of the NEH response: funding of the edition of Booker T. Washington, funding of a project on the NAACP, workshops and seminars and institutes, word of a biography of Richard Wright. In other words, editing had its brief and coincidental moment of prominence in the national agenda, but only because other possibilities hadn't been identified or made operative yet. How do matters stand at present for editing in the national consciousness? Not spectacularly well. Evidence: the archivists, effective in advancing their agenda in the NHPRC, are meeting with equal success in the NEH, where the newest division, the Office of Preservation, controlled a larger budget from its first day than the Editions Program had managed to achieve in twenty years.

Outlined this rapidly and sparely, my account may seem to reflect a naive presumption that "national priority" ought to be some kind of eternal verity, as fixed in the generalized American patriotic psyche as Mom—oops, parent—and apple pie. (Actually, if watching sports and war on television is any indication, the only eternal verity is "We're number one!") No, my point is more practical but just as devastating: even strenuous efforts to create and maintain editing as a lasting national priority have been at best only temporarily successful.

And why is that so? I could trot out any number of explanations—indeed, we could make this a classroom exercise, and everybody could contribute. But let me briefly mention a few most pertinent to the direction of my argument. One, intellectual effort, unless it has a clear and immediate practical benefit, has no widespread popular following in this country; two, of those intellectual efforts which do receive some acknowledgment because of their utility in maintaining the American cultural and historical past, preservation—keeping things as they were—is taken as more significant than editing—which changes them. Three, the decision to edit something represents an assertion of value, and in the current public environment of disagreements about cultural literacy and shared values and the hegemony of the WASP, politicized or otherwise, no such decision on that kind of value is likely to receive widespread approval or even attention.

Which new set of three points returns me to the second of the observations I introduced earlier, that "the initiative in securing the resources essential to the support of editing as nonetheless a significant and demanding intellectual activity ought to be directed elsewhere—toward institutional and private patronage." The idea is not mine, by any means. It's long been a feature even of the federal programs themselves, and also a crucial part of the efforts of various editorial projects and committees of the last thirty years. The very first year the NHPC received federal funds it established an ongoing $2 million match with the Ford Foundation; MLA was turned down by the Ford Foundation even before the NEH came into existence; both agencies, and others, are increasingly incorporating matching-grant programs—government funds awarded in proportion to monies raised from other sources—into their portfolios. Several editions—for example, the Strouse Edition of Carlyle centered at Santa Cruz—are supported almost entirely by that means. And patronage has also been advanced in critical discussions of the humanities. The commentary on the matter which I find most compelling is that of Stephen Graubard, editor of *Daedalus*, who stated his position in an overview essay in *Change* commemorating the twentieth anniversary of NEH.[7] Concluding that in matters of public policy we suffer from indecision about indecision—"an unwillingness to acknowledge that we are woefully at sea in knowing how to celebrate the past, that our opinions are both divergent and conflicting on what subjects merit attention in the present"—Graubard dismisses "the expectation that a federal agency can become the principal support for major American research and teaching in the humanities" and goes on to imagine, indeed urge, individual philanthropy as the effective alternative: "Why do millions with fortunes not assert themselves—articulate their taste, their interests, their values—in continuing patronage? What better way to express a commitment to what the humanities are, and to what they seek to do?"

And so say I. But I am after all only saying what most editorial projects already do, possibly with less consciousness of the fact. Internal institutional support is a form of patronage; our dedication of our own time to editing without pay is patronage. If federal funding is available, fine, but construe it as a welfare program, not an assertion of value or a right denied. In the end, better to be reassured by support from some person or organization following principles with resources, and more likely to adhere to them, than the resources accompanying the short-term pretense of ever-changing federal policy and committees of our peers.

That proposition, you may conclude, is political incorrectness with a vengeance. True. And equally true that what we individually or collectively value as culture is most often the gift of such conscious and committed patronage. I say we take our chances.

NOTES

1. Smock's presentation was entitled "Continuing the Bloodless Revolution: The Past and Future of the NHPRC." It is scheduled to appear later this year in the *Documentary Editing*, the ADE journal.

2. The first was my account of the implications of federal support for sanctifying

the rationale of copy-text, "Theory, Funding, and Coincidence in the Editing of American Literature," pp. 137–55 in Richard Landon, ed., *Editing and Editors: A Retrospect* (New York: AMS Press, 1988), the published proceedings of the 21st annual conference on editorial problems at the University of Toronto, 1985; the second, my presentation at last October's ADE annual meeting, "The NEH and Editing: Public Good, Scholarly Dissent, and Private Enterprise," to appear in a coming issue of *Documentary Editing*.

3. "The NEH and Editing," draft page 11.

4. National Endowment for the Humanities, First Annual Report, Fiscal Year 1966, p. 12.

5. National Endowment for the Humanities, Third Annual Report, Fiscal Year 1968, p. 16.

6. National Endowment for the Humanities, Third Annual Report. p. 2.

7. Stephen R. Graubard, "NEH at Twenty: Another View," *Change* 18 (Jan.– Feb. 1986), 24ff.

The Politics of Cooperation: A Response

Donald H. Reiman

When one turns to the word "politics" in *Webster's Third New International Dictionary of the English Language*, there seems to be only one definition that might conceivably apply to the work of editors. The only example given for this, the fifth main meaning of the word—"conduct of or policy in private affairs"—is from Fielding's *Tom Jones*, which in its expanded *OED* version reads: "Mrs. Western was reading a lecture on prudence and matrimonial politics to her niece." (In the *OED*, this—the last meaning given for the word —is labeled as figurative.) It may be, then, a mark of fairly recent usage of the word—perhaps even of an underlying social change— that nobody on this panel or, I imagine, in the audience, had any trouble seeing the relevance of the title under which we were asked to speak. Indeed, the problem of all of us who spoke on this panel was not to think of ways in which the title was appropriate to the editorial enterprise, but rather to narrow the subject to a subdivision that could be covered in the available time.

If some puzzled person who had consulted the dictionaries without enlightenment had asked me to define "The Politics of Editing," I might have responded that it is *"the art of securing the cooperation and support of those individuals and institutions whose cooperation and support are necessary for the successful completion of an editorial project."* Any of the speakers, had they wished to steal the thunder of others, could have covered various aspects of this vast subject other than those to which they chose to limit their talks. So without suggesting that their papers should have ranged over so wide a topic as my putative broad definition of the phrase, let me try to add a dimension to their insights from a perspective drawn from my own definition of "The Politics of Editing."

Each speaker has chosen to focus on some aspect of the inter-
play of politics and money. David Nordloh defines the politics he
will treat as the "identifiable, participatory process by which public
policy is formed and public resources are allocated"—or, "[m]ore
specifically, . . . the relationship between editing and federal support for editing in the United States."[1] Joel Myerson, after discussing the editorial politics of race and gender, devotes the central
part of his paper to what he terms "the politics of funding."[2] Mary-
Jo Kline argues that the historical editors had to become uncom-
monly astute politically because the great historical editions,
though having "their offices on university campuses," were so often
funded directly by grants from the National Historic Publication
and Records Commission (NHPRC) and the National Endowment
for the Humanities (NEH) that they were especially "vulnerable to
review by public agencies and public officials" whose goodwill was
necessary to assure their continued life. Speed Hill begins his presentation by asserting that "[e]very choice *is* a political choice"
because "it will favor one person or one group over another in the
division of limited resources."

The speakers then approach the question of how far the way the
spoils are divided should govern one's choices in editing. From his
perspective as a chairman of the MLA's Committee on Scholarly
Editions (CSE) and a panelist for the NEH, Hill argues that those
who wish to edit traditionally canonical authors, using methods
sanctioned by the experience and authority of the foremost scholarly editors, both should and do win the approval of such established
institutions. (He does concede that occasionally the emphasis on
methodology is more determinative than the importance of the
writer or work being edited.) He justifies his essentially conservative position by saying that "*scholarly* editions are typically the *end-
products* of an entire history of publication, . . . analysis, commentary, and consequent canon-formation," and that "[n]o institution,
academic or governmental, can be expected routinely to fund projects bent on its own subversion or displacement." Scholarly editors, he thinks, "accept" history, while those who feel that history
has been unfair to them "will *not* accept history" but "will be outraged by it" and, instead of editing tracts, "will *write* them," usually
without the benefit of institutional assistance.[3]

Myerson, though happy that an influx of federal funds in the
mid-1960s enabled "'Cadillac' editions" to replace "the 'Stude-

baker' editions of old," finds a "serpent in this . . . garden": "No longer was the importance of an edition the prime consideration for undertaking it; rather, some people needed a positive answer to the question 'Is it fundable?' before even beginning a project." Nordloh and Kline describe how politically astute historians and archivists out-maneuvered the literary scholars for control of the federal pork barrel, with Kline detailing how the political skills of historical editors and the state pride of a powerful senator helped preserve the funding of the NHPRC at a crucial stage in the initial cost-cutting rampage of the Reagan administration. Impressed by this and other successes by the historians, Nordloh suggests that those editing American literature should give up the struggle and learn to raise funds from private sources or seek support for their editing from their own universities. Both Myerson and Nordloh attribute the stimulation of editions of women and racial minorities to the national political climate of the time. Myerson—with work on Margaret Fuller and Louisa May Alcott—approves of this change, but Nordloh is more ambivalent: he sees the funding of editions of Booker T. Washington and other minority figures, together with the success of the archivists in securing money to conserve the primary manuscripts and books (which we editors need to carry out our researches) as signals that the federal government has lost or diffused the "national agenda" that once made the CEAA such a lucrative enterprise.

Let me venture some reactions to this emphasis on what Kline terms "real politics" and the real money that accompanies it. The time that the federal government of the United States has provided direct grants for "Cadillac" editorial projects is a mere twenty-five years—a very short time even in the history of scholarly editing in America. Large areas of what one might rightfully call the politics of editing have nothing to do with money or with governmental power in any conventional sense; moreover, these other political aspects of the editorial pursuit seem to me ultimately more important than the struggle for governmental financing. I do not minimize the importance of support given to literary editing by the NEH, which has been essential to my work on *The Bodleian Shelley Manuscripts* and *The Manuscripts of the Younger Romantics*. But I think that editorial scholarship can make proper use of direct governmental grants only after the editors have already solved political problems more challenging than a shortfall in money for time off, travel, and equipment.

The most important activity in the politics of editing is to find capable people and persuade them to think clearly enough about long-range scholarly values and the meaning of our profession to commit themselves to the years of disciplined work required by major scholarly editions. They must be convinced that someday— perhaps when they are old and gray—their contribution will be fairly appreciated by their colleagues and by scholar-critics of future generations. We must conduct political battles in graduate seminars and professional conventions in order to win (in the rhetoric of the era when the federal funds began flowing) the hearts and minds of the best and the brightest. We must convince star-struck potential scholar-critics that, though Structuralism, Poststructuralism, and the New Historicism may provide "Thirteen Ways of Looking at a Blackbird," critical *editing* provides the blackbird itself, while *versioning* may provide the thirteen blackbirds to be examined and compared in almost infinitely complex combinations. (What is thirteen to the thirteenth power?) And once these ambitious young scholars have been enlisted in the work, we must give them full public credit for their contributions, foster their careers, and encourage them to mature and to initiate important projects of their own. Only by showing still younger students that to work in the editorial world is to participate fully in a true community of scholars will we continue to strengthen the tradition of editorial scholarship.

The second most important political task, aside from enlisting dedicated younger editors in our cause, both to aid us now in the multivolume projects we have undertaken and to "be [our] second sel[ves], when [we are] gone," is to persuade publishers of the importance and viability of scholarly editing. There was a time, during the rapid expansion of the reading public and the book trade in England and America (that is, from about 1760 till the end of the First World War), when the chief sponsors of editions and translations were booksellers or publishers, individually or in concert. This was the age of Dr. Johnson's Shakespeare, Edward Arber's "English Reprints," Macmillan's "Globe Editions," the "Oxford Standard Authors," and Houghton Mifflin's "Cambridge Editions," when these and other editions that were scholarly according to the best lights of the time (and in the case of the editions of Arber and Harry Buxton Forman, very fine scholarship by the lights of any time), were also successful commercial ventures.

Those halcyon days are gone, but thanks largely to the market for college text-books, such successful publishers as Oxford University Press, W. W. Norton, Longman, and Penguin are still willing to undertake scholarly texts on a volume-by-volume basis, and such major academic publishers as Harvard, Johns Hopkins, Princeton, Cornell, and California have undertaken major critical editions, in the hope that a combination of subsidies and the chance to reprint or license the rights to reprint in the text-book market will enable them at least to recoup their investment. There are also academic resource publishers, such as Garland Publishing, who find it possible to publish major scholarly editions by limiting their production to the size of the potential market and then directing their sales to major research libraries around the world. Occasionally, there comes a publisher, such as John Grey Murray (*the* John Murray of our day), who both loves a writer and finds an editor whom he trusts enough—in this case Leslie A. Marchand—to launch a major, multivolume scholarly edition—*Byron's Letters and Journals*—as a commercial venture. In any case, the second political task of all serious editors is to find such a willing publisher, ideally in advance of the heavy editorial work, who will consult with them and help shape their editorial methods to take full advantage of the available technology and to navigate safely past the economic obstacles to the production and sale of the finished edition.

After the editorial team has been assembled and is in tune with a publisher (and maintaining this harmony can be a continuing test of political skill, as changes in personnel or variations in the economic climate direct a press to new priorities, or as new cycles of academic fashion discourage the members of the editorial team), the editors must also secure the cooperation of the individuals and institutions who own the manuscripts and rare books on which the edition must be based and that of the holders of copyrights to these materials. Those engaged in editing recent and contemporary writers know better than I what sorts of problems arise from individual owners and literary executors. Speaking as one who has been on both sides of the use of scholarly materials in rare book and manuscript libraries, I think that I have some insights into the causes of pitfalls in securing cooperation from them. Librarians, curators, and even clerks working at such libraries are often very knowledgeable people, certainly underpaid and probably overworked, who have human feelings and can either like or dislike a visiting scholar.

They have it in their power to tell us things about the collections in their care—both about the materials there (some of them almost certainly uncatalogued) and about other scholars' use of those materials. They may know of bibliographical publications and rare scholarly commentaries on the manuscripts, private library catalogues, booksellers' records of provenance, and other valuable data in their accession files that readers have no way of discovering unless a member of the library staff chooses to volunteer the information. It therefore behooves every researcher both to consider and to treat these people as the fellow-scholars that many of them are, and to credit and thank them, both privately and publicly, for their specific contributions to our work (just as we would credit a fellow professor in our specialty). It is not politically astute, I should add, to thank only the director of the library, or the curator of the collection, if others on the staff provided you with most of the help.

What I have been describing may be called "the politics of cooperation."[4] People are social beings whose greatest satisfactions derive from joining others in a worthwhile enterprise. Thus, at all levels, editors' chief political functions are to articulate fully the ideals of their work and to convince those whose cooperation is needed for its success that the project is important, the staff undertaking it is competent, and the plan for its completion is sensible. To be convincing, the editor must be fully convinced of the importance of the work, must enlist an adequate staff of competent co-workers, and—with their help—must devise in advance a cogent plan to carry it out. Those who believe enough in the importance of their editorial task and are able and willing to perform it superlatively will, I believe, ultimately win the support they need—from other researchers, from their own institutions, from governmental or private sources of funding, from the owners and copyright holders of the requisite materials, and—early or late—from an appropriate publisher. And if the work is really worth doing, an editor who believes in it enough will find a way to get it done, even in the absence of years of time off and months of travel support. The best political location for an editor is (like the worst spot for Œdipus) a place where three roads meet: sincere enthusiasm for the proposed edition; intelligent and dedicated singleness of purpose in pursuing the research; and humane understanding of the needs and feelings of the many others whose cooperation is necessary to its success.

NOTES

1. This paper was given as a response to four papers at a panel entitled "The Politics of Editing" organized and chaired by Trevor Howard-Hill at the final session of the STS Conference held on Saturday afternoon, 13 April 1991, at the Pierpont Morgan Library. My quotations from other speakers on the panel are drawn from the versions of papers sent to me before the Conference and on which I based my response there, but they do not necessarily correspond in literal detail either to the texts of the papers the four speakers actually gave there, or to the revised essays they have submitted to *TEXT*. (I've also revised my own comments for publication.) Let the statements attributed to the four individuals named and my reactions to them be thought of as parts of a Socratic dialogue, representing a variety of viewpoints that are here personalized for the sake of dramatic interest.

2. Those who operate in the relatively young tradition of the critical editing of American letters occasionally venture generalizations that an international gathering might find a bit parochial. Myerson declares, for example, that the "earliest editors took as their subjects white males"—"The Founding Fathers" and "The Major Writers of American Literature." As a matter of fact, the "earliest editors" worked on classical and biblical texts, and a critical edition of a female writer—R. W. Chapman's edition of *The Novels of Jane Austen* (5 vols.; Oxford: Clarendon Press, 1923; 2nd ed. 1926)—not only preceded most of those American editions by half a century, but (still in print in its text from the 1920s) retains its scholarly pre-eminence.

3. Thus, Speed Hill essentially accepts Stanley Fish's dictum that a consensus of the "interpretive community"—in this case, the council of elders of the editorial tribe—controls financial support of editorial projects, and to receive such support, one must play by their rules. While it would be personally comforting for me to agree with Hill's analysis, I don't think that the review process either always does—or should—work this way. Intellectual history contains many who, marginalized in one era, are revived in a later age—sometimes by scholarly editors of the establishment—who help make Gianbattisa Vico, Mary Wollstonecraft, and William Blake, for example, greater intellectual forces in the twentieth century than they ever were before. And a democracy that gathers strength from its capacity to evolve and grow through the open exchange of information and ideas may well deem it more important in times of crisis to help renew the vigor of its institutions by disseminating texts of both older non-canonical writings and brilliant new ones than to re-edit the familiar bromides of the troubled culture.

4. The phrase "the art or science of governing" occurs in the primary traditional definition of the word "politics." One of the social changes that has surely disseminated the use of the word into more and more areas of our everyday lives is the realization that the centers of power in our society have been ever more widely dispersed with the passage of time; another is the refusal of the "gov-

erned" to conform to the decisions reached by the traditional political process. The concept of governing itself has been so diluted by these transformations that political action to be fully successful must begin at the grass roots
and filter up to the leadership. Or, to use a figure that Shelley employs to
great effect in *Prometheus Unbound*, power in our society operates like the
hydrogen cycle: awareness of the need for change first rises up from the weak-
ness or decay of old ideas; then, after accumulating in the upper atmosphere
of society (i. e., among those who help mold public opinion), as if "discharg-
ing its collected lightning," it ultimately returns to the people through their
acceptance of massive changes in social norms and patterns of behavior that
cause, in turn, the transformation of established institutions.

Computerization, Canonicity and the Old French Scribe: The Twelfth and Thirteenth Centuries

KARL D. UITTI
GINA GRECO

In this paper we will deal with three very closely interrelated issues: (1) the use of the computer in humanistically-oriented textual research, i.e., matters of poetics and literary history; (2) certain philological traditions of textual establishment in the field of Old French (=OF) literature; and (3) a project on which we have been engaged for a few years now at Princeton University. Each of these issues raises the matter of how, both in theory and in practice, one might go about integrating computer-supported research into graduate programs of literature. By "computer-supported" we mean something other than basic word-processing or even the consultation of bibliographical and textual data bases (e.g., ARTFL), however valuable these surely are. Although matters of editorial procedures are clearly at issue in what we are doing, we are *not* primarily interested at present in textual editing; this will become clear as we explain more fully what we have been trying to do and the reasons for doing it.

Textual Research and the Computer[1]

Readings in the theory and practice of computer technology in regard to textual study have been at once encouraging and disappointing. The recent *Literary Computing and Literary Criticism: Theoretical and Practical Essays on Theme and Rhetoric* is a good case in point.[2] This volume contains a number of essays that demonstrate brilliant applications of computer resources to various stylistic issues. These essays, as Potter explains, focus primarily either on the "word" or on "rhetorically conceived" syntagma. *Literary Computing* also raises a number of problems attendant upon literary analysis and computer technology. For example, Potter herself notes that individuals trained in literary study who evince an interest in computers tend to transfer their allegiance from literary scholarship to computing, thereby writing "themselves out of the range of their natural audiences" (xviii). One readily understands this trend: computing is intellectually interesting for its own sake.

Indeed, computing quickly becomes fascinating, but all too often it does so in a fashion that leaves that part of us which is devoted to *literary scholarship* somewhere out on an intellectual limb. For instance, Richard W. Bailey's suggestive and ground-breaking article, "The Future of Computational Stylistics,"[3] divides applications of the computer "to problems of style . . . conveniently . . . into three generic types."[4] The first of these stresses the primacy of data retrieval; the second focuses upon the construction of models; the third involves the formulation of hypotheses and their testing against empirical evidence. Most use of the computer has to date been limited to matters of data retrieval (e.g., the accumulation of a great deal of information in order to construct dictionaries, linguistic atlases, and variorum editions). Bailey qualifies this kind of use, however, as "merely an adjunct to the real work of criticism."[5] In his words, the "variorum edition" is *not* the "real work" critics are called upon to perform.

Several contributors to Potter's volume restate in one form or another Bailey's axioms. Thus, for Potter herself, textual criticism—the construction of critical editions—constitutes a "merely philological" enterprise for which the computer provides invaluable assistance. It is less prone to mistakes than typing and whiting out; it constitutes a great improvement over three-by-five cards as a vehicle for storing information. However—as we read Potter—the philological exercise merely fulfills a certain propedeutical function within a more widely conceived set of grander critical activities—indispensable perhaps, but not really at the cutting edge of literary-critical scholarship.

To us, then, there seems to be developing within the activities associated both with computers and literary study an assumption—a premise—which, itself, has not yet been critically examined. And,

as we discuss below, similarly unexamined assumptions characterize the discipline we know as textual criticism. It is such assumptions that our project seeks to challenge.

Textual Philology and Old French

For about a century and a half philologists of Old French have
toiled within the constraints of a number of assumptions which, like
those of certain computer specialists, deserve to be scrutinized
more closely. The idea that a medieval literary manuscript, or an
entire textual tradition, is most properly viewed as raw material to
be transformed into a modern printed book is one such assumption. This proposition has, itself, rarely been the object of critical
inquiry, despite the fact that the canonicity we accord the printed
book today diverges from the kind of canonicity prevailing at the
time our OF manuscripts were copied.

There are basically two approaches to the editing of OF manuscripts: those principles pioneered over a century and a half ago by
Karl Lachmann, and the reaction to the Lachmannians spurred by
Joseph Bédier's 1928 analysis of the textual tradition of Jean Re-
nart's *Le Lai de L'Ombre*.[6] Yet, *both* the "common error" Lachmannians and the "best manuscript" Bédierists judge texts according to their closeness to a lost authorial original. They differ in that
the Bédierists suspect the accuracy of Lachmannian reconstructions and, consequently, tend to "edit" merely a single manuscript.[7]
Thus, Wendelin Foerster's magnificent edition of the romances of
Chrétien de Troyes—learned, intelligent and literarily sensitive as
it may be[8]—is dismissed by Bédierists as merely the creation of
modern philology and not accepted as a faithful reconstruction of
what Chrétien wrote. It strains our credulity to accept that Chrétien in fact recounted his tales in the pure *champenois* dialect in
which Foerster's linguistic expertise and inventiveness couched
them. Furthermore, we are not always sure that what we are reading in Foester's text corresponds to any authentically medieval version. Meanwhile, at its most elementary, Bédierism amounts to
preparing a manuscript for the printer; glossary, linguistic commentary, and notes are kept to the absolutely indispensable minimum.
Non-intervention is so sacred that the Bédierist agonizes over
whether to repair damage caused by, say, homoeteleuton, and he
stringently avoids any, to him purely "subjective," style-based cor-

rection, even though in some cases the scribe whose work he is editing cares little for his author's brand of expressivity. Although there is in principle nothing wrong with editing as such what a scribe wrote—Mario Roques, after all, entitled his Chrétien editions the "romances of Chrétien de Troyes edited *according to* MS Bibliothèque Nationale fr. 794 (Guiot)"—the prestige naturally accorded certain printed books and scholarly series, along with inevitable human indolence, has in effect transformed Roques's edition of Guiot into the standard text used by students and scholars who mistakenly believe they are reading the romances of Chrétien de Troyes.[9]

To be sure, partisans of medieval "orality," that is, those scholars for whom the vernacular literature of the European Middle Ages—especially the earliest such literature—remains subject to the conditions of oral diffusion and performance, long ago chose to understand variants in the written testimony that has come down to us in manuscript form as something radically other than departures from lost written archetypes. For several decades (centering on the 1960s), and following upon the earlier studies of Homeric and Yugoslav narrative poetry by Milman Perry and Mathias Murko, debates among Romanists raged as to whether it was useful to consider the OF *chanson de geste* as a properly written genre at all.[10] Manuscript variants were understood by many as more or less fortuitously preserved vestiges of the on-going "oral composition" of a given poetic matter—of the constant recasting of this matter according to the tastes and exigencies of *jongleur* improvisers and their audiences—and following certain "rules" dependent upon the requirements and possibilities of prosodic structures. Here the printed book "prejudice" operates, as it were, in reverse.

"Orality" in both "composition" and "reading" obtains, during the twelfth and thirteenth centuries, even in "written" works ascribable to specific "authors." Thus, Marie de France reports having "heard" tales which she is proud to have "set down according to the letter and the principles of writing" (*escriture* or *letreüre*);[11] others dictate their narratives to clerks.[12] We hear of written narratives being read out loud from a "book" to court audiences, like the damsel who reads a *roman* in Chrétien's *Yvain*.

Meanwhile, the *fact* of writing confers upon the performed poem a stability which constitutes the first, and indispensable, step on the path to canonization. The scribe's transcription integrates the poem into the realm of textuality even though its initial purpose might only have been to serve as a kind of *aide-mémoire*. Thus, a scribal transcription is qualitatively not different from what, as "author," Marie de France claimed to have done in her *Lais* (ca. 1160–80). By virtue of writing down what she heard, she incorporated the Breton poems into a vernacular textuality (and into the processes governing it) comprised, essentially, of the mid-twelfth-century OF *romans antiques*. This was the tradition within which, as she states in her General Prologue, she had first considered laboring.[13]

Three OF terms merit citing at this juncture: *escri(v)re*, *descri(v)re*, and *translater*.

OF *escri(v)re* translates our present-day "to write down" rather than "write" (in the sense of "compose"). The latter meaning is conveyed by *faire + de*, as in the first verse of Chrétien's *Cligés*[14] where the author-narrator identifies himself as "Cil qui *fist d*'Erec et Enide . . ." Elsewhere, the name "Crestïens" is associated with "son conte" (*Cligés*, v. 48) and "son livre," as in: "Del *Chevalier de la Charrete* / Comance Crestïens *son livre*," (*Lancelot*, vv. 24–25).[15]

Meanwhile, upon completing his transcription of *Yvain*, the scribe Guiot inserts two distichs (MS B.N. fr. 794 fol. 105r):

> Explicit li ch'rs au lyeon
> Cil qui lescrist guioz a non
> Deuant n^re dame del ual
> Est ses ostex tot aestal

[*Explicit The Lion Knight.* / He who wrote it down is named Guiot. / His lodging is located in front of Our Lady of the Valley.]

It is "Guiot" who "wrote (down)" the *Chevalier au Lion*, a "book" which was "begun" by Chrétien de Troyes, who "made" (*fist*) it "concerning" (*de*) the story of the Lion Knight, and whose book it was and, in great measure, still is.

Usages of this sort antedate Chrétien. In the early *Alexander* fragment attributed to Alberic of Besançon, the narrator claims never to have seen "written down on parchment" ("En pargamen nol vid escrit . . .") the story of a king as powerful as Alexander.[16] *Escri(v)re* may also mean "to take dictation," as in these lines from the *Didot Perceval*: "*Mais de çou ne parole pas Crestiens de Troyes ne li autre troveor qui en ont trové por faire lor rimes plaisans, mais nos n' en dirons fors tant com au conte en monte et que Merlins en fist escrire a Blayse, mon maistre*" (But of that Chrétien de Troyes does not speak, nor do the other versifiers who have made verses about it in order to compose their pleasant rhymes, but we shall say no more of it than what pertains to the story proper and what Merlin had Blaise, my master, *write down* of it.).[17]

Marie de France's "Le Chèvrefeuille" describes Tristan as having "written" (*il ot escrit*) on a wooden stick just as "the Queen had said," and, in order that the words be remembered, as having composed a new "lay" about "it" (*en aveit fet un nuvel lai*).[18] Here *escri(v)re* and *fere de* are exactly opposed. The Queen is to Tristan what Merlin is to Blaise, and what Chrétien is to Guiot, namely, the authority underlying their "writing" what they "wrote down."

More akin to the authorial "writing" of our own day is OF *descri(v)re* "to describe, write, or express a thing or being in words," defined by a late-thirteenth-century Glossary as *"maniere par lequele on fait aucune cose en aucune maniere konissavle, qui c[e]lle cose est"* (the manner by which one causes a given thing to be knowable as the thing it is).[19] *Descri(v)re / descripcïon* begin to flourish around 1150, with the rise of clerkly romance narrative. Thus, in *Érec et Énide*, Chrétien de Troyes speaks of "reading" a "description":

> Lisant trovomes an l'estoire
> la description de la robe,
> si an trai a garant Macrobe
> qui an l'estoire [ed. Foester: *au descrire*] mist s'antante,
> qui l'antendié, que je ne mante.
> Macrobe m'anseigne a descrivre,
> si con je l'ai trové el livre,
> l'uevre del drap et le portret.   (vv. 6675–81)[20]

[While reading we found in the story / the description of the robe, / and I bring forth as guarantor Macrobius / who put his understanding to work on the story's behalf [*or*: on *describing*], / and who understood it, unless I am lying. / Macrobius teaches me to describe, / just as I have found it in the book, / the workmanship of the cloth and the images.]

Subject to "reading," a description is "written," based on writing, and is the product of a teachable art pertaining to the craft of *clergie*. Also, as Tobler-Lommatzsch point out, *descri(v)re* conveys the notions of "demonstration," "enumeration," and "taking down" (as in "taking down notes, copying").[21] What the labels "author" and "scribe" refer to is comprised within the range of activities associated with *descri(v)re*. "Author" and "copyist" perform the act of "writing"; both serve a truth—the truth of what they see and/or hear (or read)—by rendering it readable anew.

Essential to the act of "writing" as practiced by both "author" and "scribe" is the idea and practice of *translation* (OF *trans-later*, from Lat. *translatio*). A written textual corpus—e.g., Einhard's account of the battle of Roncevaux in the *Vita Karoli* and various later accretions to it—undergoes a process of oral recasting, or "translation," involving meter, song, and rhythm, *laisse* structuring, and so forth, rendering what the written text said meaningful and effective to a French-speaking listening audience of ca. 1100. Conversely, frequent references to writing in the performance (as preserved, for example, by the *Roland* text of MS Digby 23)—e.g., the hemistich "*si la geste ne ment*"—endow what the *jongleur* is singing with a truth-proclaiming authority. This process does not necessarily require the elimination of writing at any stage; on the contrary, one suspects that writing forms part and parcel of the tradition associated with each *geste* subject-matter. Indeed, the so-called *Pseudo-Turpin Chronicle* (mid-12th c.) recasts the vernacular *gestes* dealing with Charlemagne, Roland, et al., into "authoritative" Latin prose, offering itself as Turpin's own eye-witness account of Charles's expeditions into Spain. The vernacular legends consequently receive canonical historiographic validity by being couched in the authoritative language associated with the "truthfully" written *Chronicles of Saint-Denis*.

The activities pertaining to "author" and "scribe" are defined as distinct and also as necessarily related in the Prologue and Epilogue to the *Fables* of Marie de France (later 12th c.):

> Romulus, ki fu emperere,
> a sun fiz *escrist* e manda
> e par essample li mustra
> cum se deüst cuntreguaiter
> que hum nel peüst engignier.
> Esopes *escrist* a sun mestre,
> ki bien cunut lui e sun estre,
> unes fables qu'il *ot trovees,*
> *de Griu en Latin translatees.*
> Merveille en orent li plusur
> qu'il mist sun sens en tel labur;
> mes n'i a fable de folie
> u il nen ait philosophie
> es essemples ki sunt aprés,

u des cuntes est tuz li fes.
A mei, *ki la rime en dei faire,*
n'avenist nïent a retraire
plusurs paroles ki i sunt . . .[22]

[Romulus, who was emperor, / *wrote down* and sent to his son, / and by example demonstrated to him, / how one might take steps / against being fooled by another. / Æsop *wrote down* (*copied?*) for his master / —he knew his nature and his ways well— / some stories he *had found* / (*and had*) *translated from Greek to Latin.* / Many wondered that he had put his talents to such a task; / but there is no story of folly / that does not contain wisdom / in the examples following here / where all the deeds recounted in the stories are present. / To me, *who must compose the rhymed version of this* (*work*), / *in no way would it have seemed proper to bring forth* / *some of the words to be found in it . . .*]

and:

Pur amur le cunte Willalme,
le plus vaillant de cest reialme,
m'entremis de cest livre faire
e de l'Engleis en Romanz traire.
Esope apelë um cest livre,
kil traslata e fist escrivre,
de Griu en Latin le turna.
Li Reis Alvrez, ki mult L'ama,
le traslata puis en engleis,
et jeo l'ai rimé en franceis,
si cum jol truvai, proprement.[23]

[For the love of Count William, / the bravest of this realm, / *I undertook to compose this book* / *and from English to bring it out into the* (*Romance*) *vernacular.* / *One calls this book Æsop,* / *who translated it and had it copied,* / (*who*) *converted it from Greek to Latin.* / *King Alvred* (*Alfred?*), who greatly loved it, / then translated it into English, / and I have rhymed it in French, / just as I found it, exactly.]

"Written" and "oral" are all tangled up here, and so are "composing," "translating," and "copying." "Writer," "patron" (or "dedicatee"), "translator," "copyist," and "maker of books" are intertwined as indispensable participants in a complex process—itself in every respect a *translatio*—begun by the person who gave his name to the "book" by "translating it from Greek into Latin" (*sic*). Yet this book is described by Marie de France as a work which she, herself, "composed" ("*m'entremis de cest livre faire*"), or, rather, perhaps as a book ("*cest livre*") concerning which she "made [a book]"

(*"de . . . faire"*). "Marie de France," the *exact equivalent* to
"Esopes," is "author," "translator / converter," and, like the scribe,
also, we believe, "'exact' copyist." She has faithfully (*proprement*)
"copied" King "Alvred" who had "copied" Æsop; others, it is
assumed, will copy her.

It is hardly surprising that scribes should appear to take pride in
their craft, as in the passage quoted above in which Guiot names
himself, nor is it at all odd that their participation in the enterprise
of writing should, in their eyes, constitute an implicit authorization—indeed, an obligation—to "gloss" the works they are copying. The fact that Chrétien's five extant romances are embedded
within a codex containing other romance-type narratives of a "historical" sort (Wace's *Brut*, Benoît de Sainte-Maure's *Roman de
Troie*, the *Empereurs de Rome* by Calendre, and Alexandre de
Bernay's *Atys et Profilias*) amounts to a form of glossing: Guiot's
codex presents a history of the *translatio imperii* from its Græco-
Trojan origins through Rome down to Arthurian Britain. Guiot
incorporates Chrétien's *oeuvre* into this historiographical construct
which responds to the "anti-romance," or "serious," tastes of his
early thirteenth-century public, and this in turn imparts special
meaning to that *oeuvre*. It should therefore come as no shock that
Chrétien's text, as given by Guiot, is among the least *literarily*
focused within the Chrétien manuscript tradition. Guiot gives short
shrift to Chrétien's love of fancy literary ornamentation like *rich
rhyme*, *adnominatio*, and alliteration; he downplays Chrétien's
playfulness and humor.

MS B.N. fr. 1450 (first half of 13th c.) offers yet another note-
worthy example of scribal self-consciousness. This Picardizing text
is even more ostensibly historiographical than that of Guiot. It
begins with the *Roman de Troie* (Greece), continues with the *Énéas*
(Rome) and with Wace's *Brut* (Britain), and then takes up Chrétien's romances; it closes with the *Roman de Dolopathos* (which
represents the "wisdom," or "clerkly," cycle integrated into the
"chivalric" *matiére antique*). However, this order is self-consciously
modified. At fol. 139*v*, right after Wace had introduced King
Arthur and described his reign, the scribe intervenes, boldly insert-
ing his own voice into the texts he is copying:

> En cele grant pais que jo di—
> Ne sai se vos l'avés oï—
> Furent les merveilles provees

Et les aventures trovees
Qui d'Artu sont tant racontees
Que a fable sont atornees:
N'erent mensonge, ne tot voir,
Tot folie ne tot savoir;
Tant ont li conteor conté
Et par la terre tant fablé
Pour faire contes delitables
Que de verité ont fait fables.
Mais ce que Crestïens tesmogne
Porés ci oïr sans alogne.

[In that great peace of which I speak / —I do not know whether you have heard— / the miracles were tested / and the adventures discovered / which concerning Arthur are so much told / that they have turned into fables: / neither lies nor completely true, / neither foolishness nor completely knowledge; / story-tellers have repeated these stories so often / and have spread their fables so broadly upon the land / in order to make delightful tales / that they have made fables out of truth. / But what Chrétien testifies to / you can now hear with no further ado.]

After interrupting Wace's *Brut* at this point, the scribe commences to provide the texts of *Érec et Énide*, *Perceval* (along with a section of the *Continuations*), *Cligés*, *Yvain* (up to v. 3974 of Foerster's edition), and some 1450 lines of *Lancelot* (the codex is missing several folios). After furnishing Chrétien's "testimony," the scribe returns to the *Brut*, with these lines:

Cil en ont mené grant joie,
Signor, se jo avant disoie,
Ce ne seroit pas bel a dire,
Por ce retor a ma matire.

[These people manifested their great joy, / my lords, but if I were to say more on this subject / it would not be appropriate, / (and) for this reason I return to my subject-matter.]

Our scribe has placed Chrétien utterly at the service of *his* codex, which recounts the pre-history and the story of the Kings of Britain. He fully participates in the medieval bookishness which we have identified with *translatio* and which implies what we have called medieval canonicity, i.e., the literary process which, unlike that fostered by printed books, includes *both* the notion of "authorship" *and* a variable textuality reflecting scribal "creativity" and refashioning. That is his "*matire*." He uses Chrétien as freely as Marie de

France had used the expressive systems of *matière antique* romances in her commemoration of Breton *lais*, or when she added to the corpus of fables included in her collection.

One understands, then, even if one cannot condone, certain present-day disciplinary tendencies to throw out the baby with the bathwater. For Bernard Cerquiglini, whose polemical *Éloge de la variante*[24] betrays hasty writing, the sole reality in twelfth- and thirteenth-century vernacular literature is scribal; truth, he asserts, lies in what he calls the "variant." The "author," he claims, is unknowable, indeed, irrelevant—as fashionably dead as Nietzsche's God. Besides, are not functions attributed by late-1970s deconstructionists to the "post-modern" reader foreshadowed by scribal readings-and-writings? A few American comparativists, stirred by René Wellek's eventually withdrawn but still shameful 1946 diatribe against "old-fashioned philology,"[25] have climbed aboard Cerquiglini's bandwagon, using it as a vantage-point from which to snipe at those of us who persist in respecting the notion of scriptural author(ity).[26] To be sure, devising plausible biographies for early vernacular authors is usually impossible ("Guillaume de Lorris" is but a name tossed off by Jean de Meun, "Marie de France" is a sixteenth-century invention attributable to *Président* Fauchet), but the presence of *authorship* remains integral to most medieval textual corpora—even, we saw, to certain *chansons de geste* traditions. Furthermore, scribes, like Guiot, who name themselves, surely mean to confer upon their "writing" a manner with which they identify themselves and which embodies *how* their writing "carries" the author they are copying. What the scribe "writes down" becomes what he "*fist*": an "authored" book to be copied by subsequent scribes.

Our present-day notions of canonicity fail to mesh with the kinds of canonicity dominant at the time in which the texts we edit were produced. In fact, modern editors have sought precisely to eliminate the variety resulting from the practice of *letreüre*. Since our printed editions of medieval vernacular works seldom make allowance for scribal creativity and participation in literary process, our philological enterprise has been impoverished and our understanding of "authorship" has also been distorted.

One deplores Cerquiglini's rash stridency and, above all, the employment to which it has been put. He is right, though to argue that our editions ought to pay more heed to the poetico-literary implications of the scribe's job. However, asserting that in order to sanction, as he does, downplaying the significance of "author(ity)" is mischievous nonsense.

The association of an authorial name with a given work or collected *oeuvre*, though admittedly far more frequent with the advent of courtly romance (Wace, Benoît de Sainte-Maure, Béroul, Thomas d'Angleterre, and, especially, Chrétien), can be found in much earlier texts. One remembers Digby 23's mysterious "Turoldus." Indeed, the ascription of specific works to given individuals constitutes an essential poetic device in *translatio studii*-type narrative (Walter Map and the *Queste del saint Graal*, for example). Rutebeuf's etymological punning on *rude* and *buef* in many poems provides the connection between his generically disparate *oeuvre* and the poetic voice underlying it. By 1350 or so, Guillaume de Machaut, the first vernacular "*poëte*" (he will be so designated by his disciple Eustache Deschamps), will assume control over the putting together of codices presenting his works. Meanwhile, the scribe takes on the features we associate with the modern printer. In conjunction with his illuminator and rubricator, he becomes part of a manufacturing process designed to produce beautiful objects to be purveyed to high-born and luxury-loving patrons.

Distortion of the notions of "author" and "scribe" has vitiated scholarly approaches to early vernacular literature. Our use of terms like "source" and "influence," as well as "translation" and "imitation," tends to obfuscate important historical issues and authentic poetico-literary relationships. Our "orality" vs. "literacy" debates have seldom been very illuminating.

Unexamined assumptions have marred even the most thoughtfully crafted of our modern editions. According to Foerster, we recall, Chrétien *must* have composed his works in *champenois* since he calls himself "Crestïens *de Troies*." Bédierism, meanwhile, has led to the canonization of Guiot's "Chrétien," probably for these three reasons: (1) his text of the romances is among the oldest extant; (2) he wrote in a heavily *champenois*-colored Old French; (3) his handwriting—and this has contributed more to his popularity than has been usually admitted—is neat and easily readable. These traits have pleased many modern editors, and yet none is relevant to the value or accuracy of his version of Chrétien. The fact that Guiot compiled an immense codex—the sheer drudgery entailed must have been overwhelming—and the likelihood that he composed it for a public whose tastes no longer ran to the ornate figurative style and the humorous word-play one associates with the *roman courtois* at its most typical have played no editorial rôle. Furthermore, Guiot-based editions of Chrétien are often rife with *bourdons* and other examples of carelessness. Amusingly, an error by Guiot (or his archetype), compounded by syntactic contaminations flawing most of that other manuscripts within the tradition, led *both* Foerster and Roques (but for different reasons) to print a line of the *Lancelot* Prologue that makes no sense at all, and to Foersters's displaying immense erudition in touching efforts to explain away the nonsense. (He proposed to relocate the *Föhn*, a wicked wind endured by Swiss and Bavarians, to the rolling plains and gentle hills of north-central France![27])

Medieval Canonicity and the Computer (with Remarks of a Pedagogical Nature)

As stated above, for several years a group of us at Princeton have been using computer technology in order *realistically* to reconcile "author" and "scribe" within a specific OF textual tradition. Going beyond the mere storage and ordering of data, we hope we are using the computer creatively; our ideal is that of an "open-ended" corpus, readily subject to correction and to constant modification and/or development. We are recording in machine-readable form the entire extant manuscript tradition of Chrétien's *Lancelot* (some eight complete and fragmentary manuscripts). Our transcriptions follow the manuscripts exactly, to the extent that we leave all abbreviations unresolved, do not add punctuation, note capital letters and even respect the scribe's word spacing. In this way, the manuscript in all of its ambiguities will be affordably and readily accessible to scholars and students of Old French literature.

Computer format not being the same as pen and paper, we have been obliged to develop a system of codes to replace the non-ASCII characters and abbreviations found in the manuscripts. We are presently using extended ASCII characters for the codes, organizing the system according to functions so that if two different abbreviations represent the same word or phoneme, the codes will reflect that likeness.[28] This is obviously useful in searching and indexing, but it can also be of interest in paleographical and codicological studies. Eventually we envisage two sets of computer files, one in which our simple codes will be replaced by characters created by bit-mapping and another in which the present codes will be replaced by tags that encode the abbreviations in a more systematic way using SGML (Standard Generalized Markup Language). That will result in one set of files which visually replicate the manuscripts exactly, even with illuminations produced by scanners, and a second set of files which will classify the abbreviations in a standard format.

In addition to reproducing the manuscripts as they appear on vellum, our replications also contain *readings*, that is, notations marking the presence of such poetic devices as chiasmus, *oratio recta*, *adnominatio*, and rich rhyme, as well as manuscript peculiarities such as hypo- or hyper-metric lines. As we have seen, variations from manuscript to manuscript in the occurrence of poetic devices can be revealing about scribal practice, and coding for such variations will enable us to compare more precisely the texts of different scribes. We will also encode the more traditional "variants," those of line sequence and alteration. To that end, we have made all line-numbering consistent by grounding each manuscript to a "base" text, presently the 1989 Foulet-Uitti edition of the poem: when a manuscript differs from the base text, we note that lines have been inverted, left out, or added. *Windows* and *Asymetrix* procedures will possibly allow users to compare specific verse lines and sets of lines—that is, such lines as are particular to manuscript subsets, as well as those relating to the "authorial" text itself.

Eventually we will substitute our own "authorial" text for the base text, but that will be a final step since we will develop that text with the help of the computerized files. Whether printed on paper and bound as a book or online as a computerized document file, such a fully annotated "authorial text," or a painstaking attempt to reconstruct it, remains indispensable to our dealing with the vernacular literature of twelfth- and thirteenth-century France. The concepts of "canonicity" prevailing then ("author[ity]") and now ("authorial 'ownership'," including financial and "artistic" rights) both require such a text although their rationale differs in each case.

Important though it may be, however, the constitution of critical editions (or texts) ought no longer to be assumed as the single, overriding purpose of philological activity to which other realities must ruthlessly be sacrificed. Scribal, codicological, and literary historical conditions are of *poetic* significance in a manner analogous to the way linguistic features are. If an OF word puzzles us, we must demystify it; the same applies to Guiot's deprecation of rich rhyme, or of the presence/absence of lavishly illuminated images in the codex. Once we grasp the *fact* that, as Gianfranco Folena has put it, the Middle Ages viewed *translatio studii* as no less noble than *translatio imperii*, we shall at last realize that our "writers" *celebrate* that very *translatio* by their participation in it.[29] Only then will we truly understand the emblematic rôle played in this celebration by our *confrère* and philological model: the scribe. The computer, we believe, offers us a fair chance to render him—and the author by whom he is served and whom he serves—their due.

For us Cerquiglini's "variants" are not that at all, but, rather, readings contextually situated within the entirety of each replicated manuscript. Since no twelfth-century Chrétien text has survived, complete data-base predicated on the thirteenth-century tradition offers not merely indispensable raw material (of the type essential for a proper critical edition) but, concomitantly, three important perspectives: (1) it provides the only path to what Chrétien must—or could—have written; (2) it furnishes a history of how Chrétien was read/rewritten during the century following his death; and (3) it offers a precious vantage-point from which we might observe the workings of medieval vernacular bookishness in all its fidelity and innovative creativity. The products of specific scribes will be made available to scholars in a form conducive to their working with accurately and intelligently recorded data in a "hands-on" fashion.

It no longer suffices, we believe, to teach our students *about* literature by presenting them only with ready-made books—especially in the field of medieval studies. How texts came to be and the uses to which they were put constitute part and parcel of what texts are and what they mean. Experiencing this "mode of being" ought to be integrated into our programs of study. (Had this been the case, say, in the training received by Bernard Cerquiglini, he might have better understood the term "variant" which, paradoxically, he uses *as though* the printed book corresponded to medieval reality.) On the other hand—especially with beginning and intermediate students—the handling of the manuscripts themselves directly and exclusively (which is logistically impractical, given where most manuscripts are to be found) or even, at first, of large swaths of photocopied material, would be overly cumbersome and uselessly time-consuming.

Let us very briefly summarize the kinds of research practice to which we hope our *Lancelot* program might introduce graduate students in French literature.

Five types come immediately to mind: (1) paleographical; (2) stylistico-poetic; (3) editorial; (4) literary-historical; and (5) linguistic.

By being able to access a machine-readable version of a given manuscript the student will find him- or herself having to deal with scribal abbreviations, irregular punctuation, paratextual information (glosses, *incipits* and *explicits*, etc.). He or she will be obliged to collate and compare divergent versions of the "same" text, as well as take stock of codicological features. Using the machine-readable ASCII text will familiarize the student with scribal handwritings confronted in manuscript photocopies. All these matters may be conveniently grouped under the rubric of paleography.

Using built-in search procedures and thanks to encoded "readings" of poetic ornamentation (tropes, figures of speech, prosodic information), the student will be able to open up each manuscript to stylistic analysis, and to compare diverse manuscript corpora. For example, is there a correlation between a paucity of rich rhyme and the neglect, say, of chiasmus and *adnominatio*? How does MS *A* shape up with respect to MS *B* or to various manuscripts taken together? Are dates and/or places of copying a significant factor? What of matters of free stylistic variation, i.e., what is changeable in regard to the putative original text and what may not be changed? (One foresees the future development of more sophisticated programs of stylistico-poetic analysis growing out of these first steps.)

The editorial implications of our *Lancelot* Project need no further detailed rehearsal. Suffice it to say that by coming directly to grips with the entire textual tradition, and by working out specific editorial problems assigned in advance (e.g., make a critical "edition" based, say, on 150 lines contained in one or two—or three—manuscripts of the tradition, with variants and suitable modern paratext), the student will naturally come to a deeper understanding of medieval bookishness than by relying merely on printed variorum texts. He will appreciate that editorial choices are largely a matter of heuristic values and considerations, as are explanatory annotations.

Since manuscripts are of their own place and time (as well as related to an authorial tradition), the literary-historical conditions under which, say, Guiot operated (e.g., distrust of rhetorical ornamentation, a taste for "historical" accuracy) are both—at least to some degree—determinative of his emphases and of his neglects; these, in turn, constitute signs of the literary climate within which he worked. Meanwhile, given the relative stylistic conservatism of MS Princeton University Library Garrett 125, a late thirteenth-century Picard codex, and, as we have learned, of many manuscripts deriving from the same place and time, Garrett 125 offers insight into the literary tastes and values predominant in that part of France where a newly-rich *bourgeoisie* constituted the clientèle of major scriptoria. Socio-economic conditions thus can be considered in respect of their literary significance. Here, once again, we expect our Project to inspire new computer-assisted research programs.

The linguistic value of our *Lancelot* data-base is indisputable. The language of each manuscript is unadulteratedly medieval. Consequently, questions pertaining to orthography, to the lexicon, to grammar, and to syntax may be put to it, provided adequate search procedures can be devised. One of the present writers of this article is particularly interested in the French literary *koiné* of the twelfth and thirteenth centuries, i.e., in the early imposition of a "French" literary *scripta* at once universal and favorable to the importation of a great variety of dialect forms, including Old Provençal (e.g., *amor* vs. *ameur*). The linguistic status of French in 1200 is not unlike that of present-day American English. The *Lancelot* corpus represents *francien*, *picard*, *champenois*, and other dialects of *oïl*, yet it is best to view each as a *manifestation* of the French *scripta*.

With proper guidance the student may now address matters like those just outlined in a "hands-on" fashion. And while he or she is learning about medieval literature and its processes, the student is also learning to use the computer—to recognize the significance and value of this marvelous research tool. Meanwhile, we believe, this kind of learning is not ancillary, or propedeutical, to literary criticism. It is itself, rather, literary criticism of the highest order; informed by knowledge and by the seeking of knowledge, it is, moreover, particularly suitable to an academic setting.

NOTES

1. Our concern here is not to provide a comprehensive discussion of the topic of textual research and the computer. Rather, we offer here some remarks on

the subject which are pertinent to a manuscript project we have undertaken at our university (see below).

2. Ed. Rosanne G. Potter (Philadelphia: University of Pennsylvania Press, 1989).

3. *Association for Literary and Linguistic Computing Bulletin*, 7 (1979) 4–11; reproduced in *Literary Computing*, 3–12, from which we cite.

4. Bailey, 5. See n.3.

5. Ibid.

6. "La Tradition manuscrite du *Lai de l'Ombre*: réflexions sur l'art d'éditer les anciens textes," *Romania*, 54, 161–96 (reprinted 1970).

7. For a comprehensive and intelligent review of these two schools (particularly in their relation to OF critical practice) see Alfred Foulet and Mary B. Speer, *On Editing Old French Texts*. The Edward C. Armstrong Monographs on Medieval Literature, 1 (Lawrence, KS: Regents Press of Kansas, 1979), especially pp. 8–24.

8. Foerster's editions of Chrétien de Troyes may be listed as follows: *Editio maior*, Halle, 1884–1899: I. *Cligés* (1884); II. *Der Löwenritter* (*Yvain*) (1887); III. *Erec and Enide* (1890); IV. *Der Karrenritter* (*Lancelot*) *und Das Wilhelmsleben* (1899). To these may be added V. *Der Percevalroman (Li Contes del Graal)* (1932, 1966), ed. by Alfons Hilka, Foerster's disciple. *Editio minor*, Halle, 1886–1911: I. *Erec und Enide* (1896, 1909 1934); II. *Cligés* (1888, 1901, 1921 [abridged, ed. A. Hilka], 1934 (ed. Hermann Breuer); III. *Yvain* (1891, 1902, 1906, 1912 1913, 1926 [ed. A Hilka], 1942 [ed. T. B. W. Reid, with Glossary and Notes (Manchester: Manchester University Press)]); IV. *Wilhelm von England* (1911).

9. The "Roques" edition, all published by Champion in the series (directed by Roques) called *Les Classiques français du Moyen âge*, consists in the following: *Érec et Énide*, 80 (1952); *Cligés* (ed. Alexandre Micha), 84 (1957); *Le Chevalier de la Charrete (Lancelot)*, 86 (1958); *Le Chevalier au Lion (Yvain)*, 89 (1960); *Le Conte du Graal (Perceval)*, 2 vols. (ed. Félix Lecoy) 100, 103 (1973, 1975). These editions have been frequently reprinted.

10. The "written vs. oral" controversy has given rise to innumerable studies in OF scholarship and is by no means exhausted today. For a classic introduction to some of the issues, see the contributions by Martín de Riquer, Angelo Monteverdi, Jean Rychner, and, especially, Maurice Delbouille in *La Technique littéraire des chansons de geste*. Actes du Colloque de Liège. September 1957 (Paris: Société d'Édition «Les Belles Lettres», 1959).

11. *Les Lais de Marie de France*, ed. Jean Rychner. Classiques Français du Moyen Age, 93 (Paris: Champion, 1969).

12. The mid-twelfth-century "author," Wace, described himself as a *clers lisant* "learned reader."

13. "Pur ceo començai a penser / D'aukune bone estoire faire / E de latin en romaunz traire; / Mais ne me fust guaires de pris: / Itant s'en sunt altre entremis! / Des lais pensai, k' oïz aveie." *Les Lais* (Prologue), vv. 28–33.

14. Chrétien de troyes, *Cligés*, ed. Alexandre Micha. Classiques Français du Moyen Age, 84 (Paris: Champion, 1957).

15. Chrétien de Troyes, *Le Chevalier de la Charrette (Lancelot)*, ed. A. Foulet and Karl D. Uitti. Classiques Garnier (Paris: Bordas, 1989).

16. *Chrestomathie de l'ancien français*, ed. Karl Bartsch, revised by Leo Wiese (New York: Hafner, 1958), text #7, v. 9.

17. Quoted by Rupert T. Pickens, *Romania* 105 (1984), 496.

18. *Les Lais*, p. 154, v. 113.

19. MS Brussels, Bibliothèque Royale Albert Ier 9543.

20. Chrétien de Troyes, *Érec et Énide*, ed. Mario Roques. Classiques Français du Moyen Age, 80 (Paris: Champion, 1952).

21. *Altfranzösisches Wörterbuch*, ed. Adolf Tobler and Erhard Lommatzsch (Berlin: Weidmannsche Buchhandlung, 1925–), 2, col. 1547.

22. "Prologue," ed. Warnke, vv. 12–29; quoted by Gianfranco Folena, *Volgarizzare e tradurre* (Turin: Einaudi, 1991), pp. 14–15.

23. "Épilogue," ed. Warnke, vv. 9–19; quoted by Folena p. 15.

24. *Éloge de la variante: histoire critique de la philologie* (Paris, Seuil, 1989).

25. The essay appeared in the first edition of his (with Austin Warren) *Theory of Literature* under the title "The Study of Literature in the Graduate School"; it was dropped in subsequent editions "partly because some of the reforms suggested there have been accomplished in many places" (in the 1955 "Preface to the Second Edition").

26. See *Speculum* 65 (January, 1990), a special issue titled *The New Philology*, ed. Stephen G. Nichols, Jr.

27. Karl D. Uitti, "Autant en emporte *li funs*: Remarques sur le Prologue du *Chevalier de la Charrette de Chrétien de Troyes*," *Romania* 105 (1984), 274.

28. A simple example is the two different abbreviations for French "et"—a ligatured ampersand-like character and the Tyronian "and"—to which we have assigned the codes &1 and &2.

29. See Gianfranco Folena, op. cit.

Annotating *Piers Plowman*

Ralph Hanna, III

I know very little about annotation except as a problem of *praxis*: with four colleagues—John Alford, Steve Barney, Traugott Lawler, and Anne Middleton—I am currently engaged in preparing some form of textual commentary to accompany the standard edition of *Piers Plowman*.[1] *Piers* is a poem in alliterative metre reflecting the compulsions, of something like a quarter century's duration, c. 1365–90, of one William Langland. His work, which never achieved anything like completion, exists in some fifty manuscript copies, more or less reducible to three separate versions (called A, B, and C)—each an apparently arbitrary representation, unsupervised in distribution, of some stage in Langland's continuing work.[2]

Because I view my annotative efforts as a *praxis*, I find it impossible not to recreate how I came to the view of annotation which I'll eventually describe. This occurred by trying to annotate *Piers*, and thus I begin with the specific, with a nitpicking, if not thoroughly captious, problem of annotative detail. In trying to recreate for you my thoughts about this detail, I hope you will come to see, as I did, that the notion of some "incontestible or normal/normative annotation" is only that—a notion; and that, although constructive annotation may proceed nonprogrammatically, mystified as to its own procedures, ultimately all annotative activity rests upon some theoretical presumptions, which should be clearly stipulated.

My exhibit is a very trivial, and easily soluble, one. At C 7.134a, amidst one of the poem's few "sublime" passages, Langland, as is frequently his wont, quotes a Latin text:

> And sethe in oure secte, as hit semed, deyedest,
> On a Friday, in fourme of man, feledest oure sorwe.
> *Captiuam duxit captiuitatem.*

> The sonne for sorwe therof lees [s]iht for a tyme,
> Aboute mydday, when most liht is, and meltyme of sayntes;
> Feddest tho with thy flesch and blood oure forfadres in helle.
> *Populus qui ambulabat in tenebris vidit lucem magnam.*
> The lihte that lup oute of the, Lucifer hit blente
> And brouhte thyne yblessed fro thennes into the blisse of heuene.
>> (*Piers Plowman*, C Version, 7.130–36)[3]

Walter Skeat, who in 1886 provided, in addition to a full edition, annotations of a variety my group has no hope of superseding,[4] typically gets things right. He provides a concise identification of the quotation, a necessity for modern non-Catholic readers estranged from the Latinity of the Vulgate; implicitly through this move, Skeat offers directions which, if followed through the whole of Langland's text, would restore to modern readers some of that sacred and echoic sonorousness medieval readers experienced as an everyday form of textual exposure:

> The quotation from Isaiah 9.2 is explained in the apocryphal Gospel of Nicodemus with reference to the "Harrowing of Hell," i.e. the descent of Christ into hell to fetch out the souls of the patriarchs. See the whole account, as there narrated, and cf. 20.366 [where Langland cites part of the verse in his description of Jesus harrowing hell].[5]

I say that Skeat is "typically" correct because it is important to realize his ongoing importance to our entire professional enterprise: his *Piers Plowman* has always been the first fully annotated text which a fledgling medievalist meets, and thus our disciplinary model.

Skeat gets things right because he recognizes exactly what biblical passage Langland has in mind, identifies it, and sees that Langland appears in this context to associate with the Harrowing of Hell the verse from Isaiah:

> (9.1) Primo tempore alleviata est terra Zabulon et terra Nephthali; et novissimo aggravata est via maris trans Jordanem Galilaeae gentium. (9.2) *Populus qui ambulabat in tenebris vidit lucem magnam*; habitantibus in regione umbrae mortis, lux orta est eius.

And Skeat recognizes (although he did not quote the text, his one modest annotational failure) that Langland associates Isaiah's verse with the Harrowing precisely on the warrant of the Gospel of Nicodemus, the authoritative text describing this apocryphal bit of Jesus's ministry:

Nos cum essemus cum omnibus patribus nostris positi in profundo in calig-
ine tenebrarum, subito factus est aureus solis calor purpureaque regalis lux
inlustrans super nos. Statim omnis generis humani pater Adam cum
omnibus patriarchis et prophetis exultauerunt dicentes, "Lux ista auctor
luminis sempiterni est, qui nobis promisit transmittere coaeternum lumen
suum." *Et exclamauit Isaias et dixit:* "Haec est lux Patris, Filius Dei, sicut
predixi cum essem in terris uiuus: 'Terra Zabulon . . . *Populus qui sedet.* . . .'
Et nunc aduenit et inluxit nobis in morte sedentibus."[6]

Matters rested with Skeat's analysis—as they should have done—
for nearly a century until a very fine annotator, Derek Pearsall,
attempted to do what is nearly impossible, to better Skeat at his
own game. Armed, I would suspect, with a biblical concordance,
Pearsall found a second scriptural reference to associate with
Langland's citation. His note begins "Isaiah 9.2, cf. Matt. 4.16"; the
passage to which he alludes reads:

Cum autem audisset Jesus quod Joannes traditus esset, secessit in Galilaeam;
et, relicta civitate Nazareth, venit et habitavit in Capharnaum maritima, in
finibus Zabulon et Nephtalim; ut adimpleretur quod dictum est per Isaiam
prophetam: Terra Zabulon . . . *Populus qui sedebat in tenebris.* . . . Exinde
coepit Jesus praedicare.[7]

Pearsall thus ostensibly improves on Skeat by adducing a richer
biblical subtext for Langland's citation at 7.134a. In doing so, he
responds to what may be taken as a basic rule of all annotation,
that of plenitude (note, informatively, Matthew's use of *adimpleretur* in the passage Pearsall cites). By this rule, full annotation (or
fuller annotation) must always be construed as an advance in textual understanding: it constructs a deeper or denser or richer text,
restores to the author a fullness of allusion otherwise lost.

But does Pearsall actually improve our knowledge of *Piers Plowman*? I don't think so; in fact, he may have adduced information of
a sort confusing for the reader who might need such a reference as
this. Langland certainly understands Isaiah 9.2 as a prophetic statement fulfilled in the life of Jesus, and for him, this fulfillment comes
at the Harrowing of Hell, as the Gospel of Nicodemus makes clear.
However, the Matthew passage is equally prophetic—and as prophecy, thoroughly irrelevant, if not perfectly distracting, from the
prophecy Langland has in mind: for Matthew, Isaiah's words are
fulfilled, not at the (from the scriptural point of view) legendary
Harrowing of Hell, but at an early stage in Jesus's ministry.

For Matthew, the sign that prophecy has been fulfilled rests pri-

marily not on the people sitting (or walking) in the dark of Isaiah
9.2 but on the confluence of Isaiah's place names in 9.1 with the
Palestinian locales where Jesus first teaches. Matthew responds to a
different portion of the prophecy and locates it in a history different from that Langland communicates. Thus, by suggesting that
Langland may have thought of this passage, Pearsall manages to
distract his reader from that history Langland most palpably considers.[8]

This is a long megillah about a tiny jot, an iota. But it forms a
salutary lesson. For a very fine annotator, Derek Pearsall, here, it
seems to me, momentarily slips at what one might have foreseen as
one of his easier moments as annotator. Identifying explicit citations, like Langland's Latin, should be one of the annotator's most
straightforward tasks. Such notes, after all, draw attention to palpable identity relationships: either the words cited agree with a pre-
existing text, or they do not agree—and the annotator keeps on
looking for the source. Moreover, such identifications form the simplest and easiest notes to write: the annotator, as Pearsall essentially does, puts a colon after the text lemma he's citing and gives a
chapter/verse reference. But, as my reading of Pearsall here suggests, even in a situation where the annotator seeks and eventually
communicates an identity relationship, such simplicity may be only
apparent.

For notice how I have gone about deciding that my annotation
of *Piers* 7.134a will not include (or will include only with a caveat)
Pearsall's reference to Matthew, no matter what fullness that citation may appear to add to this context. Essentially, I become
involved in an interpretation of my textual locus—I must develop
some sense of an immediate context, its limits and its parameters—
and ultimately I become involved with the entire text of *Piers* (and
of related biblical loci as well). I see Langland's operative context
here as an entire extended speech (it runs C 7.120–51), what he
presents as the pulpit oration of the character Repentance, here
addressing the Seven Deadly Sins. I would identify this chunk of
poetry as falling generally within the discourse of biblical salvation
history; more specifically, Repentance outlines a temporal sequence of events which indicates the godhead's beneficent relation
to man (in the B text with some precise Trinitarian distinctions
referring to the actions of different persons in procession excised in
C, e.g., C 7.136 *brouhte* appears in B 5.495 as *blewe* and refers

directly to the operation of the Holy Spirit).[9] Within that context
7.133 *tho* fuses with the acts of Good Friday Nicodemus's narration
of Holy Saturday and the Harrowing of Hell, a segue aided by the
eucharistic references of lines 133–34: for Repentance, the acts of
God's beneficent grace immediately become available to contrite
sinners, in this case the benighted prophet Isaiah who instantly
believes his words fulfilled. Repentance's overindulgent enthusiasm
is, of course, also stimulated by context—in this case dramatic: the
sins he addresses, by their nature resistant to any "grace" but that
"of gyle" (6.213), require immediate payoffs for the confessional
trouble they've been subjected to.

My analysis suggests that Pearsall here misidentifies a discursive
context. Like a number of prominent positivistic critics of *Piers*, he
describes the passage as if quotationally driven, as if Langland's
verse exists as annotation itself does, to embroider upon a previous
master-text, here the Vulgate, and as if the annotator's job is to
help elucidate that derivative relationship.[10] My sense of the passage and poem happens to be otherwise: the incarnation, here
Jesus *in oure secte* (7.130), the lord paradoxically wearing his fol-
lowers' livery, always stimulates Langland to that poetry most like
what twentieth-century readers want him to write, and of all events
associated with the Incarnation, the Harrowing of Hell does so
especially. Eventually, the one perfected piece of Christian poetry
Langland finds he can compose is precisely a grand Harrowing narrative, in C passus 20. But such an effort is emulative, appropria-
tive, at least in part an effort by the vernacular (always, in editions
of this poem, printed in Roman type) to aspire to the level of the
sacred Latin, always italicized. And such acts of vernacular appropriation in *Piers* embed and reconstitute Latinate references (here
Latin *lucem magnam* coexists within a double absence of light—
solar eclipse and infernal darkness; and Jesus, although emitting
light, is equally the darkened incarnational form, flesh and blood).
Such acts of embedding thus always turn out to be deeply problematic, most frequently (although not here) intrusions of the local and
contested, the discontents of the fourteenth century which animate
the poem, upon the very language which alleges its unique power
as a solution to such local eruptions.

I might restate the sort of confrontation I here describe as being
between a learned idealistic positivism (the world of identity relations in which equivalents may all be equal grist for the annotative

mill) and a position far more conflicted, troubled, unsure, and open-ended. And this confrontation I see as endemic to the state both of medieval textual studies and of the annotation which surrounds texts. The first view, what I have called above "normal/normative annotation," essentially posits the annotator's craft as the provision of what might be construed as matters of fact, raw information which bridges that historical divide which separates readers and work. In such a view, the annotator benignly mediates, provides a reader with that plenitude of data which restores him, so far as possible given historical loss, to some approximation of the full information an alleged contemporary reader would have possessed.

But such a procedure involves some significant theoretical ellipses. Is its invocation of plenitude appropriate to a work unfinished and oppressively concerned with its own inability (and frequently, its deliberated unwillingness) to achieve the plenitude it wants to posit as its solution—to be bible, not midrash? Is the fourteenth century (or any other period one might name) actually blessed with a noncontested and plenitudinous discourse? Was there ever such an ideal reader? Mightn't one conceive that modern scholars, especially in an age of electronic information retrieval, might know, in the midst of their incalculable losses, more (as well as less) than any posited ideal contemporary?[11] And finally, to return to the rhetoric of Skeat and Pearsall's annotation, the colon by which they link *Piers* C 7.134a to Isaiah 9.2: what does this colon of identity mean anyhow?

My bout with Derek Pearsall enacts that querulous current state of thinking among Middle English scholars about the mission of annotation as we have professionally received it. At least one thing the *Piers Plowman* group of which I am a part has spent much time considering is where to go from here.

The stance we have agreed to take to this problematic emerged out of our combined experiences as medievalists. All of us, it turns out, have had extensive experience with medieval commentaries of one or another sort. These documents take as their model the grammarians' commentary, developed in the Roman schools as a mode of analyzing great poetry. In the Middle Ages, this became a virtually universal model for analyzing writings in a wide variety of disciplines, many of which we have studied—biblical exegesis, analysis of secular literature (Boethius's *Consolation*, Walter Map's "Dissuasio Valerii"), explanations of canon and civil law. On the basis of our combined experiences, we have identified and appropriated two central features of this tradition as models for our use.

First, the classical/medieval/Renaissance commentary tradition deliberately sought to be the best and most complete critical tradition of its age. It fused in a fluid account a variety of acts which more recent practice has taken to be separate:[12] the textual critic's commentary on competing readings, the Skeat/Pearsall annotator's identification of recondite lexicon and allusions, and instructively, the literary critic's interpretative essay. This last feature, the provision of interpretation, differs from most modern presentations: it does not form a continuous argument—as the essay does—but is textually dispersed, responds to an appropriate lemma and must be rejoined by the reader to create an argument. But it nonetheless strives for a total interpretative view of the text and presupposes that no detail "makes sense" apart from the commentator's take on the whole.

Second, the mechanism whereby such interpretative dispersal proceeds forms the normal metier of medieval commentaries and their most ubiquitous critical move, "textual mapping." Medieval annotators conceived as basic to their activities the provision of a *distinctio partium*, an explanation through division of the discontinuous onward flow of language, the identification and analysis of difference.[13] The commentator's minimal contribution, the division, outlines the text's "parts," explains how each is necessary to an overall development of argument, how each functions within an ordered succession to reach a single argumentative goal. (Our commentary, I should note parenthetically, must deal not just with textual succession but with a second dimension as well: the existence of our work in three distinct versions necessitates a perpetual excavation of the work's life in its maker's. The A version, for example, lacks altogether the passage on which I predicate my discussion.)

Although conceiving annotation in this way forms an act of historical recuperation, reinstitutes an interpretative system like that Langland knew, we do not choose to adopt such a system for reasons fundamentally historical. Rather, within this derivative of the classical language arts, we choose to identify *Piers Plowman* not as a reference to a lost historical wholeness available to an idealized medieval reader but as a discontinuous linguistic flow. The discontinuities, the "parts" which we follow the grammatical tradition in separating out, do not form allusions to but emanations from a

partly recoverable polygot—the discursive practices of late medieval England (which comprehend a true polyglot: Latin, Anglo-
Norman, and Middle English). Our division of the work attempts
to position each portion of Langland's erratic flow amidst a contested range of contemporary possibilities, all equally products of poly-
glottism yet none sharing the precise parameters of Langland's
bricolage. Among these discourses are not simply those of exegesis
and theology, but also discourses whose presence within the poem
conditions the claim to primacy of such Latinate clerical master-
narratives: the discourses of canon and English civil law, of records
of agricultural practice, of manuals on religious duties—most ubiq-
uitously penitential literature but also discussion of other conflicted
duties both clerical (the controversy over Franciscan practice) and
lay (the habits of hermits).[14]

Our annotative goal is to reinsert *Piers*, a poem for us uniquely
receptive to the contemporary, and especially to contemporary anxieties, into its constituent contemporary discourses, to describe its
place within them, and thus to direct attention to their and its con-
testations and obscurities. We hope that this choice dynamizes
"normal annotation" in two ways. First, it obliterates that "colon of
identity" by which traditional annotation marks what it typically
sees as a unidirectional source-receiver relation between the text
commented and that writing which precedes/surrounds it. For us,
the linguistic flow which is *Piers Plowman* does not remain an inert
receptor of preformed meaning but a partaker within an ongoing
social linguistic contest, a problematic to which it also contributes
and of which it may provide the most explicitly formalized record.

Second, as our commentary moves between its self-designated
"parts," it answers one of the most debilitating features of "normal
annotation": in that mode, "the annotatable," the crux, presents
itself as a disruptive opacity within an otherwise pellucid textual
surround, something which requires smoothing. But "normal annotation" offers no guide for such activities: our commentary aims
toward, while inevitably falling short of achieving, a sense of the
total work, open to the fact that it can only interpret and only see
cruces on which to exercise our annotative skill on the basis of its
interpretation. And our activity does not postulate the removal of
anomaly as goal: our belief in the centrality of contestation to discursive formations allows us to accept the occluded and opaque as
productive textual moments not to be naturalized.

As I hope I've shown, interpretation is inevitable to annotation, even in the situation of the simplest identification. Our hope is to construct an annotative form uncompromised by the contemporary plurality of interpretative modes, inasmuch as it acknowledges its place within them. And our annotation, we hope, will be of equal interest to the plurality of modern interpreters, especially insofar as it presents the discursive plurality from which the poem it annotates emerges.[15]

NOTES

1. This text we did not ourselves generate: see George Kane, *Piers Plowman: The A Version* (London: Athlone, 1960); Kane and E. Talbot Donaldson, *Piers Plowman: The B Version* (London: Athlone, 1975); G. H. Russell's *C Version*, to which we have generously been allowed access, is still forthcoming. I cite C here from Derek Pearsall, *Piers Plowman by William Langland: an edition of the C-text* (London: Arnold, 1978). Pearsall's extensive notes provide the only full contemporary annotative guide, for the Athlone editors have given their full attention to the text and finally professed themselves too exhausted by its demands to offer any annotation at all. I deliberately scant the issue of our successor relationship to the Athlone editors, largely because of Middleton's fine explanation, "Life in the Margins, or What's an Annotator to Do?" *The Library Chronicle of the University of Texas at Austin* 20, i–ii (1990):167–83. I'm grateful to Middleton not only for letting me see her paper in various unpublished (and more extensive) forms but also for a thoroughly pervasive imprint on this paper—the fruit of a variety of trenchant conversations about our mutual project and of numerous (and always improving) suggestions.

2. My "more or less" equivocation here does not refer to recent efforts at identifying as the Ur-*Piers Plowman* the so-called "Z Text" (for which, see my "MS. Bodley 851 and the Dissemination of *Piers Plowman*," forthcoming in *Yearbook of Langland Studies* 6) but rather to the still unsettled question of the two B-text manuscripts R and F. Kane and Donaldson's discussion, *B Version*, pp. 63–69, does not entirely dispel the claims, made by both editors in the 1940s (see p. 64, n. 101), that these may represent some stage intermediate between B and C.

3. I emend Pearsall's text in line 132: about half the manuscripts at B 5.491 have the correct (because it rhymes) reading I intrude; *siht* has been alliteratively assimilated to preceding *lees* and to *liht* in the following line, an error probably made independently by several scribes in both B and C traditions.

4. Skeat is utterly inimitable because he had access to the complete archive of

Middle English as understood in his generation; moreover, having edited most of this material, he knew that archive with an intimacy of detail no longer attainable. The comparable modern Middle English archive (even in its printed forms, leaving aside known manuscript texts) has become so extensive as to render such control impossible by anyone today.

5. Walter W. Skeat, *The Vision of William Concerning Piers the Plowman in Three Parallel Texts*, 2 vols., (London: Oxford University Press, 1886), 2:99, 8.133n, with minor adjustments of style and reference. The same information Skeat provides occurs in J. A. W. Bennett, *Piers Plowman* (Oxford: Clarendon, 1972), pp. 185–86, 5.501n, with some additional liturgical parallels; and A. V. C. Schmidt, *The Vision of Piers Plowman* (London: Dent, 1978), p. 319, 5.494an.

6. From 18.1, cited from H. C. Kim ed., *The Gospel of Nicodemus: Gesta Salvatoris* (Toronto: Pontifical Institute, 1973), p. 36.

7. To give adequate context, I am citing parts of Matt. 4.12–16.

8. In passing, one could suggest that the actual relevance of Pearsall's extra citation is in fact to Nicodemus—for its clerical author learned how to write stories of prophetic fulfillment precisely from reading Matthew: it, and not Isaiah, is the source of his citation. But that is another story.

9. See Thomas D. Hill, "The Light that Blew the Saints to Heaven: *Piers Plowman* B, V.495–503," *Review of English Studies* n.s. 24 (1973): 444–49.

10. For the distinguished *locus classicus* urging such a reading, see John A. Alford, "The Role of the Quotations in *Piers Plowman*," *Speculum* 52 (1977): 80–99.

11. Lexicography provides an immediate example: the breadth of representation in a tool like *The Middle English Dictionary* grants a modern scholar access to a sweeping archive of lexical items probably unavailable to most dialectally limited Middle English speakers. At the same time, of course, our reconstruction of meaning is significantly impoverished vis à vis theirs: we may know more words and more examples of them in more records than any Middle English speaker, but we know only writing, only an arbitrary selection of that (what has by chance survived), and are severely limited in our ability to intuit connotation in any narrow way.

12. In a prequel to this essay, "Annotation as Social Practice," in Stephen A. Barney, ed., *Annotation and its Texts* (New York: Oxford University Press, 1991), pp. 178–84, I address directly this dissociation of functions within "normal/normative annotation" (and by extension, textual editing). I would suggest that this nineteenth-century separation is predicated precisely upon the insistence that some objective function is being served by the materials the annotator offers.

13. Howard Bloch has provided us with an excellent example, the first gloss from John of Faenza's (standard) commentary on Gratian's *Decretum*: "This distinction is divided into two parts. In the first one, he proves by four canons that the human race is ruled in two ways, namely by law and by custom. In the second part, . . . he presents seven differences among laws."

14. See generally David A. Lawton, "The Subject of *Piers Plowman*," *Yearbook of Langland Studies* 1 (1987):1–30; and for an informative analysis of one outstanding example of contested fourteenth-century discourse, that concerning poverty, labor, and wandering, see David Aers, *Community, Gender, and Individual Identity* (London: Routledge, 1988), esp. pp. 20–35.

15. I'm very grateful to Speed Hill for allowing me to read a version of this paper at the session sponsored by the MLA Division on Methods of Literary Research, 28 December 1990. In addition to my collaborators on the *Piers Plowman* annotations, who have read and responded vigorously to various versions of this paper, John Ganim and David Lawton have offered me advice. Of course, the good bits are all theirs, the remainder my refusal to heed good counsel.

Historical and Methodological Considerations for Adopting "Best Text" or "Usus Scribendi" for Textual Criticism of Chaucer's Poems.

JOHN H. FISHER

It is generally agreed that we have no manuscripts of Chaucer's poems dating from before his death in 1400 (Fisher 1988). The dating of manuscripts not internally dated is tricky business. Handwriting is the best evidence, but handwriting alone cannot date precisely. The British Library has a codex of photostats of internally dated hands running from the twelfth to the sixteenth centuries. One can compare a manuscript with these and arrive at a fairly secure date within twenty-five or thirty years but no closer since an individual scribe may write over that many years in very nearly the same hand. Before the advent of typing or printing, *ars dictaminis* was the art of producing copper-plate script in the approved format of the day. This secretary hand changed over time, and these changes help to date manuscripts, but always to a period, never to a date (Parkes 1979, 54ff). Handwriting cannot distinguish 1390 from 1400 or 1400 from 1410. On this evidence, the earliest manuscripts of *Canterbury Tales* could equally well be from the last decade of Chaucer's life as from the first decade after his death.

The one manuscript that may preserve Chaucer's own handwriting is Cambridge Peterhouse 75.1, the manuscript of the *Equatorie of the Planetis*, internally dated 1392 and now generally accepted as a Chaucer holograph.[1] It is written in the same Anglicana script as the earliest manuscripts of his poems. It does not incorporate the single compartment *a* and *g*, and short *r* and *s* that were to become

standard in the fifteenth-century English secretary hand. Chaucer
would have learned to write in the middle of the fourteenth century
before these shapes began to take hold. But in the examples accompanying this text, the Hengwrt/Ellesmere scribe preserves all of
the older forms except the oversize *s* (and that is sometimes fairly
large when it is final). Corpus has the later single-compartment *g*
and small *s*, but older double compartment *a* and long *r*. Harley has
the later small *r* and *s*, but double compartment *a* and *g*. Lansdowne has all the later forms. Cambridge Dd has all of the older
forms, even an extender on the round *s*. Cambridge Gg has all the
later forms except the single compartment *a*. So we can say that the
hands in the manuscript samples are marginally later than that of
the *Equatorie*, but only marginally. One could not by the hand date
the composition of any manuscript within a decade.

More psychologically and culturally interesting is the lack of any
presentation manuscripts from Chaucer. Before the era of printing,
rewards for writing came only through patronage (Root). An
author would commission a fine manuscript of his work and present it to a patron who would reward him with cash or appoint-
ments. We have evidence of this sort of publication from most medieval authors: Dante, Petrarch, Machaut, Deschamps, Froissart,
Christine de Pisan, Chaucer's friend John Gower, and his disciples
Hoccleve and Lydgate. How does it happen that we have no such
manuscripts from Chaucer himself? He was a member of the royal
household, and some of his poems, like *Book of the Duchess* and
Legend of Good Women, seem clearly addressed to royalty. All of
the presentation manuscripts may have been lost, but it is very
strange that Chaucer's would have been lost, when those of Gower,
Hoccleve, and Lydgate have been preserved.

The psychological evidence seems to be that Chaucer felt he had
little to gain from formal presentation of his writings during his lifetime. The cultural evidence seems to be that until after Chaucer's
death there was not enough prestige in English to warrant presentation manuscripts. English may well have been gaining as the colloquial of court and government, but French continued as the language of prestige until the reign of Henry V.

I would like to believe that it was the personal interest of Prince
Henry that influenced his relative by marriage, Thomas Chaucer, to
employ a group of scribes to assemble Thomas's father's foul papers
and produce the earliest manuscripts of *Canterbury Tales* and

Troylus. (Documentation for the relations of Thomas Chaucer, Henry Beaufort, and John Lydgate is to be found in Fisher 1991, chap. 5, and fisher 1992.) After he married the heiress Maud Bergersh in about 1395, Thomas Chaucer's seat was at Ewelme, ten miles from Oxford. From about 1397–1403 Prince Henry, age 11 to 16, may have been in residence at Oxford from time to time, under the guardianship of his tutor and later adviser and chancellor Henry Beaufort. Beaufort was, of course, Prince Henry's uncle. From about 1397 John Lydgate was in residence at Gloucester College. One would like to know what sort of discussion may have gone on in the circle around Prince Henry about the need to bolster public support for the Lancastrian usurpation. Promoting the use of English could have been one suggestion. Although there are a few English petitions and guild returns in Chambers and Daunt's *Book of London English* and Riley's *Memorials of London Life* from before Henry IV, all official records are in French and Latin, but in 1399 Chief Justice Thirnyng's addresses concerning the deposition of Richard II and the accession of Henry IV and Henry's own challenge to the throne in the *Rotuli Parliamentorum* are in English, and from then on the *Rotuli* begin to have scattered entries in English. But none of these are royal. Both Henry IV and V continued to use French for their official correspondence and promulgations until Henry V began to assemble his forces for his second invasion of France in 1416. At this time his proclamations to the citizens of London are in English. After he landed in France in August 1417, he sent a triumphant report in English back to London and his first signet missive in English to his chancellor. From this time until his death in 1422, all of Henry's official correspondence and proclamations are in English. This gave English official standing. Chancery and the guilds quickly began to adopt it, and by 1430 English had become the standard for government and business transactions (Fisher 1977, Fisher 1984).

The first manuscripts of Chaucer's poems and the first English poems by Lydgate and Hoccleve are coincident with these sociopolitical developments. Ms Morgan 817 of Chaucer's *Troylus and Criseyde*, bearing on its first page the arms of Henry V when he was Prince of Wales, must have been produced before he became king in 1413, and the seven early manuscripts from which we print samples, which form the basis for the text of *Canterbury Tales*, are dated by their scripts in the first quarter of the fifteenth century.

Hengwrt is regarded as the earliest. It has the purest text but extensive omissions and the worst order for the tales. Corpus, Harley, Lansdowne, and the two Cambridge manuscripts add material and experiment with the order. Ellesmere, written by the same scribe as Hengwrt, appears to be the last. This, the most sumptuous of all Chaucer manuscripts, is associated by internal references and illuminations with Thomas Chaucer, whom Manly and Rickert propose as "logically the person to have had made what was clearly intended as an authoritative text" (1:159).[2]

In *The Textual Tradition of the Canterbury Tales* (1985), Norman Blake has given a persuasive account of the evolution of the text from Hengwrt to Ellesmere. His argument has not been fully accepted because he contends that only the Hengwrt contains the original Chaucerian text, that the Canon's Yeoman's Tale and other added passages in the subsequent manuscripts are non-Chaucerian. Most of us are unwilling to forgo 1,028 lines of good poetry. But Blake's hypothesis that a group of friends worked to give a veneer of completeness to papers that Chaucer left in disarray at the time of his death develops in more detail ideas put forward earlier by J. S. P. Tatlock, Germaine Dempster, Charles Owen, and others, and accords with the socio-political milieu in which the first manuscripts appeared. In a word, there never was a complete and ordered manuscript of either *Troylus* or *Canterbury Tales*, only foul papers left in a state of disarray. The earliest manuscripts are independent scribal reconstructions from these papers. Hence, there is no "best text" upon which to base an edition of either poem.

Now this is a long preamble to a tale. It represents the historical conditions that argue for a "usus scribendi" method of editing Chaucer's poems rather than a "best text" method. All of the early manuscripts appear to be scribal reconstructions from Chaucer's foul papers (and from each other as they began to appear). The foul papers disappeared early on, so we must try to explain the relations of the earliest manuscripts to one another and the reasons for a scribe's using one reading rather than another. The two most attractive manuscripts remain the Hengwrt and Ellesmere, by the same scribe, the first and last of the trial series. Corpus, Harley and Lansdowne are likewise very close, the first two by the same scribe, the third copied from Corpus with reference back to the foul papers for material not in Corpus. According to Blake's scenario, the Cambridge Dd scribe made use of Hengwrt as well as the foul papers and, possibly, some of the other early manuscripts. His greatest contribution was, by close reading and good taste, to achieve the order for the tales deemed most satisfactory by modern scholars. This order, adopted by the Gg scribe and by the Hengwrt scribe when he came to produce the Ellesmere, now goes under the heading of the Ellesmere order. The claim to fame of Gg is, again following Blake, that it was the first manuscript to be illustrated with miniatures of the pilgrims (nearly all of which have been cut out). This innovation was likewise adopted for the Ellesmere. In sum, the scenario Blake develops in detail describes a judicious process of experimentation from Hengwrt onwards in the creation of text, rubrics, glosses, links, order, and illustrations leading finally to the production of the Ellesmere manuscript.

Blake's scenario is not the last word. It will no doubt be modified; but he seems to me to be on the right track. We must identify the earliest manuscripts, study their readings meticulously, and try to deduce the scribal reason for every variation. We will be left with some readings for which no scribal explanation can be given. We are then thrown back on Chaucerian practice or our own taste. We may elect in that case to adopt the Hengwrt reading as the earliest or the Ellesmere as the most considered, but we must be aware that neither the Hengwrt nor the Ellesmere readings are any more inherently Chaucerian than those of the other early manuscripts. Our text will be eclectic, as nearly all texts of Chaucer have always been, but eclectic in a more sophisticated way. The assumption that the *Equatorie* is really a Chaucer holograph would be very useful in helping decide at least about spelling and idiom.

But enough generalization. Let me exemplify "usus scribendi" editorial technique by showing briefly how readings might be selected in ten lines from the Wife of Bath's Prologue. Facsimiles of the lines in the relevant manuscripts are provided below.

Hengwrt presumably represents the earliest and least edited version. Ellesmere is by the same scribe, but with the benefit of several years and several versions in between. Both Hg and El begin with *Thow*, spelled *þou* by Cp, Ha, and Gg. The *Equatorie* regularly uses the *thow* spelling, which could be taken to indicate that the Hg scribe was staying close to Chaucer's form. (Larry Benson has prepared a computer concordance to the *Equatorie*, from which the following citations and totals are drawn.) The use of this spelling by

Dd suggests that that scribe was also looking closely at the foul papers and hence that his additions may be more than inventions. La is said by Manly-Rickert to be copied from Cp, but if so, the scribe chose to revert to the Chaucerian spelling or had a personal predilection for the *ow*. We must understand that there were no preferred spellings as long as English was considered a patois. W. C. Bolland records a case (p. 105) in 1426 in which objection was raised because the name B*a*nister was written B*e*nister. The judge disallowed the objection because "words are pronounced differently in different parts of England, and one is just as good as the other." Only after Henry V began to use English for royal missives did spelling begin to be regularized, and, not surprisingly, many of the preferred spellings today, like the *gh* in *taught* and *through*, are Henry's own (Richardson), although they are spelled *tawhte* and *thorw* in the *Equatorie*.

H*g*/E*l* continue *seyst* which both spell *seist* in line 8. These are spelled variously in the other manuscripts, but most generally *seist*. This form is not found in the *Equatorie*, but it does have *seye*, *seid*, and *seyn/sein*. In ME *i* and *y* are so interchangeable that the variation is not recorded in the *MED*, so it is no surprise that Chaucer himself spelled the forms differently. On the whole, the spelling in the *Equatorie* is consistent, but if a "usus scribendi" edition were to be normalized (as it should be) an arbitrary decision would have to be made whether to use *i* forms (eighteen occurrences in the *Equatorie*) or *y* forms (twelve occurrences) for the forms of *sein*, *seist*, and *seid*.

That, thorn *þat* and contraction *þt* are likewise completely interchangeable in ME. The regular form in *Equatorie* is the contraction *þt* (132 occurrences; *that* is spelled out three times). The H*g*/E*l* scribe interchanges them cavalierly in lines 1 and 8 in the sample. Again, a normalized text would have to decide among these spellings.

The collocation *Thou seyst* appears in lines 1, 5, and 8. H*g* and the next four MSS omit the following *that* in line 5, only to have it introduced by Gg and then picked up by E*l*. This suggests that it was not found in the exemplar but was introduced by the Gg scribe for parallel structure. The H*g* scribe was sufficiently impressed to follow along when he copied E*l*. Which reading the modern editor should prefer is problematical. *That* gives ten syllables for line 1, but eleven syllables for lines 5 and 8. It appears in all the manuscripts for line 8. So the editor must decide whether to omit it in line 5 in the interest of meter or include it in the interest of parallelism. (I omitted it in both my school edition and my Variorum edition. The Variorum is a best-text edition based on Hg, and the Holt is a best-text edition based on El, but in this case, the rhythm of the Hg reading for line 5 seems manifestly preferable, and the rhythm of line 8, confirmed by all the manuscripts, seems not so bad. In this respect, all eclectic editions are to some extent "usus scribendi.")

Houses is plural in all the MSS except Ha where we may take the singular as a scribal aberration perhaps influenced by singular *smoke*. The *ow* spelling of La is likewise in the minority but raises again questions about normalization. I do not find *house* in the *Equatorie*, but that text shows a marked preference for *ow* spelling of the modern [au] dipthong, as in *owt, rownd, bownde,* and *abowte*. However, *abowte* is twice spelled *aboute* and the preterit of *finden* as *found* and *fond*. So it is evident that Chaucer (or the writer of the *Equatorie*) was not entirely consistent in this spellings, although *ow* was his dominant form.

His lack of consistency is revealed likewise in the vowel of noun plural and verb third singular inflections, which appear in the *Equatorie* as *-es* (207 occurrences) and *-is* (16 occurrences), and *-eth* (25 occurrences), *-ith* (4 occurrences), and *-yth* (4 occurrences). Many of the plural inflections in modern editions are expansions of abbreviations. Hg/El *eyleth* in line 4 is represented with both *e/i* and *th/þ* in other manuscripts. The variations in the *Equatorie* are Chaucer's own, but again, the *e* forms are dominant and should be employed for normalization, certainly for the expansion of abbreviations. On the whole, Chaucer was careful to distinguish *e* and *i* in rhymes, but he does occasionally rhyme the plural with the verb *is*: *dedis/is* twice in WBP (1155, 1169), *goddis/forbode is* in MerchT (3395), and so on.

The *i/y* forms of *chidyng* in the MSS represent the common variants discussed above for *seyst*. The word is not found in the *Equatorie*, but it does have *deuided/deuyded, bi/by, bitwix/bytwix*, again evidence of authorial inconsistency. That Hg/El use *i* both here and at the end of line 4 leads one to suppose that *i* was Chaucer's dominant form for this word.

Wyues, on the other hand, is spelled with *y* in all the manuscripts. The *y* is dominant with *u, m,* and *n* in most ME MSS to avoid ambiguous minims, but throughout the *Equatorie iu* and *in* (particularly in the participial inflection *-ing*) are more frequent than *yu* and *yn* (gross numbers are hard to arrive at because of the frequency of particular words, e.g., prep. *in* 213 times, *aryn* 37 times, etc.). The singular *wyf* in Gg along with the plural *men* is a scribal aberration. *Maken men to* is regular through all the manuscripts.

Flee with double *ee* in Hg/El is probably a scribal form. I don't find the word in the *Equatorie*, but that text always uses single *e* for the long vowel, as in *whel, degre, sek* (seek). Hence the Cp/Ha/Gg single *e* is more probably that of the exemplar. The rhyme of the double *ee* with single *e* in Dd is simply scribal carelessness. La *flye* is similarly a scribal variant. This is a recorded ME spelling, but not usual as a rhyme for simple *e*.

Owte of La is the spelling found in the *Equatorie* suggesting that the *ou* forms in Hg/El and the other early manuscripts are again scribal. *W* and *u* are different shapes for the same letter in ME, with *u* coming in Chancery standard to be restricted to medial position and *w* to final. On the evidence of the *Equatorie*, Chaucer appears to have preferred *u* for the consonant *v*, and *w* for the vowel *u* although the *abowt/about* show that he was not entirely consistent.

The Hg/El *hir* is consistently the form in the *Equatorie* for *their*, so the *er* forms in the other manuscripts must be scribal.

Hg/El *Owen(e)*, not found in *Equatorie*, is the usual form in the samples; Ha *oughne* is a curious preservation of the Anglo-Saxon palatal (OE *agen*) sometimes found in Kentish (*Ayenbyte of Inwit*, Gower).

Houses in line 3 follows much the same pattern as in the first line. But La, the only manuscript that got it right there, here adopts the scribal *ou* and flouts parallelism by reducing it to singular, as does Gg; Ha has the singular both places. The grammatical context is plural, but the ideational context is singular. Men don't flee from their plural houses, but from their singular house, which is evidently what produced the singular forms.

Hg/El *a benedicitee* differs only in scribal doubling of the final *ee* discussed above in connection with *flee*.

What is regular throughout all the manuscripts.

Hg/El *swich* in line 4 is the regular form in the *Equatorie* and has been cited by Michael Samuels as a characteristic feature of Chaucer's spelling.

An old man for to chide is nearly regular throughout the manuscripts. La *holde* for *old* is simply a mistake; Dd/Gg omission of *for* loses a needed syllable; *i/y* in *chide* is discussed above.

Let me treat only the distinct variants in the rest of the passage. Hg/Cp/La/Dd *wil* in line 5 is El *wol*, Ha *woln*, and Gg *wele*. In Line 6 Hg/Dd/El have *wol* and Cp/Ha/La have *wil* and Gg again *wele*. *Wil* and *wol* are interchangeable forms in ME, but the *Equatorie* uses only *wole* (five occurrences—not many, and no evidence that this was the author's only form). Still, this suggests that the two *wol* forms in El are the most authentic, and that the others represent various combinations of scribal transcription.

Hg/El/Gg *oxen asses hors and houndes* of line 8 gave the other scribes various kinds of trouble. Cp/La/Dd are influenced by parallel structure to make the plural *assen*, and Ha got both the cadence and the meaning completely wrong both here and in the last line.

This is how scribal usage and the holograph *Equatorie of the Planetis* might be used to determine the text of Chaucer. I have selected a simple passage for this exercise. There are many more interesting problems in other passages. But this is enough to raise the question, whether the text of the *Canterbury Tales* and Chaucer's other poems should continue to be based on any one manuscript, corrected only for obvious errors, or should be an editorial construct, arrived at by consideration of the scribal process and the usages of the *Equatorie*? In particular, should the spelling be normalized according to the usage in the *Equatorie*? Not all of the words are to be found in the *Equatorie*, and there are minor variations in the use of *i* and *y*, *u* and *w*, *th* and *þ*, *es* and *is*, *eth* and *ith* in the *Equatorie*. But in most cases the statistics indicate the dominant form, and a normalized text would be much easier to read than texts that preserve the pointless variations found in Hengwrt and Ellesmere. There is little authorial justification for these variations; the orthography of the *Equatorie* is much more regular than that of any scribal production.

It would take a generation of analysis by a team of scholars to arrive at a satisfactory "usus scribendi" text for the *Canterbury Tales* and *Troilus and Criseyde*. The substance of such a text would not differ markedly from Corpus and Morgan for *Troylus* and Hengwrt and Ellesmere for *Canterbury Tales*, but there would be some significant differences, and the regularized orthography would be both easier to read and, on the basis of the usage of the *Equatorie*, more nearly Chaucerian than the variations between *wil* and *wol*, *swich* and *such*, *owt* and *out*, *that* and *þat*, *seyst* and *seist*, *flee* and *fle*, *hir* and *her*, and so on that we find in the best-text editions, my own included. Talbot Donaldson normalized the spelling in his edition of *Canterbury Tales* on the basis of Hengwrt, but the model of the more regular *Equatorie* seems better. The example of George Kane and Talbot Donaldson in arriving at a "usus scribendi" text for *Piers Plowman* would obviously be important.[3] Kane and Malcolm Samuels have made important suggestions about applying the principles of "usus scribendi" to Chaucer's text. I must say that I am not eager to have the Holt text superseded, but I would like to be part of a preliminary planning commission that would debate the principles of selection and the details of their application for a new kind of text of Chaucer's poems. "Scribendi recte sapere est et principium et fons," said Horace. I would like to end my career as part of Chaucerian "scribendi recte."

Samples from the earliest MSS of *Canterbury Tales*
Wife of Bath's Prologue, III.278–89

Hengwrt (Hg)

Corpus 198 (Cp)

Þou seist þat droppyng houses and eek smoke
And chydyng wyues maken men to fle
Out of here owne houses a benedicite
What eyleþ swich an olde man for to chyde
Þou seist we wyues wille oure vices hyde
Til we be faste and þanne we wille hem shewe
Wel may þis be a prouerbe of a shrewe
Þou seist þat oxen assen hors and houndes
They ben assayed at diuerse stoundes
Bacynes lauours or þat men hem bye

Harley 7334 (Ha⁴)

Þou seist þat droppyng hous and eek smoke
And chydyng wyues maken men to fle
Out of here oughne hous a benedicite
What eyleþ swich an old man for to chyde
Þou seist we wyues woln oure vices hyde
Til we ben weddid and þan we wil hem shewe
Wel may þat be a prouerbe of a shrewe
Þou seist þat assen oxen and houndes
Þay ben assayed at diuere stoundes
Bascyns lauours eek er men hem bye

Lansdowne (La)

Þou seist þat dropinge houses eeke smoke
And chidinge wyues maken men to flie
Oute of heir owen house a benedicite
What eyleþ suche an olde man for to chide
Þou seist þe wiues wil owre vices hide
Til we be faste and þan we wil hem shewe
Wele maie þis be a prouerbe of a shrewe
Þou seist þat oxen assen hors a houndes
Ri buen assaide att suche stoundes
Bascyns lauours er þat men hem bye

Cambridge Dd 4.24 (Dd)

Thou seist that droppyng houses/ & eek smoke
And chidyng wyues/ maken men to flee
Out of here owen houses/ a benedicite
That eilith swich an old man: to chide
Thou seist we wyues/ wyln oure vices hide
Til we be fast/ and thanne we wol hem shewe
Wel may this be/ a proueibe of a shrewe
Thou seist that oxen/ asses, hors and houndes
They ben assayed· at dyuse stoundes
Bacyns/ lauours, or that men hem bye

Cambridge Gg 4.27 (Gg)

þu seyst þt droppynge housis & ek smoke
And chydynge wyf makyth men to fle
Out of here owene hous a benedicite
What eylyth swich an old man to chyde.
þu seyst þt we wyuys wele oure vicis hyde
Til we ben fast & panne we wele he shewe
Wel may þt ben a prouerbe of a shrewe
þu seyst þt oxyn assis hors & houndis
þey ben asayed at dyuerse stoundis
Bacynys lauourys er þa men he bye

Ellesmere (El)

Thow seist that droppyng houses & eek smoke
And chidyng wyues/ maken men to flee
Out of hir owene houses/ a benedicitee
That eileth swich an old man for to chide
Thow seist þt we wyues, wol oure vices hide
Til we be fast and thanne we wol hem shewe
Wel may that be a gynde of a chicke
Thow seist þt oxen/ asses, hors/ and houndes
They been assayd· at diuerse stoundes
Bacyns, lauours, er that men hem bye

Folio 73ʳ, bottom 13 lines, MS. Cambridge Peterhouse 71.1

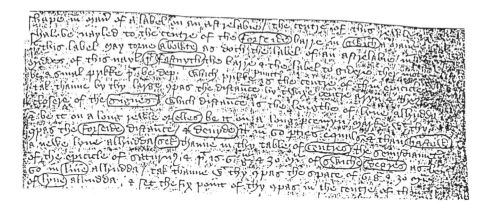

Usus scribendi text of III.278–89

Thow seyst that droppyng howses and ek smoke
And chidyng wyves maken men to fle
Owt of hir owen howses a benedicite
What eyleth swich an old man for to chide
Thow seyst we wyves wol owr vices hide
Til we ben fast and thanne we wol hem shewe
Wel may that be a proverbe of a shrewe
Thow seyst that oxen asses hors and howndes
They ben assayed at diverse stowndes
Bacyns lavowrs er that men hem bye

NOTES

1. The radix date for the tables in the *Equatorie of the Planetis* is identified on fol. 5ᵛ as "radix chaucer," which Derek Price in his edition (1955) took as indication of its authorship. Pamela Robinson has more recently (1988) observed: "It seems unlikely that anyone other than he [i.e., Chaucer] would refer to the radix date as his since anyone capable of calculating with such a set of tables as in the present MS could produce their own radices, and the date chosen, the last day of 1392, was of no particular significance" (p. 83). Robinson 1991 expands the codicological argument for Peterhouse 75.1 as a

Chaucer holograph. A. S. G. Edwards and Linne R. Mooney (1991), on the other hand, put forward codicological arguments that it is a scribal copy. Jeanne E. Krochalis (1991) disposes of most of Edwards's and Mooney's arguments and suggests that the Latin superscripts suggest that Peterhouse 75.1 is the composition of an author trying to put a Latin scientific text into accurate English, most likely Geoffrey Chaucer. To Krochalis's assessment I would add that the *Equatorie* is so technical that it is unlikely that Peterhouse 75.1 is the earliest draft. Chaucer had no doubt worked through several drafts, wrestling both with the matter and the language. Peterhouse 75.1 must have been a much later draft, although not yet the final one ready to be copied since he would still have had to deal with the "false canons."

R. M. Wilson in the Price edition concluded his analysis of the language: "There is certainly nothing in the language or style of the *Equatorie* which is definitely against Chaucerian authorship. On the contrary, there are certain facts which offer some support for such a theory; and if none of them is particularly striking by itself, taken together they may well have some significance, though the exact value of this is more difficult to determine" (p. 148). Margaret Schlauch subsequently noted the similarity of the personal voice of the *Equatorie* to that of the *Treatise on the Astrolabe*. Price compared the science in the two works, concluding that the *Equatorie* might have been composed as a completion for the incomplete *Astrolabe* (pp. 156–57). J. D. North did not at first accept the similarity of the science in the two works, but in *Chaucer's Universe* (1988, pp.177–81) he reviews the objections and concludes: "But it is in any case, in my opinion, a moral certainty that it dates from the first eight months of 1393, and is Chaucer's" (p.181).

Michael Samuels's argument that the *Equatorie* represents Chaucer's spelling has been acutely criticized by Larry Benson, "Chaucer's Spelling Reconsidered," *English Manuscript Studies III*. Using the same methodology as Samuels, Benson "proves" that the spelling of the *Equatorie* is not Chaucerian. But what this article really demonstrates is the methodological difficulty in sorting out authorial spellings from scribal transformations—as well as the very close intertextual relations in the work of the London-Westminster professional scribes (like those discussed by Doyle and Parkes) who turned out the earliest manuscripts of English poetry. If the spelling of the *Equatorie* is to be accepted as Chaucerian, it must be on the basis of the Chaucer name in the manuscript, the similarities to the style and science of the *Astrolabe*, and the holograph status of the manuscript, not on the basis of comparison with the spellings in other Chaucer manuscripts.

What impresses Price, North, and Robinson—and me—is the difficulty in imagining that there could have been two different authors writing at exactly the same time, in exactly the same place, on exactly the same limited topic, in so nearly the same language as the *Treatise on the Astrolabe* and *Equatorie of the Planetis*. A study of the facsimile in Price's edition, much less of the original MS on which the deletions and erasures are even more evident, makes it impossible for me to imagine that Peterhouse 75.1 is not a holograph.

2. The Manly-Rickert inference about Thomas Chaucer is enigmatic, but Heng-

wrt, Ellesmere, Corpus, and Harley were all produced by scribes in the group turning out copies of English poetry and prose in London and Westminster the first quarter of the fifteenth century, described by Doyle and Parkes. As envisaged by Blake, the work of these scribes in producing an evolving series of experimental texts of the *Canterbury Tales* had to be paid for by somebody. The best candidate is Thomas Chaucer, wealthy landowner, member of parliament, king's butler to both Henry IV and V, comptroller of Petty Customs. He would have had the money, presumably the motive, and access to the foul papers Chaucer left when he died in Westminster in 1400.

3. See Kane 1960, Chap IV, for a description of the "usus scribendi" method as applied to the A text of *Piers Plowman* and to the B text of Kane-Donaldson. Kane discusses application of "usus scribendi" methods to *Canterbury Tales* in his essay in Ruggiers.

WORKS CITED

Benson, Larry, "Chaucer's Spelling Reconsidered," *English Manuscript Studies III*, Ed. P. Beal and J. Griffiths Toronto: Toronto University Press, 1992, pp. 1–28.

Blake, Norman. *The Textual Tradition of the Canterbury Tales*. London: Arnold, 1985.

Bolland, W. C. *A Manual of Yearbook Studies*. Cambridge: Cambridge University Press, 1925.

Doyle, A. I., and M. B. Parkes. "The Production of Copies of the *Canterbury Tales* and the *Confessio Amantis* in the Early Fifteenth Century." *Essays presented to N. R. Ker*. Ed. M. B. Parkes and A. G. Watson. London: Scolar, 1978, pp. 163–210.

Edwards, A. S. G., and Linne R. Mooney. "Is the *Equatorie of the Planetis* a Chaucer Holograph?" *Chaucer Review* 26 (1991): 31–42.

Fisher, John H. "Chancery and the Emergence of Standard English in the Fifteenth Century." *Speculum* 52 (1977): 870–99.

———, Malcolm Richardson, Jane L. Fisher, eds. *An Anthology of Chancery English*. Knoxville: University of Tennessee Press, 1984.

———. "Animadversions on the Text of Chaucer, 1985." *Speculum* 63 (1988): 779–83.

———. *The Importance of Chaucer*. Carbondale, IL: Southern Illinois University Press, 1991.

—————. "A Language Policy for Lancastrian England." *PMLA* 107 (1992): 1168–80.

Kane, George. "J. M. Manly and Edith Rickert." *Editing Chaucer: The Great Tradition.* Ed. Paul G. Ruggiers. Norman, OK: Pilgrim Press, 1984, pp. 207–230.

—————, ed. *Piers Plowman: The A Version.* London: Athlone, 1960.

—————, and E. Talbot Donaldson, eds. *Piers Plowman: The B Text.* London: Athlone, 1975.

Krochalis, Jeanne E. "Postcript: The *Equatorie of the Planetis* as a Translator's Manuscript." *Chaucer Review* 26 (1991): 43–47.

Manly, J. M., and Edith Rickert, eds. *The Text of the Canterbury Tales.* 8 vols. Chicago: Chicago University Press, 1940.

North, J. D. *Chaucer's Universe.* Oxford: Clarendon, 1988.

Parkes, M. B. *English Cursive Hands, 1350–1500.* London: Scolar, 1979.

Price, Derek J., ed. *The Equatorie of the Planetis.* With a linguistic analysis by R. M. Wilson. Cambridge: Cambridge University Press, 1955.

Richardson, Malcolm. "Henry V, The English Chancery, and Chancery English." *Speculum* 55 (1980): 726–50.

Robinson, P. R. *Catalogue of Dated and Datable Manuscripts, c. 737–1600, in Cambridge Libraries.* Cambridge: D. S. Brewer, 1988.

—————. "Geoffery Chaucer and the *Equatorie of the Planetis*: The State of the Problem." *Chaucer Review* 26 (1991): 17–30.

Root, R. K. "Publication before Printing." *PMLA* 28 (1913): 417–31.

Samuels, M. L. "Chaucer's Spelling." *Middle English Studies Presented to Norman Davis.* Ed. D. Gray and E. G. Stanley. Oxford: Clarendon, 1983, pp. 17–37.

Schlauch, Margaret. "The Art of Chaucer's Prose." *Chaucer and Chaucerians.* Ed. D. S. Brewer. London: Nelson, 1966, pp. 140–63.

Fifteenth-Century Patrons and the Scipio-Caesar Controversy

Maria Grazia Pernis

During the 1430s in Italy, a controversy arose over the relative merits of the Roman leaders Publius Cornelius Scipio Africanus and Caius Iulius Caesar. They came to symbolize opposite styles of government. The foremost fifteenth-century protagonists on either side of the controversy were the humanists Poggio Bracciolini and Guarino Veronese. They cited ancient Greek and Roman authors, including Cicero, Livy, Plutarch, Tacitus, Suetonius, Lucian, and others. Poggio's and Guarino's arguments were also rooted in scholarly works of the fourteenth and fifteenth centuries, particularly those by Francesco Petrarca, Coluccio Salutati, and Leonardo Bruni.[1]

Because of the close intellectual ties linking humanists with their patrons, the Renaissance evaluation of Caesar and Scipio was charged with meaning that transcended the boundaries of a literary argument. In fact, this controversy dealt with a basic issue of Renaissance culture, namely liberty versus tyranny.[2] Patrons modeled themselves either on Caesar or Scipio, according to the public image they wished to project. Most often, the patrons' choice had been inspired by the views of a particular humanist. Ultimately, the literary images from the humanists' texts were reflected visually in the works of art commissioned by the patrons.

Because of the significance of this issue, the intellectual reputation of the humanists involved in it, and the political implications connected with a patron's choice of his model, the Scipio-Caesar controversy had a far-reaching impact on Renaissance art and culture.

This paper investigates the reactions of certain patrons to the controversy and focuses on the Medici, leaders of the Florentine

Republic, Leonello d'Este, Marquis of Ferrara, Federico da Montefeltro, Lord of Urbino, and Francesco Sforza, Duke of Milan.[3] The
latter was praised by Machiavelli as a "principe nuovo," who used
every political means to achieve his ends.[4] The patrons' identifications with this dispute, which depended on the historical and political conditions of their states, were widely different. By comparing
their reactions, I hope to shed new light on Renaissance patronage.

Scholars agree that the Scipio-Caesar controversy first emerged
in Poggio's letter of April 1435 to Scipione Mainenti of Ferrara.[5] In
this letter Poggio compares the deeds of the two Roman leaders; he
praises Scipio Africanus and condemns Caesar. Although both
were outstanding Roman generals, Poggio says that Scipio, unlike
Caesar, combined military success with a virtuous life. After his
final victory over Hannibal, Scipio retired in voluntary exile to Lin-
terno. In fact, he did not want his increasing power to endanger the
liberty of the Roman *res publica*. Caesar, on the other hand, was for
Poggio an extremely dangerous citizen,[6] conspiring to murder the
senators and subvert the republic. When Caesar became a Consul,
he acted as a tyrant.[7] Hav-ing been granted perpetual dictatorship
after the Civil War, Caesar ruled as a despot.[8]

Poggio appears to have been mainly concerned with the political
contrast between Scipio as a symbol of liberty and Caesar as one of
tyranny, but he also enumerates Scipio's virtues and Caesar's vices.
Poggio praises Scipio's "justice, temperance, dignity, moderation,
continence, integrity, and lifestyle." He then condemns Caesar's
shameful actions, such as "plundering, deceit, internal opposition,
civil struggle, immoderate lust for power, disgraceful behavior, and
adultery."[9]

Poggio's letter to Scipione Mainenti was, according to John W.
Oppel, directly connected with two other letters that he had previously written to Cosimo de' Medici.[10] One was the October 1433
letter of consolation to Cosimo when he was exiled by the Signoria
of Florence.The other was the November 1434 letter of congratula-
tion for Cosimo's triumphant return.[11] Oppel asserts that in the
Scipio-Caesar controversy Poggio played the role of "a Medici partisan" and "conscious propagandist" of the Medici policy.[12] Oppel
discerns Cosimo's political opponent, Rinaldo degli Albizzi, in
Poggio's Caesar and Cosimo himself in his Scipio. Like Scipio,
Cosimo, had gone into exile for the love of his country; both were
deeply committed to the "cultivation of virtue and the preservation

of peace."[13] In Poggio's opinion, in fact, peace and liberty were pre-requisites for the survival of arts and letters.

From the earliest period of his power, Cosimo's virtues were cel-ebrated by humanists and poets of the Medici circle. Their stress on Cosimo's respect for the *Florentina libertas* confirms, in my opinion, his endorsement of Scipio as Poggio's model.[14] However, as Alison M. Brown demonstrated, the nature of Cosimo's praise developed along the lines of his increasing political power.[15]

The evidence that Cosimo himself was undergoing a gradual modification in his choice of a model is provided by Poggio's letter of May 1438.[16] Poggio wrote to Andreolo Giustiniani, his Genoese friend and a collector of Greek art objects, that Cosimo would like the seal carved with the head of the emperor Trajan with which An-dreolo used to sign his letters.[17] Since the emperor Trajan was widely celebrated for his virtues, particularly that of justice, even as enthusiastic a republican as Poggio could hardly object to Cosimo's choice. Cosimo's request was proabably satisfied, since in the 1456 inventory of the collection of gems of Cosimo's son Piero de' Me-dici "uno chalcedonio con una testa di tutto rilievo di Trajano lega-to in oro" was included.[18]

After Cosimo's death, he was idealized and celebrated as "Pater patriae" in the Medici iconography (Fig. 1). Although the Roman emperors became increasingly popular with the Medici circle, Cosimo's republican models continued to be respected and exalted by his successors. A public commission executed by Domenico Ghirlandaio and assistants in 1482–85 under the rule of Lorenzo the Magnificent indicates that Poggio's praise of Scipio still had an echo several decades after the beginning of the controversy.

Ghirlandaio painted a fresco cycle of Famous Men from Roman antiquity in the "Sala dei Gigli" of the Palazzo Vecchio, the old seat of Florence's republican power. In the iconography of these fres-coes, Brutus, the murderer of Caesar, joins Scipio as a champion of liberty. The Six Famous Men are divided into two groups. Decius, Scipio, and Cicero are on one side and Brutus, Scaevola, and Cam-illus are on the other. Their names are clearly inscribed below each figure. The two groups flank the central part of the wall where a Madonna in the lunette and the Saints, who are protectors of Flo-rence, are represented. This extraordinary iconographic program, which combined religious and classical themes that glorify

Figure 1. Florentine, *Cosimo de'Medici, 1389–1464, Pater Patriae (obverse)*, Samuel H. Kress Collection, © 1993 National Gallery of Art, Washington, c. 1465/1469, bronze.

Florence, also included several medallions representing the heads of Roman emperors. But, because of their small size and arrangement in a decorative pattern, the medallions with the Roman emperors play a subordinate role. The frescoes depicting the representatives of the Roman republican past, on the other hand, dominate the walls by virtue of their large scale.

Poggio's criticism of Caesar had actually become the subject of a controversy in June 1435 when his friend Guarino da Verona sharply attacked Poggio's letter to Scipione Mainenti.[20] A learned scholar and Leonello d'Este's tutor, Guarino had already praised the accomplishments of Caesar in letters written to his princely pupil. Guarino had compared the magnificence of the House of Este with that of Caesar and Augustus.[21] He had also prepared an edition of Caesar's *Commentari* for his patron. Leonello's agreement with Guarino's opinion is attested to by the fact that he commissioned a work of art representing Caesar to Guarino's fellow-citizen, the Veronese artist Antonio Pisanello. On February 1st, 1435, Pisanello received in fact the sum of two gold *ducati* upon Leonello's order for a work with Caesar's image that he had sent to the Marquis by his assistant, "ad ipsum dominum Leonellum . . . Pisani nomine Divi Julij Cesaris [sic] effigem detulit et presentavit."[22] Mario Salmi suggests that this work may have been a wedding gift because Leonello married Margherita Gonzaga in that very month.[23] Since this work is lost, it is still an open question whether Pisanello had represented Caesar on a medal or in a painting. Salmi is inclined to favor the latter hypothesis for two reasons.[24] First, a 1494 inventory of the Este House lists a "capsa quadra in forma di libro, dov' Giulio Cesare in un quadretto di legno con le cornici dorate." According to Salmi, this small panel may have in fact been Pisanello's work, which was likely kept in the room of the Estense palace in Ferrara that was called "stanza di Cesare." Second, by general agreement Pisanello began his activity as medallist only in 1438 and, he did not represent ideal images on his medals, but real personages. Whatever media Pisanello used for his "Divi Julij Caesaris effigies," it is evident that this commission indicates Leonello's inclination to select Caesar as his model. An "enlightened despot," the Marquis of Ferrara could not in fact agree with Poggio's republican criticism of Caesar's deeds.[25]

Actually, when Leonello returned from a visit to Florence and informed his tutor of Poggio's condemnation of Caesar, Guarino was deeply disappointed. Since he as more an educator than a politician, Guarino particularly resented Poggio's assertion that Caesar had been the "parricida" of the "latinae linguae et bonarum artium."[26] According to Oppel, however, unlike Poggio's one-sided depiction of Caesar, Guarino's defense was not based on a condemnation of Scipio. In fact, Guarino directed his arguments to "redress the balance" between the two Roman generals, even though he also made his preference for Caesar very clear.[27]

There is evidence that Federico da Montefeltro, the Lord of Urbino, was impressed more by Guarino's moderate attitude in this controversy than by Poggio's sharp criticism of Caesar. In fact, Federico went even further than Guarino and tried to reconcile the two Roman generals. An educated condottiere, Federico was familiar with the intellectual circles of both the Medici in Florence and the Este at Ferrara, and he was also well acquainted with the two protagonists of the dispute, Poggio and Guarino.[28] Because of his natural disposition and political skills, Federico was inclined to prefer compromise. Although Federico, being a true Renaissance prince, was an autocratic ruler, he always tried to maintain a careful balance between his own power and the support of his subjects.[29] According to the Florentine bookseller, Vespasiano da Bisticci, Federico had modeled himself on the Roman generals from his youth. He tried to imitate the deeds of "Iscipione Africano," and, at the same time, was extremely fond of—"Iodava in infinito"—the *Comentari* of Caesar. He also combined the love of letters with military discipline.[30]

Iconographic evidence for Federico's attitude is provided by the inscription on a bronze medal, which was executed by Clemente da Urbino in 1468 (Fig. 2).[31] The obverse of the medal represents Federico's bust in mortier, cuirasse, and mantle; its reverse reproduces an eagle supporting symbolic devices of war and peace protected by a favorable conjunction of planets. Both sides of the medal bear inscriptions. That on the obverse reads:

ALTER.ADEST.CAESAR.SCIPIO ROMAN
ET ALTER.SEV.PACEM.POPULIS.SEV.FERA.BELLA.DEDIT
(On the one side [Federico} is present as the Roman Caesar-Scipio and, on the other, as the one who gave to the people either peace or cruel wars.)[32]

Figure 2. Clemente da Urbino, *Federico da Montefeltro, 1422–1482, Count of Urbino 1444, and Duke 1474,* (obverse) Samuel H. Kress Collection, © 1993 National Gallery of Art, Washington, 1468, bronze.

Laurie Schneider, who analyzed this medal in the 1990 College Art Conference, described it as a synthesis of opposing forces. I agree with Schneider's view because, in my opinion, this medal actually illustrates Federico's simultaneous identification with both Caesar and Scipio.

Federico's conciliatory attitude was celebrated publicly in a triumphal procession staged under Guidobaldo, his son and successor, in which Federico was accompanied by both Roman generals. This actual triumph appears to have been a modified version of the *Triumph* that Piero della Francesca had painted on the back of a diptych representing Federico and Battista Sforza (Fig. 3). According to a letter of July 28, 1488, to the marquis of Mantua from his secretary Benedetto Capilupi, centaurs pulled a chariot carrying Caesar, Scipio, and Federico in the center. All three wore cuirasses *all' antica* and were borne in triumph through the streets of Casteldurante. Together with a Sybil and an angel standing on the top of a ball, they all recited verse.[33]

Despite Federico's documented preference for Caesar and Scipio, he did not include either of them in the cycle of Famous Men in his *Studiolo*. In the opinion of various scholars, including myself, the iconographic program for the *Studiolo* was dedicated to the theme of the *vita contemplativa*.[34] Since Caesar and Scipio represented the *vita activa* because of their military activities, they were not suitable for the *Studiolo's* program.

Unlike Federico da Montefeltro, Francesco Sforza not only included Caesar and Scipio in a cycle of Famous Men, but also joined them, as is evident from a miniature (Fig. 4).[35] In this illustration, the Famous Men are clearly indicated by their names inscribed in the frieze above them. Francesco Sforza is seated in the center of the group between Caesar and Hannibal, the Roman and Carthaginian generals, with whom he joins hands. Sforza, however, turns his head completely toward Caesar with whom he is engaged in conversation. Scipio is also present, but he is far from the Duke suggesting that Sforza considered his virtues less worthy than those of Caesar and Hannibal.

Francesco Sforza's choice of Famous Men probably served a political and a literary purpose. Sforza had become Duke of Milan in 1450 after serving as Captain of the Milanese army during the short-lived Ambrosian Republic.[36] As the new Duke, Sforza's aim was to celebrate his predecessors, namely the Visconti Dukes, who

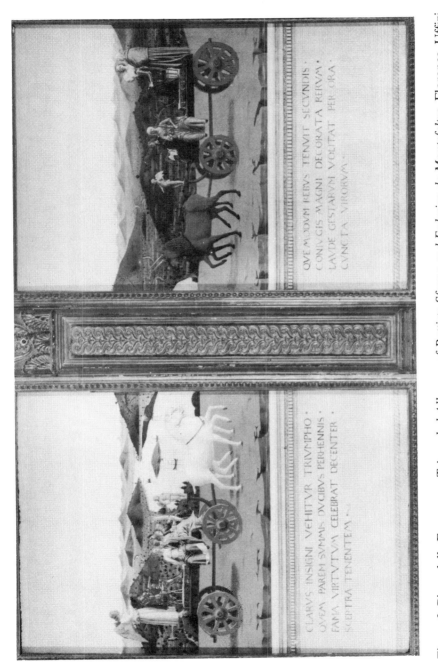

Figure 3. Piero della Francesca, *Triumphal Allegory of Battista Sforza and Federico da Montefeltro*, Florence, Uffizi (Courtesy of Alinari/Art Resource, N.Y.).

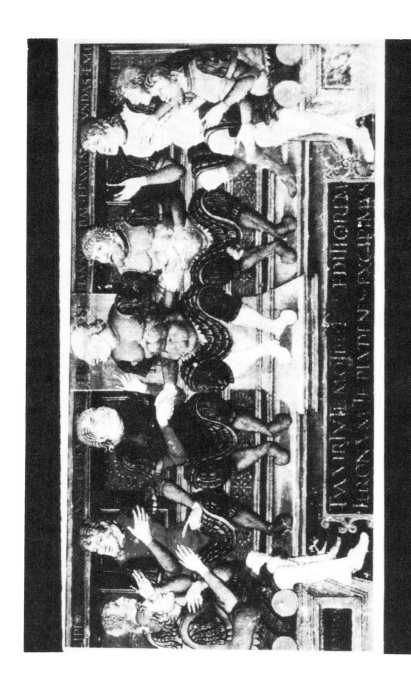

Figure 4. Giovanni Pietro Birago, *Francesco Sforza amid the Most Famous Warriors of Antiquity*, miniature, c. 1490, Florence, Uffizi (Published in *Storia di Milano*, VII, p. 223).

had enjoyed despotic power over Milan, rather than to commemorate his pseudo-Republican past. Politically, thus, Sforza's close
alliance with Caesar stressed the Duke's intentions. Cecco Simon-
etta, the Duke's secretary, compared Sforza with Caesar in a pane-
gyric saying that both had never been defeated.[37]

From the literary point of view, Sforza seems to have based his
program on the conflation of two themes. Judging from the portrayal
of the two Roman generals, one referred no doubt to the Scipio-
Caesar controversy. The preeminent position assigned to Caesar is a
visual declaration of Sforza's opinion on this issue. Because of
Hannibal's inclusion, the other theme reflected the contest for
supremacy between Alexander, Hannibal, and Scipio in the presence
of Minos. The event is described by Lucian in the XIIth of *The
Dialogues of the Dead*.[38] Lucian's dialogue had been popular among
scholars since Petrarch had treated this subject in his *Collatio inter
Scipionem, Alexandrum, et Pyrrum*.[39] Later, in his *De gestis Caesaris*,
Petrarch had also revealed his strong interest in Caesar's life. Petrarch's
works had attracted the attention of the early humanists, particularly
Salutati and Bruni. These works and Aurispa's translation of
Lucian's dialogue had aroused arguments that ultimately led to the
controversy between Poggio and Guarino.[40]

Although the humanists devoted most of their energy to the literary dispute, the patrons had a more political subtext. Their concerns were directly related to their own political systems. The different styles of the Medici, Leonello d'Este, Federico da Montefeltro, and Francesco Sforza are documented not only in humanistic
literature but also in artistic commissions. These commissions reveal the patrons' financial, political, and intellectual involvement in
the Scipio-Caesar controversy. The works examined here, including
frescoes, the bronze medal, and the miniature, all bear inscriptions,
thereby indicating that, in the Renaissance, words were used as literal signs to mediate between the humanist texts and the visual arts.

NOTES

1. For humanist learning, see Paul Oskar Kristeller, *Renaissance Thought and
   the Arts*, Princeton, New Jersey, 1990, an expanded edition of Professor
   Kristeller's *Renaissance Thought II*, 1964, 1980. For the Scipio-Caesar controversy, cf. Hans Baron, *The Crisis of the Early Italian Renaissance*, Princeton,
   N. J., 1955, 2 vols., I, particularly pp. 54 ff and 351 ff; see also John W. Oppel,

"Peace vs. liberty in the Quattrocento: Poggio, Guarino, and the Scipio-Caesar controversy," in *The Journal of Medieval and Renaissance Studies*, IV, 2, Fall 1974, pp. 221–265, and Giuliana Crevatin, "La politica e la retorica: Poggio e la controversia su Cesare e Scipione. Con una nuova edizione della lettera a Scipione Mainenti," in *Poggio Bracciolini 1380–1980*, Istituto Nazionale di Studi sul Rinascimento, Studi e Testi VIII, Florence, 1982, pp. 281–342.

2. I am more inclined to consider this controversy as dealing with the issue of "liberty versus tyranny" as proposed by Baron and other scholars than to accept Oppel's suggestion that it refers to "peace versus liberty."

3. The Medici began their rise to the leadership of Florence after Cosimo's return from exile in 1434; cf. Curt S. Gutkind, *Cosimo de' Medici, Pater Patriae*, Oxford, 1938. Leonello d'Este, Niccolo III's son and successor, was an educated prince who by his patronage of humanists and artists, including Leon Battista Alberti, contributed effectively to the establishment of Ferrarese courtly culture. Politically, Leonello continued his father's policies. He was one of the most enlightened princes of the House of Este; cf. Werner L. Gundersheimer, *Ferrara: The Style of a Renaissance Despotism*, Princeton, 1973. Federico da Montefeltro, who became Lord of Urbino after the murder of his young half-brother Oddantonio, assumed and maintained power with the consent and support of his subjects. First as a Count and then as a Duke, Federico ruled the Duchy of Urbino from 1444 until his death in 1482; cf. Walter Tommasoli, *La vita di Federico da Montefeltro 1422/1482*, Urbino, 1978. Francesco Sforza became Duke of Milan in 1450 after having reinforced his political status by marrying Bianca Maria Visconti, the former Duke's daughter. Increasingly relying on enlightened despotism, Francesco Sforza remained Duke of Milan until he died in 1466; cf. Cecilia M. Ady, *A History of Milan under the Sforza*, London, 1907.

4. Niccolò Machiavelli, *Il Principe*, ed. Ettore Janni, Milan, 1950, chapter VII, and chapter XX, 10. See also "L'eta' Sforzesca dal 1450 al 1500," in *Storia di Milano*, VII, Milan, 1956, particularly pp. 15 ff.

5. Poggio Bracciolini, "Rem sane arduam," in *Opera Omnia*, ed. Riccardo Fubini, Turin, 1964–69, 4 vols., IV, pp. 357–365.

6. "Civem perniciosissimum patriae," Poggio, *op. cit.*, p. 358.

7. "In more tyranni." *Ibid.*, p. 359.

8. Ibid., p. 360.

9. Ibid., p.364.

10. Oppel, op. cit., pp. 231–33.

11. Poggio, *Opera omnia*, III, ep. XII, pp. 37–46 and ep. XXI, pp. 64–71.

12. Oppel, op. cit., pp. 221–22.

13. Ibid., p. 241.

14. For a discussion on the ideals of republican freedom in Florence, see Nicolai Rubinstein, "Florentina libertas," in *Rinascimento*, 2nd series, XXVI, 1986, pp. 3–26.

15. Alison M. Brown, "The Humanist Portrait of Cosimo de' Medici 'Pater Patriae', " in *Journal of the Warburg and Courtauld Institutes*, XXIV, 3–4, 1961, 186–221.

16. Poggio, "Epistolae," VII, epistola XIV.

17. On Poggio's relationship with Andreolo Giustiniani and other collectors, cf. my work "Greek Sources for Donatello's 'Annunciation' in Santa Croce," in *Source: Notes in the History of Art*, V, 3, Spring 1986, pp. 16–20.

18. Eugène Müntz, *Les Collections des Medicis au XVe siecle*, Paris, London, 1888, pp. 16–17.

19. For Domenico Ghirlandaio, cf. James Beck, *Italian Renaissance Painting*, New York, 1981, pp. 265–274. For the "Sala dei Gigli," cf. Piero Bargellini, *Scoperta di Palazzo Veccio*, Florence, 1968, and Giulio Lensi Orlandi, *Il Palazzo Vecchio di Firenze*, Florence, 1977.

20. Remigio Sabbadini, *Epistolario di Guarino Veronese*, Venice, 1916, 3 vols., II, epistola 670, pp. 221–254.

21. Ibid., epistola 620, p. 165, and epistola 668, pp. 216 ff.

22. Mario Salmi, "La 'Divi Julij Caesaris Effigies' del Pisanello," in *Commentari*, VIII, II, Aprile-Giugno 1957, pp. 91–95.

23. Salmi, op. cit., p. 91.

24. Ibid., pp. 92–93.

25. Gundersheimer, op. cit., p. 5.

26. Guarino argues against Poggio's assertion in various parts of his letter, see, for instance, pp. 226 ff.

27. Oppel, op. cit., pp. 249–250.

28. Federico highly praised Poggio and his literary achievements in a letter to Jacopo Bracciolini, Poggio's son, thanking him for Poggio's *Historia Fiorentina*; cf. no. 91, pp. 105–106, in *Federico da Montefeltro, duca d'Urbino: lettere di stato e d'arte, (1470–1480)*, ed. Paolo Alatri, Rome, 1949. Federico seems to have been acquainted with Guarino since 1444; cf. Maria Moranti, "Organizzazione della biblioteca di Federico da Montefeltro," in *Federico di Montefeltro: La cultura*, Rome, 1986, pp. 19–49, pp. 25 ff.

29. For a deep understanding of Federico's personality, cf. Cecil H. Clough, *Federigo da Montefeltro: The Good Christian Prince*, Manchester, 1985.

30. Vespasiano da Bisticci, "Comentario de la vita del Signore Federico, Duca d'Urbino," in *Le vite*, ed. Aulo Greco, I, Florence, 1970, pp. 355–416; particularly pp. 355, 379, and 382.

31. Several copies of this medal exist. See *Renaissance Small Bronze Sculpture and Associated Decorative Arts at the National Gallery of Art*, catalogue, ed. Carolyn C. Wilson, Washington, 1983, no.1, p. 42; Fert Sangiorgi, *Iconografia Federiciana*, Accademia Raffaello, I, Urbino, 1982, p. 100, tav. XLI; and *Renaissance Medals from the Samuel H. Kress Collection at the National Gallery of Art*, catalogue by G. F. Hill, revised and enlarged by Graham Pollard, London, 1967, no. 100.

32. I am using my own translation.

33. A. Luzio and R. Renier, *Mantova e Urbino: Isabella d'Este ed Elisabetta Gonzaga*, Turin and Rome, 1893, pp. 44–45.

34. Cf. Luciano Cheles, *The Studiolo of Urbino: An Iconographic Investigation*, Wiesbaden, 1986; Virginia Grace Tenzer, *The Iconography of the 'Studiolo' of Federico da Montefeltro in Urbino*, Ph.D. thesis, Brown University, 1985, and Maria Grazia Pernis, "Ficino's Plationism and the Court of Urbino: The History of Ideas and the History of Art," Ph.D. thesis, Columbia University, 1990.

35. This miniature has been published in "L'eta' Sforzesca dal 1450 al 1500," in *Storia di Milano*, VII, p. 233.

36. For Sforza's activity and his relationship with the humanists, cf. Mario Borsa, "Pier Candido Decembri e l'umanesimo in Lombardia," in *Archivio storico lombardo*, 2nd series, X, 1893, pp. 5 ff and 358 ff.

37. Cf. "L'eta' Sforzesca dal 1450 al 1500," in *Storia di Milano*, VII, p. 224.

38. *Lucian*, Greek and English, tr. by M. D. Macleod, Cambridge, Mass., and London, 1969, VII, 25 (12), pp. 143–55. Lucian's *Contentio de presidentia P. Scipionis* . . . in the Latin translation by G. Aurispa had an enormous success

in the Renaissance.

39. Guido Martellotti, "La 'Collatio inter Scipionem Alexandrum Hanibalem et Pyrrum," in *Classical, Medieval and Renaissance Studies in Honor of Berthold Louis Ullman*, II, Rome, 1964, pp. 145–55.

40. Baron, *op. cit.*, also discusses the issue of Dante's different treatment of Caesar and Brutus that was a main argument for the humanists. By general consensus, the Scipio-Caesar controversy ended in a pamphlet by Pietro dal Monte; it is actually included in a letter sent by the latter to Poggio from London on January 31, 1440, published by Giovanni Mercati in his *Ultimi contributi alla storia degli umanisti*, Citta' del Vaticano, 1939, pp. 615–39, which is included in Poggio's *Opera omnia*. Pietro dal Monte provides the significant information that the English prince "Humfredus, dux Gloucestriae" had read "magna quadam aviditate" Poggio's and Guarino's dispute on the merits of Caesar and Scipio.

From Authorization to Authorship, Orality to Literature: The Case of Medieval and Renaissance Drama

JOHN W. VELZ

i

In the late twentieth century, everything is literature, in the sense that everything has its author. In our daily newspapers, even stories that just record the facts have their bylines, and the cult of personality extends to the electronic media, where we hear (to single out NPR) "This is 'Morning Edition'; I'm Bob Edwards"; "For National Public Radio this is Andy Lyman at the Metropolitan Museum of Art"; "This is Nina Totenberg at the Supreme Court"; "I'm Richard Gonzales with the President in Paris"; "This is 'All Things Considered'; I'm Linda Wertheimer"; "and I'm Noah Adams." Personal names shower down on us like leaves in autumn.[1] We are so used to such insistence on authorship that it is easy to assume that identifying authors is a natural state of cultural affairs.[2] But it need not be so. For instance, newspapers before World War II were more chary about attributing news stories to authors than they have since become. Gathering and publishing the news was once a corporate venture in which individual achievements were subsumed in the group effort, whether the group was The Associated Press, The International News Service, or merely the news desk and editorial room of a big city newspaper.

Given our culture's insistence on attributed authorship, it is not surprising that scholarship in our time has misconstrued the true nature and status of early drama in Western Europe. We are tempted to spend energy looking for authors, or at least wishing we could

identify some. Yet this quest and this wish are misguided. It is better to take the focus off "The York Realist," and "The Wakefield
Master," and the question of whether it was Gilbert Pilkington who
was that master, and whether it was Ranulf Higden who wrote the
Chester Cycle. Why? Because religious drama began as *Gemeinschaftswerk*, corporate achievement, *authorized* first by the matrix
of liturgy which generated Western drama and in which it was originally embedded; liturgical authority was unimpeachable, traceable
all the way to the Church Fathers. A reinforcing authority was the
monastic communities which were the first custodians of the liturgical drama. By the fourteenth century authorization proceeded in
many places from the enduring and stable civic guilds that produced the cycles, year after year, decade after decade. Still later
came the authorization emanating from itinerant acting companies.
With institutions like these to validate it, drama needed no authors;
it had authority without them. Drama continued as a corporate,
non-literary, oral art form for more than six centuries—even down
to the year of Shakespeare's death. In that year, 1616, Ben Jonson
made the revolutionary and iconoclastic pronouncement that his
own plays were "Works," an oeuvre worthy of being gathered up
along with his poetry—which automatically qualified as an oeuvre,
because poetry by single authors had long been gathered up and
published as literary achievements to be canonized for posterity.
Drama then and for the first time became "literature."

ii

It is appropriate to begin with comment on the means of recording and preserving drama in the Middle Ages. These comments
about medieval playtexts are perhaps in order, because A. J. Minnis
does not mention playtexts in his important book on the concept of
authorship in the Middle Ages.[3] The medieval oral tradition continued for a century and a half after the invention of printing.[4] But
then Ben Jonson altered literary history by in effect metamorphos-
ing plays into literary artifacts authorized by their authors' identities—and by readers' acceptance of these texts as works of art, not
as mere scripts.

Since drama in the West began in the form of interpolations in
liturgical ceremonies, it follows that the monastic communities in
which such interpolation took place thought of the texts of their

tropes as if they were liturgy. Indeed, in effect, these tropes *were* liturgy; their stage directions are rubrical, their dialogue is antiphonal, their action is epiphanic, and their place in liturgical contexts was tacitly sanctioned by ecclesiastical authority. These tropes are no more literary than the liturgy in which they were embedded. This being the case, the tropers that have been found in monastic and cathedral libraries are as it were liturgical manuscripts, on the order of missals and breviaries, preserved not as literature, but as codified liturgy, a written guide to oral performance. One might say that the creation of these manuscripts in the tenth century was an archival, not a literary venture.

It may be instructive to provide a much lesser modern analogue. An Episcopal parish in Austin, Texas, sometimes does chancel drama in liturgical contexts, distantly echoing the original syndrome of the tenth century. If the parish archived the scripts of successful ventures in this blending of drama with liturgy, it would certainly not be because they are "literature" but so that they could be referred to in future years for similar production.

When liturgical tropes became extra-liturgical musical plays, growing in length and complexity in the twelfth and thirteenth centuries, the attitude toward the playtexts remained what it had been. So collections like the Fleury Playbook must be thought of as the reified memory of abbeys, as reference archives, not as storehouses of literary treasures. This is true even when literary texts are interpolated into a "liturgical" playbook as the Goliardic songs are in the Carmina Burana manuscript of playtexts from the Benediktbeuern monastery in Bavaria. In this case we have a hybrid manuscript: secular and "literary" documents housed with a collection of quasi-liturgical scripts. One sees how much the playtexts are scripts, how little they are literature, when a scribe offers only the first words of an anthem in the text; he knows that the monks who will mount the production of (shall we say) the Benediktbeuern Christmas Play a year hence can and will supply the rest of the anthem from the shared trove of monastic memory. One sees it also in the common tendency to end a play with a "Te Deum," even after the plays were much too long and too elaborate to be interpolated in Matins where the "Te Deum" is always chanted.[5] Moreover, one sees it in the state of the manuscripts as they come down to us; their margins are quite barren of *commentarium* by comparison with the margins of a literary figure like Chaucer.

Contemporary literary texts were annotated in the Middle Ages on the analogy of the seriatim commentaries that surrounded classical texts; medieval playtexts lack this explicatory apparatus.[6]

There is a curious anomaly, an exception to the rule I have been spelling out. This is the solemn but ironic *Raising of Lazarus* by the wandering scholar Hilarius, the student of Abelard. This twelfth-century Lazarus play, as David Bevington has shrewdly observed,[7] is more literature than theater; it lacks necessary stage directions, and in other ways it shows that the controlling purpose of the author was literary, not theatrical, even though the last stage-direction is rubrical and ties the play to liturgical performance: "Quo finito, si factum fuerit ad matutinas, Lazarus incipiat Te Deum laudamus; si vero ad vesperas, Magnificat anima mea Dominum." Hilarius reveals how far he is from a specific quasi-liturgical monastic production when he writes in the dramatis personae that Christ is to be accompanied by "the twelve apostles, or six at least." It is significant that this play, a literary as much as a theatrical work of art, has an author, almost the only playtext to its time that does so.[8] As soon as we get outside the realm of corporate authorization and into the realm of literature, an author becomes the authority for the work.

iii

When the corporate theatrical ventures of the monasteries were paralleled in the fourteenth century by the corporate ventures of civic authorities and of guilds, no real change in *auctoritas* took place. We may find that odd, perhaps, because we have been trained to think of the Cycle Plays as increasingly secular and increasingly free of the all-encompassing Church which subsumed individual identity in the Mystical Body of Christ. But this is a misapprehension. The guilds were a corporate source of identity for medieval tradesmen not unlike the monastic communities that were contemporary with them and not unlike modern military services or fraternal organizations, in which group identity takes precedence over individual identity. Besides, as the publications of the REED research team have shown over the last decade and more, an entire community had to strain every nerve to get a vast and multiplex Cycle mounted every year at Corpus Christi time. There was no time for prima donnas, whether authors or actors, to preen them-

selves, as actors and authors now preen themselves in a strange collaboration between the Hollywood star system and the celebrity
writers whose plays or novels Hollywood turns into films.[9] It was
the guild, not a group of individuals, who were the authority—even
the *legally* responsible authority—for the production of a play about
Noah and his recalcitrant wife, or about Abraham and his sweetly
naive son Isaac. One needs an author less when a work of art is
authorized by some other agency than an individual. Besides, no
matter how brilliantly a Cycle was unified on typological or other
lines, it was in essence a *compilatio*—though it was certainly not an
anthology. So the manuscripts of the several Cycle plays were kept,
as the props and pageant wagons and costumes were, in the safe-
keeping of the several guilds until they should be needed for production in Corpus Christi seasons to come.[10] Under such conditions,
playtexts were not literary artifacts any more than the scenarios of
films or television programs are literary artifacts today. They were
carefully stored archival valuables, references for future use.

None of this is to imply that there is somehow less aesthetic
merit in these playtexts that are purely theatrical than there is in
playtexts today that we think of as literature. Indeed, we edit and
publish and anthologize and teach and study these medieval scripts
as if they were literature, and increasingly we have come during my
lifetime to admire them as art objects. The difference between literary art and oral art is not that literary art is more pleasing aes-
thetically. Nor is the difference in whether it is written down—as
we have seen, there was good reason to write down the oral liturgies of the Church and the dramatic texts that emerged from those
liturgies, good reason to copy out and carefully store the scripts of
the plays in Cycles. The difference between literature and oral art
is in how the art object is regarded, for whom and for what purpose
it is written. And always the difference is in what authorizes the
work of art. Is the authority an author? or, as in a *Gemeinschaftswerk*, is the authority a community of anonymous participants in
the creative process?

iv

The arrival of the Morality Play in the fifteenth century as a separate genre of religious drama eventually opened a path for itinerant
professional actors; and a new way with plays modified, though it

did not change radically, the attitude toward authorization, authorship, orality and literature that had prevailed since the tenth century. At first, if we are to judge by the massive *Castle of Perseverance*,
a Morality was as much a *Gemeinschaftswerk* as the Cycles were and
had been. With its vast text, its huge cast of characters, its elaborate
theatrical venue and stage décor, this grandiose play would have to
be a corporate venture of the traditional kind. But before long,
shorter, more manageable forms of Moralities began to appear, and
hence—enter the professional acting company.

Here it is well to point out that the Saint play, like the Morality
play, was a self-contained art object, brief and tight enough in cast
and stage demands to be suitable material for small itinerant companies. Though we know of some sixty-six Saint Plays before the
reign of Henry VIII, it is difficult to specify any role for the English
Saint play in the orality/literature question, because so very few
exemplars survived the ravages of the Reformation in England.[11]
But all the texts we do have are from late in the fifteenth century,
when the professional companies were becoming established. The
European Saint play dates from the twelfth century, and it had
remained in the hands of monastic actors, civic sponsors, and aris-
tocratic households until a relatively late date, at least in England;
but the professional actors, once established, were quick to incorporate this old genre in their repertories. One of the handful of surviving plays, the *Play of Mary Magdalene* in the Digby Manuscript,
is, like *The Castle of Perseverance*, massive and sprawling and possibly the work of a *Gemeinschaft* of some kind. But the others are,
like most Moralities, short, compressed, and arranged to permit
doubling—natural vehicles for small professional companies. The
Saint play can be lumped, then, with the Morality in the schema of
a history of orality and authorship in the drama.

The rise of the professional acting company coincided with the
introduction of printing into England. This was a fortuitous coincidence, because by the beginning of the sixteenth century printers
were publishing playtexts, and this encouraged the writing of plays.
But it was emphatically not as literature for a reading public that
the printers brought plays out. The press runs were small, the playtexts appeared single spies, and the intended clientele were the itinerant professional actors who used them as scripts. These printed
plays were often designated "offered for acting," and the apparatus
often included a doubling chart, a guide to casting. Their pragmatic,

non-literary raison-d'être is clear in the advertising tag that charac-
teristically appears on title pages or in colophons: "nine [or some
lesser number] can play it at ease."

The standard authority on plays "offered for acting" is David
Bevington.[12] His interest is in the designing of these plays so that
doubling could permit staging by small professional companies. He
does not concern himself with the authority/authorship/orality/lit-
erature question, but his book is the place to start in an investigation of the conception of drama in Tudor times. In a convenient
appendix he lists and describes all of the 24 surviving plays offered
for acting between the late fifteenth century and 1603; here is clear
evidence that the tradition continues down into the high years of
Shakespeare's career.

Many people In the sixteenth century must have bought printed
playtexts to read, but the ambiance in which these booklets lived
was plainly professional, not literary-cultural. The introduction of
printing paradoxically reinforced the image of drama as an oral art
form. There in stark print on title pages were tacit indications that
the text in hand was not literature, but a theatrical scenario. And
the vision of drama as non-literature pervaded all social classes, for
though the Tudor Humanists themselves wrote plays, and though
they or their printers sometimes put their names as authors on title
pages, it would not have occurred to a Heywood or a Medwall to
think of a playtext as anything more than a jeu d'esprit for actors to
put on at a banquet.

v

This conception of drama as orality rather than literature endured through the secularization of the themes of drama and
through the chartering of the Stationers' Company in 1557, as it
had endured through the rise of the professional actor and the
introduction of printing nearly a century earlier. The Stationers'
Company was focused on censorship and legal responsibility of
authors and printers; it was not primarily an advocate of literature
or a protector of the rights of authors in their literary texts.[13] And
so there were few if any forces at work in Tudor times to encourage
men and women to regard plays as literature; plays remained what
they had always been, "momentany as a sound, / Swift as a shadow,
short as any dream"—to alter Shakespeare's point of reference—

(*MND* 1.1.143–44). Though plays became more complex and more artful as dramatists learned from experience, and though increasingly the names of dramatists appeared on title pages as the century wore on, drama remained a subliterary genre. It is a suggestive fact that Sir Thomas Bodley, who died in 1613 and who began gathering his great library in 1598, instructed his Keeper of Books, Thomas James, not to purchase any quartos of English plays for his shelves. No Shakespeare, no Marlowe, no Greene or Lyly or Peele or Jonson. Plays were for Bodley to be bracketed with almanacs as "Baggage Books," mere "riff raff."[14]

A conception of the nature and status of drama that had originated in the tenth century endured through social, cultural, and technological change for more than six centuries. One man can be said to have swept away the conception and to have changed literary history abruptly. This man, Ben Jonson, deserves his place in English cultural history not just for his brilliant hard-edged comedies, but also for his insistence that a play is literature.

The moment that changed the conception of the nature and status of drama came in 1616. In that year Jonson published a folio of about a thousand pages containing nine of his plays, eighteen of his masques and entertainments, and a substantial body of his epigrams, panegyrics, and verse letters; he called this miscellany of traditional literary forms and dramatic texts *The Works of Benjamin Jonson*. The old guard laughed contemptuously at the pretentious use of the literary term *works* for mere stageplays. One wag's epigram became an in-joke in London in 1616:

> Pray tell me *Ben*, where doth the mystery lurke,
> What others call a play you call a worke.[15]

Jonson was not consciously doing literary history or drama a favor. His voracious ego and to a lesser extent his financial acquisitiveness were reason enough for the conception and execution of this epoch-making Folio. It was by no means a casual affair. He was preparing for it as early as 1612.[16] Jonson revised and in some cases entirely rewrote his plays for the projected Folio, and he worked hard at getting the book ready for the press, selecting plays and writing dedications of them to noblemen.[17] Writing dedications is a sure sign of *literary* intentions, as this is what one did with poems— for example, *Venus and Adonis* and *The Rape of Lucrece,* which Shakespeare had dedicated to the Earl of Southhampton in the early 1590s. The title page of the Jonson Folio is pretentious in its use of iconography to suggest the stature of the "works" in the Folio. The text of the Folio exists in at least five press states,[18] evidence that a very anxious Jonson was constantly meddling in William Stansby's printing shop during production of the book. The author wanted his literary book perfect.

Jonson thought he was using the Folio of his "Works" to enhance his public image as an artist and his place at Court. But actually the benefit may have worked the other way around. Jonson had been granted a pension for life by James I and was an unofficial poet laureate.[19] He had also sided with the winners in a political struggle at Court. His career was at its height.[20] All of this, and the inclusion of legitimate poetry with bastard plays seem to have conferred acceptance and even stature on the Folio. One sees the mood of the majority of the London intelligentsia in the witty reply an anonymous "friend" of Jonson made to the wag's joke about plays as works:

> The authors friend thus for the author sayes,
> *Bens* plays are works, when others works are plaies.[21]

William Shakespeare died just as the Jonson Folio was emerging from the press. Seven years later, in 1622–23, two of Shakespeare's fellow actors and sharers in the King's Men's acting company put together a Folio of his plays obviously inspired by the Jonson Folio, though not closely modeled on it. Virtually all of Shakespeare's plays were included, where Jonson had left certain plays out of his Folio for strategic reasons. And Heminges and Condell omitted both Shakespeare's non-dramatic poetry and the traditionally elaborate and somewhat florid iconography in the front matter that had been a bald-faced attempt at conferring stature on the Jonson Folio. One might hypothesize that Heminges and Condell left out the more obviously literary "works" of William Shakespeare out of some sense of modesty and decorum that Jonson lacked; but the actual effect was quite otherwise: now plays alone were sufficient warrant for the creation of an oeuvre.[22]

The Shakespeare Folio was a success at the bookstalls as the Jonson Folio had been. The public was ready suddenly and for the first time to take contemporary plays seriously as literary artifacts. There was a demand for a re-issue of the Shakespeare Folio in 1632, only nine years after its appearance. The Jonson Folio was reprinted in 1640. Evidence was piling up that drama could be a success when published as literature. When the theaters were closed down by the Puritans in 1642, an enterprising printer, Humphrey Moseley, began to put together a Folio of the plays of Beaumont and Fletcher; it appeared in 1647, unabashedly borrowing from the format and the front matter of the Shakespeare Folio.[23] The public appetite for all of these author-dramatists led to various reprintings before the end of the seventeenth century.

All of the Folios, Jonson's, Shakespeare's, and Beaumont and Fletcher's, gave prominent attention to their authors' identities. The *auctoritas* for each of these publications was the author, not some authorizing *Gemeinschaft*. Jonson had, as it were, invented "literary" drama in England. The distance between the Fleury Playbook and the three great drama Folios of the seventeenth century is some five centuries; but the distance is greater even than the hundreds of years between: the distance is the difference between authorisation and authorship, between orality and literature.

NOTES

1. Julian Wasserman has informed me that professional accountability for the facts and interpretations in a newspaper article is the important factor in the contemporary emphasis on bylines. I see the point, but continue to believe that pride of authorship is a contributing factor. (On NPR we even hear daily who composed the incidental music that accompanies the news.) Gary Trudeau certainly assumes that this media phenomenon is a matter of egotism—witness his acidulous parodies embodied in the occasional Roland Hedley episodes in his "Doonesbury" cartoon strip: "This is Roland Hedley somewhere in the Middle East." Professor Wasserman, Chairman of the panel in which an earlier form of this paper was read October 21, 1989, at the Southeastern Medieval Association convention in Houston, merits thanks for other helpful suggestions as well. It is a privilege also to acknowledge the well-informed advice of Richard Clement, of Rita Copeland, of Donald Davis, of Thelma Guion, of Krystyna Kujawinska-Courtney, of Marga Munkelt, of David Harris Sacks, of Ernest Sullivan, of Laetitia Yeandle, and of Ian Willison and the members of his seminar "The Book" for which the first version of this paper was written in February, 1989.

2. The post-modern theoreticians have come at the authorship question from a direction diametrically opposed to the momentum of journalism and other manifestations of mainstream culture in our time. The meaning of *authorship* is an important question among literary theorists in the late twentieth century. New Historicism and its cousin Cultural Materialism both have diminished

the author's "authority" by locating authorization of the work in the environing culture in which it was generated. Roland Barthes, who diminishes the authority of authorship for another reason, may be said to speak for many post-modern theorists when he insists, "As soon as a fact is *narrated* . . . the voice loses its origin, the author enters into his own death, writing begins. . . . [T]he responsibility for a narrative is never assumed by a person but by a mediator, shaman or relator whose 'performance' . . . may possibly be admired but never his 'genius'." "The Death of the Author." *Image-Music-Text.* Ed. and tr. Stephen Heath (NY: Hill & Wang, 1977), pp. 142–48. [If narrative, we may add, the more so drama.] Martin Elsky is interested in another dimension of orality, the medieval philosophical certainty about the existential priority of speech to writing that shifted its ground in the Renaissance to prioritize the written (and the printed) word; see *Authorizing Words: Speech, Writing, and Print in the English Renaissance* (Ithaca and London: Cornell University Press, 1989). Michel Foucault in a much-cited essay "What is an Author?" (1969) is closer to the historical view advocated in this essay when he asserts that the anonymous works of a bygone time were "valorized" by "their ancientness, whether real or imagined." (Revised 1979 and tr. by Josué V. Harari in *Textual Strategies: Perspectives in Post-Structuralist Criticism.* [Ithaca: Cornell University Press, 1979]: 141–60 [149].)

3. *Medieval Theory of Authorship.* London: Scolar Pr., 1984.

4. The interface between orality and literature is more often jagged than smooth, as D. F McKenzie notes, citing work by Keith Thomas, Jack Goody, and Ruth Finnegan. See "Speech-Manuscript-Print," *Library Chronicle of the University of Texas at Austin* 20, nos. 1–2 (1990): [86]–109 (87 esp.).

5. A striking instance is the *Danielis Ludus* from Beauvais, which at nearly 400 lines is probably too long for liturgical interpolation. The convention had great staying power. It is used to great dramatic effect at the end of the Harrowing of Hell play in the Wakefield Cycle. It turns up early in the fifteenth century at the end of the 3649-line *Castle of Perseverance*, and late in the fifteenth century at the end of the 1000-line *Play of Mary Magdalene* in the Digby MS. Shakespeare works it into the dramatic action of *Henry V* at the end of Act IV, after the Battle of Agincourt: the King commands that God be given all the credit for the victory-with-minimal-losses: "Do we all holy rites. / Let there be sung 'Non nobis' and 'Te Deum'. . ." (4.8.121–22; David Bevington, ed. *Complete Shakespeare,* Glenview, IL: Scott, Foresman, 1980s). By the same token, the "Quem quaeritis," with which it all began centuries earlier, appears in Gethsemane in the N-Town Passion Play I: Jesus (to the party of soldiers sent to arrest him): "Telle me, serys, whom seke ye?" (976). And moments later as the soldiers are struck to the ground by God's power: "Arise, serys. Whom seke ye? . . ." And the reply comes back as it did in the tenth-century trope: "Jhesus of Nazareth we seke . . ." (985, 989; Quotations here and elsewhere in medieval plays from the David Bevington, ed., *Medieval Drama*, Boston: Houghton Mifflin, 1975).

6. Likewise, drama (except for one brief reference to classical dramatic theory and practice) is entirely absent from the texts and discussion in A. J. Minnis and A. B. Scott, with David Wallace, *Medieval Literary Theory and Criticism c. 1100–1375: The Commentary Tradition*. Oxford: Clarendon Pr., 1988. There are exceptions, of course, to the absence of *commentarium* from playtext manuscripts. For example, the Chester "Christ Appears to the Disciples" gives in parentheses the Vulgate text of Isaiah 66:13 at line 96, the culmination of a passage in the play that has paraphrased this verse; almost certainly this is a marginal gloss which has found its way into the text of the play. It is worth noting, however, that this Chester manuscript is dated 29 July 1607, many years after the Cycle had ceased to be a living oral artifact; did the scribe in 1607 see his task of transcription as a work of antiquarian piety in which scholarly apparatus would be appropriate as it would not be in a truly oral manuscript?

7. *Medieval Drama,* Boston: Houghton Mifflin, 1975, p. 155.

8. "Almost" because Hilarius also wrote a play on Daniel in the manner of the Beauvais "Danielis Ludus." Hrosvitha of Gandersheim is, of course, also an identifiable author; but her roots are classical, not liturgical.

9. Budd Schulberg complained in his address to the Deauville Festival of American Films, September, 1989, that the director supplants the author in Hollywood's credit-giving. See "The 'Auteur' Syndrome," *New York Times,* Op-Ed Page (i.e., p. 27), 4 Dec. 1989. But Schulberg was speaking of the authors of screenplays, not the authors of the best sellers Hollywood lives on.

10. Here it may be instructive to compare the rubrics for any modern secular liturgy—say, the rituals of a Commencement exercise at a given college or university. The reason for preserving the guide to the formalities is merely practical, not literary.

11. John Wasson, "The Secular Saint Plays of the Elizabethan Era," *The Saint Play in Medieval Europe*, ed. Clifford Davidson, Early Drama, Art, and Music Monograph Series 8 (Kalamazoo, Michigan: Medieval Institute Publications, 1986). pp. 241–60 (241–42 & nn. 1, 2, esp.).

12. *From* Mankind *to Marlowe: Growth of Structure in the Popular Drama of Tudor England.* Cambridge, MA: Harvard Univ. Pr., 1962.

13. See D. F. McKenzie, "Printing in England from Caxton to Milton," *New Pelican Guide to English Literature*, ed. Boris Ford, Vol. 2, *The Age of Shakespeare* (Harmondsworth: Penguin, 1982): pp. 207–26 (216): In the period following the chartering of the Stationers' Company, "[a]fter religion and the law most translations were not of the great classical or learned humanist works but of texts with a practical bias and broad appeal."

14. Letter CLXVII, *Reliquiae Bodleianæ; Or Some Genuine Remains of Sir Thomas Bodley*. London: Printed for John Hartley, 1703, pp. 277–78: "I can see no good Reason, to alter my Opinion, for excluding such Books, as Almanacks, Plays, and an infinite Number, that are daily Printed, of very unworthy matters [p. 278]; and handling, such, as methinks, both the Keeper and Underkeeper should Disdain to seek out, to deliver to any Man. Haply some Plays may be worthy the Keeping: But hardly one in Forty. For it is not alike in *English* Plays, and others of other Nations. Because they are most esteemed, for Learning the Languages, and many of them compiled, by Men of great Fame, for Wisdom and Learning: Which is seldom or never here among us. Were it so again, that some little profit might be reaped (which God knows is very little) out of some of our Play-Books, the benefit thereof, will nothing near Countervail, the harm that the Scandal will bring upon the Library, when it shall be given out, that we stuff'd it full of Baggage Books. . . ." [dated June 15, no year given, but very probably after 1603. The 229 letters almost all omit the year; they are not arranged in chronological order, apparently, and therefore it is very difficult to infer a year for any letter with the help of others. References in other letters nearby in the sequence to the King and to the impending election of an Archbishop of Canterbury (Richard Bancroft, 1604?, George Abbott, 1610?) are not definitive.] Cf. Letter XXIV, ibid., p. 82: "In any wise take no riff raff Books (for such will but prove a Discredit to our Library). . . ."

A pastoral letter from Archpriest William Harrison 9 March 1617/18 forbids Catholic secular clergy under his direction in England from attending without license "playes acted by common plaiers upon common stages" on pain of suspension of their priestly faculties (Folger MS V.a.244). But here the issue is not that plays are sub-literary but rather the conventional rationale of the Puritans. (Harrison's prohibition evoked a challenge from Thomas Le[a?]ke, a priest speaking for two others, and a lengthy answer from the Archpriest's secretary.)

15. As quoted in David Riggs, *Ben Jonson: A Life*, Cambridge MA: Harvard Univ. Pr., 1989. pp. 226–28.

16. Herford, C. H., and Percy Simpson, edd. *Ben Jonson*. Oxford: Clarendon Pr., 1925, 1:64.

17. Richard Dutton. "Introduction: The 1616 Folio and its Place in Jonson's Career," *Ben Jonson: To the First Folio* (Cambridge: Cambridge Univ. Pr., 1983): pp. 1–22 (pp. 12 et passim). See also Michael Warren, "The Theatricalization of Text: Beckett, Jonson, Shakespeare," *Library Chronicle of the University of Texas at Austin* 20 nos. 1–2 (1990): 41–46.

18. W. W. Greg. *A Bibliography of the English Printed Drama to the Restoration* Vol. III *Collections, Appendix, Reference Lists*, London: Oxford Univ. Pr. for the Bibliographical Society, 1957, III, 1070–73.

19. Dutton, p. 11.

20. Riggs, pp. 220–21 et passim in Chapter Eleven: "The Making of a Jacobean Poet."

21. As quoted in Riggs, p. 238.

22. For a variety of other views of the semiotics of the front matter in the First Folio of Shakespeare, see Leah S. Marcus, "The Art of the Uncomely Frontispiece," in her *Puzzling Shakespeare: Local Reading and Its Discontents.* (Berkeley & Los Angeles: Univ. of California Pr., 1988), pp. 2–25.

23. See the author's "Topoi in Edward Ravenscroft's Indictment of Shakespeare's *Titus Andronicus*," *Modern Philology* 83 (1985): 45–50 (p. 50 & n. 23).

WORKS CITED

Bevington, David, ed. *The Complete Works of Shakespeare.* Third Edition. Glenview, Illinois: Scott, Foresman, 1980.

———. *From* Mankind *to* Marlowe: *Growth of Structure in the Popular Drama of Tudor England.* Cambridge: Harvard University Press, 1962.

———, ed. *Medieval Drama.* Boston: Houghton Mifflin, 1975.

[Bodley, Sir Thomas]. *Reliquiae Bodleianae; Or Some Genuine Remains of Sir Thomas Bodley.* London: Printed for John Hartley, 1703. [Includes 229 letters from Bodley to his Keeper of Books at the Bodleian at Oxford.]

Dutton, Richard. "Introduction: The 1616 Folio and its Place in Jonson's Career." *Ben Jonson: To the First Folio.* Cambridge: Cambridge University Press, 1983: pp. 1–22.

Elsky, Martin. *Authorizing Words: Speech, Writing, and Print in the English Renaissance.* Ithaca and London: Cornell University Press, 1987.

Greg, W. W. *A Bibliography of the English Printed Drama to the Restoration.* Vol. III: *Collections, Appendix, Reference Lists.* London: Oxford University Press for the Bibliographical Society, 1957.

Harrison, William. "A Prohibition" (9 March, 1617/18). Folger Shakespeare Library, MS V.a .244.

Herford, C. H., and Percy Simpson, edd. *Ben Jonson.* Oxford: Clarendon Press, 1925, I.

McKenzie, D. F. "Printing in England from Caxton to Milton." *New Pelican Guide to English Literature*, ed. Boris Ford. Vol. 2, *The Age of Shakespeare* (Harmondsworth: Penguin, 1982), pp. 207–26.

————. "Speech-Manuscript-Print." *Library Chronicle of the University of Texas of Austin* 20, nos. 1–2 (1990): 86–107.

Minnis, A. J., *Medieval Theory of Authorship*. London: Scolar Pr., 1984.

Minnis, A. J., and A. B. Scott, with David Wallace. *Medieval Literary Theory and Criticism c. 1100–1375: The Commentary Tradition*. Oxford: Clarendon Pr., 1988.

Riggs, David. *Ben Jonson: A Life*. Cambridge. MA: Harvard Univ. Pr., 1989.

Schulberg, Budd. "The 'Auteur' Syndrome." *New York Times*, Op-Ed Page (i.e., p. 27), 4 Dec. 1989.

Velz, John W. "Topoi in Edward Ravenscroft's Indictment of Shakespeare's *Titus Andronicus*." *Modern Philology* 83 (1985): 45–50.

Warren, Michael. "The Theatricalization of Text." *Library Chronicle of the University of Texas at Austin,* 20 nos. 1–2 (1990): 41–46.

Wasson, John. "The Secular Saint Plays of the Elizabethan Era." *The Saint Play in Medieval Europe*, ed. Clifford Davidson. Early Drama, Art and Music Monograph series 8. Kalamazoo, Michigan: Medieval Institute Publications. 1986, pp. 241–60.

The Editor of Letters as Critic: A Denial of "Blameless Neutrality"

BETTY T. BENNETT

Mrs. Julian Marshall, when preparing her 1889 edition of *The Life and Letters of Mary Wollstonecraft Shelley* at the request of Mary Shelley's son and daughter-in-law, Sir Percy and Lady Shelley, had available to her all the letters belonging to Mary Shelley's heirs.[1] Frederick L. Jones, in his 1944 edition of *The Letters of Mary W. Shelley*, had collected "All the available correspondence" for his edition.[2] My 1980–88 edition of *The Letters of Mary Wollstonecraft Shelley*[3] more than doubled the number of letters in Jones and is generally regarded as presenting a new, far more complex and accomplished Mary Shelley.[4] One might be led to believe that the additional letters in my edition were the sole factor in this revised perspective. But there was a second significant factor, related not to the transmogrification of the subject herself—all such transmogrifications having ceased with her death in 1851—but to the transmogrification of editors.

Editors of letters, however, are not generally recognized as influencing the way in which documents are interpreted, an outgrowth of the concept that documentary editors do not change the text itself. In fact, any document not a photofacsimile represents editorial alteration. Tanselle's assertion that "any text that a textual critic produces is itself the product of literary criticism,"[5] is thus applicable to letters as well. Moreover, it can be unquestionably demonstrated that editorial commentary and annotations do modify, for better or worse, biographical and literary perceptions about an author. In an era in which the issue of editor as critic of primary texts has stimulated lively discussion in scholarly circles, it is lamentable that we generally continue to exempt documentary editors from these larger considerations. By discarding the artificial dichotomy between documentary and critical editors, we could also more fully recognize the influence and problems of documentary editing. Though I am certain that no one set of standards would or should meet the problems of all documentary editing projects, at the least such focus could bring to the issues the scholarly perspective they warrant.

The primary source of the idea that editing is somehow less than criticism or theory was the New Criticism. Its notion of intentional fallacy, by separating the text from biography and history, made the sole relevant critical act a meditation upon the text. But even that meditation depended upon a stable text. An editor who established that text did so on the basis of the principle of recovering an author's intention, historical significance, aesthetics, or on some other principle of what would be "best." Despite New Critical dicta, therefore, the editor as explained by the New Critic also engaged, however camouflaged, in a critical process.

Though deconstruction has the reputation of fostering hyperformalism in both theory and practice, in fact it has led to a greater use of documents such as letters and biographies as tools of criticism. After all, if one argues that an author's intention is not sufficient to control a text's meaning, one will logically have to know both what the author's intention was and what forces worked against that intention. Those forces would include biographic, psychoanalytic, and historic elements as well as linguistic ones.

Further, since any text is subject to these forces, the criteria one uses to decide what constitutes the proper literary text would also necessarily play a part in deciding what constitutes the proper text of a letter. How can the situation of an author's life not have meaning for choices regarding what the text of a particular letter should look like and what annotations are necessary to understand the significance of that letter? The concept that "there is nothing outside the text" means that all decisions are critical ones, not that only some kinds of decisions are critical.

In recent years, New Historicism has brought biographical and historical issues into the interpretation of texts in an obviously more intense way that makes questioning the distinction between text, letters, and lives a prerequisite for its form of historical and critical interpretation. Thus Foucault questions what he calls the unity of a book: "the frontiers of a book are never clear-cut: beyond the title, the first lines, and the last full stop, beyond its inter-nal configuration and its autonomous form, it is caught up in a sys-tem of references to other books, other texts, other sentences."[6] To suspend the unity of the book would, for example, make of Mary Shelley's *Letters* a text against which or with which to read *Frank-enstein* rather than merely some form of secondary background. And decisions about the text of both would be fully critical ones. To be sure, Foucault is also skeptical about the unities of author and *oeuvre*, but not in ways that call into question the practice of editing or its critical responsibilities.

How knowledge gained from letters affects our understanding of biography may be illustrated through two particulars that appear in all three editions of Mary Shelley's letters. The first concerns Mary Shelley's friends, the Robinsons; the second, Mary Shelley's 1828 trip to Paris. In Marshall, the Robinsons are dispatched in two lines: "During most of this autumn [1827] Mrs. Shelley and her boy were staying at Arundel, in Sussex, with or in the near neighbor-hood of her friends, the Miss Robinsons. There were several sis-ters, to one of whom, Julia, Mrs. Shelley was much attached" (II, 183). Marshall's commentary on the trip to Paris, the result of an invitation from a source unidentified, acknowledges that Mary Shelley would be lionized there but concentrates on the smallpox that felled her on arrival (II, 188). The editor makes no connection between the Robinsons and Paris.

Jones includes additional letters that refer to both the Robinsons and Paris, letters that were in the collection of the Shelley heirs but were not used in Marshall. Mary Shelley's letter of 25 September [1827] relates that Mr. and Mrs. Douglas (Mrs. Douglas noted as the former Isabella Robinson), along with several others, plan to go to Paris. To assist them, Mary Shelley writes to her friend John Howard Payne, who lives in London, to procure a group passport for them. Mary Shelley's own Paris visit of a year later is cited to Marshall, with the explanation that the friend Mary Shelley pined to see was Julia Robinson.[7] Mr. Douglas remains unidentified. Nor is any comment made on the fact that Mary Shelley had requested Payne, an actor, accompanied by an actress, to impersonate the Douglases at the passport office or that, equipped with descriptions of the Douglases as well as samples of their signatures supplied by Mary Shelley, Payne successfully obtained the illegal passports and is heartily thanked by Mary Shelley for the deed.

The Robinsons and the 1828 trip to Paris are in my edition as well. Notes regarding the Robinson family are extended to include identification of a large number of offspring who play parts in Mary Shelley's life; Isabella, not Julia, Robinson is now the favorite friend. A series of new letters offer more details of Mary Shelley's friendship with Mr. and Mrs. Douglas, amplifying the letters regarding the illegal passports. The trip to Paris is clarified as a visit to the Douglases, with Mary Shelley *accompanied by* rather than intending to visit Julia Robinson. In addition to Mary Shelley's bout with smallpox, the notes deal with an elite social circle she met in Paris. And, in a full-page footnote, Mr. Douglas is identified as a man who never existed, actually being the disguise of a woman named Mary Diana Dods, who in the first volume of this edition is identified as a woman who successfully and secretly passed into history as the author David Lyndsay. The notes further explain that Isabella Robinson was "married" to Miss Dods; and that Mary Shelley was a co-conspirator in aiding this original couple to pass as husband and wife among a sophisticated Anglo-French set that included General Lafayette, Prosper Mérimée, Stendhal, and the Misses Garnett.[8]

How we perceive the widowed Mary Shelley is considerably altered by the additional information about her central role in an international transvestite plot that was not only unusual, but, in a variety of ways, illegal. Discovery of this plot, in an era when a woman pretending to be a man was subject to imprisonment for fraudulently impersonating a superior being, held potentially dire consequences for Mary Shelley. Besides the social opprobrium the Godwin-Shelley family would again suffer, Mary Shelley was likely to lose custody of Percy Florence, her one surviving child, to Sir Timothy Shelley, her father-in-law who earlier had tried to wrest the child from her. At the least, Sir Timothy would revoke the repayable allowance he provided for Percy Florence, in accordance with Sir Timothy's strict injunction that the Shelley name not be brought to public attention. But the letters reveal—covertly and overtly—Mary Shelley's active participation in the plot. Thus, in place of the commonly held view of Mary Shelley as a woman who after Shelley's death spent the remainder of her life unimaginatively conforming to the mores of Victorian society, we discover a daring Mary Shelley who mid-wifed a transvestite foray against Victorian mores and legal codes.

Taking this as an example—admittedly an extraordinary one—of the influence of annotations, one may readily dismiss the illusion that editors of letters and journals do not exercise critical authority over their texts. And since editors of letters are critics, their methodology should be considered within the context of some theoretical standards as much for evaluation of the individual project as for better conceptualization of the art of editing.

Most critics would probably now grant that letters, in providing evidence about lives, also furnish new information and new insight into those lives, thus attributing to letters critical significance. But it is also true that determining the texts of letters is itself a critical act. The very act of setting in print the text of a letter requires editorial decisions, with appropriate explanations of *why* as well as *what* editors have altered. Unfortunately, many editors who themselves complain about a past editor's misdeeds of alteration, often forgive their own. So an editor may indicate preservation "as a general rule" of "punctuation and accentuation" but then go on to advocate regularizing idiosyncratic capitalization, supplying commas "where absolutely necessary," and the decision to "ventilate" with the loan of "a few commas" and "a full stop or two" letters that are unusual in their lack of punctuation.[9] However, because an author's idiosyncratic spelling, punctuation, or cancel scores and underlines represent the way that an individual regarded words, style, etc., a first standard of editing should require that such irregularities be scrupulously retained.

Which leads to another requisite standard for editors of letters: the transcription of the letters by the editor. Many editors regard transcription as a mere mechanical operation. Hence, the differences in editorial style that slip in even within single editor projects; and the inflated NEH grant applications that commonly request funding for graduate assistants or junior colleagues to transcribe the letters. In fact, the act of transcribing the letters may be one of the most valuable tools the editor has for reviewing the subject. In transcribing word after word, one comes as close to the act of writing the letters as possible and can consider words as they unfold into a thought, a thought into a series of thoughts. One sees themes initiated, dropped, alluded to, denied, enhanced. In a kind of intellectual voyeurism, the physicality of acknowledging, piece by piece, the structure of the words into sentences, paragraphs, and letters constitutes the microscopic study of a subject that allows one the opportunity to organize the meaning of those pieces in a closer approximation to what the subject intended.

The above discussion addresses how letters may illuminate a life and how editorial decisions about letters are also critical decisions. Although the theoretical questioning of the barrier between text and context may allow us to see the critical effects and practices of editing more clearly, these considerations, of themselves, do not completely question that barrier. But letters in fact also exist in the context of literary works and of the historical period that surrounds them both. A larger reconsideration justifying the retrieval process, then, is that it leads to a reconsideration of an author, and proves particularly valuable in situating female authors. In Mary Shelley's case, my justification in 1973 for wanting to know more about the author and her works resulted from the scores of mostly peculiar critical essays written about her masterpiece *Frankenstein*. By "peculiar" I mean for the most part that explanations of *Frankenstein* are couched in biographical, personal terms, based largely on speculation rather than fact, and with a marked absence of recognition of the author's intellect. If this was true of *Frankenstein*, it was all the more true of commentary about Mary Shelley's five other novels, one novella, two travel works, short fiction and essays, which when not considered biographically have been all but ignored. My agenda to get to the works themselves, announced in my introduction, was to treat the author as author, with focused consideration on her intellectual and artistic achievements, as opposed to what I call the "biographical hurdle" that confuses or distorts the way Mary Shelley's, and most other women's, works are generally read and critiqued.

The strongest claim for the critical implications of editing occurs, therefore, in the editorial process of accurately determining a context in order to grasp a letter's significance and then finally to turn that significance into a further judgment about historical context. Thus, a documentary technique finds reflection in Jerome McGann's larger thesis of the interactive nexus of people and forces, without the abdication of authorial intention.[10]

Again, I will return to Mary Shelley's life as illustration, with reference to the veil that Percy Bysshe Shelley sought to tear away from life that became instead the veil that obscured much of nineteenth-century biography. Ironically, nowhere was this more true than with Mary Shelley, who was transmuted into the perfect angel/

mother/wife at the instance of her daughter-in-law and son. Marshall's introduction indicated that her Mary Shelley study would not suffer that veil. She depicts Mary Shelley as someone who "would have been eminent among her sex at any time, in any circumstances, and would, it cannot be doubted, have achieved greater personal fame than she actually did but for the fact that she became, at a very early age, the wife of Shelley."

Marshall's biography, however, was undertaken at the request of Sir Percy and Lady Shelley in order to refute the negative biography recently published by Trelawny. As "official" biographer, she worked with whatever documents they provided, and she elucidated whatever was thought proper.[11] Marshall neatly omitted or glossed over the many aspects of Mary Shelley's life in which she appears as anything but a Victorian lady. For example, her elopement with the married Shelley is justified on the basis that the estrangement between Shelley and Harriet, his first wife, resulted from Harriet's "cold," "frivolous and extravagant," nature (I, 58–59) as well as through Shelley's belief that Harriet "had been misled" by one of "her admirers" (i.e., had an affair [I, p.60]). Marshall acknowledges Mary Shelley's own disregard, bred by her family, of the idea of "marriage as a divine institution"; (I, p.64). But she does not mention that Mary Wollstonecraft was five months pregnant before she and Godwin married; or that Mary Shelley's beloved daughter-in-law, a prime mover in having Marshall's biography written, was herself one of nine illegitimate children and the guardian of the illegitimate child of her first husband, who though legitimate was one of only two legitimate children of his father's fifteen children.

Clearly, our era of far greater permissiveness invites the resituating of an author. But this too has pitfalls as we resee our subjects today and in our own context. An example: in dealing with the story of Mary Diana Dods, the question arose of whether she and her circle were lesbians. When we say "lesbian" today we know more or less what we mean. However, the term did not exist when Dods existed; "homosexual" and "lesbian" are modern terms. According to the law, and received custom in Dods' era, it was held that women could be sexually attracted to men, men could be sexually attracted to men, but it was believed that a woman could not be attracted to another woman since women were regarded as inferior beings. In recognition of this sexual distinction, men who had sexual relationships with other men were charged with sodomy; women suspected of sexual relations with other women, as noted earlier, were charged with fraud for impersonating a superior being. The modern editor must make heroic efforts not to assign to an author our own modern social or personal biases; to guard, to the extent possible, against the superimposition of our own veils in the act of removing those of other peoples' or centuries'.

To what extent are editors responsible for placing their author within the author's socio-political context? And should that context extend beyond what the author consciously acknowledged? Again, Mary Shelley as an example. In pre-1980 biographies, despite the fact that Shelley, Byron, Godwin, and even Mary Wollstonecraft's life and works were considered within a socio-political framework, Mary Shelley's were not, thereby denying both the political turmoil of the period and her own engagement with that turmoil. Without this context, hundreds of references in her letters to political events went unnoted: from the youthful "Are not the events in Spain wonderful" and "What a Joan Bull I am" to the comments on the 1830 French revolution and the 1840 letters with their highly informed commentary on Australian as well as British politics.

The omission of such annotations led biographers to assert that Mary Shelley's interest in politics died with Shelley. This in turn allowed critics generally to misread Mary Shelley's novels after *Frankenstein*, condescendingly dismissing them as, at best, romantic romans à clef. The failure to recognize her intellectual accomplishments has even influenced criticism of her masterpiece. The argument still persists in some quarters that Shelley reworked it sufficiently to be regarded as co-author. And, as suggested above, *Frankenstein* generally suffers from narrowly biographical readings that do justice to neither book or author. But a close reading of Mary Shelley's letters—annotated to draw the reader's attention to her many political comments—provides substantial evidence of a lifelong fascination with politics, which calls for a reassessment of her works in terms of her reformist politics, and will, I believe, materially add to our understanding of English Romanticism, the English novel, and women's studies.

If context illuminates letters, though, letters also illuminate context. As the meaning of a poem often reveals itself only when we understand the one part of the poem we initially fail to fathom, so, too, in letters new perspectives are often couched in seemingly inexplicable phases or references—it took me seventeen years to unravel the story of the Douglases. The editor must establish a commentary that is in fact a set of clues, to establish one's own perspective and subject it to the test of other people's perspectives.

John Matthews, in arguing for the inclusion of "important" as well as "trivial" letters of Disraeli in his edition, maintains that only when *all* the letters "are collected in chronological order" can one be made "aware for the first time of the complexity of a personality in which the sum is greater than and different from the parts."[12] His argument for inclusion of *all* the letters is by extension an argument for recognizing and contextualizing those aspects of the author's life that were important to that author—however significant or trivial they may appear to the editor.

In Mary Shelley's life, and in the life of other women authors as well, writing, reading, art, language, literature, politics, and nature were as integral to her as her family and the paraphernalia that support family life. It is as much the editor's as the biographer's responsibility to understand how this conjunction of commitments took its place in her letters and in her works. Editors must also deal with the idea of the recipients of letters as unacknowledged collaborators, their distinctive presence necessarily influencing the letter writer.

Editors of letters, therefore, must recognize that they are, intentionally or not, critical biographers. Approaching their subject as if they are writing a biography—though that biography appears in the staccato form of bite-size pieces of information—means that editors are responsible for discovering *everything* there is to know about a subject.

Editors should be expected to test themselves comprehensively against past publications and editions. At the same time, editors must test against prior established beliefs about the author. If there are no existing good biographical or critical studies—by a good biography I mean one that provides reliable, substantiated insights and depth of understanding of the author's works and life—the editor of letters must exercise even more responsibility for maintaining editorial objectivity.

This does not make for a quick read. The productivity of some authors may preclude comprehensive knowledge in one editor's lifetime—hence, justification for the concept of multiple editors. But these circumstances call for editorial meetings that are themselves mini-conferences regarding information, perspective, and intention. For the individual editor, working with published and unpublished texts provides a major reality check but also a major danger. Plainly, it is a great aid to see what biographers and editors have earlier adduced. But editors must retain their own perspective. They must in fact read as if no one has ever read the material before.

In a sense, I am suggesting that one take a well-known figure about whom much is known and thought and believed and un-know and un-think it after one has deliberately taken the time and trouble to know it. If the edition is scholarly, intended to add to the body of knowledge about the author, an editor of letters must first take responsibility for a skeptical approach to past perspectives in order to reaffirm, further develop, or supersede those perspectives. The failure to undertake so comprehensive a methodology leads to a disservice to the individual subject and the world of letters.

We are too accustomed to think of theory as a thing separate from information and of editing of letters as the retrieval of theoretically neutral facts. But just as modern theory questions the separation between fact and interpretation, it invites reconsideration of the role and responsibility of the editor of personal writings as well as texts. There are no neutral facts or neutral editors; there are only theoretical and interpretive editorial processes that, like "the awful shadow of some unseen Power," should not float unrecognized among us.

NOTES

1. 2 vols. (London: Richard Bentley & Son), I, Preface, v.

2. 2 vols. (Norman: University of Oklahoma Press), I, Preface, v.

3. 3 vols. (Baltimore: The Johns Hopkins University Press), I, xii, hereafter cited *MWSL*.

4. See, for example, Richard Holmes, "Poetic Injustice," *New York Times*, 18 May 1980. Holmes writes: "The injustice of her fate—the poetic injustice, as it were—is even more disturbing in Mary Shelley's case, for she was clearly a wonderfully gifted (and indeed tormented) writer on her own terms, and an altogether remarkable and complex personality.". . . "What is new so far? Apart from the vivid central perspective it brings to Mary Shelley's predicament as one writer married to another, this first volume shows much more

clearly—and sympathetically—the breadth and independence of her character. I had never fully appreciated the degree of her interest in the political
freedom movements of the day . . . or her gossipy but highly professional
inside knowledge of literary and theatrical life in London."

5. G. Thomas Tanselle, *A Rationale of Textual Criticism* (Philadelphia: Univer-
    sity of Pennsylvania Press, 1989), p. 35. For a further discussion of emendation
    of documentary texts, see G. Thomas Tanselle, *Textual Criticism Since Greg:
    A Chronicle 1950–1985* (Charlottesville: University of Virginia Press, 1987),
    pp. 109 ff.

6. Michel Foucault, *The Archaeology of Knowledge*, trans. A. M. Sheridan
    Smith (New York: Harper, 1972), p. 23.

7. Jones, I, 373.

8. *MWSL*, I, 540, 533–534, 556–575; II, 1–15, 32–59.

9. Ralph A. Leigh, "Rousseau's Correspondence: Editorial Problems," *Editing
    Correspondence*, ed. J. A. Dainard (New York: Garland Publishing, Inc.,
    1979), pp. 56–57.

10. *A Critique of Modern Textual Criticism* (Chicago: University of Chicago
    Press, 1984), p. 81; see also Jerome J. McGann, "The Monks and the Giants,"
    Textual Criticism and Literary Interpretation, ed. Jerome J. McGann
    (Chicago: University of Chicago Press, 1985), p. 198. For a discussion of the
    limitations of McGann's approach, as well as an overview of the issue of
    social contextualization, see Tanselle, *Textual Criticism*, pp. 127–154.

11. Marshall, I, 2–3.

12. "The Hunt for the Disraeli Letters," *Editing Correspondence* (New York:
    Garland Publishing, Inc., 1979), pp. 83–84.

Varieties of Textual Change in the Victorian Era

ALLAN C. DOOLEY

As Robert Browning muses in "Transcendentalism" about the superiority of poetry over philosophy, he warns of the seductive, impenetrable difficulty of Jacob Boehme's mystical writings:

> But by the time youth slips a stage or two
> While reading prose in that tough book he wrote
> (Collating and emendating the same
> And settling on the sense most to our mind),
> We shut the clasps and find life's summer past.

The larger point of the passage has to do with the relentlessness of life's changes, but Browning shrewdly observes in his parenthesis that texts also change and vary, requiring subsequent "collating"; that they undergo alteration, and will need "emendating." And what a text may signify seems to be variable too, a matter of critical consensus or of individual judgment as to the sense most agreeable to our notions. Twentieth-century textual critics have come to recognize this situation as clearly as the nineteenth-century poet, and where the former aim of scholars was to produce a pristine, authoritative, single text of a given work, textual editors are now interested in representing the growth, the life, the history of a text. Thus the scholarly study of texts has become more than ever a study of differences and variations, attended by broader, more flexible ideas of authority.[1]

During the nineteenth century, a series of improvements in printing technology occurred which constituted, by the end of the century, a revolution in printing. This revolution touched every aspect of book production, from initial typesetting through reprinted editions, and it changed the relations of authors to the printed texts of their works so significantly as to render inadequate some scholarly methods which were effective for earlier texts. Both the occasions and the nature of textual change were altered by printing technology, as the following observations indicate:

(1) Conventional wisdom asserts that before our century, a printer's compositors closely followed the author's manuscript as to its wording, but freely altered and regularized spelling, capitalization, and punctuation. In fact, though Victorian printers tried to continue this common practice of earlier eras, Victorian authors, even when they were neophytes, often demanded and achieved substantial control over the so-called "accidentals" of their printed works.

(2) The fact that Dickens revised extensively during the proof-stages of his first editions, while Arnold revised heavily for his collected editions, could be attributed to differences in their personalities, circumstances, and writing habits. That different authors compose differently is true, but in the Victorian era this may not be a complete explanation. The state of printing technology at a given date determined whether an author could receive proofs in complete sets or piecemeal, whether those proofs would be galley slips or sheets of pages, whether the manuscript or printed copy could be sent along with the proofs, how many stages of proof were available, and how much alteration was possible in each.

(3) Scholars have customarily assumed that stereotype printing, which became almost universal during the nineteenth century, so stabilized a printed text that reimpressions of an edition are of minor or no textual significance. While publishers and printers since the introduction of stereotyping promoted this supposed fixing of the printed text as a great advantage of the process, there is plentiful evidence that stereo plates could be freely altered. Many authors knew this and sent their printers or publishers lists of changes intended to make each subsequent impression of an edition conform more exactly to the author's desires than the last. Running counter to this stereotype plates were subject to an insidious typographical entropy, through which textual changes that nobody intended could and did occur.

An extensive investigation into the histories of Victorian texts reveals a multiplicity of identifiable stages of textual change and a variety of kinds of changes ranging from the meticulously deliberate to the utterly accidental. But while many Victorian authors had frequent opportunities to revise, correct, and otherwise alter their works, the picture that usually emerges is of a discontinuous process, not a smoothly-graded development. Such discontinuities are the obvious norm in the hand-press period, when the entire history of a text might have consisted of a single manuscript (now lost), a single set of page proofs (also lost), a first edition, and perhaps a much later collected edition. The era of machine printing and stereotyped reprints certainly multiplied the number of discrete stages a text went through during a span of time (the author's life, perhaps, or the use of a set of plates), but it did not enforce any particular model of textual change. Nineteenth-century texts do not necessarily change a bit at a time over many editions and impressions, nor do they always show a steadily increasing or decreasing number of alterations over a given period. What they do show—and show more clearly than earlier texts simply because there are more stages and thus more surviving evidence—is subtly differing kinds of changes which appear and get dealt with on various occasions. To discuss these and suggest their implications for textual criticism, I must attempt some definitions. To some readers these will appear elementary, but I beg their indulgence for the sake of assuring that we are, in the athlete's idiom, all on the same page.

Variant Readings

A *textual variant* or *variant reading* is simply a difference between one text and another at a given point of the same passage of the work at hand. The degree of difference may be very small (the spelling of a word, the placement of a hyphen, the use of a colon rather than a semicolon) or quite large (the insertion, deletion, or rearrangement of passages or entire chapters). Scholars disagree to some extent about the minimum amount of difference required to define a variant, and to a great extent about the amount of difference necessary to make a variant significant or meaningful. Texts from the Victorian era tend to display large numbers of small variants, occurring over numerous sequential iterations; over a span of editions and impressions, these variants may accumulate until they constitute a pattern of revision (or decay and corruption, for that matter). Questions about the origin—and thus the authority—of variant readings are never far from the textual critic's mind, be-

cause declaring a reading an error, a correction, or a revision requires deciding how the variant came to exist. A variant may be
characterized as a *substitution* (*had* in one text for *has* in another),
an *insertion* (a punctuation mark, a word, a phrase, a sentence, or
much more, added to a preexisting text), or a *deletion* (textual material, small or vast, removed from a preexisting text). When a variant reading occurs, the scholar customarily assigns a human origin
to it by calling it an author's slip of the pen, a compositor's error, a
reader's change, an author's revision, an editor's imposition, or
some other human act. The study of Victorian texts makes it plainly
apparent that variant readings can and repeatedly do appear as the
result of the mechanical processes of printing, having no origin in
any human choice and arising in spite of a uniform desire that there
be no change to a text.

Errors

When we scrutinize a printed work with an eye toward determining its accuracy, all sorts of things may strike us as wrong in one
way or another. From the mechanics of book-manufacturing to the
subtleties of rhetoric and intricacies of subordination, faults often
abound. Sheets get gathered out of sequence, inadequate inking or
uneven plates cause portions of pages to disappear; even if the
work is complete and coherent, we may encounter strange spellings, odd punctuation, confused references, even misstatements of
fact. All of these are errors, and all may have their interest, but
some of them fall beyond the realm of textual scholarship and
belong to the biographer or historian. A detailed history of every
aspect of the text of *Pippa Passes* cannot determine for us whether
Browning—who knew his Chaucer—truly thought that *twat* was
part of a nun's attire, or whether he might have been attributing
this confusion to the utterly innocent Pippa. All the record shows is
that on at least eight occasions over forty-eight years Browning
chose not to change the word, which can hardly be a misspelling of
some other word. If this was an error from first to last, it was not a
textual error. On the other hand, where Browning's Bishop
Blougram asked for decades, "You criticize the *soil*? it reared this
tree—" in the authoritative edition of 1888–89, soil is replaced by
soul.[2] A compositor's error, surely—yet Browning passed up several chances to correct it; and despite the arboreal metaphor, "Bishop

Blougram's Apology" is about the soul, not soil; and thus what initially appears to be a simple typographical mistake can become so problematic as to lose the name of error.

Of course, some kinds of textual error—those, for instance, which printers term "literals"—are so obvious that they defy worthwhile definition (*waht* or *what*), but in more interesting cases things are usually not so clear. Certainly, to identify an error is to point out a difference between a faulty reading and a correct one, but the correct reading may be only putative or virtual, not actual. This would be the case when an author misspells a common word in a compositional manuscript: when the juvenile Jane Austen repeatedly wrote *freind* and *freindship*, the correct spellings existed in the realm of linguistic convention, if not in Austen's lexicon, and her error does not represent a deviation on her part from a prior state of correctness. The nature of a textual error becomes less ethereal when a written work enters the process of development and comes to exist in more than one stage. A fair copy may contain errors that are readily identifiable as inaccurate transcriptions of the preceding compositional manuscript. A set of proofs will almost inevitably manifest errors that arise with the compositor and exist as deviations from his copy. These the author or printer's reader will mark for correction, and indeed even the most cautious scholar would have to admit that an erroneous reading—even one that makes sense, such as *soul* for *soil* or *human* for *humane*—is proved to be an error if the author corrected it. This most common sort of *textual error*, then, is a species of undesired variant reading: a reading which does not conform to the intentions of the person having authority over the text. Such intentions can be represented by a previously-approved iteration of the text (a manuscript or other printer's copy, a set of prior proofs, corrections on proofs, an earlier edition, etc.) or by one subsequent to the erroneous text (a list of errata, a later edition, etc.).

Since our ordinary understanding of erroneousness carries with it an implication of human agency, it would be natural to think that behind every error lies a slip, a mistake, a misunderstanding. But some kinds of variants (textual differences) that quite rightly get called errors do not necessarily arise from human actions. Pick up one copy of the fourth volume of Browning's 1888–89 *Poetical Works* and it appears that someone has removed the word *but* from line 837 of "Bishop Blougram's Apology," creating a rhythmic, if not syntactic, error. Collate four or five more examples and you will see how *but* disappeared piece by piece as the stereo plate of page 271 disintegrated.

Textual errors are not always confined to the level of the individual word or punctuation mark; if a sentence or a paragraph has been marked by the author for deletion but reappears in the next iteration of the text, the passages's continued presence is a textual error. (To decide to remove it was probably an act of revision, as discussed below.) The well-known reversal of chapters 28 and 29 of James's *The Ambassadors* was an enormous but straightforward textual error, irrespective of any aesthetic or critical consequences. What the offending words or passages actually say is largely unimportant to this definition of the erroneous. True textual errors inhabit a category quite separate from an author's mistake in wording or error of fact, such as writing "Cortez" when you mean "Balboa," or believing that Cortez was the first European to see the Pacific.

Corrections

From this narrowed concept of error, we may draw more than one definition of *correction*. At the simplest functional level, a correction is a variant which consists of a restoration, replacing an erroneous reading with the approved prior reading from which the error deviated. When a printer's reader or an author makes a set of proofs conform to copy, he or she performs this sort of routine correction. Seemingly little more than this is involved in a second kind of correction, that which occurs when a printer's reader or an editor makes a text conform to the basic elements of common spelling and usage; but difficulties and uncertainties can arise as the functional slides toward the conceptual. An apparent error may actually have some artistic purpose. For example, it seems obvious that the spelling in Austen's "Love and Freindship" should be corrected. Yet one might also argue that such changes could be counter to the author's possible intention: what better way to represent the hilarious silliness of the inexperienced young lovers who are the butt of the story's comedy than by suggesting that they can hardly understand what they cannot even spell?[3]

Out of such possibilities grew the compositor's maxim, "follow your copy," and it is tempting to limit the term *correction* to those variant readings which witness an effort to make a text conform to its approved immediate predecessor. However, since it is a primary characteristic of language that it must make literal sense before it can become ironic or figurative, we may still rightly describe many authors' insertions, deletions, and substitutions as corrections. To replace the period in "When did you leave." with the question mark is to correct; so is to insert *his* after *tried* in "After he tried grey suit on," or cancel *on* in "He later went on into the house." But when a change does more than restore the preceding approved reading, or involves more than the basic rules of grammar or the requirements of simple idioms, it goes beyond correction and verges on revision.

Revisions

If many a publisher has trumpeted a somewhat corrected impression as a "thoroughly revised edition," so too has many an author characterized a detailed revision as "minor corrections of the press." The publisher's motive is to persuade the buyer that the book is something new and improved; the author aims to assure the publisher that the book will not have to be redesigned, or perhaps hopes to avoid paying for the alterations. The printer traditionally bore the cost of "corrections"—i.e., changes made to conform to copy—while the author or publisher paid for any other insertions, deletions, or substitutions. While modern textual experts can hardly accept a distinction between correction and revision based on who pays the bill, another kind of quantitative notion still prevails. A revision, as usually imagined, comprises a significant number of variant readings between two texts, not just a few; furthermore, revision involves something fairly substantial, and correction by restoration would not qualify. Most scholars would probably agree, however, that a large number of corrections—particularly of the kind described at the end of the preceding section—eventually add up to a revision. Enough revisions and you might find yourself with a new version of a work.

The advantage of these notions is that they allow certain kinds of intellectual problems to be solved by counting, but clearly an arithmetical grasp of the evidence of textual change is only the merest beginning for a valid approach to revision. A purely quantitative approach fails to take adequate recognition of three highly important aspects of revision: the possible sources of a textual change, the nature of the change, and the intention behind it.

Of all the sources and agents of change to a text—author, copyist, compositor, reader, publisher, printing machine, stereotype process, plate damage or decay—only an author can truly revise. This does not mean that readings which *look* like revisions always come from or through the author of a text. I have before me a volume of Browning's 1888–89 *Poetical Works* in which lines 60–61 of "Fra Lippo Lippi" read (in part): "And a face that looked up . . . zooks, sir, flesh and blood. / That's all I'm made of!" Collations show that in every typesetting supervised by Browning, including this last one, *blood* was followed by a comma; the period was created when the tail of the comma loosened from the stereo plate, curled around, and ultimately disappeared. This textual change, created entirely by the mechanical processes of printing, would surely have the standing of a revision (rather than an error) if its origin were not known. The change from comma to full stop makes a distinct change in the syntactical coordination and the rhetoric of the lines, thus qualifying as a revision in substance.

Other persons may suggest revisions, and mechanical processes and technological faults may prompt them by creating new opportunities for alteration, but a textual variant earns its status as a genuine revision by virtue of a particularly authorial activity. Other agents of change may correct, rearrange, censor, corrupt, or mutilate, but authors alone can create or sanction a revision. To select but one of the hundreds of examples of the composite nature of some revision, consider George Eliot's response to her publisher's evaluation of one of her poems. She sent the manuscript of "How Lisa Loved the King" to Blackwood in February of 1869, characterizing the draft as "*absolutely* unrevised"; Blackwood apparently had it set in type immediately and sent her a proof bearing his suggestions for alterations. She wrote on 19 February: "I do not return the proof as you requested; though I have read it and made every correction that I see my way to now, except those lines about which you are doubtful and which I will reconsider." A few days later she announced: "I have made various verbal corrections of importance, and have rewritten the passage you had marked." However closely Eliot did or did not follow Blackwood's suggestions, the changes she made for the succeeding printed text were, in my view, her own revisions.[4]

I have already used the phrase "correction by restoration" for the act of replacing an erroneous reading with a reading from an immediately prior approved text (such as printers' copy or marked proofs). Another kind of restoration, involving more than two iterations of a text, constitutes a fairly common kind of revision, likely to be encountered in authors who superintended numerous editions of their works. The pattern can be easily illustrated by the following imaginary variants:

1. printers' copy MS in author's hand:
    Since thou didst hold thy father in thy heart,

2. author's proof of first edition, printed reading:
    Since thou didst hold thy fahter in thy heart,

3. author's MS alterations on proof:
    If thou didst ever thy dear father love—

4. revised proof of first edition, printed reading:
    If thou didst ever thy dear father in love—

5. author's MS alteration to revises:
    If thou didst ever held thy father dear:

6. first edition:
    If thou didst ever hold thy father dear:

7. collected edition, set from copy of first edition
    as revised by author:
    If thou didst ever thy dear father love—

Variant 7, the author's final version of the line, is identical to variant 3; what the author performed in preparing the collected edition was a restoration, even though variant 3 was not previously published. Having revised reading 2 into 3, the author discovered a new error in 4; on the occasion of correcting this, the author tried out a further revision, which was faithfully reproduced in the first edition as published. A literal error in variant 2 is corrected in 3, and someone has corrected the verb tense between 5 and 6.

Few would disagree that variant 3 represents a significant autho-

rial revision of a preexisting text. But what kind of difference between the two underlies our recognition of revision? The substitution of one or more words for others cannot be the key, since such
an act may constitute no more than a correction. A new line added
to a passage or five lines marked by the author for deletion certainly must be revisions, but even tiny changes may have substantial
weight. In the case of "Bishop Blougram's Apology,"[5] Browning's
alteration of line 267 from

> That's the first cabin-comfort I secure—

in 1855 to

> That's the first-cabin comfort I secure:

in 1865 accomplishes with the movement of a mere hyphen a shift
from one scale of value (acquiring something immediately) to
another (acquiring something of the highest quality). We might say
that this is a revision because it seems to involve a change of meaning, but the very term *meaning* is too broad and controvertible to be
of much use. Besides, is there any genuine difference in meaning
consequent on this change? Blougram is still characterized as greedy
for his comforts, despite the emphasis on taste in the revised version. To revert to the earlier example, the alteration from "Since" to
"If" in variant 3 represents a falling-off from confident presumption
to uncertain hope, yet our essential understanding of the line is not
deeply affected.

I believe that what we recognize as different, as revised, is not
just words or punctuation, and not some generalized thing called
"meaning"; it is the rhetoric of the passage. The nature of revision
is that it changes the expression of an idea, not the idea itself. A
revision, no matter how small, always involves a rhetorical shift, not
a shift in underlying conception. Since only an author can claim a
full grasp of the ideas and conceptions behind his or her work, only
an author can *revise*, that is, change expression without betraying
his or her broader intention.

A particular kind of authorial intention manifests itself in revision, one which goes beyond striving to conform an iteration of a
text to an existing standard (i.e., correcting) but does not aim at
making a new iteration say something quite different from its predecessors. Thackeray's revisions of *Vanity Fair* in 1848 and 1853
offer a clear example of how an author can make numerous changes

throughout a text with no intention of changing a work into something other than what it had been. Thackeray made the novel more fully expressive, a more complete manifestation of his conception, without altering the novel's direction, tone, or balance.[6] On a similar scale, the thousands of changes Browning made over the years to *The Ring and the Book* constituted an elaborate, careful finishing and polishing of the poem as it was, a vast and extended process of revision.

Revisions and Versions

Whitman's changes to *Song of Myself*, James's reworking for the New York edition of his works, and Wordsworth's modifications to *The Prelude* represent something more than finishing or completing a text. The authorial process of revision has in these cases given way to wholesale rewriting. Such works come to exist in two or more versions containing numerous variant readings, but the crucial degree of difference between one version and another does not result solely from numerous corrections and revisions. A new version is the work of an author who has changed his or her intentions toward the work. When an author's view of a work's statements, ideas, structures, and themes has shifted significantly, and the author sets out to alter the text of that work in accordance with this shift, what occurs will be not so much revision as re-creation. The re-created text is intended by the author not to improve the existing work as it has been, but to replace it with a version which has been altered in an essential way.

Authors usually create substitute versions in the belief that they are offering the public a better product or are being truer to their own talents. If pressed, most authors would assert a proprietary control over their works that entitles them to rewrite however they like, though few would offer a completely different work under the old title. The balance of old and new in the case of James's multiple versions has been neatly described by Robert Bamberg: "Although there is only one novel by Henry James called *The Portrait of a Lady*, we have what amounts to two separate 'Portraits.' The first appeared in 1880–81, and the other, with extensive retouching, was unveiled over a quarter century later in 1908."[7] Ultimately, one must conclude that to denominate a text as a new version, rather than a revision, of another involves an informed critical judgment, not just counting or calculating percentages.

Authorial Control of Textual Changes

Textual scholars struggle to detect precise distinctions between correction and revision or revision and re-creation, but authors seem to recognize the differences instinctively, despite the occasional inexactitude of their terms. When trying in 1847 to convince Moxon to put out a collected edition of his earlier works, Browning wanted to claim the right to revise without alarming the publisher with the possibility of major changes: "But the point which decided me to wish to get printed over again was the real good I thought I could do to *Paracelsus*, *Pippa*, and some others; good, not obtained by cutting them up and reconstructing them, but by affording just the proper revision they ought to have had before they were printed at all. This, and no more, I fancy, is due to them."[8]

Many years later, when preparing the collected edition of 1888–89, Browning sent his printers a set of proofs on which the poet had extensively revised his first published poem. The sheer number of changes must have made it appear that Browning wanted to print a new *Pauline* in place of the old embarrassing one, but the poet insisted—correctly, in my view—that he had not in fact created a new version of the work. His letter to his publisher, which defensively employs the word *correcting* for what was in anyone's definition a concentrated revising, reveals Browning's sense of the outer limit of revision and his presumption of textual control:

> My dear Smith,—When I received the Proofs of the 1st. vol. [in which *Pauline* was to appear] on Friday evening, I made sure of returning them next day—so accurately are they printed. But onlooking at that unlucky *Pauline*, which I have not touched for half a century, a sudden impulse came over me to take the opportunity of just correcting the most obvious faults of expression, versification and construction,—letting the *thoughts*—such as they are—remain exactly as at first: I have only treated the imperfect expression of these just as I have now and then done for an amateur friend, if he asked me and I liked him enough to do so. Not a line is displaced, none added, none taken away. I have just sent it to the printer's with an explanatory word: and told him that he will have less trouble with all the rest of the volumes put together than with this little portion.

This letter and the record of Browning's revisions to *Pauline*[9] make explicit the hierarchy of levels of thought and expression on which this discussion has depended. To a considerable extent, the distinctions between various levels are based on the degree to which a competent user of language consciously attends to them. Thus the basic features of written language, such as grammatical necessities, spelling, and capitalization, are automatically observed by a competent writer unless his or her aim is to be deliberately unconventional. Punctuation, particularly if it is complex and unorthodox, is often more consciously selected. Above this is the level of rhetoric, which includes diction, rhythm, and sound as well as sentence length and structure, patterns of coordination and subordination, and figurative language. At the highest level of conscious direction stands what Browning calls "thoughts," what the author wants us to grasp more than anything else: the cluster of ideas, statements, judgments, and structures we call meaning. All the lower levels serve to forward the writer's aim to get something across, to stimulate and then control the reader's emotions and thoughts.

No author can completely control a reader's associations and interpretations, but the most effective means of trying to is to control the printed text that reader encounters. Controlling the fundamental, compulsory elements of written language often involves the correction of textual errors, though when artfully used, these basic features may become part of rhetoric, and changes to them then become revisions. Clearing up a minor confusion at the rhetorical level—by rearranging word order, for example—may be called correction, but most changes in rhetoric must be seen as revisions, because they result from the author's conscious attention and intention. Deeply considered revision, of a kind which manifests a substantial change in what a work has to say, usually attends the re-creation of a work into a new version; the substitution of a new version for an older one testifies most powerfully to an author's control of a text.

In two fundamental ways, then, the revolution in nineteenth-century printing technology shaped the way texts were constructed and the way we read them today. First, technology dictated the processes by which texts were transmitted and books were made and had the potential to alter, create, and destroy readings by itself. Second, the ingenious employment of this technology by printers and publishers multiplied the number of occasions on which textual changes—errors, corrections, and revisions—could occur. The corresponding increase in documents at every stage of a text's history often provides ample evidence of a Victorian author's efforts to alter and control how a work read. With careful research and sufficient labor, the scholar of texts can determine which documents and iterations of a work must be scrutinized (all of those, surely, over which the author exercised any degree of control). Collation will then yield a list of all textual variants, and from these variants the scholar must decipher a pattern of textual change and detect within it the best evidence of authorial intention.

All textual critics, no matter what their theoretical stances and axioms, are committed to the effort to identify and recover authors' intentions, variable though they may be, toward their texts. But rueful experience teaches us that intentions, whether of authors or scholars, are neither uniform, nor consistent, nor particularly stable. Intentions may be unconscious or conscious; impulsive or considered; fleeting or fixed; initial, interim, or final. The tasks of textual criticism include deciding what kinds of intention must be taken most seriously, determining which iterations of a text best represent a work as the author intended it to read, and attaining a grasp of what the history of a work's text signifies. As twenty years and more of intense scholarly discussion has shown, these are anything but settled questions.[10]

Initial Intentions

The best-known mode of textual criticism goes by several names: the "Greg-Bowers" school, from the names of two of its founders; the "Anglo-American" school, so called because both basic theoretical work and landmark applications were done in England and America around the middle of the twentieth century; and the "first-edition" school, reflecting the emphasis these critics put on the early stages of a text's history. Critics in this camp confer the highest textual authority on the manuscript or, if a complete manuscript is lacking, on the first edition of a work. They locate the apex of authorial control in these early stages of a text's history and see later phases as occasions for the intrusion of unauthorized readings and textual corruptions. The success of this approach to scholarly editing, especially for literary works from the sixteenth through eighteenth centuries, is widely acknowledged; its rationales and methods are succinctly described by Philip Gaskell in his *New Introduction to Bibliography*. Scholarly editors working on these principles have cleared great literary works of gross inaccuracies and restored unauthorized cuts.

Textual critics of this school aim to recover an author's initial intentions about a text, which they privilege because they stand closest in time to the creation of the work. The Anglo-American school developed as a means of establishing texts for the great works of the English literary Renaissance, a period during which an author typically exercised very limited control over a text once the manuscript was handed in. Under such circumstances, authorial intention often will be best represented by the earliest text, on the grounds that it will bear the smallest number of nonauthorial readings (though this may still be quite substantial). Of course the earliest text may not derive directly from any authorial document, and some later text may better reflect what the author intended, as in the case of the first and second quartos of *Hamlet*. This famous example alone points up one problem inherent in any view of textual authority which depends exclusively on chronology.

As printing technology, the book trade, and the nature of authorship all changed during the ensuing centuries, authors increased their command over their printed works. By the nineteenth century, authorial control often increased over a writer's career, so that the history of a text is one of increasing accuracy, not spreading corruption. Leading scholars trained in the Greg-Bowers school have been reluctant to alter their theoretical framework to incorporate these historical changes. Even when dealing with nineteenth-century texts which were carefully revised by their authors for later editions, some textual critics strongly assert the primacy of the manuscript or first edition. They take a view of textual development which rests, I think, on the romantic concept of inspiration, in which it is posited that the unconscious (or preconscious) artistic impulse can never be adequately realized in words. The image of the inspired artist, feverishly working to grasp the fragments of a vision before it fades, has been very powerful indeed in recent centuries. If art begins in transcendent visions, if a work of art is whole and radiant only as a dream, inspiration, or other phenomenon of the mental realm, then no text can truly represent what the artist originally intended. With this premise, we will come closest to the original artistic intention by hewing to the earliest complete manuscript or printed text; earlier is always better, whether we are considering revisions of unknown origin or a genuine authorial second version. An extreme version of this theory, proposed by a few scholars, sees *all* revision—by anyone, including the author—as corruption, a falling away from the pristine original.

Final Intentions

The rival position seeks to recover an author's final intentions about a text, not the original inspiration. Textual critics of this school, which has no agreed-upon name, elevate not the first edition, but the last edition of a work seen through the press by the author, to the position of greatest textual importance. To these scholars, an author's revisions, especially when spread over many years and editions, are part of a creative process which ends only with the author's death. They grant privileged standing to the revising author, who becomes a specially-qualified editor in a life-long attempt to bulwark a text against agencies of corruption.

Taking their cue from Tennyson, Browning, George Eliot, and other Victorian authors who prepared their own collected editions, a few modern textual critics and editors have applied this approach to nineteenth-century authors. A very late or even final edition is taken as the copy-text to be followed, and earlier editions provide variant readings, which inevitably contain numerous compositorial errors and other non-authorial material. But where the adherent of Greg-Bowers sees corruption, the "final intention" critic sees development—perhaps even, to misapply an Arnoldian tag only slightly, "the pursuit of perfection." (Certainly Arnold himself saw his meticulous revisions to the many editions of his poems in these terms.) To trace this development, however, this critic must pay close attention to many documents which the Greg-Bowers critic would see as secondary in importance. The proliferation of evidence about nineteenth-century authors, printers, and publishers almost guarantees that the modern scholar will find that a text exists in a substantial number of incremental stages. The exact sequential order, as well as the textual significance, of intermediate proofs and editions may be anything but obvious.

This kind of textual critic needs more than the basic notion that a succession of revised editions constitutes a developing text, rather than a disintegrating one. The choice of a late copy-text must repose on historical and biographical evidence about the habits of the author under study and on an informed judgment about how fully this author sought and achieved textual control. The scholar who enshrines an author's final intentions must have confidence that the process preserved in the particular textual history represents an accumulation of authorial revisions and a diminution of textual errors. That is, it should be demonstrable that the author's desire and ability to control the text of a work increased through the series of editions that culminates in a final edition. Indications of an author's desire to control a text are often plentiful; many writers have fulminated against publishers' or printers' alterations to even the most minute aspects of their works, and many a writer has averred that every particular in a set of proofs has been attended to.[11] But such claims and desires are not necessarily commensurate with ability, and a high degree of both is required for a textual process to be rightly described as driving out, rather than accumulating, textual errors and non-authorial readings. Certainly the technological advances of nineteenth-century printing increased the author's chances of doing just that, if the author was willing to work assiduously and swiftly. In turn, as technology gave authors opportunities to revise repeatedly through multiple stages of proof and to make still further revisions in later impressions, their desire to do so may have increased.

Maximum Authorial Control

Experience and vigorous scholarly argument have shown that neither of these two approaches is satisfactory for all authors. Each carries within it propositions about the nature of artistic creation, the manifestation of authorial intention, and the processes of book-production that cannot fit every case. Indeed, some of these propositions are subject to shifts in literary taste, as seen in the recent changes in attitude toward the "bad" quartos of Shakespeare. Scholars have not arrived at, and may never agree upon, a single critical system which will give adequate status and proper importance to an author's initial artistic intentions, while recognizing and respecting that author's developing textual intentions and proprietary right to revise unto death.

Nevertheless, I want to describe a third view, one which takes into account the effects of changing printing technology and the expanded body of evidence that are encountered with nineteenth-century works and authors. This proposal sanctifies neither original intention or final intention and does not dictate a uniform choice of preferred text. The Greg-Bowers approach, it seems to me, often depends too much on chronology and on a belief in inspiration. It also tends to elevate the textual critic's judgment over the author's in matters of revision, and I am never completely at ease with the notion that an accomplished, talented author didn't know what he or she was doing in this case or that. On the other hand, the critical scheme seeking and emphasizing final intention depends just as heavily on chronology and on a belief in textual progress, and consequently it may over-value revisions which any sensitive reader will see as tantamount to distortions. We should not grant privileged standing to one stage of a text solely because it is the first or the last in a historical sequence, because history alone does not govern the expression of intention.

The fullest, most important, most valuable expression of authorial intention toward the text of a work occurs—if indeed it occurs on a single occasion at all—when: (1) the author is working at maximum concentration on the accurate preparation of a written or printed text; (2) the author is most interested in and capable of governing the presentational features of the work, such as spelling, punctuation, chapter arrangement and length, stanza indentation, and so on; (3) the author is most free from external compulsion or limitation as to how the work will read; (4) the author is bent on perfecting and finishing the work at hand, not on changing it into another work; and (5) the author has the maximum control over the outcome of the labor, the text which will be produced. An alert and imaginative scholar, given sufficient surviving documents, diligent research, and sound bibliographical knowledge, will be able to see these conditions when they obtain. In most cases, this full and intense effort will be signaled by numerous textual variants.

A given iteration of a text may well meet some of these criteria and not others; most manuscripts, for instance, rate high in terms of authorial freedom, but proofs and revises will be worked over before the first printed edition is produced. An intermediate revised edition may represent an author's most concentrated review of a particular work as a whole, but the degree of alteration possible may have been constrained by printing and publishing limitations. At the time of a final collected edition, an author may have been constrained by printing and publishing limitations. At the time of a final collected edition, an author may have absolute command over what the works will say, but lack the stamina for an exhaustive revision. The situation will vary from author to author and from age to age, but the object of the scholar's labors does not vary. The textual critic seeks that text which most fully embodies the author's best, most complete, most successful effort to get the work right, even if that effort occurred years after the work was created, even if the author's taste and judgment differ from ours, and even when the author revised further (if less successfully) in later editions.

To a scholar working on these lines, all iterations of a text which an author worked on are of primary interest, and any one of them may emerge as the representation of the author's maximum concentration and control. This approach properly respects an author's proprietary rights over a text, while not necessarily taking all authorial revisions as "improvements." Instead of beginning with a model of textual change as disintegrative corruption or evolutionary progress, this last view emphasizes the recoverable and inferential history of the individual text and author; it does not employ an *a priori* notion about which text ought to be superior. Perhaps, since textual criticism depends on textual history, we should accept gracefully some of the axioms and limitations of the historian and dispense with this kind of judgment. No competent historian is likely to argue seriously that the events of one year or decade are superior to another, or that one era is preferable to an earlier one; such terms are practically nonsensical.

In the study of the arts, of course, we make a little more room for pleasure, taste, and systematic aesthetic judgment. An art historian might find the finished version of Turner's "Rain, Steam, and Speed" indeed superior to the sketches that preceded it and by this would mean not so much that the sketches were faulty, but that the finished painting manifests the artist's most concentrated attempt to get the thing right, to control every brush-stroke and swipe of the knife, to leave nothing undone that lay within his power to execute his idea. Turner "published," as it were, his finished painting in 1844; he did not publish his sketches, interesting though they might be. I think that multiple, revised texts of a literary work can be sorted out on such bases as these. Presented with the whole intricate textual history of a work and all its revisions and alterations, we can, with diligent enough research, answer the questions: "Which texts did the author publish? Which of these did the author concentrate on the most? Which one did the author control most completely? Was the author attentive and meticulous at the time? Was the author revising freely, without compulsion or limitation? Was the aim to finish and perfect the work, not to turn it into another work?" We can find that text which most fully embodies the author's best and most successful effort to make the work come out right: that text we can fairly declare "superior." But it may be neither the earliest text nor the final one, and it may not always be the one endorsing "the sense most to our mind," in Browning's phrase.

Because nineteenth-century printing technology multiplied the stages of textual development and expanded the opportunities for both authorial control, it also increased the burdens of the modern textual scholar. The longer the history of a work's text, the more successful the career of its author, the more editions and documents there are to be collated and sifted for variants. Concealed impressions are the rule with stereotyped editions, and any impression may contain important authorial changes to the text. Careful scholars have long taken each individual impression (whether acknowledged or concealed) as a discrete stage in the history of a typesetting. Within an impression an editor must be alert for "stop-press" corrections, but it has been a conventional belief that the rest of the text remained fixed. This assumption, or hope, has been clung to with quiet fervor by past authors and publishers, as well as the scholars who study them. In light of what we know about printing techniques in the age of mechanized type-founding, stereotype plating, and machine printing, this belief must be abandoned. Every time the bed of a printing machine passes under the cylinders, an opportunity for textual alteration occurs: letters and words disappear; punctuation transforms itself; in consequence, grammar, rhetoric, and meaning can be changed. With luck, the Victorian pressman saw the edge of a plate collapse, stopped his machine, and called for a replacement to be cast from the matrix. The next sheet printed off will offer the scholar a text in which the pages printed from the fresh plates revert to the level of press proof and reflect closely what the author approved, while others have decayed away from the intended readings.

Fortunately, twentieth-century technology offers powerful means of dealing with the multiplicity of documents and subtlety of textual changes. The Hinman and Lindstrand collating machines use simple principles of optical comparison to highlight any differences between one exemplar of a typesetting and another; these devices have assisted in proving the use of stereotype plates, detecting concealed impressions from them, and tracking decay and repair of the plates. The combination of optical character recognition systems ("reading machines") with moderately powerful computers has made possible the electronic collation of different typesettings, the output being a highly reliable list of variants culled from multiple editions.

The late twentieth century is proving to be a great age of preservation and restoration in Europe and North America, as a visit to any major city shows. People everywhere strive to preserve old buildings; no sizable art museum is without its conservation expert; the market in antiques expands yearly; the Sistine chapel is renovated; millions of public dollars are spent to stop the disintegration of our library collections, rendered fragile in part by Victorian paper-making practices. Textual scholarship, with its roots reaching back to the Fathers of the Christian church, is one of the oldest and noblest forms of preservation and restoration, and like its kindred enterprises of later date, it has turned to technology to accomplish its task. As with the crumbling of nineteenth-century paper, modern technology can provide a solution only when we understand the previous technology that caused the problem. Our optical scanners and computers will enable us to restore and preserve nineteenth-century texts when we have come to a thorough understanding of how the technology that reproduced them also shaped them.

NOTES

1. This essay is a revised portion of my study of the impact of changing printing technology on nineteenth-century authors, *Author and Printer in Victorian England*, published in 1992 by the University Press of Virginia. I wish to offer my thanks to the Press for permission to publish this material in *Text*, and to ask for the reader's forbearance of any faults resulting from lifting the present discussion out of its original context.

2. *The Complete Works of Robert Browning*, ed. R. A. King et al. (Athens, Ohio, and Waco, Texas: Ohio University Press and Baylor University, 1969–), 3:82, l. 96; 3:351; 5:315, l. 608; 5:356.

3. To the detriment of this ingenious proposition, Austen frequently spelled the word *freind* in letters and in other circumstances where no potential irony is likely. But within the text of this one juvenile work, the seeming error can readily be taken as deliberate. Authors from Plato to Joyce have employed deliberate errors, often at their peril. Thousands of readers have ignored the dramatic framework of Browning's "The Bishop Orders His Tomb at St. Praxed's Church" and pointed out the poet's supposed blunder in line 95, "Saint Prazed at his sermon on the mount." George Eliot once received from an assiduous and admiring reader, William MacIlwaine, a list of the errors he found in *The Spanish Gypsy*; Eliot gently replied to MacIlwaine: "Some of the passages marked by Mr MacIlwaine for revision were deliberately-chosen irregularities." Browning, *Complete Works,* 4:192; *The George Eliot Letters*, ed. Gordon S. Haight, 7 vols. (New Haven and London: Yale Univiversity Press and Oxford University Press, 1954–55), 4:463.

4. *Eliot Letters*, 5:16–17.

5. Browning, *Complete Works*, 5:302.

6. See William Makepeace Thackeray, *Vanity Fair*, ed. Geoffrey and Kathleen Tillotson (Boston: Houghton Mifflin, 1963), xxiii–xxvii; Peter L. Shillingsburg, "Final Touches and Patches in *Vanity Fair*: The First Edition," *Studies in the Novel* 13 (1981): 40–50; idem, "The Printing, Proof-Reading, and Publishing of Thackeray's *Vanity Fair*: The First Edition," *Studies in Bibliography* 34 (1981): 118–45.

7. Henry James, *The Portrait of a Lady*, ed. Robert C. Bamberg (New York: Norton, 1975), vii.

8. *Letters of Robert Browning*, ed. Thurman L. Hood (London: John Murray, 1933), 14.

9. Alexandra [Leighton] Sutherland Orr, *Life and Letters of Robert Browning*, 2d ed. (London: Smith, Elder, 1891), 403–04; Browning, *Complete Works*, 1:9–52.

10. For an overview and discussion of various concepts of authorial intention, see G. Thomas Tanselle, "The Editorial Problem of Final Authorial Intention," *Studies in Bibliography* 29 (1976): 167–211; Hershel Parker, *Flawed Texts and Verbal Icons* (Evanston, Ill.: Northwestern University Press, 1984), chapters 1 and 2; and Jerome J. McGann, *A Critique of Modern Textual Criticism* (Chicago: University of Chicago Press, 1983).

11. Equally, some authors have been—or were said by others to have been, or have themselves claimed to be—indifferent to their writings once the manuscripts had left their hands. Despite the careful proofreading she always did, George Eliot once denied any interest in revision: "I could no more live

through one of my books a second time than I can live through last year again" (*Eliot Letters*, 4:396).

The Edition as Art Form: Social and Authorial Readings of William Cullen Bryant's *Poems*

C. Deirdre Phelps

> To him who in the love of Nature holds
> Communion with her visible forms, she speaks
> A various language. . . . [1] (*fig. 1*)

While the "visible forms" of William Cullen Bryant's "Thanatopsis" are to be found in "Nature," the book forms in which the poem historically appeared are those of culture, which are as various and can be as variously read as those belonging to "Nature." They are subject equally to mood and feeling, and can be described critically, as objects of philosophical and historical understanding. To explore the possibilities and limitations of such readings, I will survey significant examples of the presentation history of Bryant's Poems, with "Thanatopsis" as my example. Not only was Bryant at the center of the professional development of literary and artistic work in nineteenth-century America, but his responses to the linguistic and presentational forms of his work exemplify the potential discrepancy between private/authorial and public/social requirements. The poem is really about space and time itself, and its presentation history demonstrates the relations of those qualities to their embodiment in book form. I consider points of form in relation to both an authorially intended textual presentation and to a non-editorial socio-critical interpretation of particular examples, emphasizing the separate but equal validity of each approach.

My terminology is based on that of G. Thomas Tanselle in *A Rationale of Textual Criticism* and that of Jerome J. McGann, in his review of D. F. McKenzie's work.[2] Tanselle's use of "work" for the intangible meaning, conceptually unembodied in any one particular form, is adopted here. In McGann's schema, variant physical forms are referred to as "versions," and I use that terminology (in reference to specific documentary versions) because of its inclusion of the idea of difference from other forms of the same category, as opposed to Tanselle's "instructions," which serves mainly to distinguish any single example from that opposite concept of "work." I will use "text" only in reference to the typography representing the work in any given physical form, as one component within a version. It is useful thereby to separate it from non-linguistic visual forms, in which I include typographical ornament, illustration, spatial arrangement (or layout, or *mise en page*), format, and binding.[3]

In September of 1817 "Thanatopsis" appeared for the first time in print in the *North American Review* (*fig. 2*), with a second poem erroneously printed as its opening and without fifteen additional lines of the ending as we now know it, offering nevertheless a contemplative break from denser matter. The manuscript page shown, composed between the poem's first printing and first book publication, illustrates some of Bryant's frequent early reworking of it, which, as Tremaine McDowell's critical examination showed in 1937, suggested some conflict with his celebration of poetic inspiration. Bryant himself worried that some of the revision was at the expense of the poetry, but as McDowell concludes, the changes are consistent with the initial intention for the poem and often in fact strengthen it. Furthermore, the changing physical forms in which one poem appears parallel the textual revisions they embody.[4] The physical book and the order it brought to Bryant's work were part of the romantic attempt to discover the order of Nature, to make sense of its vastness and of the feelings of death, loneliness, and humility it could engender. But his editions also confirm his seminal position as the foremost American poet and central figure in an extensive network of journalism, art, publishing, and other social and political interests.

In 1821, as a young barrister in the Berkshires whose poetry and other work had already been making his reputation, Bryant was invited to Cambridge to give the Phi Beta Kappa address, for which he wrote the poem "The Ages" in thirty-five Spenserian stanzas. With the help of the *North American Review* editors, including his friend Richard Henry Dana, Sr., the poem was printed with others by Hilliard and Metcalf (*fig. 3*). As William Charvat pointed out,

> That [Bryant] had [his *Poems* of 1821] printed in Cambridge was prophetic,
> for Cambridge skill in poetry printing was to lead to a country-wide convic-
> tion within the next thirty years that in no other place could printers set up a
> page of poetry properly, and that only in Boston could poetry be published
> with adequate dignity and prestige.[5]

But Charvat also refers to the volume as professional poetry's "in-
auspicious beginning" in America, certainly in part because of its
rather rough unfinished appearance, which perhaps mirrored the
incipience of Bryant's own career. Much later, in "The Poet," he
described the creative experience of his original period of composition as "the dark power" that stole over him, "though artless and
rude." The darkness of his romantic vision was represented in the
title, with "POEMS" in large capitals in a combination outline/
shadow font that was repeated on separate poem subtitle pages.
The capitals throughout the title page, the spacing, the finality of
the periods after each title, and the heavy black inking all contribute to an inscriptional memorial effect, emphasized more when
printed on brown paper wrappers, with an added box rule, which in
some further copies was pasted over boards and stiffened.[6]

Here, for the first and last time, "Thanatopsis," the meditation
on death, appears at the end of the volume, succeeded appropriately by the nothingness of a final blank. Its invocational tone fits the
presentation's typographical reference to seventeenth-century
tracts, and here we first have the strong opening reference to an
expected darkness. But while death is composed of "pale realms of
shade" suggested by the type, it is also modified through faith and
trust, and the contrast of light and dark also figures Bryant's idea of
Nature's "various language"—both fearful and benevolent.[7] The
framing of the poem by its title page with shaded type on the white
field and the final blank also suggests the final enjoinder to the
poet to "lie down to pleasant dreams" as he "wraps the drapery of
his couch/ About him" (lines 80–81); the poem is wrapped or
couched in the white space around the text. The movement of ideas
in the poem from the view of the natural scene through reflection,
conflict, mediation, and resolution is emphasized too as the poem is
spread over several pages. As D. F. McKenzie has suggested, type
and layout in effect transform all poetry into concrete poetry, and
all type figures the work it represents.[8]

Nicolas Barker has shown how the simple style and plain boxed border suitable for the small sheet size of the seventeenth century in England (and of course in America) gave way to what he calls the "unconstricted vigour" of eighteenth-century title pages, where perhaps an inserted typographical ornament will coordinate with a pleasantly proportioned text arrangement that as a whole radiates out from the center rather than in from a border. And Hugh Amory equates the new openness in the typography of Fielding's works with the author's good nature and the Enlightenment itself. In America, with more limited printing facilities, it is easier to see that transition taking place in the romantic context of the nineteenth century, where it results from the continuous cultural dialectic of which books are the seminal agents. The open eighteenth-century style met new cultural concepts that were forced to assimilate it, and their intensity shaped the reading of books by transforming their design as it did the literature contained within it.[9]

In 1832, with Bryant now resident in New York and editor of *The Evening Post*, an augmented collection of his poems appeared in London with Washington Irving's help, followed by American editions in New York and Boston. By 1836 Bryant, already well established among and honored by the New York literati, arranged with Harper's to turn out a fourth edition that included the first illustration to accompany the *Poems* in a separate printing—a vignette by Robert F. Weir on an engraved title page (*fig. 4*).

With artist friends like Durand, Morse, Dunlap, Weir, and Cole, Bryant was deeply involved in promoting literary as well as artistic professionalism through associations like the American Art-Union and the Sketch Club. Some of his poems had already been illustrated in book form, in particular in *The Talisman*, the pioneering miscellany he undertook with Robert Sands and Gulian Verplanck in the late 1820s. He was certainly sensitive to its physical form, writing to friends that it was "beautifully printed and embellished."[10]

According to Ralph Thompson, *The Talisman* was the second American gift book, and "in some ways the best" of them.[11] It used paintings from the collections of New York merchants engraved by local artists as well as original work. Bryant explained the difference in conception from those "regarded as a kind of New years toy." *The Talisman* was to be more of a small *Sketch Book* or *Salmagundi* with plates. His sensitivity to presentation was also apparent when he enthusiastically wrote to Verplanck of an annual planned by the Sketch Club in 1832 that it would have a "splendid" appearance, with "six copper plate engravings of larger size than is common in the American annuals—and several more cuts by Mason for head and tailpieces. The book is to have a larger page than any other of our Annuals, and but half the matter."[12]

In May of 1836 Bryant wrote Weir to suggest the scene to accompany the quote from his "Inscription for the Entrance to a Wood": "I have thought that an opening into a thick wood, with a human figure retiring up the avenue, and an old tree or two uprooted, with some other accessories suggested by the poem, would do."[13] An engraving of Weir's painting of the "View of Hudson Highlands from the West Point" was just then circulating in the current number of the *New-York Mirror*, and in July during a visit to Weir Bryant described a similar scene as they rode horseback through the woods to a mountain lake:

> We stood on a steep precipice several hundred feet above it— the rocks about us were black as ink with a peculiar kind of moss; and were crowned with rough looking pitch pine trees full of large cones and black as the rocks; below us lay the lake, quiet and glassy . . .[14]

Weir's title vignette for Bryant's *Poems* maintains this sense of darkness from the natural scenery, and the edition quite successfully evokes the dark spirit in Bryant's work. Engraving at this period is invested with a darkness that matches the accompanying typography well, and Weir renders both the "vraisemblance" and "chiaroscuro" of the poetry itself. The "pale realms of shade" in the poem's text has now been changed to the more Romantic phrasing of "that mysterious realm."[15]

The typography now shows a far greater control in both proportion and workmanship. Harper's stereotyping has rendered a clean, dark impression on a crisp, parchment-textured paper in a type size more commensurate with the format. Bryant himself announced in a letter that he found this edition "better printed" than the previous one.[16] Perhaps even "nature" could be said to be more controlled in it, since in the opening line it is now uncapitalized. As he would with almost every edition, Bryant added a number of poems and included the notes he first compiled for the 1832 edition, although during his lifetime there was never one for "Thanatopsis."

The idea of the stereotype and its repeated images certainly correlates here with the French word for the process, *clicher*, and the related *cliché*, since through Harper's extensive distribution system, their repeated editions made Bryant's work so widely popular that it became the standard representation of American romantic poetry.[17]

Lest these comparisons seem too baldly associative, we should remember the importance of romantic associationist philosophy to Bryant in his own view of nature's forms. Whereas Jonathan Edwards had used objects in his typology so that "words were obliged to stand in the place of engendering objects," in Bryant they are now engendering objects themselves.[18] An extreme modern example is the generative fiction of the French novelist Jean Ricardou, in which his own title-page words and typography are the source for his plot and characters.[19] But just as all type forms are concrete, so are they all generative. Consciously or unconsciously, the mind of the reader responds to their shape, color, and arrangement.

This careful mechanical product of 1836 might seem to lend itself to a Marxist reading as a reification of a bourgeois ideal, but the contribution of the accompanying art to the organic aesthetic form of the text marks it rather as the professionalization of the romantic vision through its immersion in the market—one that in its assertion of Bryant's status would later allow him to reject the excess of later editions. A mechanical devaluation was something he would identify in the next important presentation of the *Poems*, Carey and Hart's media event of 1847.

Book forms by themselves fit neither the Whig myth of progressive improvement (as final authorial intentions are sometimes associated with) nor Walter Benjamin's idea of reproductive degeneration (which Hershel Parker applies to texts).[20] But while each form, early or late, has its own individual circumstantial integrity, it cannot help but support or detract from the way we read the state of the text. Disparaged for its "outward garnish of mechanical elegance," this edition came to appear rather as a commercial stain on the purity of Bryant's work, and detractors might also say that it matched what was now becoming the rather mechanical feel of his later poems.[21] The large and thick octavo volume was advertised as

> Bryant's Poems, illustrated by Twenty Superb Engravings, from designs by E. Leutze expressly for this volume, engraved by American Artists, and printed on fine vellum Paper . . . Price $5.00 bound in scarlet, gilt edges; or Beautifully Bound by S. Moore in calf or Turkey Morocco, $7.00.[22]

Figures 5 and 6 show the third edition, in the "Turkey Morocco" binding, which identified it with the similar volumes in the publisher's

"Illustrated Poets" series. In this way the poet's identity begins to be incorporated with that of the publisher, as when in the first edition of *Moby-Dick* Harper's name was stamped inside the shape of a life-preserver on the cover.[23] It also coordinated with Carey and Hart's presentation of Griswold's anthology of 1842, in which Bryant's poems had appeared. Such editions now helped to canonize the poet, reinforcing his identification with the aesthetic, moral, and democratic mission Alan Golding locates in the earlier anthologies in which he had appeared, such as Kettell's *Specimens of the American Poets* and Cheever's *American Common-Place Book of Poetry* of 1831.[24]

This new extravagance in the *Poems* for the first time enshrined them within a sequence of accoutrements of opening plate, engraved illustrated title, typographic title, and address "To the Reader," contents, detailed list of illustrations and engravers, author portrait, 344 pages of text and plates, fourteen pages of notes, and often several pages of publisher's advertisements, each page enclosed in a box rule which, while meant to unify the book, separated even sections of poems from each other. The long primer type of the text might also pose a problem of both "perspectivism" and "textualism," as Hugh Amory terms the typography's relations to format and content.[25] The octavo size of the volume would more naturally require a pica type. Although necessitated by length and bulk and made to seem more appropriate by the generous leading and the duodecimo illusion of the box rules, the relatively small type within them can only suggest an unsuitable constraint on the poetry itself. As professional as the engravings were, the overall impression was one of polished greyness. The series format might be equated with editorial normalizing, limiting the individuality of the text, and imposing on it implicit commentary less intended by the author than elicited by the market it served. William Spengemann has noted that the canonical emphasis in American literature also shares the faults of the Whig myth, so that works preceding mid-nineteenth century high points are read inadequately if seen only as cruder forms on the road to their realization.[26] By analogy this more "advanced" physical form in fact accentuates the integrity of the earlier ones.

In its imposition of society's technical development on his art, this edition's production parallels Bryant's own liberal theme of progress as divided between aesthetics and social advancement. The mechanical idea with its heavy dependence on illustration suggests faith in the kind of Macaulayan Whig myth dependent on a pictorial cultural view—the optimism of a new pictorial narrative and the artistic panorama. Bryant equated the national democratic expansionist faith in the frontier with a panorama of it when he toured it and wrote "The Prairies," and the expansion of sales networks for books became part of that vision.

In then contemporary social philosophy, where the purity of nature was to improve degenerate manners and morals, the presentation of those ideas and their mass production in highly finished form should promote the same lesson, even as its embellishments would appeal to those ambitious to acquire evidence of their personal status. Even if the physical book was a product of circumstances that artists of the period were attempting to cancel—the decadence and monotony of commerce and cities—it successfully conveyed the idealistic message.[27] Just as they saw nature offering the continual renewal that cities could not, so the book form both perpetuated their saving views of nature and was a metaphor for that renewal, as works shed the forms of earlier editions to take on new ones. At the same time, in a period of fragmentation and dangerous sectarianism in religion, where Bryant's poem has a social role to play in its calming statement of belief on the border of the transcendental, so its mechanicalizing serves to reinforce that social restraint.[28]

Bryant had looked forward to the edition, responding when first approached about it that he was sure "the publication would be got up in the best manner, I should be glad to see what I have written given to the world in such a form. . . ."[29] But the results were disappointing, as he wrote Dana:

> I grow fastidious in regards to illustrations; there is scarcely one in a score, in the books of poetry that I take up which does not displease me. I have seen eight of those intended for my book and with one or two exceptions cannot say I take much delight in them. . . . I think very well of the talents of Leutze who makes the designs, but what can be expected of an artist who works to order in that way? What sort of verses should I make if I were to sit down to put his pictures into verse? Worse than I make now I fear.[30]

In fact Bryant's generative associationist ideas about nature necessarily extended to the pictorial representation of it he saw. But Leutze, known for his *Washington Crossing the Delaware*, was the kind of artist who would be praised for his "rationality and industry," who displayed no "undue amount of imagination" or susceptibility to "fancy."[31] Apparently Bryant also found the typographic design objectionable, since having reluctantly agreed to a simple edition from Carey and Hart, he wrote Dana, "they have published them in a cheap form, a duodecimo volume, the engravings left out and the black lines taken off, and it is an ugly book after all."[32]

What was successful, however, was the author's portrait by S. W. Cheney (*fig. 6*), and when Bryant had posed for it, he said he thought it would be "the best thing in the book."[33] A later writer likened the "graceful and delicate head . . . in which taste and sensitiveness are legible at a glance" to portraits by Rubens—as seems apt if we think of Rubens' book illustrations for the Plantin-Moretus Press. Cheney's brother John, who engraved the portrait, had himself been called by a contemporary "the best engraver of the female head in America" for his combined restraint and delicacy, based in part on the work he had done for Bryant's *Talisman*.[34] Bryant's portraits exemplify E. H. Gombrich's concept of the perceptual mask, which he correlates with Aristotelian accidents of momentary modification of a person's substance:[35] we see the substantive author in momentary or accidental form, in each of what are also momentary forms of the work—that is, in each version. This more mechanical version might be commensurate not only with the restraint imposed on the romantic imagination itself by all real forms, but with Bryant's own character as well. In spite of his celebration of poetic spontaneity and his general sociability, the temperament Lowell characterized as "ice-olation" in "A Fable for Critics" was one of quiet dignity, balance, and restraint.[36] And when Bryant later recovered his rights and consigned the next issues of his poems to Appleton, he stipulated an unillustrated edition, the plain, open, and modest two-volume edition of 1855, in brown publisher's cloth, which best expresses the idea of contemplative space in his work (*fig. 7*).

In this century, André Maurois commented on the eminent suitability of the *mise en page* of Proust's work as it appeared in the *Nouvelle Revue Française*, where he found that the "massive paragraphs of lengthy lines . . . filled with characters . . . prepare the reader's mind for their wealth of subject matter, so that just like Proust's bedroom, his masterpiece lacked air."[37] If we can say that the massing of type lends itself to density of narration, wide margins, extra leading, and the space around uneven lines in poetry leave us room to think. Here, with the deep sinkage of the poem openings and the delicate open type on the thicker yet lightweight wove paper, the entire effect is one of space and air that allows for the mental liberation of the "panorama of the mind," as James T. Callow calls it, that appears in "Thanatopsis," where the poet soars freely into the past and the future, or in the "illimitable air" of "To A Waterfowl." As Donald Ringe has shown, in "Thanatopsis" the poet alternates from the expanse of historical time, as with his "hoary seers of ages past," to an earthly spatial description that could be as local as the Berkshires, and then back to a continental and even cosmic immensity.[38] So, as the eye moves from the "local" area of the poem into the expanse around it, the fixed type seems to function as nature's "still voice" (line 17) with "the vales/ Stretching in pensive quietness between" (lines 38–39).

W. J. T. Mitchell cites Wendy Steiner's idea of an ekphrastic poem like the "Ode on a Grecian Urn" that in content suggests that art overcomes time while in form is prevented from doing so because it is organized linearly and temporally. He focuses on the ways space is evoked by poetic language itself, noting as well that its material written existence is spatial. If the poem's whole concrete form is included, it can then appear to challenge time in form as well as in content.[39] "Thanatopsis" itself becomes successful in these ways: it is a portrait of the artist seeking through a "picture" of nature a resolution to the problem posed by the inevitability of his personal extinction in time, while seeking a perpetuation of his art in its concrete as well as its linguistic form.

The contemporary interest for nineteenth-century artists and writers in the vastness of native scenery often positioned the viewer so as give him a perspective from which he could see the broad sweep of life. But while artists were only occasionally able to suggest the passage of time successfully (as Cole did in *Course of Empire*), the spatial form of the book itself in its progression of pages offered an historical foreshortening that allowed the reader to survey days, centuries, or even infinity within the space between two covers. Space in a text, then, can be as effective as pictorial representation. As Ronald Paulson found with Keynes's facsimile of Blake's *Songs*, where the words are separated and placed opposite their illuminated settings (in which they can seem cramped), they "expand to fill the empty space with their energy" of connotation and context.[40]

In spite of his reservations, Bryant had acquiesced in Appleton's production of an illustrated issue of his poems, which eventually appeared in a large format. The publisher also offered an unillustrated single volume small format, and with all of these available in a variety of bindings, the public as well as the author was confronted with a potentially disjunctive view of the work. The illustrated edition announced on the title its "Seventy-one Engravings from Drawings by Eminent Artists" (engraved by the Brothers Dalziel), most of whom were British. Bryant found that they had failed as much as Leutze to realize the Americanness of the landscape and the sensibility of his poems. He had already written to Dana:

> As to my poems with illustrations; that is an idea of my bookseller's. There is, I suppose, a class of readers—at least of book-buyers, who like things of that kind; but the first thing which my bookseller—it is Appleton's—has promised to do, is to get out a neat edition of my poems in two volumes *without* illustrations. The illustrated edition is a subsequent affair, and though I have as great a horror of illustrations as you have, they will I hope hurt nobody. I am not even sure that I will look at them myself.[41]

This was in part a formula, since he often used similar terms about his poetry: "I hope, at least," he wrote in 1864, "that my verses, if they have done no good, have been the occasion of no mischief to any of my fellow creatures."[42] Regardless of his feelings, the repeated appearance of these illustrations over many editions would render them almost inseparable from the poetry in the perception of many readers.

The non-British artists in this edition in fact included Durand, for whom Bryant was at this same time expressing his fervent admiration. Comparing him with Cole, Bryant wrote that he "seems to love art more for her own sake. . . . Durand, in general, imitates nature with truest paint. . . . If I were to be asked what other painter in that department I would prefer to Durand, I should say—no one."[43] But for his two contributions, for "Green River" and "Monument Mountain," Durand actually supplied only sketches that were then fully drawn by Birket Foster and later engraved. The more successful of the other illustrations might include the one for "To A Waterfoul" (by William Harvey), especially since the poem itself is so graphic.

By this time Bryant's artist friends had often painted scenes from his poems, and "Thanatopsis" had already been a subject for Durand (*fig. 10*) when Appleton finally included an illustration for it in their 1876 edition (*fig. 8*), now advertising the poems as "Illustrated with One Hundred Engravings from drawings by Birket Foster, Harry Fenn, Alfred Fredericks, and Others."[44] The author's portrait in the volume has now become the familiar bearded one, which seems to be connected with the figure in the landscape of the "Thanatopsis" illustration by Fenn. It also recalls an early drawing of Bryant's own (*fig. 9*) and evokes as well the "gray-headed man" (line 70) who is gathered to death with the poet and who first appeared in Bryant's manuscript about the time his drawing was done.

Bryant's art criticism showed his admiration for the softening effects of shadow in the paintings of Cole and others, and W. S. Mount recorded that in his painting of "Thanatopsis" Durand had aimed for repose, so that objects in shadows were to be flat to create an effect of distance, as engraved illustrations require (*fig. 10*). Although a Durand painting might for Bryant better represent his work by adding depth and shadow, perception theory also explains that what is most characteristic about an image is often rendered more clearly in line than with detail, as a caricature, for example, reduces a figure to its essentials.[45]

What is significant about the insertion of many of these illustrations within the text is the romantic unity of art and text realized by the vignette, which

> presents itself both as a global metaphor for the world and as a fragment. Dense at its center, tenuous on the periphery, it seems to disappear into the page: this makes it a naive but powerful metaphor of the infinite, a symbol of the universe; at the same time, the vignette is fragmentary, sometimes even minute in scale, incomplete, mostly dependent upon the text for its meaning, with irregular and ill-defined edges. . . . It is the perfect Romantic formula, not unlike Schlegel's hedgehog.[46]

Its advantages had been recognized by Poe, one of Bryant's greatest admirers, who in his attempts to establish his *Penn Magazine* in Philadelphia in 1840 and 1841 specified that he would have "no engravings, except occasional wood-cuts . . . and when so required, they will be worked in with the type—not upon separate pages as in Arcturus."[47] Such a treatment had been initiated with the 1836 title vignette carrying a quotation below it, and there had occasionally been others, such as in John Keese's anthology of 1840, where the illustrator was Bryant's friend John G. Chapman and the poem "Green River," for instance, was broken up with his line engravings.[48]

Ann C. Colley's idea that space paradoxically both separates and connects people and objects, in literature and art, certainly applies to the space between text and vignette.[49] Rosen and Zerner cite a Bewick example of the two-part vignette, a dog below baying at a moon above with only blank page space to represent the intervening air, demonstrating the extension of space into the page where it may encounter other inked forms, including type.[50] The tentativeness of such an illustration thus renders it in the same position in relation to the whole book as the dwarfed figure has in the illustration. Its perspective accents the sublime but is not the major statement of it. "Thanatopsis" may be better served by that emphasis than Bryant's other poems, where the poet remains the speaker. Here the poet is silent for much of the time: Nature herself provides the lesson, and Nature's dominance in the art is appropriate.

As in Cole's or Durand's paintings, the figure dwarfed by the landscape remains in a position of safety from which only reason and imagination can resolve the immensity suggested by the canvas's unbounded margins. Bryan Jay Wolf finds the sublime used as a reinvention of "older systems of meaning" in which the artist's own struggle with past forms resolves into a beauty of harmony.[51] Bryant's poem also uses these "older systems of meaning," both for his subject and his formal verse articulation of it, in order to work through the question and resolve it within the natural scene, which he never in fact leaves. These older systems, which Donald Pease refers to as a "cultural reserve" of persons and forms from the past that are awaiting "renewal or activation" in order to establish a "visionary compact" or sense of community among writers and readers, are recreated as well in book forms, which draw on their own "cultural reserve."[52]

A better illustration style for Bryant, then, was one that integrated pictorial suggestion with typography. In the late seventies and eighties, the vogue years of portfolios such as F. O. C. Darley's 1879 *Scarlet Letter* for the Riverside Press, when the new-school wood engravers were providing suites of carefully delineated and photographically toned prints of literary scenes, Bryant's interpreter in a portfolio for Putnam's was fortunately W. J. Linton, who, while admitting the importance of tone and shadow, adamantly defended "old-school" expressiveness in wood-engraving, discoverable in what he called "the intention of the lines." His rather Blakean illustrations also appeared in Putnam's issue of "Thanatopsis" alone,

THANATOPSIS

To him who in the love of Nature holds
Communion with her visible forms, she speaks
A various language; for his gayer hours
She has a voice of gladness, and a smile
And eloquence of beauty, and she glides
Into his darker musings, with a mild
And healing sympathy, that steals away
Their sharpness, ere he is aware. When thoughts
Of the last bitter hour come like a blight
Over thy spirit, and sad images   10
Of the stern agony, and shroud, and pall,
And breathless darkness, and the narrow house,
Make thee to shudder, and grow sick at heart;—
Go forth, under the open sky, and list
To Nature's teachings, while from all around—
Earth and her waters, and the depths of air—
Comes a still voice—Yet a few days, and thee
The all-beholding sun shall see no more
In all his course; nor yet in the cold ground,
Where thy pale form was laid, with many tears,   20
Nor in the embrace of ocean, shall exist
Thy image. Earth, that nourished thee, shall claim
Thy growth, to be resolved to earth again,
And, lost each human trace, surrendering up
Thine individual being, shalt thou go
To mix for ever with the elements,
To be a brother to the insensible rock
And to the sluggish clod, which the rude swain
Turns with his share, and treads upon. The oak
Shall send his roots abroad, and pierce thy mould.   30

Yet not to thine eternal resting-place
Shalt thou retire alone, nor couldst rhou wish
Couch more magnificent. Thou shalt lie down
With patriarchs of the infant world—with kings,
The powerful of the earth—the wise, the good,
Fair forms, and hoary seers of ages past,
All in one mighty sepulchre. The hills
Rock-ribbed and ancient as the sun,—the vales
Stretching in pensive quietness between;
The venerable woods—rivers that move   40

Fig. 1 All items illustrated and not otherwise credited are
        from the collection of the author.

In majesty, and the complaining brooks
That make the meadows green; and, poured round all,
Old Ocean's gray and melancholy waste,—
Are but the solemn decorations all
Of the great tomb of man. The golden sun,
The planets, all the infinite host of heaven,
Are shining on the sad abodes of death,
Through the still lapse of ages. All that tread
The globe are but a handful to the tribes
That slumber in its bosom.—Take the wings   50
Of morning, pierce the Barcan wilderness,
Or lose thyself in the continuous woods
Where rolls the Oregon, and hears no sound,
Save his own dashings—yet the dead are there:
And millions in those solitudes, since first
The flight of years began, have laid them down
In their last sleep—the dead reign there alone.
So shalt thou rest, and what if thou withdraw
In silence from the living, and no friend
Take note of thy departure? All that breathe   60
Will share thy destiny. The gay will laugh
When thou art gone, the solemn brood of care
Plod on, and each one as before will chase
His favorite phantom; yet all these shall leave
Their mirth and their employments, and shall come
And make their bed with thee. As the long train
Of ages glide away, the sons of men,
The youth in life's green spring, and he who goes
In the full strength of years, matron and maid,
The speechless babe, and the gray-headed man—   70
Shall one by one be gathered to thy side,
By those, who in their turn shall follow them.

    So live, that when thy summons comes to join
The innumerable caravan, which moves
To that mysterious realm, where each shall take
His chamber in the silent halls of death,
Thou go not, like the quarry-slave at night,
Scourged to his dungeon, but, sustained and soothed
By an unfaltering trust, approach thy grave,
Like one who wraps the drapery of his couch   80
About him, and lies down to pleasant dreams.

His harm to compass, and his good oppose ?
No ; one alone, the hapless being spares,
Wages no war, and no resistance dares.
    Yes, earth, kind earth, her new-born son beholds,
Spreads a soft shelter, in her robe enfolds,
Still, like a mother kind, her love retains,
Cheers by her sweetness, with her food sustains,
Paints her fair flow'rs to wake his infant smile,
Spreads out her fruits to sooth his hour of toil,
Renews her prospects, versatile and gay,
To charm his eye, and cheat his cares away,
And if her roseate buds, a thorn conceal,
If some sharp sting the roving hand should feel,
A med'cine kind, the sweet physician sends,
And where her poison wounds, her balm defends.

    But when, at last, her drooping charge declines,
When the dear lamp of life no longer shines,
When o'er its broken idol, friendship mourns,
And love, in horrour, from its object turns,
E'en while affection shudders, as it grieves,
She to her arms, her mould'ring son receives,
Sings a low requiem, to her darling birth,
' Return ! thou lov'd one, to thy parent earth.'
Safe in her bosom, the deposit keeps,
Until the flame that dries the watery deeps,
Spreads o'er the parching skies its quenchless blaze,
Reddens her features, on her vitals preys.
Then struggling in her last, convulsive throes,
She wakes her treasure from his deep repose,
Stays her last groan, amid dissolving fires,
Resigns him to his Maker, and expires.

In Bryant

Thanatopsis.

Not that from life, and all its woes
The hand of death shall set me free ;
Not that this head, shall then repose
In the low vale most peacefully.

Ah, when I touch time's farthest brink,
A kinder solace must attend ;
It chills my very soul, to think
On that dread hour when life must end.

In vain the flatt'ring verse may breathe,
Of ease from pain, and rest from strife.

There is a sacred dread of death
Inwoven with the strings of life.

This bitter cup at first was given
When angry *justice* frown'd severe,
And 'tis th' eternal doom of heaven
That man must view the grave with fear.

———————— Yet a few days, and thee,
The all-beholding sun, shall see no more,
In all his course ; nor yet in the cold ground,
Where thy pale form was laid, with many tears,
Nor in th' embrace of ocean shall exist
Thy image. Earth, that nourished thee, shall claim
Thy growth, to be resolv'd to earth again ;
And, lost each human trace, surrend'ring up
Thine individual being, shalt thou go
To mix forever with the elements,
To be a brother to th' insensible rock
And to the sluggish clod, which the rude swain
Turns with his share, and treads upon. The oak
Shall send his roots abroad, and pierce thy mould.
Yet not to thy eternal resting place
Shalt thou retire alone—nor couldst thou wish
Couch more magnificent. Thou shalt lie down
With patriarchs of the infant world—with kings
The powerful of the earth—the wise, the good,
Fair forms, and hoary seers of ages past,
All in one mighty sepulchre.—The hills,
Rock-ribb'd and ancient as the sun,—the vales
Stretching in pensive quietness between ;
The venerable woods—the floods that move
In majesty,—and the complaining brooks,
That wind among the meads, and make them green.
Are but the solemn decorations all,
Of the great tomb of man.—The golden sun,
The planets, all the infinite host of heaven
Are glowing on the sad abodes of death,
Through the still lapse of ages. All that tread
The globe are but a handful to the tribes
That slumber in its bosom.—Take the wings
Of morning—and the Borean desert pierce—
Or lose thyself in the continuous woods
That veil Oregan, where he hears no sound
Save his own dashings—yet—the dead are there,
And millions in those solitudes, since first

Fig. 2   New York Public Library Manuscripts Division

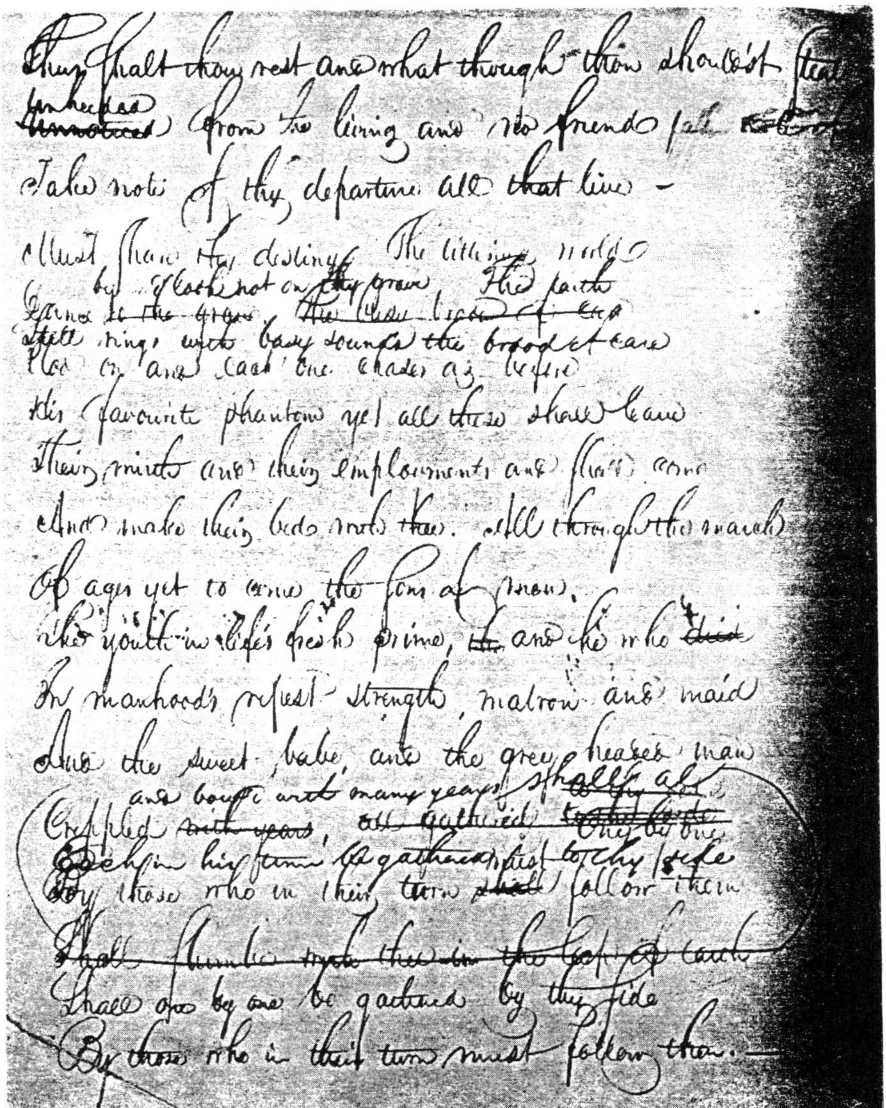

Thus shalt thou rest and what though thou shouldst steal
Unheeded from the living and no friend
Take note of thy departure all that live
Must share thy destiny. The
Looks not on thy grave. The earth
Still rings with busy sounds the brood of care
Plod on and each one chases as before
His favourite phantom yet all these shall leave
Their mirth and their employments and shall come
And make their beds with thee. All through the march
Of ages yet to come the sons of men,
The youth in life's fresh prime, and he who
In manhood's ripest strength, matron and maid
And the sweet babe, and the grey headed man
Crippled
Each in his turn be gathered to thy side
By those who in their turn follow them
Shall one by one be gathered by thy side
By those who in their turn must follow them.

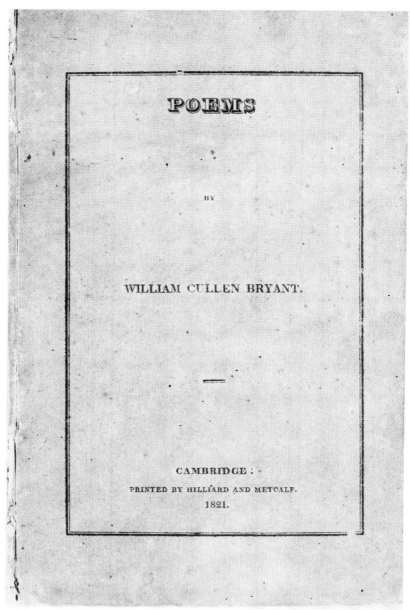

Fig. 3   Massachusetts Historical Society

POEMS

BY

WILLIAM CULLEN BRYANT.

CAMBRIDGE:
PRINTED BY HILLIARD AND METCALF.
1821.

THANATOPSIS.

To him who in the love of Nature holds
Communion with her visible forms, she speaks
A various language ; for his gayer hours
She has a voice of gladness, and a smile
And eloquence of beauty, and she glides
Into his darker musings, with a mild
And gentle sympathy, that steals away
Their sharpness, ere he is aware.   When thoughts
Of the last bitter hour come like a blight
Over thy spirit, and sad images
Of the stern agony, and shroud, and pall,
And breathless darkness, and the narrow house,
Make thee to shudder, and grow sick at heart ;—
Go forth under the open sky, and list
To Nature's teachings, while from all around—
Earth and her waters, and the depths of air,—
Comes a still voice—Yet a few days, and thee
The all-beholding sun shall see no more
In all his course ; nor yet in the cold ground,

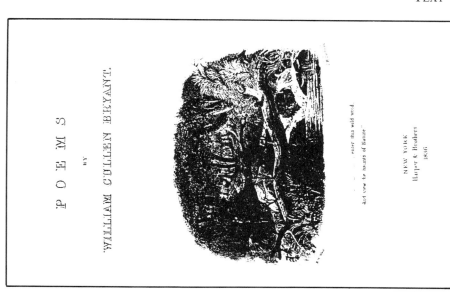

POEMS

BY

WILLIAM CULLEN BRYANT.

enter this wild wood
And view the haunts of Nature

NEW-YORK
Harper & Brothers
1836

Fig. 4

POEMS

BY

WILLIAM CULLEN BRYANT.

FOURTH EDITION.

NEW-YORK:

HARPER & BROTHERS, CLIFF-ST.

1836.

30   TO THE PAST.

They have not perished—no !
Kind words, remembered voices once so sweet,
      Smiles, radiant long ago,
And features, the great soul's apparent seat ;

      All shall come back, each tie
Of pure affection shall be knit again ;
      Alone shall Evil die,
And Sorrow dwell a prisoner in thy reign.

      And then shall I behold
Him, by whose kind paternal side I sprung,
      And her, who, still and cold,
Fills the next grave—the beautiful and young.

THANATOPSIS.

———

To him who in the love of nature holds
Communion with her visible forms, she speaks.
A various language ; for his gayer hours
She has a voice of gladness, and a smile
And eloquence of beauty, and she glides
Into his darker musings, with a mild
And healing sympathy, that steals away
Their sharpness, ere he is aware.   When thoughts
Of the last bitter hour come like a blight
Over thy spirit, and sad images
Of the stern agony, and shroud, and pall,
And breathless darkness, and the narrow house,
Make thee to shudder, and grow sick at heart ;—
Go forth, under the open sky, and list
To Nature's teachings, while from all around—
Earth and her waters, and the depths of air,—
Comes a still voice—Yet a few days, and thee
The all-beholding sun shall see no more
In all his course ; nor yet in the cold ground,
Where thy pale form was laid, with many tears,
Nor in the embrace of ocean, shall exist
Thy image.   Earth, that nourished thee, shall claim
Thy growth, to be resolved to earth again,

POEMS

BY

WILLIAM CULLEN BRYANT.

WITH

ILLUSTRATIONS BY E. LEUTZE,

ENGRAVED BY AMERICAN ARTISTS.

Third Edition.

PHILADELPHIA:
CAREY AND HART.
1847.

Fig. 5

POEMS.

THE AGES.

I.

WHEN to the common rest that crowns our days,
Called in the noon of life, the good man goes,
Or full of years, and ripe in wisdom, lays
His silver temples in their last repose;
When, o'er the buds of youth, the death-wind blows,
And blights the fairest; when our bitter tears
Stream, as the eyes of those that love us close,
We think on what they were, with many fears
Lest goodness die with them, and leave the coming years.

II.

And therefore, to our hearts, the days gone by,—
When lived the honoured sage whose death we wept,
And the soft virtues beamed from many an eye,
And beat in many a heart that long has slept,—

1:

William Cullen Bryant.

Fig. 6

32

POEMS.

THANATOPSIS.

To him who in the love of Nature holds
Communion with her visible forms, she speaks
A various language ; for his gayer hours
She has a voice of gladness, and a smile
And eloquence of beauty, and she glides
Into his darker musings, with a mild
And healing sympathy, that steals away
Their sharpness, ere he is aware.   When thoughts
Of the last bitter hour come like a blight
Over thy spirit, and sad images
Of the stern agony, and shroud, and pall,
And breathless darkness, and the narrow house,
Make thee to shudder, and grow sick at heart ;—
Go forth, under the open sky, and list
To Nature's teachings, while from all around—
Earth and her waters, and the depths of air,—
Comes a still voice—Yet a few days, and thee
The all-beholding sun shall see no more
In all his course ; nor yet in the cold ground,
Where thy pale form was laid, with many tears,

THANATOPSIS.

33

Nor in the embrace of ocean, shall exist
Thy image.   Earth, that nourished thee, shall claim
Thy growth, to be resolved to earth again,
And, lost each human trace, surrendering up
Thine individual being, shalt thou go
To mix for ever with the elements,
To be a brother to the insensible rock
And to the sluggish clod, which the rude swain
Turns with his share, and treads upon.   The oak
Shall send his roots abroad, and pierce thy mould.

Yet not to thine eternal resting-place
Shalt thou retire alone—nor couldst thou wish
Couch more magnificent.   Thou shalt lie down
With patriarchs of the infant world—with kings,
The powerful of the earth—the wise, the good,
Fair forms, and hoary seers of ages past,
All in one mighty sepulchre.—The hills
Rock-ribbed and ancient as the sun,—the vales
Stretching in pensive quietness between ;
The venerable woods—rivers that move
In majesty, and the complaining brooks
That make the meadows green ; and, poured round all,
Old ocean's gray and melancholy waste,—
Are but the solemn decorations all
Of the great tomb of man.   The golden sun,
The planets, all the infinite host of heaven,

POEMS

BY

WILLIAM CULLEN BRYANT.

COLLECTED AND ARRANGED

BY THE AUTHOR.

IN TWO VOLUMES.

VOL. I.

NEW YORK:
D. APPLETON AND COMPANY,
346 & 348 BROADWAY.
LONDON: 16 LITTLE BRITAIN
M.DCCC.LVII.

Fig. 7

That trample her, and break their iron net.
Yes, she shall look on brighter days and gain
The meed of worthier deeds ; the moment set
To rescue and raise up, draws near—but is not
    yet.

XXXV.

But thou, my country, thou shalt never fall,
Save with thy children—thy maternal care,
Thy lavish love, thy blessings showered on all—
These are thy fetters—seas and stormy air
Are the wide barrier of thy borders, where,
Among thy gallant sons that guard thee well,
Thou laugh'st at enemies : who shall then de-
    clare
The date of thy deep-founded strength, or tell
How happy, in thy lap, the sons of men shall
    dwell ?

THANATOPSIS.

To him who in the love of Nature holds
Communion with her visible forms, she speaks
A various language ; for his gayer hours
She has a voice of gladness, and a smile
And eloquence of beauty, and she glides
Into his darker musings, with a mild
And healing sympathy, that steals away
Their sharpness ere he is aware. When thoughts
Of the last bitter hour come like a blight
Over thy spirit, and sad images
Of the stern agony, and shroud, and pall,
And breathless darkness, and the narrow house,
Make thee to shudder, and grow sick at heart ;—

2

POETICAL WORKS

OF

WILLIAM CULLEN BRYANT.

COLLECTED AND ARRANGED

BY THE AUTHOR.

ILLUSTRATED BY ONE HUNDRED ENGRAVINGS

FROM DRAWINGS BY

BIRKET FOSTER, HARRY FENN, ALFRED FREDERICKS, AND OTHERS.

NEW YORK:
D. APPLETON AND COMPANY,
549 & 551 BROADWAY.

W. C. Bryant

Fig. 8

But thou, my country, thou shalt never fall,
Save with thy children—thy maternal care,
Thy lavish love, thy blessings showered on all—
These are thy fetters—seas and stormy air
Are the wide barrier of thy borders, where,
Among thy gallant sons who guard thee well,
Thou laugh'st at enemies: who shall then declare
The date of thy deep-founded strength, or tell
How happy, in thy lap, the sons of men shall dwell?

THANATOPSIS.

To him who in the love of Nature holds
Communion with her visible forms, she speaks
A various language; for his gayer hours
She has a voice of gladness, and a smile
And eloquence of beauty, and she glides
Into his darker musings, with a mild
And healing sympathy, that steals away
Their sharpness, ere he is aware. When thoughts
Of the last bitter hour come like a blight
Over thy spirit, and sad images
Of the stern agony, and shroud, and pall,
And breathless darkness, and the narrow house,
Make thee to shudder, and grow sick at heart;—
Go forth, under the open sky, and list

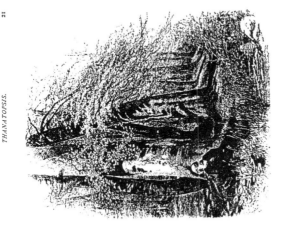

To Nature's teachings, while from all around—
Earth and her waters, and the depths of air—
Comes a still voice—Yet a few days, and thee
The all-beholding sun shall see no more
In all his course; nor yet in the cold ground,

Fig. 9 Trustees of Reservations, William Cullen Bryant
Homestead, Cummington, Massachusetts

Fig. 10 The Metropolitan Museum of Art, Gift of J.P. Morgan,
1911. (11.156)

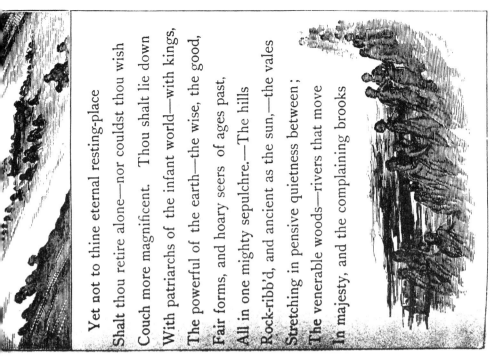

Yet not to thine eternal resting-place

Shalt thou retire alone—nor couldst thou wish

Couch more magnificent.   Thou shalt lie down

With patriarchs of the infant world—with kings,

The powerful of the earth—the wise, the good,

Fair forms, and hoary seers of ages past,

All in one mighty sepulchre.—The hills

Rock-ribb'd, and ancient as the sun,—the vales

Stretching in pensive quietness between;

The venerable woods—rivers that move

In majesty, and the complaining brooks

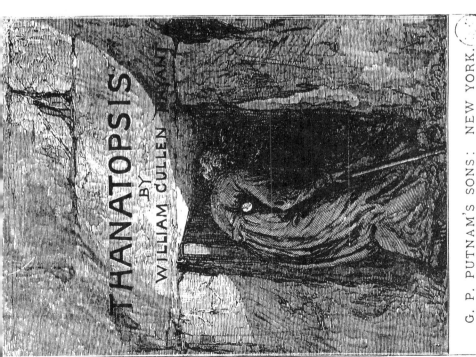

THANATOPSIS
BY
WILLIAM CULLEN BRYANT

G. P. PUTNAM'S SONS: NEW YORK.

Fig. 11

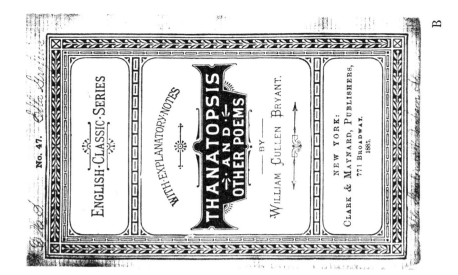

English·Classic·Series

No. 47.

With·Explanatory·Notes

THANATOPSIS
AND
OTHER POEMS

BY

William Cullen Bryant.

New York:
Clark & Maynard, Publishers,
771 Broadway.
1885.

B

BRYANT'S Poetical Works.

BRYANT'S POETICAL WORKS

PS
1150
E78a

Fig. 12

BRYANT

BRYANT'S
COMPLETE
POEMS

ILLUSTRATED

APPLETONS

D

BRYANT'S POEMS

THE ELECTRIC SERIES

BUTLER BROTHERS,
NEW YORK & CHICAGO.

C

Fig. 13

TO THE READER.

THIS edition contains several of the author's poems which have not appeared in any previous collection. These, as well as the others in the volume, have been made to follow each other in the order in which they were written, the author deeming this arrangement to be quite as satisfactory to the reader as any classification founded on the nature of the subjects or their mode of treatment.

NEW YORK, *June*, 1871.

POEMS.

THE AGES.

I.

WHEN to the common rest that crowns our days,
Called in the noon of life, the good man goes,
Or full of years, and ripe in wisdom, lays
His silver temples in their last repose;
When, o'er the buds of youth, the death-wind blows
And blights the fairest; when our bitter tears
Stream, as the eyes of those that love us close,
We think on what they were, with many fears
Lest goodness die with them, and leave the coming years.

II.

And therefore, to our hearts, the days gone by,
When lived the honored sage whose death we wept,
And the soft virtues beamed from many an eye,
And beat in many a heart that long has slept—
Like spots of earth where angel-feet have stepped,
Are holy; and high-dreaming bards have told
Of times when worth was crowned, and faith was kept,
Ere friendship grew a snare, or love waxed cold—
Those pure and happy times—the golden days of old.

Seek'st thou the plashy brink
Of weedy lake, or marge of river wide.
TO A WATERFOWL. p. 29.

And oft he turns his truant eye,
And pauses oft, and lingers near;
But when he marks the reddening sky,
He bounds away to hunt the deer.

TO A WATERFOWL.

WHITHER, midst falling dew,
While glow the heavens with the last steps of day,
Far, through their rosy depths, dost thou pursue
Thy solitary way?

Vainly the fowler's eye
Might mark thy distant flight to do thee wrong
As, darkly seen against the crimson sky,
Thy figure floats along.

Seek'st thou the plashy brink
Of weedy lake, or marge of river wide,
Or where the rocking billows rise and sink
On the chafed ocean-side?

There is a Power whose care
Teaches thy way along that pathless coast—
The desert and illimitable air—
Lone wandering, but not lost.

All day thy wings have fanned,
At that far height, the cold, thin atmosphere,
Yet stoop not, weary, to the welcome land,
Though the dark night is near.

THE

POETICAL WORKS

OF

WILLIAM CULLEN BRYANT.

EDITED BY

PARKE GODWIN.

IN TWO VOLUMES:

Volume first.

NEW YORK:
D. APPLETON AND COMPANY,
1, 3, AND 5 BOND STREET.
1883.

Fig. 14

THANATOPSIS.

TO him who in the love of Nature holds
Communion with her visible forms, she speaks
A various language ; for his gayer hours
She has a voice of gladness, and a smile
And eloquence of beauty, and she glides
Into his darker musings, with a mild
And healing sympathy, that steals away
Their sharpness, ere he is aware. When thoughts
Of the last bitter hour come like a blight
Over thy spirit, and sad images
Of the stern agony, and shroud, and pall,
And breathless darkness, and the narrow house,
Make thee to shudder, and grow sick at heart ;—
Go forth, under the open sky, and list
To Nature's teachings, while from all around—
Earth and her waters, and the depths of air—
Comes a still voice.—

　　　　　Yet a few days, and thee
The all-beholding sun shall see no more

where most pages of text are enclosed by boxed illustrations at the head and foot (*fig. 11*)[53]

In later years, Bryant's poems appeared, variously illustrated and decorated, in both cheap paper series and the so-called "pedagogically inspired" ones, some of which are shown below (see *fig. 12*).[54] The 1878 illustrated edition had appeared in a floral binding (*fig. 12a*) that echoed the Victorian busy-ness of its dense interior assemblage of plates, biography, poems, and notes in small, crowded type. A homier presentation of the poems, meant to return them to a sentimental or fireside mode, was a 1909 version of Appleton's Household Edition (*fig. 12d*), with its plain interior and simple garlanded binding.

A *via media* between the plain and the elaborately illustrated was the popular red-line edition of 1871 (*fig. 13*). Here the red-line borders coalesce with the ornaments to exemplify the romantic-organic view of the Gothic. Within these embellishments, Bryant structures his individual poems carefully, while the blank verse of the poems ensures a Ruskinian naturalness of construction. The sermonic plain-style of "Thanatopsis" has been called "as eminently lucid as the village steeple" in its architectural articulation, with its simple language and division into doctrine, reason, and use.[55] At the same time the poet demonstrates his interest in the sublimity of Gothic effects. Here man is entwined in time and in dialogue with nature, where its forms, metaphors themselves, "Are but the solemn decorations all/ Of the great tomb of man" (lines 44–45).

The 1871 edition is a comfortable small square octavo in a discretely ornamented red cloth, with only occasional illustrations relegated to separate pages. The ornaments carry into the design the idea of the vignette,

> a term originally used to describe the little "vines" or tendrils, the ornamental flourishes, that crawl along the margins of codices. The freedom and fantasy, the complete integration of the visual and the verbal, which was supposed by the Romantics to be characteristic of medieval bookmaking, became their ideal.[56]

Here the gothic image that Neil Fraistat observes in an authorial order in poetic collections is carried through into the graphic design, where the twining of the tendrils suggests an integral arrangement from which no part can be easily detached.[57]

The now established order of the poems also meets Fraistat's idea of a poetic book's synchronic "contextual architecture."[58]

"Thanatopsis" followed "The Ages" and was succeeded by "The Yellow Violet," "The Inscription for the Entrance to a Wood," "Song," "To a Waterfowl," and "Green River." As Ian Jack has noted:

> When William Cullen Bryant told his readers that his poems had been "made to follow each other in the order in which they were written, the author deeming this arrangement as satisfactory to the reader as any founded on the nature of the subjects or their mode of treatment," it is clear that he was reacting against other methods of arrangment, and perhaps in particular against Wordsworth's characteristically idiosyncratic pronouncements.[59]

Although Jack contrasts such an order with Wordsworth's comparison of his arrangement in "The Recluse" to a Gothic church, the chronological order does not prevent such a volume from having the same effect: whatever the opening poems are, they will still serve as the "ante-chapel." Bryant's prefaces indicate that the value of this order for him was precisely its illustration of the very Wordsworthian idea of his own mental growth, since ". . . at different periods of his life, an author's style and habits of thought may be supposed to undergo very considerable modifications."[60] He had been satisfied to hear of the likely destruction of the plates of the 1839 edition, noting that "[t]hey are not well arranged and the alterations I have since made are considerable."[61] The value of chronology (or at least inclusiveness) was also important to Poe, who reacted to Duyckinck's selection for Wiley and Putnam's 1845 edition of his *Tales* of mainly his "analytic" stories: "In writing these Tales one by one, at long intervals, I have kept the book-unity always in mind—that is, each has been composed with reference to its effect as part of *a whole*."[62] In Bryant's arrangement, the poems largely maintained their individual integrity, the "inner" structure as it has been called, so that any one could be read alone and in any actual order, but the very persistence of that order over time emphasized the "outer" structure, the poem in relation to the others around it.[63] Overall, then, this edition becomes a visual manifestation of what Mary Ann Caws calls "architexture," defined as "the combination of structure and texture visible in a given work and its constructive attachment to other works in an overall building developed in the reader's mind."[64]

Several years after Bryant's death, his son-in-law Parke Godwin assembled the materials for a two-volume collected edition for

Appleton that significantly altered the reader's experience of the work by providing it with the perspective of a scholarly editor, adding notes that included a composition history of "Thanatopsis" and appending composition and publication dates at the end of each poem. He saw his work historically since, he said, it "has a biographical as well as a literary purpose, and the editor therefore has not felt at liberty to omit any of his acknowledged pieces which may illustrate the qualities of his mind or the variety of his culture."[65] Godwin chose a more strictly chronological arrangement for the poems than Bryant had, so that "Thanatopsis" now came first. In 1935, in the *Representative Selections* of Bryant's work in the American Book Company's American Writers Series, Tremaine McDowell corrected Godwin.[66] He kept the chronological order, which has its scholarly uses, but he pointedly excepted from that order "The Ages." Bryant's 1847 Preface makes clear that Bryant saw this poem as an introduction to the rest of his work because of its encompassing view of life, "a survey of the past ages of the world, and of the successive advances of mankind and knowledge, virtue, and happiness," intended "to justify and confirm the hopes of the philanthropist for the future destinies of the human race." Such a sentiment also clearly contributes to the reader's comprehension of the limitations of darkness in "Thanatopsis," as he comes upon it next.

Godwin's typography (*fig. 14*) was simple, clean, and well-positioned, but so generous in size that it seems rather too loud and demanding. A modern editor would certainly want a median of type size and leading, and generosity rather in space on the page to allow for a suitable sense of quiet discovery and thought. Periods after titles were retained in all Appleton editions until well into this century, when modern typographical conventions had long since allowed space and upper case alone to set off titles from texts.

Before the poems, Godwin usefully assembled Bryant's prefaces in order, although the repetition of similar sentiments means that reading them through has a somewhat dizzying fast-forward effect. An editor might better choose one to represent them all, reserving the whole run for an appendix. The placement of the *Poems* as the central two volumes in a six-volume set, between the biography of the first two and the prose works of the last two, made them still more architectonic, as they retained their own integrity, yet were identified with and by the whole set.

In 1903, Appleton's Roslyn Edition of Bryant's poems combined the popular and the scholarly. Accompanying the collected poems, the familiar illustrations, and Bryant's original notes, there was extensive editorial material including bibliographies. In McGann's terms, we have here a series of spatially and radially readable arrays, comprising different levels of the author and work—biography, titles, prefaces, poems, and notes.[67]

Whether in appreciation of fragmentation or in search of unity, the eye and mind of the critic must range among physical forms of the text in order to engage an author's intangible *work*. As Bryant's work recognizes, Nature, too, is an intangible concept, but it speaks to man through forms and images, just as the poet speaks through the "still voice" of those of the book.[68]

NOTES

1. The text cited throughout is from Tremaine McDowell's edition, *William Cullen Bryant: Representative Selections* (New York: American Book Company, 1935), which takes its copy from *The Poetical Works of William Cullen Bryant* (New York: Appleton, 1876), the last edition the poet himself prepared.

2. Tanselle, *A Rationale of Textual Criticism*. The Rosenbach Lectures, 1987 (Philadelphia: University of Pennsylvania Press, 1989); McGann, "Theory of Texts," *London Review of Books*, 18 February 1988, pp. 20–21; also cited in his *Towards a Literature of Knowledge* (Chicago: University of Chicago Press, 1989), p. ix.

3. Tanselle's discussion of McGann's terminology appears in his "Textual Criticism and Literary Sociology," *Studies in Bibliography*, 44 (1991), 100–101. But there is really not such a discrepancy between their terms as Tanselle suggests. McGann's "work" is equal to Tanselle's, and his "version" equals Tanselle's "instructions." McGann realizes that the linear text is part of the spatially read physical version but wishes to distinguish between its physical embodiment and the linguistic work it represents. That he uses the word "text" for both of those, and problems with his exposition, lead Tanselle to find him inconsistent.

4. Tremaine McDowell, "Bryant's Practice in Composition and Revision," *PMLA*, 52 (1937), 474–502. Dana was continually making suggestions for changes, for which Bryant expressed his thanks and respectful consideration. See for example "To Richard H. Dana," 25 September 1846, Letter 599, *The Letters of William Cullen Bryant*, ed. William Cullen Bryant II (New York:

Fordham University Press, 1975–), II, 474.

5. William Charvat, *Literary Publishing in America: 1790–1850* (Philadelphia: University of Pennsylvania Press, 1959), p. 34.

6. Nicolas Barker notes a similar effect in a mid-eighteenth century printing of Young's "Night Thoughts," when, despite the general replacement of seventeenth-century typography by eighteenth-century light and space, the title typography showed a recurrent use of black-letter, possibly intended to suggest the content. See "Typography and the Meaning of Words: The Revolution in the Layout of Books in the Eighteenth-Century," in *The Book and the Book Trade in Eighteenth-Century Europe: Proceedings of the Fifth Wolfenbütteler Symposium*, ed. Giles Barber and Bernard Fabian (Hamburg: Hauswedell, 1981), p. 135.

7. The "pale realms of shade" was a phrase that Bryant, responding to Dana's criticism, confessed he had "no particular liking for" ("To Richard H. Dana," 15 September 1821, Letter 74, *Letters*, I, 110). He appeared to accept—after the fact—Dana's revisions at press. This reading nevertheless does appear in 1821, as McDowell reports in his 1937 article. But in his 1935 notes in *Representative Selections*, McDowell reported the 1821 reading as "pale realms of death," and that information is repeated in the editorial note to Bryant's letter. It was in the 1832 edition that the phrase was changed completely to the final reading of "that mysterious realm" (line 75).

8. See for instance D. F. McKenzie's consideration of seventeenth-century examples in "Typography and Meaning: the Case of William Congreve," in *The Book and the Book Trade*, pp. 101–3.

9. Barker, pp. 131–32. [Hugh Amory], *New Books by Fielding: An Exhibition of the Hyde Collection* (Cambridge, MA: The Houghton Library, 1987), p. 50. See also the discussions of the significance of French typographic development in *Histoire de l'édition française*, Henri-Jean Martin, Roger Chartier, and Daniel Roche, gen. eds., 4 vols. (Paris: Promodis, 1981–86); Roger Laufer considers relations of typography, space, and the work of the philosophes in "Les espaces du livre," e.g., II, 128; Frédéric Barbier discusses the interaction of the emergent romanticism with typographic classicism in "Les formes du livre," II, 577.

10. "To Richard H. Dana," 13 August 1827, Letter 183, *Letters*, I, 250. For a contextual survey of Bryant's activities among New York artists, see Neil Harris, *The Artist in American Society: The Formative Years, 1790–1860* (New York: George Braziller, 1966).

11. *American Literary Annuals and Gift Books, 1825–1865* (New York: H. W. Wilson, 1936), p. 58.

12. "To Jared Sparks," 16 November 1827, Letter 190, *Letters*, I, 254. "To Gulian C. Verplanck," 30 March 1832, Letter 236, *Letters*, I, 322.

13. 17 May 1836, Letter 318, *Letters*, II, 20.

14. Engraving by James Smillie, *New-York Mirror*, 14 May 1836, facing p. 362. "To Frances F. Bryant," 15 August 1836, Letter 329, *Letters*, II, 51.

15. The black/white contrast in this edition also suggests the scribal metaphor of the page as a white field on which the plow of the quill deposits black seed. See the section on "The Book as Symbol" in E. R. Curtius, *European Literature and the Latin Middle Ages*, trans. Willard R. Trask (New York: Pantheon, 1953), pp. 313–14.

16. "To John Howard Bryant," c. 15–20 September 1836, Letter 334, *Letters*, II, 60.

17. Charvat, *Literary Publishing*, p. 34. For details of Bryant's relationship with Harper, see Eugene Exman, *The Brothers Harper: A Unique Publishing Partnership and Its Impact on the Cultural Life of America from 1817 to 1853* (New York: Harper and Row, 1965).

18. Perry Miller, *Errand Into the Wilderness* (1956; rpt. 1964), quoted in Harris, *Artist*, p. 171. As Harris notes, "Edwards himself was the spiritual father of many nineteenth-century art enthusiasts."

19. In the novel *La Prise de Constantinople*, he derived ideas from the star in the Éditions de Minuit publisher's device and from that name created the character Ed Word. For a summary, see the chapter, "Postmodern Generative Fiction," in Bruce Morrissette, *Novel and Film: Essays in Two Genres* (Chicago: University of Chicago Press, 1985).

20. Walter Benjamin, "The Work of Art in The Age of Mechanical Reproduction," in *Illuminations*, ed. Hannah Arendt, trans. Harry Zohn (New York: Harcourt Brace and World, 1955), pp. 219–54. Hershel Parker, *Flawed Texts and Verbal Icons* (Evanston: Northwestern University Press, 1984). See also S. M. Parrish, "The Whig Interpretation of Literature," *TEXT*, 4 (1988), 343–50.

21. The evaluation of the presentation appeared in *Homes of American Authors: Comprising Anecdotical, Personal, and Descriptive Sketches by Various Writers* (New York: G. P. Putnam and Co., 1853), p. 77.

22. Publishers' advertisements, bound in, following the text of Bryant, *Poems* (Philadelphia: Carey and Hart, 1847), 3rd edition (collection of the author).

23. Exman, *The Brothers Harper*, p. 297. Included is an illustration and details of

the planning for the presentation.

24. Alan C. Golding, "A History of American Poetry Anthologies," in *Canons*, ed. Robert von Hallberg (Chicago: University of Chicago Press, 1984), 282, 288–90. Bryant himself had compiled *Selections from the American Poets* for the Harpers in 1840.

25. Amory, *New Books*, p. 35.

26. *A Mirror for Americanists: Reflections on the Idea of American Literature* (Hanover, NH: University Press of New England, 1989), pp. 131–32.

27. Harris, *Artist*, p. 118, discusses the use of nature by artists to counter cultural decadence.

28. Perry Lewis, in his *Intellectual Life in America: A History* (New York: Franklin Watts, 1984), pp. 229–30, considers ways in which form mirrors restraint in religion, and the idea extends to that of the book as bible. Both Curtius and Walter J. Ong, have traced some of the philosophical correspondences here with the book as symbol of such social roles. The book as the Word, and as immortalized form of the poet, as well as the idea of the poet as priest, common on through Flaubert and Joyce, have too many implications to follow through here. A recurrent one is the idea of the book as a literal pilgrimage or as a voyage into an interior world. The symbolism of the Book of Nature would certainly be more appropriate for the 1821 or 1836 edition, as we have read them, or for the 1855 edition discussed below.

29. "To Rufus W. Griswold," 16 August 1844, Letter 499, *Letters*, II, 273.

30. "To Richard H. Dana," 25 September 1846, Letter 599, *Letters*, II, 473.

31. Charvat, in *The Origins of American Critical Thought: 1810–1835* (Philadelphia: University of Pennsylvania Press, 1936), discusses the associationist ideas in the period. Donald A. Ringe applies them to Bryant in *The Pictorial Mode: Space and Time in the Art of Bryant, Irving, and Cooper* (Lexington: University of Kentucky Press, 1971). The judgement of Leutze is given in Harris, *Artist*, p. 250, citing *Lippincott's Magazine* of November 1868.

32. "To Richard H. Dana," 12 September 1848, Letter 647, *Letters*, II, 531.

33. "To Richard H. Dana," 25 September 1846, Letter 599, *Letters*, II, 473.

34. *Homes of American Authors*, p. 77. Frank Weitenkampf, *American Graphic Art*, 2d ed. (New York: MacMillan, 1924), p. 81. The comparison to Rubens was made in part with his hatted portrait in mind, since Bryant wore a similar hat on his country estate. On Rubens's book illustration, see Otto Benesch, *Artistic and Intellectual Trends from Rubens to Daumier As Shown in Book*

Illustration (New York: Walker and Company, for the Department of Printing and Graphic Arts, Harvard College Library, 1969); and Julius S. Held,
"Rubens and the Book," in *Rubens and His Circle: Studies by Julius S. Held*,
ed. Annie W. Lowenthal, David Rosand, and John Walsh, Jr. (Princeton:
Princeton University Press, 1982), pp. 166–84.

35. E. H. Gombrich, "The Mask and the Face: The Perception of Physiognomic
    Likeness in Life and Art," in E. H. Gombrich, Julian Hochberg, and Max
    Black, *Art, Perception, and Reality* (Baltimore: Johns Hopkins University
    Press,1972), p. 8.
       An interesting modern example of author-book representational corre-
    spondences is Harcourt Brace Jovanovich's six-voume set of Virginia Woolf's
    letters, in which the top of the jacket on the spine of each volume carries a
    portrait of the author at the stage of her life covered in it , so that the volumes
    are linked on the shelf by a series of presentations in person as well as on the
    page, all in one version. *The Letters of Virginia Woolf*, ed. Nigel Nicolson and
    Joanne Trautmann (New York, 1975–80).

36. One critic sees Bryant's very discussion of his publishing business in his let-
    ters as a mask behind which to avoid presenting his feelings about his work,
    although he was sincere and open in his answers to those who asked about his
    writing; see Albert F. McLean, *William Cullen Bryant* (New York: Twayne,
    1964), pp. 24–25. But what he wrote in his letters corresponded with what he
    wrote in his works. For the meaning both had for him, see McLean's idea of
    the expanding Emersonian circles of sensibility in Bryant's development (pp.
    25–38).
       With Bryant's interest in both sculpture and landscape, and his many years
    as supporter of Olmstead and the public park movement as well as of New
    York libraries, we might even compare his poem in its *mise en page* to the
    artistic "text" of Bryant's own statue in the space of the eponymous park
    (*mise en parc?*) behind the New York Public Library. "Thanatopsis" itself
    suggests this because it reassures us of our immortality, returning us to the
    idea of the whole book and the common symbolic understanding of it as the
    writer's immortal embodiment, his place in the pantheon of writers (he said
    he imagined himself so when he first wrote it). Just as the statue perpetuates
    his personal image, so the poem itself is the fixed image of that concept.

37. "French Books," in *The Dolphin*, No. 4, Pt. II (Winter 1941), 133–34. Proust
    initially specified his desire to make the pages dense—"of thirty-five lines with
    fifty-five characters to the line"—because he wanted the work to be cheap
    enough to reach a wide audience. His correspondence is cited in Pierre
    Assouline, *Gaston Gallimard: A Half Century of French Publishing*, trans.
    Harold J. Salemson (New York: Harcourt Brace Jovanovich, 1988), p. 37; this
    account includes a sampling of other author specifications for typographical
    treatment, e.g., "The great Flaubert himself often pestered his publisher,
    Michel Levy. 'The circumflex accent on Salammbô has no sweep; nothing could
    be less Punic. I demand a broader one', he had written Levy in 1862" (p. 30).

38. James T. Callow, *Knickerbocker Writers and American Artists, 1807–1855* (Chapel Hill: University of North Carolina Press, 1967), p. 147. Ringe, *Pictorial Mode*, pp. 213–14. The reader's private relation to the poems would also be enhanced by the comfortable duodecimos, as opposed to the gaudy public octavo of 1847 (although the copy illustrated has been rebound in polished calf with marbled endpapers). Bryant might even have been influenced by such an idea, since he owned a copy of the 1834 Boston edition of D'Israeli's *Curiosities of Literature*, with its disquisition on "Little Books" with "seem to pay a deference to the reader's quick and great understanding" (3 vols.[Boston: Lilly, Wait, Colman, and Holden], II, 86). Bryant's copy was item 123 in Anderson Galleries, Inc., *Catalogue of a Portion of the Library of William Cullen Bryant, Poet and Editor* (New York: Anderson Auction Co., 1908).The choice of the brown cloth binding was probably influenced by its association since about 1848 with the literary works produced by Ticknor and Fields in Boston; see John William Pye, *James T. Fields, Literary Publisher* (Portland, Maine: The Baxter Society, 1987), pp. 16–17, 26–27.

39. W. J. T. Mitchell, "Space and Time: Lessing's Laocoön and the Politics of Genre," in his *Iconology: Image, Text, Ideology* (Chicago: University of Chicago Press, 1986), pp. 95–115, esp. pp. 99–100. See also David Rosand, "*Ekphrasis* and the Generation of Images," *Arion*, 3rd ser., 1 (1990), 61–105; and the idea of "notional" ekphrasis in John Hollander, "The Poetics of *Ekphrasis*," *Word and Image*, 4 (1988), 209–17. Mary Ann Caws, in *The Eye in the Text: Essays on Perception, Mannerist to Modern* (Princeton: Princeton University Press, 1981), p. 5, n. 7., cites Murray Krieger's affirmation of the paradox of a poem as "unmoving movement at the heart of the stillness of the Keatsian urn" from his "Mediation, Language, and Vision in Literature," in *Interpretation, Theory and Practice*, ed. Charles S. Singleton (1969), p. 234.

40. Ronald Paulson, *Book and Painting: Shakespeare, Milton, and the Bible: Literary Texts and the Emergence of English Painting* (Knoxville: University of Ten-nessee Press, 1982), p. 123. In "Typography and Meaning," McKenzie shows what a difference white space and scene divisions make to theatrical visualization in the 1710 Congreve. For treatment of the wider context of McKenzie's ideas there, see Julie Stone Peters, *Congreve, the Drama, and the Printed Word* (Stanford: Stanford University Press, 1990).

41. "To Richard H. Dana," 26 May 1854, Letter 868, *Letters*, III, 334.

42. "To John H. Woods," 21 April 1864, Letter 1407, *Letters*, IV, 364.

43. "To Estelle Anna Lewis," c. 20 July 1854, Letter 870, *Letters*, III, 336.

44. A number of these artists, and the ones in the next edition discussed (1876), collaborated with Bryant on Appleton's 1872 magnum opus, *Picturesque America*. Harry Fenn was its principle instigator (Weitenkampf, p. 188), and it carried a plate of Bryant's country estate at Roslyn, Long Island, as a fron-

tispiece.

45. Vince Clemente, "Bryant's 'To a Waterfowl' and the Painter W. S. Mount," in *Under Open Sky: Poets on William Cullen Bryant*, ed. Norbert Krapf (Roslyn, N.Y.: Stone House Press, 1986), pp. 17–28. Julian Hochberg, "The Represen-tation of Things and People," in Gombrich, et al., *Art, Perception, and Reality*, p. 72.

46. Charles Rosen and Henri Zerner, *Romanticism and Realism: The Mythology of Nineteenth-Century Art* (New York: Viking Press, 1984), p. 75.

47. "To Washington Irving," 21 June 1941, Letter 113, *The Letters of Edgar Allan Poe*, ed. John Ward Ostrom (Cambridge: Harvard University Press, 1948), I, 162.

48. *The Poets of America, Illustrated by One of Her Painters*, ed. John Keese (New York: S. Colman, 1840).

49. *The Search for Synthesis in Literature and Art: The Paradox of Space* (Athens: University of Georgia Press, 1990).

50. Rosen and Zerner, p. 87.

51. See Bryan Jay Wolf, *Romantic Re-Vision: Culture and Consciousness in Nineteenth-Century American Painting and Literature* (Chicago: University of Chicago Press, 1982), pp. 182–84, 178–79.

52. Donald Pease, *Visionary Compacts: American Renaissance Writings in Cultural Context* (Madison: University of Wisconsin Press, 1987), p. 66.

53. Rita Gollin, "The Scarlet Letter," in "From Cover to Cover: The Presentation of Hawthorne's Major Romances," *Essex Institute Historical Collections*, 127 (1991), 12–30 (16). Linton is discussed and cited in Weitenkampf, pp. 121–23, 127–29. See also David Woodward, "The Decline of Commercial Wood-Engraving in Nineteenth-Century America," *Journal of the Printing Historical Society*, 10 (1974–5), 56–82; and F. B. Smith, *Radical Artisan: William James Linton, 1812–97* (Manchester: Manchester University Press, and Totowa, N.J.: Rowman and Littlefield, 1973).

54. "From Cover to Cover," p. 6.

55. McLean, p. 78.

56. Rosen and Zerner, p. 75. See also the discussion of related forms, and the significance of black and red type in Roger Laufer, "L'espace visuel du livre ancien," *Histoire de L'édition française*, I, 483.

57. Fraistat, *The Poem and the Book: Interpreting Collections of Romantic Poetry* (Chapel Hill: University of North Carolina Press, 1985). See also Fraistat, ed., *Poems in Their Place: The Intertextuality and Order of Poetic Collections* (ibid., 1986).

Just as the interlaced structure of Anglo-Saxon artwork has been found in the interlaced textual pattern in *Beowulf*, these ornaments embody Hawthorne's idea of the romance as a woven tapestry of intricate patterns. D. F. McKenzie and D. C. Greetham both discuss the implications of the common etymologies of *texere*, *textus*, texture, textile, and text, and the comparison of the weaving of physical materials with patterns of words. See Thomas H. Ohlgren, "Visual Language in the Old English Caedmonian Genesis," *Visual Language*, 6 (1972), 253–76, who cites the Beowulf example (255) and makes a similar interpretation. For Hawthorne, see the Preface to *The House of the Seven Gables*, vol. 2 of the Centenary Edition of the Works of Nathaniel Hawthorne, ed. William Charvat, Roy Harvey Pearce, and Claude M. Simpson (Columbus, Ohio: Ohio State University Press, 1965), p. 2. See also the correlations made with Hawthorne's idea in "From Cover to Cover"; McKenzie, *Bibliography and the Sociology of Texts*, The Panizzi Lectures, 1985 (London: British Library, 1986), pp. 5–6; and Greetham, "[Textual] Criticism and Deconstruction," *Studies in Bibliography*, 44 (1991), 29.

58. Fraistat, *Poem and Book*, pp. 4–5.

59. Ian Jack, "A Choice of Orders: The Arrangement of 'The Poetical Works,'" in *Textual Criticism and Literary Interpretation*, ed. Jerome J. McGann (Chicago: University of Chicago Press, 1985), 127–43 (129–30). Jack cites the London 1877 edition.

60. *Thirty Poems* (New York: Appleton, 1864).

61. "To Messrs. Carey and Hart," 13 November 1846, Letter 607, *Letters*, II, 486.

62. "To Philip B. Cooke," 9 August 1846, Letter 240, *Letters*, II, 328–329.

63. Fraistat, *Poem and Book*, citing Floyd Allport, p. 10. Although Fraistat focuses on author-determined structures, patterns can of course result from publisher- or other-determined orders, and can be read within reasonable limits; Fraistat gives some useful examples of possible and questionable readings (pp. 15–16).

64. Caws, p. 9.

65. Parke Godwin, ed., *The Poetical Works of William Cullen Bryant*, Vols. 3 and 4 of *The Life and Works of William Cullen Bryant* (New York: Appleton, 1884), p. 6. He added that it was to be understood that new items he included were "presented without having received the final revision of the author."

66. In the McDowell edition, there was one illustration as frontispiece, an adaptation of the Cheney portrait of Bryant, in a sketchy rendering by the well-known illustrator Kerr Eby.

67. *The Poetical Works of William Cullen Bryant, with Chronologies of Bryant's Life and Poems and a Bibliography of His Writings by Henry C. Sturges, and a Memoir of His Life by Richard Henry Stoddard* (New York: Appleton, 1903). McGann, in *Social Values and Poetic Acts, The Historical Judgment of Literary Work* (Cambridge, Ma: Harvard University Press, 1988), pp. 139–45.

68. Tanselle cites Eliot for the idea of the book form as "the still point" in the continual flux of the intangible work's appearances; *Rationale*, p. 65.

Yeats's Letters, Eliot's Lectures: Toward a New Focus on Annotation

Ronald Schuchard

When in 1978 I became a co-editor, responsible for the annotation, of two volumes of Yeats's *Collected Letters*, I had a pathetic sense of the work before me. Two years, I thought, would easily see the task to completion, and that was the time allowed in the ever-extended contract. After all, I said in eager innocence to John Kelly, the general editor, Allan Wade had already annotated the published letters.[1] John, who was himself becoming steeled in the precision of annotation under the tutelage of Catharine Carver, just looked at me for a long time and generously said nothing. Little did I know that I would spent the next six summers, and most of an academic year, in Colindale, the dreaded repository of British newspapers, that I would visit every major library in England, Ireland, and America (some several times), that I would write hundreds of letters to heirs, executors, and historical societies, that I would write and revise so many drafts of so many notes, or that in pursuing annotations I would uncover over a hundred new letters to annotate. After twelve years of pursuing every kind of fugitive person, object, and event in and out of the flux of print, one poor volume is now annotated and in press. How excessive and unjustifiable such work must seem to some: all that delay of the letters just for notes? As I was to learn, extensive time is crucial to intensive annotation.

In 1988, I became the editor of an annotated edition, still in progress, of T. S. Eliot's unpublished Clark Lectures on Metaphysical Poetry, delivered at Trinity College, Cambridge, in 1926. Eliot originally planned to enlarge the eight lectures into a book entitled *The School of Donne*, but after some deflating criticism from Mario

Praz he became disillusioned by the burden of scholarship and then frustrated by the futility of the project. "I dont [sic] want these lectures ever to be published," he wrote to his brother in 1936. "They are pretentious and immature."[2] They also represent an immense demonstration of learning and the most sustained body of criticism at the heart of his career, on the eve of his conversion. They are also filled with difficult allusions, misattributions, misquotations, peculiar editions and unqualified assertions that cry out to be placed in the larger critical and historical context of his work. Back to Colindale, et cetera. Though many of the daily procedures are the same, the task of annotating Eliot is largely the antithesis of annotating Yeats, in that Yeats requires more notes of recovery, Eliot of explanation. But as I move back and forth from letter to lecture, often with some anxiety and uncertainty to be sure, I try to reassure myself that common principles of exacting scholarship underlie the different notes, and that as an annotator I know who I am and what I am about with my separate audiences.

That has not always been the case among annotators of modern texts. Certainly we have not benefited from the clarity of purpose, technique, and procedure provided to textual editors by the collective rationale of Greg, Bowers, Tanselle, McGann, and others. Indeed, for the past fifty years the art of annotation generally seems to have been in a controlled state of repression and neglect, and the intimidated cries for liberation have been modest and infrequent. Of the few articles recommended for their "useful suggestions about annotation" in the CEAA *Statement of Editorial Principles and Procedures* (1972), the earliest by Arthur Friedman defined the plight of a conscientious editor who observed a general lack of rigor and rationale among editors attempting to place works in historical contexts and who found that in most critical editions "the text is usually more satisfactory than the annotation."[3] Friedman was curious to discover that there had been "little theorizing" about annotation, "possibly because so many of the annotator's problems seem purely particular questions of research" (p. 116). He obviously knew to coax rather than to admonish resistant editors at the English Institute, allowing from the outset that "the primary question of what needs to be annotated . . . will always depend to a large extent upon the erudition and tact of the editor" (p. 117). To bring some sense of definition and procedure to the disarray of annotation, he distinguished usefully between "notes of recovery" and "explanatory notes," showing some pitfalls that await the unwary editor. And though he recommended resourceful ways of making perfunctory notes "really enlightening," he was cautious to emphasize that such desirable information could often be provided "with little additional labor" (p. 126). Clearly aware that his was not a timely call for more precise and intensive annotation, Friedman made his concluding observation and assertion rather apologetically: "allusions which at first sight seem to call for only a little inform-ation can often be satisfactorily explained only by a thorough search through the author's background. So I fear we have to conclude that for cases in doubt we should try to do our historical annotation the long and hard way" (p. 128). Had Friedman seen examples of Wilmarth Lewis's thoroughly annotated edition of the Horace Walpole correspondence, announced as a project at MLA in 1932, he might have taken courage, but when his five-volume edition of the *Collected Works of Oliver Goldsmith* finally appeared at the Clarendon Press in 1966, his earlier "principles" seemingly forgotten or advised against, the annotations were extremely spare and conservative.

Friedman's address elicited no response for forty years, and from the forties to the seventies most annotators remained gun-shy of asserting any larger responsibility to text and reader. Nowhere in this better illustrated than in a second article recommended by CEAA, Robert Halsband's "Editing the Letters of Letter-Writers," in which he warns the would-be editor that in the bout over annotations "he will find even less agreement than in textual style."[4] But what is striking about the article, which argues that the editor must remain subservient to the text and which praises notes that exemplify brevity, directness, simplicity, and lucidity, is that he expresses a longing admiration for the annotation of the Walpole and Mann correspondence, in spite of unfavorable criticism of both editions:

> Mr. Lewis's Walpole annotations are considered by many to err on the side of generosity; and in England one hears quips about the full genealogies attached to everyone mentioned in the text. This tendency to annotate Walpole widely and deeply has become more pronounced in the Mann correspondence, so that the volumes are becoming not a source for political history but a veritable reference collection. Whether or not one agrees with this objection, there can be no doubt as to the balance, tact, and efficient accuracy of these annotations. (p. 35)

Admiration aside, Halsband could but revert to his own premise

that if letters are to be readable "then the annotations must remain
subservient." Though the annotator cannot disregard names, quotations or allusions merely on the ground that "his main job was to
present the text," he must still practice "extreme self-effacement"
while keeping his notes adequately "serviceable to readers." Wandering Arnold-like between the two worlds of nineteenth-century
readability and twentieth-century scholarship, "one dead, / The
other powerless to be born," Halsband contented himself with ad-
monishments against the temptations that beset contemporary
annotation. At all costs the "vivacious editor" should avoid "editorial exhibitionism," refrain from "cozy chats," and resist the opportunity to indulge in "sly quips" and "oblique jokes" (p. 36). Such
were the passing habits of the gentleman-annotator.

Not until the early eighties was the annotator elevated to the
more diplomatic position of "mediator," as characterized by Martin
Battestin: "The task of the annotator . . . is to mediate between the
text which the editor has thus established and the reader who wishes to recover its meanings wherever they are obscure."[5] But in his
belief that the mediator cannot achieve objectivity, and due to the
variable nature of each text and audience, Battestin voices his conviction "that there can be no single rationale of literary annotation
that will prove universally practical and appropriate" (p. 3). In the
absence of a rationale, the mediator needs guidelines and procedures to help him fulfill his role, which is to supply the reader "with
essential information only and in the briefest compass possible" (p.
14). Battestin thus returns to Friedman's "pioneering study" to re-
fine and expand some guidelines outlined forty years earlier. "We
ought at least to be able, " he writes, "to agree on what we are trying to do as annotators and on how we can best go about doing it"
(p. 7). Battestin provides a comprehensive and suggestive discussion of procedures that lead to more valuable notes, but for him the
purpose of the mediator is the singular one of clarifying the
author's specific meaning and intention in specific instances. Should
we not have a more demanding role for the modest mediator?

By 1990, in a radical reversal of his traditional image, the passive
but restless annotator was declared to be an "aggressor," a self-jus-
tifying textual intruder whose annotations are viewed as an act of
aggression directed at the text, the reader, even society itself. In a
recently published collection of essays, *Annotation and its Texts*,
some of our contemporaries affirm that the noisome fact of annota-

tion is determined by various sources of authority and power: "it is solely the great engine of university functioning that powers the pistons of scholarly annotation."[6] The relation of annotation to text, we are told, is less a relation of meaning than it is of power: annotation is "a procedure of political appropriation of the power of the text; it is an apparatus for reproducing knowledge in a form than legitimates the annotator, the annotation, and the social structures within which they exist. . . . Therefore the multiplication of critical apparatus does not enhance the authority of the text itself but achieves the recognition of the annotator within the academic discipline" (pp. 186–87).

It is a surprising irony that annotation should suddenly be seen not as the sissy but as the bully of text and scholar. The fact that some annotation does derive from academic power games unfortunately highlights some of the darker motives and realities of contemporary scholarship, but the fact that a lack of high standards for annotation invites such self-seeking enterprises is no cause to make annotation guilty by association with the perpetrators. The greater irony of the new arguments is that the attempt to relegate annotation to the dismal arena of petty politics and passing fashion is fueled in part by some of the least attractive motives of careerism, especially when the critic expressly desires to circumvent the conventional annotation of his or her own work in order to protect the sources that he or she mines for critical authority from being raided by "claim jumpers" and "predatory readers" (pp. 168, 170).

On higher ground, we know that annotation is more a handmaiden than an aggressor, that it aims to enhance the clarity and accessibility of the text more than its own recognition; however, the portrayal of the annotator as a nihilistic, status-seeking egoist may continue to have a deleterious effect on the editorial scholarship before us. In place of timid guidelines for laconic notes, we are now advised of the myth, the subjectivity, the impermanence, and the ultimate futility of annotations. Underneath the changing rhetoric is the unchanging distrust that the annotator will somehow desecrate the sacred text or, in more secular terms, that he will engage in a power struggle with its authority. The greater pity is that the annotator seldom regards himself as an objective scholar whose authoritative presence and skill are essential to a full representation of the text and to the leveraged movement of that text in time. Seldom does he consider that the virtue of brevity may be a dishon-

orable excuse for avoiding the detailed attention that the text requires; seldom does he entertain the possibility that rigid conventions of apparatus may be fortified barriers designed to fragment
and foil his proper role.[7]

The practice of annotating texts in 1991 exhibits the same state
of anarchy that Donald H. Reiman found in the editing of Shelley's
texts in 1971: a fortunate extension of the parallel is that there is
again no entrenched orthodoxy to rebel against. Moreover, the no-
vice annotator finds no helpful dogma in the materials of the
Committee on Scholarly Editions, whose seventeenth guiding question for inspectors is simply, "annotations adequate?" Adequate to
whom, one wants to know, and when is adequacy ever a desirable
standard, especially when one recalls the severe criticism of some
unevenly annotated CEAA and CSE editions?[8] When one turns to
the Clarendon Press one finds no standards common to the Press
but a smorgasbord of editions in which editors appear to have cut
their own deals for annotations—from the Hardy letters, a paean to
brevity, to the Dickens letters, where the full particulars are nonetheless limited by various compromises.

Nor does one find consistency at the Yale University Press,
where for the editors of the Yale edition of Samuel Johnson "no
matter has given rise to more diversity of opinion . . . than the question of how much explanatory annotation to provide."[9] For the
edition of *The Rambler* the editors surrendered to the interests of
time, contending that a thorough job of annotation, admittedly
needed, "would be a tremendously taxing job, the work of a great
many years of patient research. . . . [P]erhaps in time a scholar will
be found who is willing to give the best years of his life to the task
of producing the 'definitively' annotated edition of *The Rambler*"
(p. 106). In preparing a "readable" edition, the editors would "at
least . . . explain the more prominent allusions," but as an editorial
rule, formed in reaction to Birkbek Hill's excesses, they would not
let the Yale Johnson become "an exercise in ingenuity of bibliographical annotation" (p. 101). Fortunately, we have the Yale edition of *Horace Walpole's Correspondence* (48 volumes), rejected as
a model of annotation by the Johnson editors as too "encyclopaedic," to show us what scholarly ingenuity is all about. It was the
editor of that colossal undertaking, Wilmarth S. Lewis, who told
members of a Toronto editorial conference on the eve of the edition's completion: "It is no longer acceptable for an editor to stop

at routine identification of persons or casual annotation. His goal is complete understanding, and he hopes to give to his work the final grace of art."[10]

I made reference earlier to Reiman's "Editing Shelley" (1971), recently reprinted in his *Romantic Texts and Contexts* (1987). It can hardly be said that this is a neglected essay, for it stimulated two decades of rigorous textual criticism, but Reiman's early views on the editor and his annotations, as informed by his work on the catalogue-edition of *Shelley and His Circle*, have been neglected by unmoored annotators. I turn to Reiman because he was one of the first to dismiss totally conventional views of annotation and to declare that the editor and the annotator, be they not the same, must be consummate scholars and equal partners in the editorial enterprise, must be in complete command of text and context, lest "the work of an entire generation . . . turn out to be little more than a furious spinning of wheels."[11] Reiman was joined on the platform that day by another vehement editor, W. J. B. Owen, who in joint refrain pleaded in "Annotating Wordsworth" not only for annotations that provide crucial information for the reader and the literary critic but for a revision and liberation of annotation theory: "In short," he concluded, "I plea for the commentary as a means to a knowledge of the poet's knowledge, so that we may the better understand his art and his wisdom."[12] In a chorus that is no less daring today, Reiman declared that it is not only each commentator's duty "to track down particular information that has eluded his predecessors, but also to raise new questions and problems that, if solved by researchers in the future, will result in fuller knowledge not only of the *actions* of poets but of their unstated reasonings as well."[13] Here at last was a view of the editor as the master custodian of text and context for his time, undeterred and undisturbed by the prospect that some of his labor would be revised as a result of projecting the text into another generation. One thing more: Reiman and Owen, like Lewis before them, insisted on admitting into the annotation process a new level of exactitude and detail. "Besides noting such customary details as literary and historical allusions," wrote Reiman, "we delve into printing and publishing techniques, the operation of the postal system, banking and business practices, relevant medical and legal information, and, in general, the web of daily affairs in the early nineteenth century that underlay the lives and literary works of the major figures" (p. 21). For those listening then, no longer could annotations be casually put in the hands of graduate assistants and reference librarians. The un-yielding and untraced problems of many editions are solved when years of immersion in "the web of daily affairs" suddenly allow a leap of imagination that no assistant can make for any scholar.

It is in the spirit of Lewis, Reiman, and Owen that I return to Yeats's letters and Eliot's lectures, though I must limit my focus to a few principles of time, pursuit, and detail at work in some notes of recovery and explanation. But first I want to underscore the perti-nence to annotation of Reiman's timely call in this volume for a more humanistic orientation in the editorial process, in which he characterizes the editor's relation to the "person" that is the text as analogous to a "family physician," the literary historian's to a "bio-grapher," the literary critic's to a "family friend."[14] If I draw the implication and extend the analogy of those relations correctly, that one of the annotator's large roles should be, when needed, to human-istically represent the private world to the public, then as annotator I should be prepared to serve as "family confidant" to Yeats, even as "attendant lord" to Eliot, discreetly providing glimpses of their per-sonal worlds to illuminate both text and context for the reader. The once subservient annotator must thus serve the author and the work more intimately than editor, historian, or critic.

My immediate purpose as Yeats's annotator, however, is to re-construct and portray the rich context of the letters, to indicate the roles of the recipients in Yeats's intellectual life, to allow the reader to participate fully in their dialogue, to identify and capture the implications of allusions and references. But it is also my purpose to recover sources that open up the scholarship without intruding on the text, to enrich the literary and social history without creating a narrative, to inform precisely without interpreting, to identify fully without being pedantic or patronizing, and to make decisions about opportunistic inclusions as objectively as possible.

From 1901 to 1904 Yeats journeyed back and forth from London to Dublin trying to realize his various dramatic enterprises. The fleeting surface of his daily reading is often seized in the letters, a fact that requires the annotator to trawl through the daily London and Dublin papers for these years and to live with the agony of time required to discover that a sentence said to be quoted from the *St. James Gazette* last week was slightly misquoted from the *Westminster Gazette* the week before. But for the moment I want to focus on some notes of recovery for known and unknown figures in the text. In obvious dislike of the deadly primer note that had progressed from "See DNB" to the minimalist birth-death-occupation entry, Arthur Friedman urges us to consult contemporary sources rather than reference sources for identified figures, a rewarding lesson for Yeats's letters. With his bad eyes, Yeats occasionally refers to his Dublin oculist, identified simply as Dr. Charles Fitzgerald (1843–1916) by previous editors. But why, the attentive reader asks, is Fitzgerald sometimes alluded to in non-ocular contexts? Extensive familiarity with contemporary memoirs leads us to Paige Dickinson's *The Dublin of Yesterday* (see Illustrations, note 1). With the addition of selected details—the location of his office and his love of John Butler Yeats's paintings—Fitzgerald is brought to life again in a note that clarifies his presence in Yeats's life for future appearances.

A less obvious use of contemporary sources occurs in annotating the concluding lines of Yeats's letter to Wilfred Blunt from Coole Park on 4 July 1902, in reference to Robert Gregory's coming of age (see note 2). Some annotators, subjective as we are, might choose not to annotate this passing occasion at all, but when one discovers that Robert actually came of age six weeks earlier, some objective explanation is required. Lady Gregory's unpublished diary in the Berg was a start, but what society magazines, one might ask, carried reports of such Ascendancy festivities? The letter invites the account found in the ladies' weekly, *Hearth and Home*, and we allow the length of the note in deference to the nonessential but satisfying description of an elaborate social ritual in which Yeats was witness and participant, a hitherto unrecorded dimension of his life at Coole. Do we not savor the close of the letter more through the note?

Some of the most significant recoveries are to be made only in the unpublished diaries of Yeats's friends, and it is of course the annotator's responsibility to track them down: Lady Gregory in the Berg; Sturge Moore in Senate House; Henry Nevinson in the Bodleian; Ricketts, Shannon, and Cockerell in the British Library; Violet Hunt at Cornell, and so on, with many others in private hands. When, for example, Yeats writes to John Quinn early in July 1904 of "a very fiery Irish address" that Maud Gonne had recently given in London (see note 3), it is one thing to track down the details of the unreported lecture, but it is a divine gift to find an account in the diary of his friend Nevinson, who probably described the evening to Yeats. Nor could I be persuaded to exclude a rare and apt portrait by Nevinson of Arthur Symons's offensive wife, Rhoda Bowser (see note 4), as a woman with "viper mouth, very cruel & full of lust," especially in view of Yeats's expressed hatred of her when Symons went mad in 1908.[15]

Yeats's friends were often struck by aspects of his conversation, and an astonishing amount of it is quoted or recorded in their diaries, which often provide spectacular contexts for routine letters, such as Yeats's to Sturge Moore on 10 January 1901 (see note 5). Re-covering from a bout of flu, Yeats wrote to delay dinner to "one evening shortly." Since the future evening is left open, and since Sturge Moore's diary records two subsequent meetings, a tea on 21 January at which dinner was planned for Friday the 25th and a dinner that actually took place on 4 February, the letter invites both entries, thereby providing an opportunity to give the reader-critic two strikingly different views of Yeats in conversation. Should the annotator, fearing a charge of subjectivity, keep from the reader Yeats's earthy story of the man whose trade was biting the testicles off calves? Not this annotator.

Many fine editors have written "untraced" more times than they would wish because their publishers have taken away their time. It takes several years of intensive research on a project to provide opportunities and situations for hopelessly untraced items to reveal themselves at the least expected moment, whether by serendipity, chance, or sudden illumination of context. I held little hope of ever identifying the very mysterious object that Yeats called "my Shrine" in a letter to Lady Gregory of 13 January 1903 (see note 6). All such fugitives become embedded in the annotator's desperate subconscious, ready to seize upon the slightest shard of hope. Left untraced, Yeats's request for Lady Gregory to bring him his Shrine could lead to all sorts of mischievous speculation and abuse. Going through George Russell's unpublished autobiography in the Lilly Library one day, I came across his bizarre description of Yeats's relation with a man named Fitzpatrick, whom I had never encountered in researching the letters. A curious inquiry led to an ecstatic revelation—Fitzpatrick was the editor of a short-lived symbolist periodical, *The Shrine*! And as the note explains, further examination convinced me that it was the object of Yeats's baffling request—as simple as that.[16]

And for months I had gnawing doubts about my note on a book titled *Silver Drops* that Yeats had returned to a Mrs. Rogers Rees in Wales (see note 7). Two nineteenth-century books by that title were unearthed, both so irredeemably bad that one could not account for Yeats reading either, and the temptation was to suggest that the title was probably a slip for Somerville and Ross's *Silver Fox* (1897). Further work revealed the unrewarding news that the husband was John Rogers Rees, a banker, and even more digging showed that Yeats had stayed with the Rees's when lecturing in Cardiff, when he obviously borrowed the book. But why this book? Much later my hungry eye seized on the name John Rogers Rees, author of *The Pleasures of a Bookworm* (1886) and *With Friend and Book* (1889), in the context of collecting rare books. Of course! Wing's *Short-Title Catalogue*! And there it was in the title index of *Accessing Early English Books 1641–1700* (1981)—*Silver Drops*, undated, by one William Blake, borrowed by Yeats the Blake scholar to investigate any possible relationship. Simple as that.

I turn now to Eliot's Clark Lectures, which require more explanatory annotations but make no less exacting demands. Eliot was reluctant to publish them in their unexpanded form because, as he says in his preface, many of his remarks needed qualification, clarification, and details of fact and authority. The unrevised text is, however, a crucial document in his intellectual life: much of his reading and writing for the twenty years preceding the lectures is funneled into them; much of his reading and writing in the twenty years following the lectures flows out of them. I have thus attempted to annotate the lectures in the larger intellectual context of Eliot's critical writings, drawing upon his own earlier and later comments on a specific subject to provide the qualification of clarification that he desired. As there are hundreds of oblique allusions and references that enrich the lectures, the annotations aim not only to assist the reader with text and context but to illuminate the range and depth of Eliot's learning in the lectures. When Eliot says that Donne occasionally quotes Bonaventura, for example, the notes indicate what prose works of Donne he had to read to make that observation. A guiding principle in annotating references is to keep the reader in the text, so that when Eliot begins discussing "Sappho's famous ode" the ode is not only identified but printed in the translation Eliot likely used.

The fact that Eliot wrote the lectures in haste and drew spontaneously on his memory for illustrations is exemplified on nearly every page, where we encounter a continuous flow of errors, slips, and misquotations. He misremembers and thereby misinterprets a scene in the *Iliad*; he has Elpenor falling overboard and drowning in the *Odyssey* rather than falling off the roof of Circe's palace and breaking his neck; he refers to Marvell's "famous Marlborough House poem" when he means Appleton House; he quotes a dramatic sentence said to be from Huysman's *En Route* when it is actually from *Là-Bas*; he quotes from the *Purgatorio* when it is actually from the *Paradiso*, and he sometimes gets the canto numbers wrong.

The numerous misquotations will be preserved in the text and corrected in the notes, for it is of great interest to see in what form Eliot held such a vast amount of memorized material for instant recall. Many of the misquotations require extended explanation, as when he misquotes two lines from Swinburne's "Before the Mirror" (1865), "Snowdrops that plead for pardon/ And pine for fright." He had got them right in *The Sacred Wood* six years earlier, but here he writes "Violets that plead for pardon," and when he later revised the typescript for delivery as the Turnbull Lectures (1933), he added a passage on the significance of the violets. What is not obvious to the reader, as Eliot makes comparative references to Donne's "The Extasie," is that Eliot has confused Swinburne's snowdrops with the central image in Donne's poem, "The violets reclining head." Necessary explanation, I would argue, not interpretation.

In checking all the quotations, and in locating every instance in which Eliot used a certain quotation in print, it becomes obvious that he habitually quoted from memory, that some of the misquotations in the Clark Lectures appear repeatedly and undetected in his published works, including the dedication to Jean Verdenal from Canto XXI of the *Purgatorio*, which was substantively misquoted in *Poems 1909–1925* and in *Collected Poems 1909–1935* and not finally corrected until *Complete Poems and Plays, 1909–1950*:

la quantitate
Puote veder del amor che a te mi scalda,
Quando dismento nostra vanitate
Trattando l'ombre come cosa salda.[17]

No telling how many scholars have also misquoted this un-checked passage in which Eliot conflated lines from the *Purgatorio* and *Paradiso* (XXVIII, 50). In the midst of the errors, however, there are many misquotation traps for the incautious annotator, set by Eliot in his use of the idiosyncratic edition that he had at hand. Once these editions are identified and located in his personal library and among his personal books in the Houghton Library, what appears to be a misquoted passage turns out to be an exact transcription. I refer you to note 8, where Eliot, having concluded his remarks on Dante's *Vita Nuova*, turns to an eccentric printing of a passage in Chaucer's *Troilus* to conclude his lectures.

Finally, I want to point to one of Eliot's vague references to his previous lectures and essays, some of which are presently lost (see note 9). In such instances it becomes the annotator's responsibility, after an exhaustive but unsuccessful search, to record such information about the missing document that is pertinent both to the context and to the one literary scholar who may be prompted to recover it with new information on another day. Thus in the Lewis-Reiman-Owen spirit do we aim to make our notes not untraced but obsolete.

I think all of us must consider it an historical privilege to be editors of modernist texts and to be preparing them for a new century of readers. But to be worthy of that privilege, we must all insist that the profession abandon Dr. Johnson's lingering view that annotations are necessary evils, and reject the disaffected view that they are merely power-plays. It may be that this Society, which is "for Textual Scholarship," cannot describe a universal rationale for annotated editions, but we can define a universally high level of scholarly expectation. We can say to annotators, as textual theorists have been saying to would-be editors, and as Yeats said to would-be poets, "learn your trade/ Sing whatever is well made."

Illustrations

Note 1: WBY in Dublin to Lady Gregory at Coole Park, 3 August 1904:

I shall probably return Saturday morning. I see Fitzgerald on Friday afternoon.[1]

[1.] Dr. Charles Edward Fitzgerald (1843–1916), a Dublin oculist

with a surgery at 27 Upper Merrion Street, prescribed new glasses
for WBY. He was an early admirer of JBY's paintings and presented two of them, "My Daughter" and "The Bird Market," to Hugh
Lane's Municipal Gallery of Modern Art in 1905. In *The Dublin of
Yesterday* (1929), P. L. Dickinson describes him (31–32) as "one of
the best-known figures in the life of the Irish capital in the years
about 1900. He was an oculist, but looked like a Parisian artist of
the Du Maurier period. He invariably wore a black suit, with a
wideawake hat with an enormous brim, and a long flowing bow-tie.
He wore a pointed beard and walked rapidly with a light and
swinging step. He was . . . to me a romantic figure of picturesque
adventure in my younger days."

   Note 2: WBY at Coole Park to W. S. Blunt, 4 July [1902]:

Lady Gregory, who is typing this, has been very busy over Roberts coming
of age. All went off well, Robert made a very good speech, very simple very
sincere, and effective merely as a speech.[1]

   [1.] Robert Gregory had come of age on 20 May 1902, but, since he
and AG were in London for Edward VII's Coronation (subsequently postponed because of the King's ill-health), the tenants'
celebrations did not take place until his return to Coole on 24 June.
Reviewing the main events of 1902 in her diary on 4 January 1903
(Berg), AG recalled "Robert's coming of age homecoming—bon-
fires—torches—dinner & dance—presentations—Thank God he is
so well received & on such good terms with his people & has so
good a name." The celebration was reported in *Hearth and Home*
on 24 July 1902 (570): "The tenantry assembled at the gates of the
Coole Park domain, and presented an address and some valuable
gifts of plate, &c. The household also presented some handsome
silver, which Mr. Gregory suitably acknowledged; the road from
Gort Station being gay with bunting, the flags of all nations being
included."

   Note 3: WBY in London to John Quinn in New York, c. 6 July
1904:

Mrs. Macbride gave a very fiery Irish address here the other day. It was really very fine, I hear, quite self-restrained, for her, at least, and eloquent as
ever.[1]

   [1.] On 25 June MG lectured on "The Shan Van Vocht" [*i.e., "The*

Poor Old Woman," a traditional personification of Ireland] to the
Irish National Club in Holborn Town Hall, with John O'Leary in
the chair. After the lecture Nevinson wrote admirably in his diary
(Bodleian): "She was most lovely—more beautiful even than I
remem-bered—the mops of loose tawny hair, the strong face and
frank eyes, the sudden transformation of the smile. In black with
open neck showing her splendid throat. Only ornament the Tara
broach at the waist belt. So tall she is, her voice most beautiful.
Read or rather recited her address on the Shan Van Vocht—in
exquisite language."

Note 4: WBY in London to Lady Gregory at Coole, [13 April
1901]:

> I dined with Symons yesterday. I think he is a little anxious about his
> expenses. He pays £80 a year rent for his flat, & his wife looks no house-
> keeper. I told Mrs Old that I wanted to ask them to diner & she said 'I don't
> mind Lady Gregory or Miss Symons but cooking for her!'—she then
> became inarticulate.[1]

[1.] After marrying Rhoda Bowser (1874–1936), the daughter of a
Newcastle shipbuilder, on 19 January, Symons took up residence at
134 Lauderdale Mansions, Maida Vale. His wife was not generally
liked: after a dinner party on 21 June 1903, Nevinson recorded
(Bodleian) meeting "Arthur Symons—pallid, heavy-eyed, unwhole-
some & soft, with conspicuous little wife—pale, thin, bright brown
eyes, viper mouth, very cruel & full of lust." Symons's elder sister
was Anna Martyn Symons (1864–1933).

Note 5: WBY in London to T. Sturge Moore in London, [10
January 1901]:

> My dear Sturge Moore: I am much better, indeed had I known yesterday
> evening I was going to be I would have ventured to go to you after all, I
> think. Let me go to you one evening shortly.[1]

[1.] WBY evidently dined with Sturge Moore on Friday, 25 January, for the latter recorded in his diary (London) on 21 January:
"Met Yeats at tea he walked with me to Miss Dickens talking about
his spiritual theory of Shelley & other poets, I trying to convince
him that reason was the sole ground for my preferences. No success, though I think he understood my objection to Countess

Kathleen. He said he would come on Friday." They also dined on 4 February when the conversation was apparently more earthy: "With Binyon out to have dinner with Yeats, felt quarrelsome & thought Masefield very dull. Yeats brother had seen an old man bite off the testicles of calves when a boy. He did one after another. It was his trade."

Note 6: WBY in London to Lady Gregory at Coole, 13 January [1903]:

Will you be able to find room for my Shrine when you come?[1]

[1.] *The Shrine*, a short-lived quarterly, edited in Stratford-upon-Avon by the Irish-born R. H. Fitzpatrick, was dedicated to the belief that Shakespeare had been the Second Coming of Christ, but that the world was only now ready to receive this momentous news. On discovering himself to be Shakespeare's disciple, Fitzpatrick, a relative of the theosophist, D. N. Dunlop, had sold his Dublin business to devote himself to preaching the new gospel. AE told WBY of him, and, in an unpublished fragment of autobiography (Indiana), relates that at a meeting of The Three Kings "Yeats began to speak . . . about myself that I was a magnet who gathered about him all the wild characters of Ireland. Then he told them the story of Fitzpatrick. Now said Yeats feeling he too was a magnet 'If there was such a man in London he would be bound to be here'. A figure rose up, at the end of the room. 'I am he.' It was Fitzpatrick."   The first number of *The Shrine* (May 1902) shows Fitzpatrick's affinities with WBY's symbolism of the late nineties: "the Spirit of Beauty is abroad again in the world" he proclaimed (2–3), "we are on the brink of a new supernatural revelation of the Oversoul . . . this re-extension of the human mind . . . will lead to a fuller comprehension of Shakespeare. For he too, was a symbolist in his dawn before the dawn." WBY was probably asking for No. 3 (November 1902), which contained "An Epistle on Nietzsche" by Thomas Concannon, and which he may have loaned to AG in Dublin the previous autumn. His friend Edwin Ellis was to contribute "Keats's Shakespeare" to the final number, which appeared in February 1903.

Note 7: WBY at Coole to Mrs. Rogers Rees in Llandaff, 16 April 1903:

Dear Mrs Rees—I hope your husband got his book 'Silver drops' all right.[1] I posted it before I left London.

^{1.} *Silver Drops, Or Serious Things* (?1670) by William Blake (fl. 1650–70), housekeeper to the Ladies Charity School of Highgate. WBY had probably borrowed the undated book out of curiosity about the author's possible connection with the poet William Blake (1757–1827). Prefaced by Blake's appeal to the "Many Noble, Well-Disposed" lady subscribers, the book presents for their "pious thoughts" and "Lilly Hands" four epistolatory sermons, his "Silver drops" on Charity, Truth, Religion, and Virtue, to persuade them to support the charity school in Highgate which caters for "some 30 or near 40 poor and fatherless Boys".

Note 8: the concluding lines of the Clark Lectures:

As I have not, in a series of lectures necessarily compressed and abbreviated, had occasion to mention Chaucer directly, I should like to pay him the tribute of ending with his own ending and invocation—

> Thou oon, and two, and three, eterne on-lyve,
> That regnest ay in three and two and oon,
> Uncircumscript, and al mayst circumscryve,
> Us from visible and invisible foon
> Defende; and to thy mercy, everychoon,
> So make us, Jesus, for thy grace, digne,
> For love of mayde and moder thyn benigne! Amen.[1]

^{1.} The concluding stanza of *Troilus and Criseyde*, Book V, 1863–70, as printed in TSE's annotated copy (Houghton) of *The Student's Chaucer*, ed. Rev. Walter W. Skeat (New York: Oxford Univ. Press, 1894), p. 325. Aside from differences in punctuation and spelling, Skeat's edition is the only one to read "grace" for "mercy" in the penultimate line. In his review of R. K. Root's edition of *The Book of Troilus and Criseyde* later in the year, TSE was to illuminate his choice of Chaucer's poem to conclude his Clark Lectures: "It may be said without exaggeration that 'Troilus and Criseyde' is a document second in importance, in its kind, only to the 'Vita Nuova.' It is a pendant to the latter, and the two are perfectly consistent" (TLS, 19 August 1926, 547).

Note 9: From Lecture V of the Clark Lectures:

I have always been impressed, and once discussed in a paper, by the sense of a "double world" in the tragedies of Chapman, and which made me compare him to Dostoevski.[1]

[1.] TSE gave his lecture on Chapman before the Cam Literary Club at Cambridge University on 8 November 1924. The next day I. A. Richards wrote to his fiancée, Dorothea Pilley: "In the evening I heard Eliot's paper. Stuff about Chapman. Not very definite but we had a good deal of discussion on general topics and he seems to have some sound views (mine I mean)" (*SL*, 31). On 12 November TSE wrote to Virginia Woolf (private) that after all the labor it had not proved worthy of publication, but subsequently he planned to revise and publish it in the *Criterion*, where he announced to his readers that due to illness the editor had been "unable to prepare his essay on 'A Neglected Aspect of George Chapman' for this number" (April 1925, 341). The essay is lost, but TSE may have given a summary of it in a recent review, "Wanley and Chapman" (TLS, 31 December 1925, 907): "In Chapman we have a dramatist by accident, who was a poet and a man of thought as well as a scholar. Ideas, and the 'sensibility' of thought meant more to Chapman than to any of his contemporary dramatists; he was much more of an "intellectual" than Ben Jonson, and in his way far more a mystic than any. He is a precursor of the metaphysicals. Chapman himself is mixed; his classical stoicism is crossed with a strain—perhaps out of Marsilio Ficino and similar writers— of otherworldliness; resulting, here and there in his tragedies, in a sense of double significance which gives him here and there a curious resemblance to Dostoevsky." TSE did not return to the manuscript, writing regrettably in the preface to a new edition (1955) of *Elizabethan Essays* (1934) "that I did not, during that period of my life at which these essays were written, have occasion to write about the work of that very great poet and dramatist, George Chapman. It is too late now: to attempt to repair such a gap, after many years' neglect, would be almost as futile as to attempt to remove the blemishes . . . in one's early poems" (p. x).

NOTES

1. Allan Wade's selected and partially annotated edition of *The Letters of W. B. Yeats* (New York: Macmillan) was published in 1955. The first of at least twelve volumes of *The Collected Letters of W. B. Yeats*, ed. John Kelly and Eric Domville (Oxford: Clarendon Press) appeared in 1986.

2. Unpublished letter of 30 December 1936 to Henry Ware Eliot, Houghton
Library, Harvard University, quoted by permission (copyright Valerie Esme
Eliot).

3. "Principles of Historical Annotation in Critical Editions of Modern Texts," in
English Institute Annual 1941 (New York: Columbia University Press, 1942),
p. 116.

4. *Studies in Bibliography*, Vol. 11, ed. Fredson Bowers (Charlottesville, VA:
Bibliographical Society of the Univ. of Virginia, 1958), p. 35. The third article
recommended by CEAA, Alice Walker's "Principles of Annotation: Some
Suggestions for Editors of Shakespeare," *SB*, 9 (1957), 95–105, is limited solely to the annotation of vocabulary.

5. "A Rationale of Literary Annotation: The Example of Fielding's Novels,"
Studies in Bibliography, Vol. 34, ed. Fredson Bowers (Charlottesville:
University Press of Virginia, 1981), p. 4.

6. Ed. Stephen A. Barney (New York: Oxford University Press, 1991), p. 162.

7. In relation to footnote conventions, annotators should consider Patricia S.
White's recent discussion of note-placement strategies in "Black and White
and Read All Over: A Meditation on Footnotes" (*Text* 5, pp. 81–90). As this
essay goes to press, I have not received the discussion of annotation in *The
Theory and Practice of Text Editing*, eds. Ian Small and Marcus Walsh (New
York: Cambridge University Press, 1992).

8. See, for example, Robert C. Bray's review of a CEAA edition, Vol. IV of *The
Works of Tom Sawyer*, in *Review 3*, ed. James O. Hoge and James L. W. West
III (Charlottesville: University of Virginia Press, 1981), where he begins a
detailed discussion of the notes: "Yet *Tom Sawyer* is on the whole too much
annotated. The edition is encumbered with superfluous notes which do not
elaborate or clarify anything necessary to the story, which posit some autobiographical connection where none is implied, or which are otherwise miscon-
ceived" (p. 83).

9. Donald Greene, "No Dull Duty: The Yale Edition of the Works of Samuel
Johnson," *Editing Eighteenth-Century Texts*, ed. D. I. B. Smith (Toronto:
University of Toronto Press, 1968), p. 105.

10. "Editing Familiar Letters," in *Editing Correspondence*, ed. J. A. Dainard
(New York & London: Garland, 1979), p. 36.

11. *Romantic Texts and Contexts* (Columbia: University of Missouri Press, 1987),
p. 24.

12. In *Editing Texts of the Romantic Period*, ed. John D. Baird (Toronto: A. M.

Hakkert, Ltd., 1972), p. 71.

13. *Romantic Texts and Contexts*, p. 22.

14. See "Public and Private in the Study of Manuscripts" (p. 58, above).

15. Yeats wrote to Lady Gregory about his view of Symons's mental illness, and Rhoda's role in it, in an unpublished letter of 13 October 1908, quoted by John Kelly in *Lady Gregory Fifty Years After*, ed. Ann Saddlemyer and Colin Smythe (Totowa, NJ: Barnes & Noble, 1987): "He [Symons] had the subtle understanding of a woman & his thought flowed through life with my own, for many years, almost as if he had been one of the two or three women friends who are everything to me. And now he has been eaten like a fish by that kingfisher & his bones flung out of doors" (p. 257).

16. Not quite so simple: since writing the annotation (Illustrations, note 6) and this essay I have learned from letters recently acquired at the Berg that Yeats did indeed possess a "Shrine" and that it is visible in a photograph of Yeats in his study that appeared in the *Tatler* in 1904, now included as an illustration in the volume. With these discoveries came one of the annotator's great frustrations, that of having to cancel, though with no lack of gratitude for having come upon the truth, an informative note that took many hours to construct. Thus in time does plausible ingenuity sometimes give way to pressing fact. The note now reads:

> WBY had a small shrine, which he usually kept at Woburn Buildings, but which could be folded for travelling, and which he had taken on his latest visit to Coole. It can be glimpsed just behind his right elbow in plate OO. Replying to this letter on "Saturday" [14 January 1903; Berg], AG told him that even before "yr little note came I had discovered the picture—& given it to the manager & asked him to take care of it for you. Perhaps yr sister wd. have it packed & sent on? Worse still, on undoing by own hold all, I found that wretched Shrine which I had brought up for you—& which is now landed here again!"

17. The correct quotation is the reply of the shade of Statius to Virgil, lines 133–36:

> Or puoi la quantitate
> comprender dell' amor ch' a te mi scalda,
> quando dismento nostra vanitate,
>
> trattando l'ombre come cosa salda.

("Now canst thou comprehend the measure of the love which warms me toward thee, when I forget our nothingness, and treat shades as a solid thing.")

Richard Wright's Communisms: Textual Variance, Intentionality, and Socialization in *American Hunger*, "I Tried to Be a Communist," and *The God That Failed*

CHRISTOPHER Z. HOBSON

Upon its posthumous publication in 1977, *American Hunger*, the excised concluding portion of Richard Wright's 1944 autobiography, became firmly established in the Wright canon.[1] In the process, it displaced an earlier published version of part of the same text—Wright's section of *The God That Failed*, the influential 1949 anthology of writings about communism by six ex-communists and ex-communist sympathizers. Wright's fellow contributors were Louis Fischer, André Gide, Arthur Koestler, Ignazio Silone, and Stephen Spender, prominent cultural figures associated with what was then called the "non-Communist Left"; the volume was edited by R. H. S. Crossman, a noted British Labour MP. Hailed by such liberal opinion-makers as Reinhold Niebuhr and Arthur Schlesinger, Jr., the volume was reprinted nineteen times by the mid-Sixties; a generation of politically literate people learned of Wright's views on communism through its pages. Today, though *The God That Failed* remains in print, it is little known except to Wright specialists and cultural historians. *American Hunger*, on the other hand, exists both as a separate work, published in 1977 and reprinted numerous times; and as the concluding section of the reassembled 1944 text, included in the Library of America's edition of Wright's *Later Works* under the title *Black Boy (American Hunger)*. This last has won some endorsements as an "authoritative"

307

text,[2] though it is too early to tell if it will become predominant in general circulation and scholarly reference. In either version, *American Hunger*, an unpublished manuscript in 1949, has become the medium through which students learn of Wright's young adulthood in Chicago and his involvement with the Communist Party.

The multiple ironies in this situation are my subject. Publication of *American Hunger* gave this text canonical authority for several reasons: it possessed intrinsic interest as an original part of Wright's autobiography; it dealt with Wright's life as a whole in his Chicago years, not just with his political involvements; and even the material dealing with communism was fuller than in *The God That Failed*— which was, in fact, a condensation of three chapters of what became *American Hunger*, made originally for magazine publication (in the *Atlantic Monthly* in 1944, as "I Tried to Be a Communist"). Further, the fuller version of this material had a nuanced and moderate quality—a generosity in assessing communism's positive features even in an account of disillusionment—that was missing from the condensation, whose compression increased the harshness of its tone. Yet scope and subtlety do not automatically give *American Hunger* the status of an authoritative expression of Wright's views. Which version of Wright's text should be taken as authoritative—if either—is a question that can be established only by comparing the versions, both textually and contextually, in terms of what Wright says in each and in terms of their relation to Wright's evolving outlook and his other writings.

No account of Wright's life or works has yet done this work. Keneth Kinnamon, for example, reconstructing Wright's early life in 1973 with the aid of the then-published fragments, did not compare them to the longer version already available in a limited-circulation reproduction at several libraries (Kinnamon chap. 2 *passim*). Later writers have relied on *American Hunger* without comparing it to the published fragments. Some commentators (e.g., Herbert Leibowitz in his study of American autobiography, *Fabricating Lives*) fail to mention these earlier pieces at all. Others give the impression that the fragments represent a virtually complete if piecemeal publication of the later text of *American Hunger*. John M. Reilly, for example, asserts that in reading *American Hunger* "we are actually reassembling its familiar anecdotes and episodes into a continuous narrative, rather than receiving a new text" (214); later, he refers without qualification to "the three chapters of the manuscript that constitute [the 1944 *Atlantic Monthly* article] 'I Tried to Be a Communist'" (219). Michel Fabre, Wright's major biographer, states that in "I Tried to Be a Communist" the *Atlantic* editors "included everything from the original text dealing with communism. They added only a few transitional sentences with the result that 'I Tried to Be a Communist' does not distort the message of the complete autobiography as it was originally written in 1943." And he adds, erroneously, that the appearance of "I Tried" and two other segments of the original manuscript during 1944–45 left "only a few pages of "The Horror and the Glory' [Wright's initial title for the deleted section] still unpublished" (255, 538n.). The Library of America's version of the autobiography, finally, treats the fragments as lacking intrinsic importance. It contains only a bare notion of their publication, and no consideration of their significance (*Later Works* 857, 869).

In the absence of close study of these texts, *American Hunger* has been accepted as definitive by default. Despite questions about factual accuracy, the portions of the narrative dealing with the Communist Party have been accepted without qualification as Wright's imaginative representation of his communist experience; as Reilly puts it, gaps between "fact and narrative" serve only "to direct our attention away from [*American Hunger's*] presumed reference value as an account of objective happenings and toward its salient features as a literary reconstruction" (214–15).[3]

American Hunger's assumed status as Wright's definitive account of his Communist experience rests, then, partly on a failure of critics to examine it in relation to associated texts. When the comparisons are made, and considered in the light of textual history and Wright's other contemporary treatments of communism, a different picture from the standard one emerges—one that sheds light on issues of textual variance, authorial intention, and the social meaning of texts. It becomes apparent that "I Tried to Be a Communist"/ *The God That Failed* is a distinct version of Wright's text, differing from *American Hunger* in its more harshly negative treatment of communism. Further, even though this version originated fortuitously as a magazine condensation, Wright showed his acceptance of it by choosing to reprint it in 1949—in preference to writing a new piece for Crossman's anthology, proposing inclusion of the *American Hunger* version, or making revisions to establish a new version. Wright's reasons for this choice, though not revealed by correspondence or journals, can be established by inference: the harsher treatment of communism in T*he God That Failed* corresponds both to Wright's needs in 1949 when he was under pressure to establish his anticommunist credentials and to the evolution of his thought as shown a few years later by *The Outsider*. Inferably, then, this version is one that represented Wright's politics in 1949 and was not merely chosen for convenience. Hence, *The God That Failed* should be recognized as an independent expression of Wright's outlook as of 1948–49, and discussions of his intellectual evolution should refer to it as well as to *American Hunger*; the seeming authority of *American Hunger* as Wright's assessment of communism is an artifact, the result of canonizing a text that records an early stage in his political evolution.

* * *

Much but not all of what became *American Hunger* did see print in 1944 and 1945. A condensation of the final three chapters, dealing with the Communist Party, appeared in the *Atlantic Monthly* as a two-part serial (August-September 1944), under the title "I Tried to Be a Communist." The bulk of the first three chapters was published as "Early Days in Chicago" in the 1945 edition of *Cross Section*, an annual compilation of works by new writers. Some remaining snippets of the first two chapters (overlapping slightly with "Early Days") came out under Wright's original title for the entire work, "American Hunger," in *Mademoiselle*, September 1945. Much later, Wright republished "Early Days in Chicago" as "The Man Who Went to Chicago" in *Eight Men* (1961). "I Tried to Be a Communist," in the meantime, had appeared in French in Sartre's magazine *Les Temps Moderne* in 1949 and in English later that year in *The God That Failed*. As part of this anthology, it was subsequently reprinted and translated many times. In addition, the entire deleted section was circulated, with Wright's permission, in a limited offset edition in 1946.[4]

Contrary to Fabre's statement, cited above, that the published fragments account for all but "a few pages" of the deleted section, these pieces amount to only about 70 percent of the original text. The material that made up "I Tried" was cut even more radically than the rest, by more than one-third.[5] Moreover, the nature of the cuts was different. In "Early Days," one minor and two major cuts (pp. 1–2, 19–30, and 37–42 of *AH* as published in 1977) account for all the deletions, leaving the tone and content of the remaining sections basically unchanged. In "I Tried," in contrast, there are nearly a hundred cuts ranging from a single word to nearly two pages of the 1977 *American Hunger*; inevitably, this radical trimming affects the tone and substance of the text.

In some cases the cuts removed mild profanities ("bastard," *AH* 128/*IT* 2:55) or were mere tightening, as in Wright's description of his activity in a committee on the high cost of living:

> I gritted my teeth as the daily value of pork chops was tabulated, longing to be at home with my writing. I felt that pork chops were a fundamental item in life, but I preferred that someone else chart their rise and fall in price. (*AH* 108)

The *Atlantic*, perhaps out of an analogous preference, deleted the second sentence. In other cases, however, the cuts substantially altered the tone of Wright's text, as in this description of a confrontation with "Nealson," a CP official:[6]

"[T]hey tell me you write . . ."	"[T]hey tell me you write."
"I try to," I said.	"I try to," I said.
"You can write," he snorted.	"You can write," he snorted.
"I read that article you wrote for the *New Masses* about Joe Louis. Good stuff . . . First political treatment of sports we've yet had. Ha-ha . . ."	"I read that article you wrote for the *New Masses* about Joe Louis. Good stuff. First political treatment of sports we've yet had. Ha-ha."
"I'm trying to reveal the meaning of Negro experience," I said.	
"We need a man like you," he said flatteringly.	
I waited. I had thought that I would encounter a man of ideas, but he was not that. Then perhaps he was a man of action? But that was not indicated either. As we talked, I tried to grasp the frame of reference of his words, so that I would know how to talk to him.	I waited. I had thought that I should encounter a man of ideas, but he was not that. Then perhaps he was a man of action? But that was not indicated either.
"They tell me that you are a friend of Ross," he shot at me. (*AH* 101–102)	"They tell me that you are a friend of Ross," he shot at me. (*IT* 2:49)

In the second version Wright's effort to explain himself and his attempt to intuit Nealson's mental frame are deleted; the result is flatter in tone, more polemical, less reflective. The official's flattery and the subsequent small talk are also omitted, making Nealson's question about the dissident Ross even more peremptory. Even changing Wright's ellipses to periods contributes to a more "decisive," less ruminative tone.

Many of the cuts, and all of the longer ones, sharpen what might be called the political tone of the work. Sometimes this is a matter of dropping a sentence or two:

I had not read any of Trotsky's works; indeed, the very opposite had been true. It had been Stalin's *The National and Colonial Question* that had captured my interest.

Stalin's book showed how diverse minorities could be welded into unity, and I regarded it as a most politically sensitive volume that revealed a new way of looking upon lost and beaten peoples. Of all the developments in the Soviet Union, the method by which scores of backward peoples had been led to unity on a national scale was what had enthralled me. (*AH* 81–82)

I had not read any of Trotsky's works; indeed, the very opposite had been true. It had been Stalin's *National and Colonial Question* that had captured my interest.

Of all the developments in the Soviet Union, the method by which scores of backward peoples had been led to unity on a national scale was what had enthralled me. (*IT* 1:67)

Elsewhere, comments that offset negative statements about CP members or officials, or placed their actions in context, were omitted in the course of larger deletions:

Ed Green [an official who has been browbeating Wright] was afterwards killed in action while fighting for the Spanish Loyalists. He knew how to die better than he knew how to live. He was organically capable of only the most elementary reactions. His fear-haunted life made him suspicious of everything that did not look as he looked, that did not act as he acted, that did not talk as he talked, that did not feel as

[Not in *IT*.]

he felt. His existence both glad-
dened and frightened me. I was
glad that he was militant, but I
was frightened when I pondered
upon what he could do with his
militancy. (*AH* 85)

[. . .] I felt that it was the fear of   [Not in *IT.*]
their enemies that made Com-
munists—unconsciously compen-
sating for their fear—fight one
another so doggedly and persist-
ently. But I did not tell them that;
they would not have understood.
(*AH* 118)

The effect of such changes is cumulative and subtle, rather than blatant. It is not that "I Tried" omits all favorable statements about communists; some remain, and negative statements are among those cut. The overall effect, however, is that "I Tried" moves rapidly from one disillusioning experience to the next, in all of which the party members and officials seem to act with arbitrary malignity.

An extended example will best convey these tonal shifts. A climactic episode in Wright's narrative is the party trial of Ross, a CP dissident.[7] In both *American Hunger* and "I Tried," the episode leads up to the closing sequences in which Wright is hounded by the CP and thrown out of a May Day parade; and it brings to a head Wright's mounting feelings of alienation from CP intolerance and bureaucratism. But there are crucial differences in the two versions, as shown when the "I Tried" reduction is read in conjunction with *American Hunger*:

It was a rule that once you had   It was a rule that once you had
entered a meeting of this kind   entered a meeting of this kind
you could not leave until the   you could not leave until the
meeting was over; it was feared   meeting was over; it was feared
that you might go to the police   that you might go to the police
and denounce them all.   and denounce them all.

Acting upon the loftiest of impulses, filled with love for those
who suffer, urged toward fellowship with the rebellious, committed to sacrifice, why was it that
there existed among Communists

so much hate, suspicion, bitterness, and internecine strife? I
stood in the midst of people I
loved and I was afraid of them.
I felt profoundly that they were
travelling in the right direction,
yet if their having power to rule
had depended merely upon my
lifting my right hand, I would
have been afraid to do so. [...]
I was determined not to participate in any way, for that would
have surely, by implication, im-
plicated me in a network of guilt
which I did not share.

Ross, the accused, sat alone at
a table in the front of the hall, his
face distraught. I felt sorry for
him, yet I could not escape feeling that he enjoyed this. For him,
this was perhaps the highlight of
an otherwise bleak existence.

I was for these people. Being
a Negro, I could not help it. They
did not hate Negroes. They had
no racial prejudices. Many of the
white men in the hall were married to Negro women, and many
of the Negro men were married
to white women. Jews, Germans,
Russians, Spaniards, all races and
nationalities were represented
without any distinctions whatever.
[...] Yet a new hate had come
to take the place of the rankling
racial hate. [...] I had fled men
who did not like the color of my
skin, and now I was among men
who did not like the tone of my
thoughts.

In trying to grasp why Communists hated intellectuals, my
mind was led back again to the
accounts I had read of the Rus-
sian Revolution. (*AH* 118–19)

Ross, the accused, sat alone at
a table in the front of the hall, his
face distraught. I felt sorry for
him; yet I could not escape feeling that he enjoyed this. For him,
this was perhaps the highlight of
and otherwise bleak existence.

In trying to grasp why Communists hated intellectuals, my
mind was led back again to the
accounts I had read of the Rus-
sian Revolution. (*IT* 2:53)

The trial begins with a series of speakers who outline the world scene, the state of the Soviet Union, the U.S. and Chicago situations, and the tasks of the CP; only after these lengthy preliminaries are charges made against Ross. Wright reflects:

This presentation had lasted for more than three hours, but it had enthroned a new sense of reality in the hearts of those present, a sense of man on earth. With the exception of the church and its myths and legends, there was no agency in the world so capable of making men feel the earth and the people upon it as the Communist party.

I knew, as I watched, that I was looking at the future of mankind, that this way of living would finally win out. I knew that in no other way could the emotional capacities, the passional nature of men be so deeply tapped. In no other system yet devised could man so clearly reveal his destiny on earth, a destiny to rise and grapple with the world in which he lives, to wring from it the satisfactions he feels he must have. I knew, as I watched and listened, that but few people understood the essence of Communism, its passional dynamics; but a few knew that Communism was more important than any of its individual parties, than the sum of all its tactics, strategies, theories, mistakes, and tragedies. I knew that once this system became entrenched on earth, for good or bad, it could not fail, that all Europe and her armies could not destroy the Soviet Union, that the spirit of self-sacrifice that Communism engendered in men would astound the world.

[. . .] I had wanted to tell others what these men felt. I un-

This presentation had lasted for more than three hours, but it had enthroned a new sense of reality in the hearts of those present, a sense of man on earth. With the exception of the church and its myths and legends, there was no agency in the world so capable of making men feel the earth and the people upon it as the Communist Party.

derstood their impulses, the long
years' privation and hurt out of
which they had come to Communism. I had wanted to make
others seee what was in the Communist heart, what the Communists were after; but I was on trial
by proxy, condemned by them.
   Toward evening the direct
charges against Ross were made
[. . . .] (*AH* 122–23)

   Toward evening the direct
charges against Ross were made
[. . . .] (*IT* 2:54)

In the first sequence, the deletions in "I Tried" omit the extraordinary ambivalence in Wright's feelings: Wright's tributes to the
communists' idealism and nonracialism in *American Hunger* are
generous, even fulsome, yet his references to "suspicion, bitterness,
and internecine strife" and to "a new hate" are more hostile than
what appears in "I Tried." The deletions in the second passage eliminate an important affirmation of Wright's politically-centered concept of human destiny, and his faith as of 1943–44 in some version
of communism. They eliminate, as well, his conflation of the communist ideal with the Soviet Union and with the communist apparatus ("this system"). Altogether, the trial episode is shortened by
nearly 50 percent. No important narrative "facts" have been omitted; the cuts have been made skillfully to present the maximum of
"hard" information. But this very method of condensing means
that taken together, the deletions sharply alter both the tone and
the substance of Wright's account. Throughout this and other
episodes, reflections that present a careful judgment on the positive
and negative aspects of communism have been cut out, resulting in
a text that is more a one-sided polemic, an anticommunist tract, less
an introspective meditation on communism and Wright's hopes and
fears, than the original.

   Wright's ambivalence about communism and its devotees is not
the only casualty of the excisions. At the very end of the manuscript, "I Tried" excerpts Wright's original in a way that eliminates
his continuing commitment to a radical social vision. In both versions, Wright sits alone after being physically thrown out of the
CP's May Day parade contingents, and is glad that his writings glo-
rifying the party have already been published.

For I knew in my heart that I
should [. . .] never again make

For I knew in my heart that I
should [. . .] never again make

so total a commitment of faith.

[Five paragraphs follow, including the following passage:]

Somehow man had been sundered from man and, in his search for a new unity, for a new wholeness, for oneness again, he would have to blunder into a million walls to find merely that he could not go in certain directions. No one could tell him. He would have to learn by marching down history's bloody road. [. . .]

A better world's in birth . . .

The procession still passed. Banners still floated. Voices of hope still chanted.

I headed toward home alone, really alone now, telling myself that in all the sprawling immensity of our mighty continent the least-known factor of living was the human heart, the least-sought goal of being was a way to live a human life. Perhaps, I thought, out of my tortured feelings I could fling a spark into this darkness. I would try, not because I wanted to but because I felt that I had to if I were to live at all.

[Four paragraphs follow, including the following passage:]

I heard a trolley lumbering past over steel tracks in the early dusk and I knew that underpaid, bewildered black men and women were returning to their homes from serving their white masters. In the front room of my apartment our radio was playing, pouring a white man's voice into my home, a voice that hinted of a coming war that would consume millions of lives.

Yes, the whites were as miser-

so total a commitment of faith.

"A better world's in birth . . ."

The procession still passed. Banners still floated. Voices of hope still chanted.

I headed toward home alone, really alone now, telling myself that in all the sprawling immensity of our mighty continent the least-known factor of living was the human heart, the least-sought goal of being was a way to live a human life. Perhaps, I thought, out of my tortured feelings I could fling a spark into this darkness. I would try, not because I wanted to but because I felt that I had to if I were to live at all.

able as their black victims, I
thought. If this country can't find
its way to a human path, if it can't
inform conduct with a deep sense
of life, then all of us, black as
well as white, are going down the
same drain . . .

[One paragraph follows, stat-
ing Wright's determination to
write.]

I would hurl words into this
darkness and wait for an echo;
and if an echo sounded, no matter how faintly, I would send
other words to tell, to march, to
fight, to create a sense of the hunger for life that gnaws in us all, to
keep alive in our hearts a sense
of the inexpressibly human.
(*AH* 133–35)

I would hurl words into this
darkness and wait for an echo;
and if an echo sounded, no matter how faintly, I would send
other words to tell, to march, to
fight, to create a sense of the hunger for life that gnaws in us all, to
keep alive in our hearts a sense
of the inexpressibly human.
(*IT* 2:56)

The sequence in which these passages occur has several functions (as befits its original placement as the conclusion of the entire
autobiography): it alludes briefly to Wright's childhood and years in
Chicago, and looks forward to his future as a writer. Aside from
these aspects, and some incidental detail, the major difference is
that the references to "man" as "sundered" and to "history" state,
by allusion, Wright's continuing acceptance of Marxist ideas of
alienation and redemption, while the evocation of the Chicago
evening leads to a restatement of Wright's belief in the reality of
exploitation, a foreshadowing of World War II, and a linking of
white perpetrators and Black victims of racism in a complex formulation that does not deny white responsibility but sees whites also
as victims. The omission of these passages in "I Tried" creates an
impression simultaneously more polemical—because the words
hurled into darkness are hurled mainly at the CP—and less political, an affirmation of humanism without the social dimension supplied by the missing paragraphs.

Cumulatively, the differences between "I Tried" and *American
Hunger*—only some of which I have cited here, though they are
among the more dramatic—are sufficient to qualify the two texts as
distinct versions of the same work. True, "I Tried" covers the same
events in the same order and (with very minor exceptions) in the

same words, since the compression has been achieved almost exclusively by deletion. Moreover, the overall picture "I Tried" gives of Wright's experience with communism is similar. Yet it makes a definably different impression when read independently: the CP presented in "I Tried" is more unambiguously negative than that in *American Hunger*, owing to the excision of the qualifying reflections in the longer manuscript, and "I Tried" conveys a more single-mindedly polemical impression, largely as a result of the removal of passages in which Wright describes his developing, inevitably am-biguous feelings about the party.

What now must be discussed is the *status* of this version. Is it to be regarded as authorial or nonauthorial, and in what sense—as a significant variation in Wright's account of communism or as a merely exigent production dictated by market needs and possessing no importance in the evolution of Wright's views? To answer these questions, it will be convenient to look at the work's textual history, and then to compare the "communisms" in *American Hunger* and "I Tried" with other roughly contemporary treatments by Wright of the same question.

* * *

The production of a shortened and politically altered magazine text from Wright's original may seem to suggest editorial censorship. Indeed, as a professional author working in the commercial market, Wright was never free from editorial interference. Ironically, however, textual and other evidence shows that in this case editorial shortening produced a text that ultimately suited Wright's purposes better than the longer original.

The evidence is necessarily inferential. Wright is not known to have directly expressed satisfaction or dissatisfaction with either the "I Tried" or *American Hunger* texts, in 1944–49 or later; nor did he indicate an attitude indirectly by such actions as trying to secure publication of *American Hunger*, or expressing a wish that it eventually be (or not be) published.[8] From bibliographical evidence and correspondence, however, a fairly clear picture emerges: in 1944 Wright approved a condensation he did not personally prepare, while in 1949 he actively chose this same condensed text for republication.

No setting text for "I Tried" has been preserved, but it is possible to determine the way the changes were made from their intrinsic character and from correspondence between Wright, his agent, and the *Atlantic*.[9] The character of the changes themselves suggests that they were made by the *Atlantic* editors. Except for a handful of word changes and the shift of a few lines to an earlier position,[10] the changes are entirely excisions, the sort of thing magazine editors do skillfully; if Wright had made the changes, it seems likely that he might have done some rewriting. Correspondence between the *Atlantic* and Wright's agent, Paul Reynolds, confirms that the cuts were made by the *Atlantic* and—at least for the first installment—approved by Wright, who also suggested the title. Wright was offered the opportunity to restore "any of his favorite passages," provided he made equivalent cuts elsewhere, but apparently suggested no changes.[11]

No particular significance need be assigned to Wright's agreement to the *Atlantic's* truncation of his manuscript. The most likely reason for the cuts is space. The Atlantic editors serialized Wright's piece over two issues, a rare procedure; at ten and nine pages, respectively, even the severely condensed installments were pressing the *Atlantic's* space limits. (Only five out of more than a hundred other prose features published between January and September 1944 ran as long as ten pages.) When the cuts were made, the autobiography was expected to appear in its entirety sometime in 1944. Even after the decision to divide the book, Wright's intention, concurred in by Reynolds and his editor Edward Aswell, was to expand the second section for later publication by including more material on his apprenticeship as a writer. As late as July 1945, in a letter to Reynolds reporting his decision to supply *Mademoiselle* with the "American Hunger" excerpt, Wright still spoke of this as an active intention (July 8, 1945, Reynolds files). Wright, then, was agreeing in May 1944 to a magazine condensation and no more.

The picture changes, however, over the following few years. Wright did not complete the intended expansion of the excised chapters. Nor, so far as his correspondence with Reynolds shows, did he make any effort to publish the deleted chapters in full, though he did agree to their reproduction for limited circulation. In November 1948, Wright was asked to contribute to what became *The God That Failed*. The initial proposal did not refer to "I Tried," but asked simply for an article of 6,000 to 10,000 words, guaranteeing each author "complete freedom in his handling of the subject." Wright did not raise either to Crossman or to Reynolds the possibility of reprinting or reworking the relevant portion of *American Hunger*. His initial response, indeed, was not concerned with his own contribution at all, but with expanding the scope of the project to include material by or about "workers, organizers, doctors, scientists, women, etc.," a proposition Crossman rejected rather peremptorily. Although by March 1949 Wright's U. S. publishers were still assuming that he was writing a new piece for the anthology, by May he had decided to use "I Tried," without revision, as his contribution.[12]

Wright's choice places the question of "authorization" (in the sense of the text's status as an utterance of the author) in a different light. In 1944, despite the offer to let him readjust the cutting, Wright was essentially limited to the role of passively approving a reshaping carried out by others. In 1949, he had more options. He was invited to contribute whatever he wished, and was free to compose a new piece, to propose reprinting the *American Hunger* chapters on communism in full, to revise "I Tried" by restoring "favorite passages," or to reprint "I Tried" unchanged. Printing the chapters in full might have been ruled out by space considerations (at 48 pages, even the shortened version was longer than any other contribution except Arthur Koestler's, which ran 61), but the other options were live ones. Hence, Wright's decision to use "I Tried" constitutes a definite choice in favor of this version, an "active" rather than "passive" authorization of its text.[13]

It is, of course, possible that with other writing in progress, Wright did not wish to devote a major effort to the project. But even allowing for this, Wright's decision cannot have been a casual one, a throwaway choice about a reprint: his political instincts were sharp enough to know that with contributions by Koestler, Silone, Gide, and the rest, Crossman's anthology would be an important and controversial book.[14] And it should be emphasized that a few very minor revisions in the "I Tried" text could have shifted its tone somewhat back toward that of the 1944 manuscript. For example, the following hypothetical revision, made by reintroducing only five sentences from the 1944 text, would have restored an important element absent from the condensed version:

With the exception of the church and its myths and legends, there was no agency in the world so	With the exception of the church and its myths and legends, there was no agency in the world so

capable of making men feel the earth and the people upon it as the Communist Party.

capable of making men feel the earth and the people upon it as the Communist Party.

I knew, as I watched, that I was looking at the future of mankind, that this way of living would finally win out. In no other system yet devised could man so clearly reveal his destiny on earth, a destiny to rise and grapple with the world in which he lives, to wring from it the satisfactions he feels he must have. I knew that once this system became entrenched on the earth, for good or bad, it could not fail, that all Europe and her armies could not destroy the Soviet Union.

I had wanted to tell others what these men felt. I had wanted to make others see what was in the Communist heart, what the Communists were after; but I was on trial by proxy, condemned by them.

Toward evening the direct charges against Ross were made [. . . .] (*IT* 2:54, *GF* 155)

Toward evening the direct charges against Ross were made [. . . .] (see *AH* 122–23)

Neither space considerations (stringent though they might be) nor the press of work could have kept Wright from making such changes had he felt it essential to include some affirmation of faith in a communist future and the attractive power of communism in a statement of his views on the topic. For whatever reasons, Wright must have felt that the portrayal of communism and his relationship to it in the *Atlantic* articles was one he was ready to stand by.

* * *

I would now like to argue that *The God That Failed* represents Wright's evolved intentions, and that *American Hunger* should be *provisionalized* as an artistic representation of Wright's communist experience. By provisionalizing, I mean simply that whatever is in *American Hunger* needs to be weighed against the corresponding material in *The God That Failed* as a later, autonomous version of the same text. The reasons for regarding *The God That Failed* as an evolved text, rather than simply a cut-down version of the 1944 text that Wright reprinted for convenience, lie in a consideration of the two autobiographical texts in relation to Wright's life and his other statements regarding communism.

During the 1940s and 1950s Wright, like many other independent radicals, reacted sharply against communism. He remained on the left and did not support the cold-war camp of "the West" as many ex-communists did, yet at times he collaborated actively in efforts to limit the influence of communists. In 1946, for example, he agreed to run for the governing council of the Authors Guild on a slate intended to "liberalize [the] League avoiding [the] extreme left and extreme right."[15] As late as 1956, according to State Department documents, he gave the Department information on possible communist influence within African nationalist groupings (Gayle xv). This reaction against communism was part of a more complex movement over the next decade, in which Wright's views eventually evolved toward pan-Africanist radicalism. Yet even in a late work such as *White Man, Listen!* (1957), echoes of the postwar anticommunism of the "non-Communist Left" remain. Although this work is primarily concerned with explaining the anticolonial movements of the 1950s, Wright identifies himself in it as "a man of the West" (78), rejects the idea of a "Third force" (80), and expresses concern that the anticolonial revolts not be "captured by the Communists" (17; see also 72–73, 157–18, 160), phrases that retain the tang of their origin in the political arguments of the "non-Communist Left" even though Wright uses them in a more general (and socially radical) sense.

Like other ex-communists, Wright was under considerable pressure to show his anticommunism; he avoided visiting the U.S. from his Paris home partly from fear that his passport would be lifted and he would be unable to leave, and at least some instances in the 1950s in which he provided information to the State Department were prompted by the need to renew his passport (Gayle *passim*).[16] But Wright's opposition to communism was principled and not merely pragmatic, as shown by his continuing redefinition of his positions in his writing.

Wright's most extended treatment of communism in this period was his fictional one in *The Outsider* (1953). Communism is of course not the only theme in a work whose overall concern is nothing less than a philosophical view of modern humanity; but it is a very important one. *The Outsider* is relevant to a discussion of Wright's autobiographical texts both because it shows the direction in which his view of communism was evolving when he sent "I Tried" to Crossman (he had begun work on the novel at this time, but it had not yet jelled in his mind) and because of the parallels and contrasts it contains to these works. Overall, *The Outsider* extends and reworks the treatment of communism in *American Hunger* in a more bitterly hostile fashion; the specific parallels, too, are developed in a more sharply negative way.

The Outsider shows fascism and communism as twin totalitarian "monsters" (414), yet communism is seen as more intellectually insidious and is given by far the fuller treatment. In an interview with the CP official Blimin late in the novel, Wright's persona, Cross Damon, characterizes Russia as a state in which "ruthless men" seized power and established "a dictatorship" in order to "rationaliz[e] human life to the last degree"; the actual aim, industrialization, "could have happened under a dozen different ideological banners," and communism's ideological pretensions, Damon insists, are "for the workers, for the public, not for me. I look at facts, processes" (452). The communist movements are guided simply by the will to power. "At the heart of all political movements," Damon reflects earlier in the novel, "the concept of the basic inequality of man was enthroned and practiced, and the skill of politicians consisted in how clever[l]y they hid this elementary truth" (210). The communist use of power is "more recondite than mere political strategy; it was a *life* strategy using political methods as its tools. . . . Its essence was a voluptuousness, a deep-going sensuality that took cognizance of fundamental human needs and the answers to those needs" (253–54). Communists work at "organizing and exploiting the raw stuff of human emotions" and are "akin to priests" in their closeness "to the common impulses of men, in their cynical acceptance of the cupidities of the human heart" (312–13). Damon insists that Blimin and other communists are conscious of what they are doing, "convinced that you know how the game goes," offering as programs "crude translations of the daydreams of the man in the street" in which they themselves "do *not* believe!" (464–65) Though communism and fascism are different, "the degree of difference is not worth arguing about"—communists "are more intelligent, more general in their approach, but the same power-hungry heart beats behind the desire to rule! I'm on prepolitical ground here, Mr. Blimin. And you know I'm speaking the truth" (464–65). Communism, Damon summarizes to Blimin, is a "horrible totalitarian reptile" (469).[17]

Into this overall portrayal Wright introduces numerous echoes of *American Hunger*. Many, one feels, are not so much intentional references as matters of a word, a look or tone that lingered in Wright's mind for years after his exit from the CP. Thus, Blimin begins his interrogation of Damon with a phrase recalling Nealson's interview with Wright: "Say, they tell me you are a friend of Gil" (445). Yet Gil himself—a CP functionary whom Damon has murdered, though Blimin isn't sure of this yet—is introduced earlier in the novel in a way that also recalls Nealson; though physically unlike Nealson, he resembles him in being "intellectual without partaking of the processes of thought" (221.) ("I had thought that I would encounter a man of ideas, but he was not that"—*AH*, 102.) The major parallel, however, may well be intentional; in the character of Bob Hunter, a Black CP rank and filer betrayed by the party, Wright provides a reworking of the Ross material in the earlier work.

Like Ross, the "street agitator" and urbanized "peasant" (*AH* 78), Hunter is a naïf, honestly trying to organize Black dining car waiters for the party. He is accused, like Ross, of "ideological factionalism," and, just as Wright himself "gaped" when he heard the charges against Ross, Hunter is "incredulous" (279; *AH* 87). But there are differences in the portraits as well. Ross is accused of being "anti-leadership" and a "nationalist," and of a "long list of political offenses" (*AH* 102, 117). Hunter is *just* a militant, whom the party betrays by cancelling his organizing campaign for unstated reasons and then informing on him to U.S. customs to get him out of the way (he is an undocumented West Indian immigrant). There are differences, as well, in the treatment the two characters receive and in their responses. Ross is formally tried, Hunter browbeaten by a party functionary in a nighttime visit. Ross's responses, though pitiable, possess some dignity as well: he "wilt[s]" during the trial, but under "moral pressure" rather than shouting and abuse (123); he stands "trembling," guilt "written in every pore of his black skin" and his personality "obliterated," yet he has been humbled by "the common vision that bound us all together" and "talk[s] on, outlining how he had erred, how he would reform" (124). Ross's sense of "oneness" with "all the members there,"

Wright emphasizes in a famous summing-up, makes the trial "a spectacle of glory" as well as "a spectacle of horror" (124–25). By contrast, Hunter in *The Outsider* is allowed not even a shred of dignity. "'But what am I gonna do?' Bob wailed. 'I want to organize my union like the Party told me'" (232). He speaks "in a wail," he "grinned, wagged his head, and crooned," and later in the novel— when the party has ratted on him to the government—his face "twitch[es]," he speaks "in a broken whimper," and "a large drop of mucus formed at the tip of his flat, brown nose, hovered there for a second, then dropped to his upper lip. He licked at it, unaware that he did so" (233, 235, 278, 280, 279).[18]

There is, of course, a political meaning to both portraits: in their original context, the passages about Ross, which appear in "I Tried" as well as the longer text, were related to Wright's attempt to convey what the latter, but *not* "I Tried," calls the "loft[y] impulses," the "love for those who suffer," the "fellowship with the rebellious," the "spirit of self-sacrifice," the overall "passional dynamics" that make communism, despite its "suspicion, bitterness, and internecine strife," the "future of mankind" (118, 122; not in "I Tried"). The portrait of Hunter is politically meaningful as well. Hunter does *not* partake in the communist "fellowship with the rebellious," because in *The Outsider* it is not found; other than Hunter, all the communists who appear in the book are bureaucrats, thugs, and murderers, and there is no sense of a rank and file communist *movement*. The "passional dynamics" are purely those of the will to power, Hunter is caught in a horrible machine, and his abject squirming is of a piece with this presentation. In *The Outsider* communism, like other totalitarian systems, has the aim of crushing the human spirit; Hunter's collapse enacts this conception.

It should now be clear that the demonized portrait of communism in *The Outsider* has more in common with "I Tried" and *The God That Failed* than with *American Hunger*. This becomes particularly clear when the Hunter sequences in *The Outsider* are viewed as a reworking of the earlier Ross material. In *American Hunger*, Ross's humiliation was a "spectacle of glory . . . [and] of horror." In "I Tried" and *The God That Failed*, that phrase is retained, but most of the glory has been edited away, letting the horror stand out more boldly. In *The Outsider*, horror is *all* that remains. What is true of the Hunter episodes is true of the treatment of communism generally. *The Outsider* is a kind of systematic intensification of the most negative material in *American Hunger*; all nuance and shading have been left behind. And this is no mere accident, no matter of omission or haste on Wright's part. Over and over in their interview Blimin brings up communism's positive ideology, its links to the workers, etc., and Damon insists that all this is mere deceptive public show: "Again, Mr. Blimin, if you want to talk to me, please understand that I'm not naive. Your propaganda is *not* for me" (453).

Much that appears in the earlier works—some in "I Tried," but especially the passages that occur only in *American Hunger*—is what Damon would consider "naive." To Wright in *American Hunger* the party goes wrong because it is "impatient of extended processes," an attitude that reflects a typically American materialism (*AH* 123; not in "I Tried")—it errs because it is *like* the rest of us in our need for quick fixes. To Damon the party opposes the "illnesses of independence, freedom, and individuality" (460) not because it shares human frailties but because it has risen breathtakingly but dangerously above them, has leapt into a future where traditional values have fallen before utter nihilism, is a nursery for the "last men" (562) who have freed themselves from all mental fetters yet gone sickeningly astray from humanity. From this perspective, *American Hunger's* idea that communism embodies "the future of mankind," that "all Europe and her armies could not destroy the Soviet Union" (122; not in "I Tried"), can only sound naive. It is not clear whether in 1949, or 1953, Wright would still have endorsed the assessment that communism represents the future; what *is* clear is that the value sign placed over such statements would be negative—not a sign of hope, but a warning of cultural decline.

Indeed, on the most mundane level, such assertions might well have been embarrassing to Wright in the aftermath of the events of 1945–48. By November 1948, when Wright was approached about what became *The God That Failed*, the establishment of communist rule in Eastern Europe was complete, a process marked by cancelled and falsified elections and climaxed by the coup in Czechoslovakia nine months earlier. In such a situation Wright might well have preferred "I Tried" to his 1944 text (or to working some statements from the latter into "I Tried") precisely *because* "I Tried" was less qualified and nuanced. In any case, "I Tried"/*The God That Failed* is closer politically to Wright's other major contemporary treatment of communism, *The Outsider*, than is *American Hunger*. However it may be assessed artistically, in terms of Wright's political theme *American Hunger* is a transitional work; "I Tried," because of the accident of its editing, has jettisoned some of the ideas and attitudes that Wright attacks in *The Outsider*, and thus it and *The God That Failed* lie closer to the endpoint of the transition.

* * *

The publication history of these works, and the broader question of their place in Wright's intellectual evolution, touch on two issues that have been much discussed in recent years by textual theorists. The first is the conception of the linear descent of texts stressed by theorists in the Greg-Bowers tradition. This conceives the most typical situation in the evolution of a text to be that of a succession of editions following the first and incorporating, variously, corrections of errata, textual corruptions, and substantive authorial changes. The methodology of "eclectic" editing as developed to deal with such situations stresses acceptance of the author's demonstrable "final" intentions with regard to substantive readings, disregard of so-called neutral variants, and return to an early state for "accidentals" (either manuscript or first edition, depending on which version of this approach is accepted).[19] This approach has been powerfully challenged by the methodology of "versions" (Hans Zeller), according to which editors should respect the autonomy of distinct states of a text and not introduce discrete substantive revisions from later states into an earlier text in the manner of "eclectic" editing. Zeller's approach rests theoretically on the conception of the text as "a complex of elements which form a system of signs," which any revisions "transform . . . into another system," i.e., a new version; and practically on the observation that an author may tacitly accept unauthorized variants and even respond to them with further changes, making the disentangling of authorized variants impossible (240–41, 249 ff.) Partly in response to such problems, Greg-Bowers methodology has elaborated ways of dealing with texts with multiple authority and has recognized that revision can produce texts so distinct from the original as to be considered new works, which Bowers has called "rewritten single-texts"

("Mixed Texts" 67). This approach, however, does not solve the problem of the degree of change that is sufficient to constitute a text as "rewritten"[20]

The second aspect of textual methodology worth noting here is that of "intentionality." The Greg-Bowers methodology normally discounts changes that result simply from publishers' interference, editors' condensations, etc., in an effort to reconstitute the author's "final and uninfluenced artistic intentions" (Bowers in the Virginia edn. of Crane's *Works*, I, lxxvii, cited by Zeller 247). This approach has been challenged both by Zeller's theory of versions and by Jerome J. McGann's conception of "social textuality," which have in common the idea that nonauthorial influences on a text are the norm. These viewpoints dissolve the insistence on "final and uninfluenced artistic intentions" in a recognition that authors customarily work in a web of influences comprising family, friends, publishers/editors, and their intended audiences. McGann is commenting on this point, as well as that of the nonlinear descent of texts, when he notes in reference to Byron, "Many works exist of which it can be said that their authors demonstrated a number of different wishes and intentions about what text they wanted to be presented to the public, and that these differences reflect accommodations to changed circumstances, and sometimes to changed publics" (*Critique* 32). In a closely related point, social-textual methodology legitimates, or rather takes factual note of, the contribution of nonauthorial hands to the constitution of a work. In an illustration directly appertaining to Wright, Zeller notes that magazine editors often intervene in shaping article texts, yet "even authors who have protested against such changes often adopt them when they publish their periodical contributions in book form, and seem to give them some kind of authority" (249).[21] Finally, McGann stresses that texts are "social" in two overlapping senses: they are normally produced by authors in a web of social obligation and expectation; and they may take on a social significance of their own, irrespective of the author's intentions.

The Wright works discussed here provide a test of these approaches. Within Greg-Bowers methodology, one is immediately faced with a question of which text to accept as "final." To choose "I Tried"/*The God That Failed* on mere chronological grounds would mean excluding *American Hunger* from the Wright canon, an unsatisfactory solution. On the other had, the later texts could be accommodated to Bowers's conception of "rewritten single-text" ("Mixed Texts" 67). According to this idea, the various parts of *American Hunger* published in Wright's lifetime would be considered single-texts because each descends in successive steps from distinct sections of the initial prepublication text of *American Hunger*.[22] And "I Tried," at least, would be regarded as "rewritten" because of the distinct character resulting from its line-by-line shortening; G. Thomas Tanselle has recognized that some condensations belong in this category ("Final Intention" 192). Such an approach, however, cannot be squared with the attempt to segregate authorial intention from nonauthorial influence. The attempt to recover Wright's intentions prior to the series of interventions that divided his manuscript and truncated the unpublished portion must lead back to the *American Hunger* text of 1944, as recognized by the Library of America edition of Wright's works, which restores this text on intentionalist grounds.[23] If a decision is made to accept "I Tried"/*The God That Failed* as a "rewritten single-text," intentionalist methodology has become unavoidably contaminated with social textuality. The sequence of decisions that produced this and the other fragments is a product of "expectation" as well as "intention"; that is, Wright's decisions were in several cases "second-best" choices influenced by what the market would allow. It seems clear that Wright did not decide on *artistic* grounds that the Chicago material in *AH 1944* should be separated into three texts ("American Hunger," "Early Days," "I Tried"); that the material that now appears on pages 19–30 and 37–42 of *American Hunger* was inferior to the rest and should be excluded; or that the material on pages 1–2 was best handled as a separate piece. Wright's aim manifestly was to get as much of the *American Hunger* text into print as possible, and in the case of the *Mademoiselle* "American Hunger" (as bibliographical examination confirms) to cook up a text from unused material to earn an easy $500 (Wright to Reynolds, July 8, 1945, Reynolds file). Nevertheless, these pieces contrived for market purposes become parts of the Wright corpus; in the case of "Early Days" and "I Tried," their status is ratified by Wright's subsequent decisions to reprint.

As this review suggests, the place of these pieces in the whole body of Wright's work is most easily accounted for by accepting the role of nonauthorial influence and the idea of multiple textuality. "I Tried," for example, was nonauthorially constructed, yet later became "authorial" when republished in *The God That Failed*. And it is multitextual insofar as Wright authorized it for publication even though, during some parts of the period 1944-49, he intended or allowed the dissemination of other versions of the same text (the expansion of *American Hunger*, which was dropped; the noncommercial reproduction of *American Hunger*). Wright, then, worked within a skein of social relations and influences within which his "uninfluenced" artistic intentions are not only hard to discern but ultimately irrelevant—the intentions that count are the ones formed within this context.

Further, as social-textual methodology would suggest, "I Tried" and *The God That Failed* must be dealt with on the level of their social significance, apart from their status as Wrightian revisions. These works are significant not merely because Wright caused them to be published, but also because they had a palpable public impact both on Wright's reputation and on larger political debates. The publication of "I Tried" completed the deterioration of Wright's relations with the Communist Party, provoking a series of polemical responses (Fabre 255–56, Gayle 167–68); and it threw Wright, willy-nilly, into the new political milieu of the liberal and social democratic "non-Communist Left," of which he nevertheless remained profoundly suspicious. *The God That Failed* brought Wright's political experiences and ideas to a major audience, exceeding those of his later works; as part of this anthology, Wright's text helped influence the political conceptions of a generation. Hence both "I Tried" and *The God That Failed*, and particularly the latter, possess an independent *social* significance, apart from their textual significance.

Regardless of how Wright's views had evolved between 1944 and 1953—even if he had somehow returned to communism—a social-textual approach would still argue that "I Tried" and *The God That Failed* are significant social texts; as with Auden's "September 1, 1939," which he later suppressed, these texts would still constitute a significant moment in their author's life and in the political history of the period. But the actual development of Wright's views and the treatment of the communist theme in *The Outsider* suggest that these texts reflect Wright's evolved intentions. They do not indeed represent his intentions for the words of a continuation of his autobiography, but rather for the words of a treatment of communism drawn from it. *Two* texts continue to coexist (a relatively frequent situation, as McGann notes in the statement quoted above). "I Tried" and *The God That Failed* deserve recognition as representing a distinct stage in Wright's political and literary development, intermediate between the dissident communism of *American Hunger* and the developed anticommunism which is a major thread in *The Outsider*.

Recognizing the significance of these texts should not simply change what is perceived as the significant corpus of Wright's work; it should also affect the way his ideas, and their development in thematically related works, are discussed. To take one example, Michel Fabre has noted that conservatives welcomed "I Tried to Be a Communist" as showing the intolerance and bigotry of communism; in such responses, Fabre contends, the "nuances" of Wright's presentation, his "enthusiasm" for some accomplishments of the party, "everything, in fact, which softened his criticism of the Party" was "ignored in favor of polemic" (256). Yet the nuances and softening which Fabre refers to are largely present in the *American Hunger* text, rather than "I Tried";[24] it follows that the conservatives' response was not so off-base as he contends, and that critical assessments of Wright must deal with the fact that "I Tried" and *The God That Failed* could legitimately be seen by conservatives as lending support to their conceptions. Another example of how discussion of Wright's ideas might be affected touches on thematic relationships among Wright's works. In an essay comparing *American Hunger* to Wright's African writings, John M. Reilly treats the former as a drama of conflict between the ideals of communism that Wright affirmed and the denial of individuality in communist practice. "[C]ommunism possesses the highest ideals based on historical analysis," Reilly paraphrases. "It holds the key to the future of the world. . . . Wright yearns as strongly as anyone for the communal world created in vision and practice by the Party, but . . . [c]ommitted as he might be to the dynamics of communism, he will not equate them to the dynamics of his personality. So *American Hunger* necessarily moves to its conclusion in tragedy," a tragedy of separation from the collective that is reflected in *The Outsider* and overcome only in Wright's African experiences and writings (220–22). The sentences Reilly is paraphrasing, however, are drawn from passages in *American Hunger* (118, 122–23, and elsewhere) that do not appear in "I Tried" and *The God That Failed*. The problem is not a trivial one. These affirmations are ones Wright sharply modified after 1944; recognizing this suggests that the wholehearted endorsement of collectivist ideology in *American Hunger* represents a specific stage in Wright's thinking rather than a permanent conviction. If so, *The Outsider's* rejection of all collective ideologies, indeed all human ties, precariously balanced by a final call for human interconnectedness, is less easily categorized as an "intellectual crisis" from which Wright advanced to the positive affirmations of his writings on Africa (Reilly 222). Instead, the tensions at the end of *The Outsider* appear as an important statement in their own right of an unresolved polarity in Wright's thought.

Although the importance of "I Tried" and *The God That Failed* can be argued on bibliographical grounds alone, in reality the question has a political aspect as well. The 1977 publication of *American Hunger* belongs to an identifiable moment in recent intellectual history, that of the resurgence of left-wing thought in the 1960s and 1970s, with its emphasis on anti-imperialist themes and its openness to what were seen as independent strands of Marxism. In this atmosphere the continued radicalism of Wright after his break with communism—unfamiliar to audiences who knew *The God That Failed* but not Wright's anticolonial writings of the 1950s—was emphasized in Michel Fabre's 1973 biography and a number of other texts, including Addison Gayle's study of Wright's conflicts with the U.S. government (1980). While such works differed in their own emphases, they agreed in rejecting as oversimplified the view of Wright as a repentent ex-communist that had been fostered by his bracketing with Koestler, Silone, and the other contributors to *The God That Failed*.

Publication of *American Hunger*, in addition to bringing to light a long-buried text, contributed to this reevaluation. It presented a Wright whose judgments of communism were more judicious, and whose appreciation of communism's attractions was more generous, than in *The God That Failed*—and whose faith in communism as an ideal was altogether missing from that text. This Wright was one that fit the temper of the 1970s, and the intellectual-political issue posed in his pages—that of the intolerance of official communism for dissident communism within an overall left-wing radicalism—also fit the preoccupations of those years. In effect, the ambivalences of Wright's first formulation of his intellectual differences with communism made the Wright of 1944 attractive to the 1970s, just as the relative harshness of *The God That Failed*—com-

pounded by its coupling with acerbic accounts by other contributors—had made the earlier text suitable to the 1950s and early
1960s. The virtual acceptance of this Wright as *the* Wright is thus a
social event as well as a textual one, a product of the web of social
circumstance in which the production and dissemination of any text
occur.

Ironically enough, this recuperation of an earlier, less trenchant-
ly anticommunist Richard Wright blocked sight of Wright's post-
1944 evolution, attested by his selection of the "I Tried" text for
The God That Failed and by the affinities of the latter with *The
Outsider*; and it obscured the political-intellectual issue opened up
in these autobiographical texts and drummed home in *The Outsider*—the fundamental hostility to human personality that Wright
then saw in all collective ideologies. The resulting bibliographical
and political problems are only increased by the Library of America's *Black Boy (American Hunger)*. The intentionalist approach
used in this edition accurately recreates the text Wright *intended* to
give the world in the first half of 1944, but obscures the fact that the
abbreviated and toughened text of "I Tried" / *The God That Failed*
is Wright's *intended* assessment of communism as of 1949. Here, use
of intentionalist methodology effectually suppresses Wright's later
views.

To base discussion of Wrights intellectual evolution on *American
Hunger* alone is to emphasize and validate a dissident-communist
philosophy that he subsequently distanced himself from; to recognize the equal claims of "I Tried" and *The God That Failed* is to
acknowledge Wright's movement toward a more strident anticommunism, one that brought him close to the liberal anticommunists
whom he nevertheless did not join and from whom he ultimately
diverged. While such an acknowlegment runs the risk of producing
yet another remodeling of Wright, this one for today's antiutopian
moods—which may not, however, be tomorrow's—it is also a recognition of the complexity of Wright's thought.

Accepting "I Tried"/*The God That Failed* as revisions of Wright's
account of communism, and "provisionalizing" the account in
American Hunger, should lead to further consideration of the rich
intellectual content of Wright's works.

Appendix

1. **Filiation.** Materials for a stemmatic filiation of the Wright texts discussed here include:

A. *American Hunger,* draft, typescript, setting typescript (with corrections) and galley proofs. Beinecke Library, Yale Univ. These are listed together since I have not discussed the development of the text in ms.

B. *American Hunger,* corrected page proofs, 1944. Beinecke. (Plate proofs do not appear to influence subsequent texts.)

C. "I Tried to Be a Communist," *Atlantic Monthly*, Aug., Sept. 1944.

D. "Early Days in Chicago," *Cross Section*, 1945.

E. "American Hunger," *Mademoiselle*, Sept. 1945.

F. *American Hunger*, privately reproduced version, 1946.

G. *The God That Failed*, 1949.

H. *Eight Men*, 1961.

I. *American Hunger,* published edn., 1977. Edited text of chapters 15–20 of B. With afterword by Michel Fabre.

J. *Black Boy (American Hunger)*, Library of America edn., 1991. Edited text of B.

Apparent filiation is as follows:

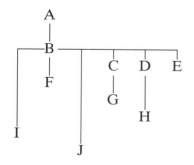

2. Variation in accidentals. The relation of B, C, G, is established by dating and general content and can be verified by comparison of recurring accidentals and a few substantives:

<u>B</u>	<u>C</u>	<u>G</u>
,—	,—	—
the party	the party	the Party
. . .	.	.
Communist party	Communist Party	Communist Party
section on 101 of I	moved to earlier position	same as C
The National and Colonial Question	*National and Colonial Question*	*Marxism and the National and Colonial Question*

C varies from B in two accidentals and G from B in four, tending to establish the sequence B, C, G (which we would expect based on external evidence), rather than B, C I G. The variation in Stalin's title is consistent with a house-style change in C and an editorial change later.

A small number of checked corrections in B are rejected in I; for example, B inserts "then" on Galley 101, p. 307, "going on then in the ranks," but I prints "going on in the ranks" (*AH* 99). I then is an edited text, not a transcript. J is reedited from B as a restoration of the pre-division text; all changes subsequent to the division of the ms. are rejected, including those by Wright himself.

NOTES

1. The longer first section was published in 1945 as *Black Boy*. Wright died in 1960. In what follows, *American Hunger* or *AH* refers to the concluding section as first published in 1977; "I Tried to Be a Communist," "I Tried," or *IT*, to the 1944 *Atlantic Monthly* articles; *The God That Failed* or *GF* to Wright's untitled contribution to that volume (unless the context indicates that the whole volume is meant); and *AH 1944* to the corrected page proofs of the full autobiography, now in possession of the Beinecke Rare Book and Manuscript Library, Yale University. I would like to express my appreciation to the Beinecke Library for access to Wright's manuscripts and correspondence in possession of the library; to John Hawkins & Associates, successors to Wright's literary agency, Paul R. Reynolds & Son, for permitting examination of Wright's correspondence with Paul R. Reynolds, Jr., in their possession; to

the Library of America for allowing me to examine their edition of Wright's *Later Works* prior to publication; and to Michel Fabre and Julia Wright for kindly responding to my inquiries. I wish also to acknowledge the suggestions and encouragement of Addison Gayle, Jr., whose sodden death while this paper was in preparation prevented me from thanking him in person.

2. E.g., by Jerry Ward, Jr., of Tougalou College, at a 1992 MLA session, "Finding the right Texts: The Library of America's New Editions of Richard Wright's Major Works." Louis Menand has offered a similar endorsement for general audiences: the works in the LOA editions have been "expertly restored to their original condition" ("The Hammer and the Nail," *New Yorker*, July 20, 1992: 79–84, at 80). In what follows, *American Hunger* can be taken as referring equally to the relevant portion of the LOA text and to the 1977 separate edition. Both use chaps. 15–20 of the 1944 corrected page proofs (*AH 1944*) as copy-text. Both correct typographical errors (*AH* silently, *Later Works* with apparatus); *Later Works* rejects two later alterations by Wright that *AH* accepts (see n. 9 below). The major differences between the *Later Works* text and previous versions occur in the *Black Boy* section, with the restoration of a censored sexual passage and the deletion of a summary passage Wright supplied to conclude the shortened work. (The passages printed in 1945 appear in the apparatus.)

3. The most prominent misrepresentation concerns the date of Wright's break with the Communist Party. Wright's text appears to show a definitive rupture with the CP in 1937 (datable from external evidence; given in the text as 1936). Wright did resign from the party in Chicago but rejoined after moving to New York and remained a member until 1942. More subtly, Wright's text presents his conflicts with the party in Chicago as focusing on his adherence to communism as such; in Michel Fabre's biography, these conflicts appear more as struggles with a particularly factional local apparatus. Fabre (chaps. 5–6 *passim*) notes a number of discrepancies between Wright's text and apparent fact, but in other cases, while establishing apparently more accurate versions of events, does not note the divergences from Wright's own account. A few are noted briefly by Reilly (214–15) and by Keneth Kinnamon (based on the previously published fragments; Kinnamon 63–67). George Breitman (*passim*) has traced some inaccuracies in Wright's presentation of the shifts in CP politics. It should be noted, however, that the distinction between "fact and narrative" is by no means so clearcut as Reilly's comment assumes. As an example, consider Wright's and Fabre's accounts of the 1935 American Writers' Congress, at which Wright unsuccessfully opposed the CP's decision to disband the John Reed Clubs in favor of a broader grouping. As Wright presents the incident, after he was outvoted, "New York held no further interest and the next morning I left for home" (*AH* 98). Fabre, in contrast, notes Wright's election to the national council of the newly formed League of American Writers and adds, "The intransigence of the Chicago officials and their severe treatment of writers now appeared to have been a local error. . . . Wright even joined the League's contingent of the May Day parade and knew

the exhilaration of participating in a mass demonstration" (119–20). Wright's reference to "the next morning" is a revision of fact for artistic purposes (in plain English, a lie); the tone of Wright's text would have been different if he had referred, in whatever fashion, to the national council and the parade, and the reader should be aware of the factual omissions. Nevertheless, if Wright's version is an imaginative reconstruction, so is Fabre's, at least in part— "appeared to have been a local error" is his own interpretation. The relationship between "narrative" and "fact," then, is one between Wright's imaginative truth and other reconstructions established or attempted by his biographers.

4. Davis and Fabre, *Richard Wright: A Primary Bibliography*, lists the published versions of "I Tried" as items 1944.7, 1949.9, 1949.10, 1950.6; item 1977.1 lists the published text of *American Hunger* and its prior 1946 circulation in a photo-offset reproduction of the 1944 galleys with notes by Constance Webb. Fabre 538n. traces the publication history of these and the other fragments. Davis and Fabre record fourteen foreign editions of *The God That Failed* in eight languages between 1950 and 1965.

5. Approximately 436 out of 1868 lines of text in chapters 1–3 of *AH* (the basis for "Early Days" and the *Mademoiselle* excerpt) remained unpublished, or 23.3 percent; approximately 826 out of 2415 lines in chapters 4–6 (the basis for "I Tried") were deleted, or 34.2 percent. In this and in textual comparisons, below, I refer to the 1977 published text for the reader's convenience. The 1944 corrected page proofs on which the 1977 text is based (*AH 1944*) are discussed below.

6. In the excerpts that follow, equivalent portions of the two texts are aligned. This makes for some jumpiness in reading the *IT* text but shows the extent of its omissions. My own omissions are shown by bracketed ellipses, to distinguish them from Wright's frequent use of ellipses as punctuation.

7. "Ross" was based on David Poindexter, whom Wright had interviewed extensively and whose memories of the South were used in some of the stories in *Uncle Tom's Children*. For differing accounts of their relationship and Poindexter's disagreements with party policies, see Fabre 106–107, 137, 542–43n.; Gayle 73–74; Walker 116. Wright's treatment fictionalizes Poindexter to some degree, characterizing him as a "street agitator" and a relatively apolitical "peasant in the city" and omitting any discussion of his views, so that the party charges of "anti-leadership tendencies" and "ideological factionalism" appear "so fanciful that I gaped when I heard them" (*AH* 78, 87). In fact, Poindexter was a seasoned dissident who probably taught Wright "about Trotskyism and the Party's opposition to it" (Fabre 107). Similarly, Wright glosses Nealson's charge of "nationalism" against Ross disingenuously: Nealson "meant that Ross's militancy was extreme" (102). Nationalism in the context of the so-called "Negro question" had, of course, a much more specific meaning; Wright here is depoliticizing Ross with the result that his

victimization looks more gratuitous. It is not until the trial scene itself that Wright tells us definitely that Ross had fought the leadership (123). Other portraits in *AH* are fictionalized to greater or lesser degrees; see Fabre 546n. and Gayle 89, 167 for some possible identifications.

8. Wright correspondence, 1944–49, Beinecke and Reynolds files; communications from Michel Fabre (undated; Aug. 1991) and Julia Wright (Sept. 19, 1991). Wright did refuse permission in 1960 to use his contribution in a new edition of *The God That Failed*, and declined to speak on a commemorative program about the book for Canadian radio. His reason was opposition to Western anticommunist hysteria (and in particular, anger at the British government for denying him an immigration visa and harassing him and his family), rather than dissatisfaction with the text. He explained in a letter, "My attitude toward Communism has not altered, but my position toward those who are fighting Communism has changed" (Wright to Oliver Swan, Oct. 24, 1960, quoted in Fabre *Quest* 517).

9. Despite the lack of a setting text for "I Tried," the corrected page proofs of *American Hunger*, preserved in the Wright Archive at the Beinecke Library, Yale University, do provide relevant indirect evidence about Wright's working methods. The page proofs consist of 111 galley sheets comprising three pages each, with the date of printing (April 19–27, 1944) in a slug at the top of each sheet; each sheet is also rubber-stamped in red at the top: AUTHOR'S PROOF | MAY 12, 1944 | H. WOLFF BOOK MFG. CO. (apparently the date the sheets were returned by Wright). What appear to be in-house proofs are marked in red pencil and either checked or x'd in blue or black pencil, which may represent different hands. A very few substitutions for proof corrections are made in blue pencil, in what seems to be an editorial hand (not Wright's). (Corrections not in Wright's hand may, of course, have been checked with him.) Each page has been marked by a thick blue line through its entire length, presumably as marked corrections were typeset. (The checked red corrections, and not those x'd, plus the few blue substitutions, are incorporated in the plate proofs—sets of eight pages numbered consecutively in two rows of four pages each per sheet. The plate proofs are dated April 19–21, 1944; as the last printing date on the page proofs is April 27, and they are stamped May 12, the plate proofs appear to have been corrected without re-dating.) Two out-of-sequence sets of galleys are stamped July 31, 1944: a substitution by Wright for a sexually suggestive passage on pages 164–65, and a new sequence of three pages added as a conclusion when the decision was made to divide the book. In the early pages of the cancelled material—chapters 15–20 of the longer work—a series of passages is marked off by solid pencil lines, squared at the ends, in the right margin, and numbered; these correspond roughly, but not exactly, to material *not* used for "Early Days in Chicago," as printed in *Cross Section* in 1945. These markings do not carry through to the end of the "Early Days" material. A second set of markings in wavy lines, again squared at the ends, appears in the left margin; except in one sequence of a few lines, these markings occur only in passages already marked in the right margin but do not account for all of those pas-

sages. The passages marked with wavy lines correspond exactly to the material printed as "American Hunger" in *Mademoiselle* in September 1945 and
show penciled corrections in Wright's hand to create continuity in that
excerpt. (See *Mademoiselle's* "American Hunger" 165, 301. The changes were
adopted in the 1977 *American Hunger. Later Works* 880n. notes the corrections, which it does not incorporate, but not that they were made for
Mademoiselle.) Apparently, then, Wright first marked some but not all of the
material from chaps. 15–17 that had *not* been used for "Early Days" and then
selected passages from this unused material (except for the brief overlap) for
submission to *Mademoiselle*. Much the same method of marking galleys for
excerpting, but on a different set of galleys, would seem to have been used by
the *Atlantic* to make their selections for "I Tried"; see below.

10. A sentence explaining the character Nealson's position in the CP and the
Comintern, which Wright had inserted just prior to the account of their inter-
view, was moved to coincide with an initial reference to Nealson slightly earli-
er in the text (*AH* 101, *IT* 2:48). In addition, house-style changes in "acciden-
tals" were made throughout; the most important are listed in my Appendix.
Wright's error in referring to a work of Stalin as *The National and Colonial
Question* was kept; in *GF* this was corrected to *Marxism and the National and
Colonial Question*.

11. The cuts were first marked by brackets on a set of *AH* galleys Reynolds had
sent to the *Atlantic* and were intended to result in two eight-page installments.
Wright approved the proposed first installment. The *Atlantic* then added back
some deleted material, increasing the length of both installments, and again
offered Wright the opportunity to approve or suggest changes; no reference
to a response by Wright appears in the correspondence, indicating that at
least he proposed no changes. (Edward Weeks [*Atlantic* editor] to Paul R.
Reynolds, May 17, 1944, quoted above; Reynolds to Wright, May 25, 1944;
Dudley Cloud [*Atlantic* managing editor] to Reynolds, June 7, 1944, Beinecke
Library.) A small contretemps occurred subsequently when the *Atlantic*
learned, apparently not from Wright or Reynolds, that the material they had
accepted as an excerpt from Wright's autobiography was not to appear in the
published book. In a letter to Wright, Dudley Cloud of the *Atlantic* refers to
their "lucky break" in hearing this, just before going to press with incorrect
information. Apparently the hint of double-dealing was not lost on Paul
Reynolds; a subsequent letter to Reynolds from Edward Weeks, acknowledging the lateness of the decision to divide *American Hunger*, seems an attempt
to smooth the waters. (Cloud to Wright, July 14, 1944; Weeks to Reynolds,
July 31, 1944, Beinecke Library.)

12. John Fischer (editor-in-chief of Harper & Bros.) to Wright, Nov. 26, 1948,
quoted above; Wright to Reynolds, Dec. 20, 1948; Fischer to Wright, March
29 and May 19, 1949; Wright to Reynolds, May 20, 1949, all in Reynolds files;
R. H. S. Crossman to Wright, Dec. 28, 1948, Beinecke. Crossman was replying
to a Dec. 20 letter from Wright, not in Beinecke or the Reynolds files, that

apparently contained the proposal outlined in Wright's letter of the same date to Reynolds, quoted above. After informing Reynolds on May 20 of his decision to use "I Tried," Wright visited London on May 21–26 to work out details (Fabre 330). *The God That Failed* was published in 1949 in England and in January 1950 in the United States. Interestingly, midway in this process Reynolds received (and had to turn down) a request to reprint "I Tried" in another proposed ex-communist/noncommunist anthology (Julien Steinberg to Wright, May 17, 1949, Reynolds files; Reynolds to Wright, May 19, 1949, Beinecke). Seemingly the time was ripe.

13. On this distinction see Zeller 232, 234. Zeller is here discussing "eclectic" editing but repeats the conception of active authorization, though not the term, in discussing the editing of versions, 260.

14. Kinnamon et al., *A Richard Wright Bibliography*, lists more than forty reviews of *The God That Failed* in English, and more than thirty in French, in the year after publication (301–314). William Henry Chamberlin, Reinhold Niebuhr, V. S. Pritchett, Arthur M. Schlesinger Jr., Norman Thomas, and Rebecca West were among the political and cultural figures who praised it.

15. The characterization is Reynolds's, in a telegram seeking Wright's agreement to be included (Wright was in Paris from May to December 1946, before moving there permanently in August 1947). A second telegram the following day reassured Wright that the slate if elected would "avoid politics . . . and stick to attempting to benefit authors." Put forward by the official nominating committee, the slate also included a number of prominent liberals, such as Paul Gallico, John Hersey, Charles Jackson, Elizabeth Janeway, and Irwin Shaw. The rival ticket "nominated by 15 members" included only a few well-known names, notably Howard Fast (then a CP member), Stefan Heym (then more or less a party-liner), and Philip Van Doren Stern. The official slate, including Wright, was elected. (Reynolds to Wright, Oct. 15 and 16, 1946; official Authors Guild ballot; Reynolds to Wright, Dec. 26, 1946, all from Reynolds files.) Fabre mentions this incident (309) but refers to the Authors League rather than the Guild; the League was the umbrella organization for the Authors Guild, Dramatists Guild, and the "payroll guilds" of radio and screenwriters.

16. The State Department had power to lift passports under the McCarran Act of 1950 and used it on other independent radicals such as the socialist Max Shachtman.

17. Since *The Outsider* was itself cut by about 20 percent before publication (mainly by Wright but with some final cuts not authorized by him), the question arises whether its treatment of communism was thereby altered. Although I have not attempted a full collation of cuts made by Wright, comparison of some salient sections does not show this. Naturally some material dealing with communism has been excised, but it does not differ markedly in tone

from what remains. The unauthorized cuts made by Harper's also do not substantially change Wright's tone or emphasis. (The most extensive occur in material not dealing with communism.) In particular, the 20-page sequence giving Cross Damon's extended exposition of his views on the topic (449–68) was printed from Wright's final draft without change. One publisher's cut that does partially change Wright's tone is a passage in which Damon condemns Western imperialism and affirms "Marxism as an intellectual instrument"; but even here he adds that he "loathed the Communist attempt to destroy human subjectivity," so the difference from other discussions is not marked (Beinecke ms. JWJ Wright 856, combined p. 301/302). The passage is restored in the Library of America edition.

18. It is striking how frequently Wright associates cringing behavior by Black characters with stereotypes of Black physicality and action. Ross's guilt is associated with his "black skin," Hunter's grovelling with the flatness and brownness of his nose; Hunter's crooning resembles "darky" stereotypes.

19. Greg "Rationale," esp. 384–87; Tanselle *Rationale, passim.* The literature is enormous; for a summary see McLaverty "Concept," *passim.*

20. It should be noted that neither approach handles the issue of versional change very well. Zeller's method gives all versional changes equivalent status, yet to equate a change which renames a character appearing only in Chapter 16 with one which rewrites a text front to back is counterintuitive. (Tanselle answers Zeller's point by treating it, in effect, as trivially true; "Final Intention" 196–97 and n.) Zeller's difficulty is a variety of the problem of change in philosophical nominalism, his underlying method. On the other hand, Bowers's method shows the same problem as it affects philosophical realism: he cannot specify when accumulating material changes in a text change its essence. This problem is perhaps greater because of the dualism that divides texts into the categories of "new" and "recognizably the same" (67). Bowers offers a disarmingly pragmatic solution: a text should be seen as a "rewritten" new version when the differences from previous versions are too great to be accommodated by a normal textual apparatus (67); this solution, however, would exclude Wright's "I Tried," since the excisions that distinguish it from *American Hunger* can easily be noted in the apparatus. At bottom Bowers's criteria for recognizing "newness" can only be common-sense ones and are not likely to satisfy everyone.

21. In a statement that seems more restrictive than some of his illustrations, Zeller specifies that a published text is to be viewed as authorized "if the author desired or approved [its] production, *and* if he influenced the text by supplying the printer's copy or by personal revision, or by revision undertaken at his request during the printing process" (260, my emphasis; Zeller is in turn adopting a formulation by Siegfried Schiebe). If *and* is to be taken in a restrictive sense, this criterion seems overly narrow: "I Tried" was certainly authorized by Wright although he did not influence the shaping of the text. (He did,

however, supply the title, which Zeller would view as part of the text.) *The God That Failed* clearly does fit Zeller's criterion, since Wright supplied the text.

22. With the exception, as noted earlier, of a tiny overlap between *Mademoiselle's* "American Hunger" and "Early Days in Chicago." The 1946 limited-circulation reproduction of *American Hunger* is not involved as an authority for any of these texts. See Appendix.

23. See *Later Works* 868–69 for the methodology employed.

24. Fabre's language suggests that he is referring specifically to discussions of the nonracialism of the Party, its appeal to impulses of solidarity, and its power as transforming ideology (*AH* 118, 119, 122), none of which appear in the magazine text.

WORKS CITED

Bowers, Fredson. "Mixed Texts and Multiple Authority." *Text* 3 (1987): 63–90.

Breitman, George. Review of *American Hunger* (1977 edn.). *The Militant/International Socialist Review* 38 (Aug. 5, 1977), 12.

Crossman, Richard, ed. *The God That Failed.* First U.S. edn. New York: Harper, 1949 [Jan. 1950].

Davis, Charles T., and Michel Fabre. *Richard Wright: A Primary Bibliography.* Boston: G. K. Hall, 1982.

Fabre, Michel. *The Unfinished Quest of Richard Wright.* Tr. Isabel Barzun. New York: William Morrow, 1973.

Gayle, Addison. *Richard Wright: Ordeal of a Native son.* Garden City: Anchor-Doubleday, 1980.

Greg, W. W. "The Rationale of Copy-Text." 1950-51. *The Collected Papers of Sir Walter W. Greg,* ed. J. C. Maxwell. Oxford, 1966. 374–91.

Kinnamon, Keneth. *The Emergence of Richard Wright: A Study in Literature and Society.* Urbana, Chicago, London: University of Illinois Press, 1972, 1973.

———, Joseph Benson, Michel Fabre, Craig Werner. *A Richard Wright Bibliography: Fifty Years of Criticism and Commentary, 1933–82.* Westport: Greenwood, 1982.

Leibowitz, Herbert. *Fabricating Lives: Explorations in American Autobiography.*

New York: Knopf, 1989.

McGann, Jerome J. *A Critique of Modern Textual Criticism*. Chicago and London: University of Chicago Press, 1983.

——. "Interpretation, Meaning, and Textual Criticism: A Homily." *Text* 3 (1987): 55–62.

McLaverty, James. "The Concept of Authorial Intention in Textual Criticism." *The Library*, Sixth Ser., 6 (1984): 121–38.

Reilly, John M. "The Self-Creation of the Intellectual: *American Hunger* and *Black Power*." *Critical Essays on Richard Wright*. Ed. Yoshinobu Hakutani. Boston: G. K. Hall, 1982, 213–27.

Tanselle, G. Thomas. "The Editorial Problem of Final Authorial Intention." *Studies in Bibliography* 29 (1976): 167–211.

——. *A Rationale of Textual Criticism*. Philadelphia: University of Pennsylvania Press, 1989.

Walker, Margaret. *Richard Wright: Daemonic Genius: A Portrait of the Man; A Critical Look at His Work*. New York: Warner, 1988.

Wright, Richard. *American Hunger*. 1977. New York: Harper & Row (Harper Colophon edn.), 1983.

——. "American Hunger." *Mademoiselle*, Sept. 1945: 164–65, 299–301.

——. "Early Days in Chicago." *Cross Section. A Collection of New American Writing*, ed. Edwin Seaver. [Annual.] New York: Book Find Club/[L. B. Fischer], 1945, 306–42.

——. *Eight Men*. 1961. New York: Thunder's Mouth, 1987.

——. "I Tried to Be a Communist." *Atlantic Monthly*, 174 (1944): Aug., 61–70; Sept., 48–56.

——. *Later Works: Black Boy (American Hunger); The Outsider*. Ed. Arnold Rampersad. New York: Library of America, 1991.

——. *The Outsider*. 1953. New York: Harper & Row-Perennial Library, 1965, 1989.

——. Selected correspondence in Richard Wright Archive, Beinecke Rare Book and Manuscript Library, Yale University.

Editing the Bilingual Text at Cross-Cultural Purposes

John V. Antush

John Glavin's article, "Bulgakov's Lizard and the Problem of the Playwright's Authority" in volume 4 of *TEXT*, vividly, even brilliantly, calls attention to the special problems of editing dramatic texts. "Why," asks Glavin, "should a playwright, unlike a novelist or poet, have no claim to an author's customary authority?" (383). Because, he answers, the real text of the play is the performance and not the script. "The text becomes the play as it is produced" (387). To support his case he quotes the Preface to *Jumpers* where the playwright, Tom Stoppard, concedes, "I have tried with some difficulty to arrive at something called a 'definitive text,' but I now believe that in the case of plays there is no such animal" (387; Stoppard 11). While fully appreciating the breadth and subtlety of Glavin's article, my own feeling is that a playwright's preparation of a script for performance has quite a different intention from a playwright's conscious construction of that same script for publication. Tom Stoppard's published version of his play *Travesties* may be only a "marked up photo-copy of the original script" including "some but not all of the changes made for the performance text" (Gaskell 247; Howard-Hill 274). This published text may suggest "alternative methods of production" and "cuts" for future performances. But this text itself is not performance oriented; the very act of offering this text for publication rather than relinquishing it to the theater makes all this dramatic machinery a literary convention subject to the same editorial treatment as a novel or a poem.

Playwrights generally write for production not publication, and only a small fraction of produced plays are ever published. Nevertheless, plays are read and criticized as literature. The problems arise when textual critics try to recover authorial intentions and seek to "establish the text as the author wished to have it presented to the public" (Tanselle 172). This kind of criticism has involved careful discriminations among authorial intentions which we need not go over again.[1] The problems of recovering authorial intention are especially complicated for playwrights like Shakespeare, who never wrote for publication, and for many others, like Chekov and Wilde, whose original intentions were so radically subverted by their respective acting companies that by the time of publication the playwrights themselves had disavowed their own plays (although they acquiesced to the published versions). However, those playwrights fortunate enough to find a publisher and who oversee the publication of their own plays seem to me much less problematic than the others. T. H. Howard–Hill cuts through the fine points of intentionality to the heart of one editorial problem when he says, " . . . a fundamental question to be addressed—one which has far-reaching implications for the editing of plays—is whether editors should regard an author of a play as intending to compose a work or intending to write a script for the theatre" (271–72). When a playwright collaborates with a director, stage manager, actors, and others to realize a performance, his "programmatic intention" is to write a script that is "incomplete as a glyph" (Glavin 386), and the production itself becomes the text of the play. However, when he himself helps prepare that same script for publication, he is choosing to freeze that text in the literary form of the drama. If we speak of theater as a performance form and drama as a literary form, then theater exists only in the evanescent production on the boards, and drama exists on the pages of the published work.

George Bernard Shaw is the modern playwright usually credited with introducing the general public to the reading of plays (other than closet dramas not intended for performance). Shaw printed at his own expense his first play, *Widowers' Houses*, in that "ridiculous French convention" of theatrical jargon. When nobody bought it, he "set to work to make plays readable," he wrote to his German translator, Siegfried Trebitsch, in 1903. He began by eliminating all the technical terms of the theater, even "enter" and "exit," and replacing them with elaborate and concise descriptions that without shattering "the readers' dream provided technical specification for the stage manager far more detailed and complete than any author has ever given before." The terms "stage left" and "stage right," for

example, normally refer to the actors'" left and right and are therefore the opposite for the audience facing them. But Shaw obviates
this confusion with a fuller description of the set for the reader. At
the opening of the second act of *Pygmalion*, for example, he tells us
". . . the double doors are in the middle of the back wall; and persons entering find in the corner to their right . . ." (230). Nevertheless, Shaw had been writing plays for thirteen years before he finally found a publisher, Grant Richards, who published his plays
pleasant and unpleasant in 1898. Shaw boasted, in that same letter
to Trebitsch, ". . . one of the most important things I have done in
England is to effect a reform in the printing of plays" (56).

Indeed, Shaw certainly represents a major step toward popular-
izing the drama for the reading public. His influence can readily be
seen in the plays of Arthur Miller, Tennessee Williams, and many
others. Lorraine Hansberry, for instance, sets the opening scene of
Raisin in the Sun this way:

> . . . we can see that at some time . . . the furnishings of this room were actually
> selected with care and love and even hope. . . . Now the once loved pattern of
> the couch upholstery has to fight to show itself under acres of crocheted
> doilies and couch covers which have themselves finally come to be more
> important than the upholstery. (11)

Such poetry gives the set decorator a theme to work with, but lines
like these could have been written only with a more generalized
reader in mind.

Now that playwrights have become more aware of publishing
opportunities, their writing has become more literary (in the good
sense). Sometimes, even when they write for production, they have
one eye cocked toward the book sales. If a play has a good run, its
published version might sell fifteen thousand to several hundred
thousand copies. For every theater-goer who sees a play, a hundred
might read it. Random House recently rushed the publication of
Six Degrees of Separation by John Guare to coincide with the play's
move from the smaller Mitzi Newhouse Theater at Lincoln Center
to the Vivian Beaumont on November 8, 1990—another opening,
another round of reviews. By March 1, 1991, book sales had topped
10,000 with no end in sight. The economic power and popularity of
the written text also give playwrights the opportunity to take
revenge on what they consider the frustrations of the theater, or to
set the record straight. Tennessee Williams felt pressured by his di-

rector, Elia Kazan, to write a completely new third act for *Cat on a Hot Tin Roof*. He hated this new ending, which he instinctively felt was not "dramatically proper" (*Memoirs* 169). However, the play went on to become a great theatrical success; it won the Critics' Award and the Pulitzer in 1954. Although the critics raved, he considered the play that was performed on opening night "a failure." When he published it, he published his own version with the original third act restored, along with the revised third act for the New York production and a note of explanation. His published version has been easily as great a literary success as his performance version was a theatrical success.

The discrete levels of "superseded authorial intention" (Cook 81) between the play as performance text and the play as published text became more vivid to me in my recent efforts to edit for publication previously unpublished plays that had survived several productions. The project is the editing of a series of plays in English by Puerto Rican playwrights living in the U.S. So far, two volumes of plays have been published, a third is with the publisher, and two more are in preparation. Almost all of these plays have been written and produced in both English and Spanish. However, this project concerns only the English version, which is bilingual in the sense that the plays are liberally sprinkled with Spanish phrases, sometimes a few sentences, from island dialects, Spanglish, and assorted "Nuyoricanisms" from Brooklyn to the Bronx. Sometimes these phrases capture a peculiar tonality of meaning untranslatable into English. These plays are cross-cultural in their intent to appeal to a broad audience outside the Puerto Rican community and to introduce the linguistic and cultural dynamics of Puerto Rican culture to non-Hispanics. Thus, the ordinary job of establishing a copy-text for these plays is complicated by the problems of editing a significant amount of foreign language text for readers who may be adequately bilingual but are not bicultural, who may be aware of the literal face value of the foreign words but are not aware of the complex meanings such words have in their cultural context.

The Puerto Rican playwrights I have been working with were very production-oriented before I suggested publication to them. At first most of them gave me variant copies and asked me to choose. As we got into the preparation of the manuscripts for publication, their attitude changed. They became aware of composing a literary work instead of another script. In substantive matters of

meaning they spoke of remaining true to their cultural roots while
still appealing to a broad readership. I sensed that their collaboration with me as a kind of semi-scholaly, literary editor was different
from their previous collaborations with directors and actors. By
changing only a few words of the script—in the stage directions or
the Spanish phrases or the dialogue—they sometimes altered the
whole play. Under the rubric of "published version" this manuscript sometimes became neither a variant nor even another version of the script; it became a different play, one that probably
might never be produced in a theater. The highly successful production of *Midnight Blues* by Juan Shamsul Alam, for example, a
play originally about a macho father who drives his healthy homosexual son to suicide, metamorphosed into a play about AIDS and
the whole family's response to the son's death. *Midnight Blues*,
however, lost none of its dramatic power in the evolution from
script to literary work; it will undoubtedly be reincarnated on stage
again. Therefore, of the many difficult, but often happy, challenges
of this project, I would like to focus on these two: establishing the
copy-text and maintaining the bilingual, cross-cultural intentions of
the playwright.

Establishing the copy-text is the more familiar problem; however, it is not as simple as one might think, even when dealing with a
single, living author who is available to resolve any choices in
emending the text. True, there are not those ordinary problems of
distinguishing between non-authorial revision or between multiple
authorship. But the difficulty remains of choosing from among several artistic intentions. The recent evolution of textual criticism has
shifted some attention from the gloss to the problems of text production. The widespread use of the copy machine (not always a
reliable tool) and the computer, coupled with modern developments in linguistics, semiotics, and structuralist and post-structuralist literary theory, has stimulated editorial interest in problems of
textual genesis by means of the apparatus of variants. These playwrights wrote for production not publication; they modified their
texts for actors, directors, audiences, and others. What played well
on a given night before a specified group with a carefully chosen
cast may not be the text that best expresses the author's intentions
in print. Therefore, although these plays were previously unpublished, they still exist in variant manuscripts adapted for different

stage productions before different audiences. These variants constitute in part what Jean Bellemin-Noel in 1974 called the "avant-
text" or "pre-text," all of which inhabit the published text but are
not necessarily integrated into it nor necessarily subsumed by it.

The living author of these pre-texts, however, to use Gary Taylor's phrase "has passed away" (44), and his latest intentions need
to be regained or reformulated. In these situations the editor sometimes plays a special, more complicated, role in the creative process
itself. In reconstructing what Fredson Bowers calls the author's
"latest intention" as opposed to "final intention" (7), one may have
to negotiate among priorities of intention. When the text itself is at
cross-cultural purposes, it can sometimes be at cross purposes with
itself. One of the author's several latest intentions may be cross-cultural, that is, to bridge the gap of understanding between, say,
Latino and Anglo cultures. When the intention appears to be at
cross purposes to the performance requirements of the script, some
attention must be paid to aligning the two intentions so that aesthetic value or integrity is not lost.

One example will illustrate what I mean by the difficulty and
special creativity in establishing the copy-text of these plays. Early
in the project a playwright, Edward Gallardo, gave me a copy of his
play, *Women Without Men*, that he said was his latest revised version. The typescript was in fair but not finished form, with typos,
misspellings, deletions, and so on, and with several pages on a different typewriter marked "revised as of June 1986." The reviews
and production notes he gave me indicated that the script had been
in a constant state of flux for four years and that two complete variant texts had emerged. When I asked about the changes, he gave
me the other version and explained his rationale for the revisions.
The original version won the New York Shakespeare Festival's contest for Latino plays. The second version resulted from Joseph
Papp's production of the play at the New York Public Theater.
Papp himself, who directed the play, and others at the Public made
substantive but not extensive changes. The play then went on to
more success in Puerto Rico, Mexico, and elsewhere in the United
States. I prepared an elaborate edition of the play with footnotes
translating the Spanish phrases, explaining the wartime references
(the play was set in the forties), and showing the dramatic meaning
of the wartime songs. I also wrote an introduction with a succinct
literary critique of the play but without any mention of the original

version or of the textual changes. To my chagrin, the playwright objected to all the footnotes, so I removed them. He agreed to a glossary of Spanish terms at the back of the book, which the publisher later did away with. So, by default we ended up with the "clear text" that the CEAA calls for, that is, a text page without all the burdensome machinery of textual commentary and translation.

When I received the word-processed version from the publisher which he sent me for further editing and proofing before the galleys, I was stunned by the unexpected changes. The compositor had taken it upon himself to omit many of the vulgarisms and references to the deity in Spanish or English and to make other arbitrary changes in diction and punctuation. Between the two of us, Gallardo and I managed to repair that damage. More importantly, there were two major variations in the text that substantially changed the ending and the meaning of the play. I recognized this as the earlier ending of the play. The playwright, without informing me, had sent his earlier version to the publisher. He had agreed to—but did not like—the changes suggested at the Public Theatre. Upon reconsideration, he felt the first fully developed script better expressed the reality of the Puerto Rican character that he wanted to dramatize for Hispanic as well as non-Hispanic audiences. I argued that from a literary point of view the ending we had originally agreed on expressed more ambiguity and was more integrally consistent with the complex emotional response the play demanded throughout. He disagreed. He felt that the other ending had more of a dramatic edge to it: it more sharply defined the break between the two main characters, the mother and the daughter. He wanted the sense of loss to be absolute, without comfort, without hope of rapprochement. Of course, I deferred to his wishes. However, I told him I would have to change my introduction because it no longer applied to the play. He was very upset because he really liked my interpretation of the play. We negotiated still another ending (and other changes) that allowed him to keep my introduction and the dramatic impact of his original ending.

Much later I was struck by Gary Taylor's contention that even the living authors we edit are dead in the sense that "the phase of the author's existence which brought the work into being has already passed away" (44). He struck an even more responsive chord in me when he said that editors "cannot escape from their own presence or from the absence of that author whose passing away they commemorate" (54). Last week Gallardo informed me that the play is presently rehearsing for a Los Angeles production with more changes and still another ending. He expressed doubts about this ending, but he also confirmed his satisfaction with the published version of the play. If a critical edition is ever done, the critical editor will have the original version, the New York variant, and the Los Angeles variant to his edition.

Another second aspect of bilingual cross-cultural communication surfaced in the editing of Richard Irizarry's play *Ariano*. I first became aware that there might be a problem when I took a group of students to see the play in New York City. They liked the play very much; they found it humorous as well as serious. But they complained that all the punch lines were in Spanish, and even though most of them had studied Spanish they missed the jokes. They saw the humor because every Spanish phrase is repeated in English, but the timing was off. This limitation of the performance text for a non-Hispanic audience may seem minor. After all, something is always lost in translation, and laughter is one of the early casualties. As it turned out, this was only the tip of the iceberg.

Ariano is a very complex play about the American dream, *machismo*, the fragility of the male ego, the low self-esteem—even self-hatred—engendered in everyone by racial prejudice, and other related themes. One strand of the play deals with racial bigotry, the most difficult cultural adjustment Puerto Ricans must make when moving to the mainland. In my Introduction to the play I make a point about this clash of cultures.

> Puerto Ricans are the first large group ever to immigrate to the United States with a tradition of widespread racial integration. When they arrive, Puerto Ricans encounter a type of racial discrimination and segregation they do not experience on the island. Moreover, Puerto Ricans find they themselves are simplistically placed into one of two categories: white or non-white. Finding their acceptance into the larger, more affluent white community much more difficult if they are non-white, Puerto Ricans soon realize the social and economic advantages of being white in America. This newly discovered color awareness often triggers identity confusion and extreme distortions of Puerto Rican cultural values. One distortion involves an unnatural tension among Puerto Ricans themselves. Those who can pass for white may assimilate with the white community and separate themselves from those who cannot pass for white. The incredible force of American racial bigotry can sometimes overcome even blood ties. The color barrier may split husbands and wives, brothers and sisters, even children and parents. (20–21)

Ariano (whose name means "Aryan") is a young, light-skinned Puerto Rican whose wife is darker than he is and whose son is even darker, with kinky black hair. A financially successful man, Ariano finds that he can pass for white if he does not identify himself as Puerto Rican, but his wife and son cannot. The conflict this social division causes within Ariano perhaps cannot be fully appreciated by, say, some in an Anglo audience whose color perceptions run only to black and white. In Puerto Rico, where racial commingling and intermarriage are more common than in the United States, a person's identity never depends solely on color. The racially sophisticated culture factors in many other characteristics. Education, occupation, wealth, nurture, and other facets of personality all contribute to social acceptance.

Nevertheless, color discrimination does exist on the island in a very complicated way, and Ariano has been infected with the prejudice that "you better the race the lighter you marry." Some Spanish terms depicting racial and color characteristics prepare the reader/viewer for the climax. The language here, a source of cross-cultural confusion for the characters, can become a potential bridge of understanding between cultures. For example, *blanco/blanca* or *hincho/hincha* refers to a white person; *mulatto/mulatta* refers to a person with black and white features; *trigueño/trigueña* (wheat-colored) refers to persons of tanned skin but perhaps straight hair and white features; *grifo/grifa* refers to a white person with kinky hair; and *negro/negra* refers to a black person. Many people who have studied Spanish may understand the meaning of these terms and still be fairly unaware of the nuances of personal and social identity the culture attaches to them. For example, one of the revealing ironies of the play is that throughout, even while adamantly denying his and his family's racial mix, Ariano frequently refers to his wife as "negritta" and to his son as "negritto, " which in Puerto Rico are intimate terms of endearment. The affection and positive quality of these terms are apparent in the context, but the untrained ear of a non-Hispanic may not quite "hear" the word in performance. The paradox of Ariano calling his son "negritto" after scolding him severely for drawing a picture of the family in brown colors may be more apparent to the Hispanic viewer who operates within the cultural given of the language, but it is not likely to be lost on anyone who sees the word on the page. At the moment of crisis in this play, interlingual communication produces the dramatic cross-cultural insight.

The experience points up a major difference between the performance text and the published text. In performance, the non-Hispanic audience, like the bilingual students who did not get the jokes, may see one play while the Hispanic audience sees another. The non-Hispanics may emphasize the crudeness of the color barriers in the United States and the terrible effects they have even on people from a more discriminating culture who are set adrift from their basic cultural moorings. The Hispanics may see that even in the fabric of their own language and culture the seeds of racial prejudice make them vulnerable to the blatant bigotry of the mainland. The cross-cultural intention of the playwright is that with a minimum of editorial apparatus both audiences will read both plays at once.

The editor is, after all, only another instrument in the elaborate orchestration of the play. Like the set designer, the lighting technician, and the rest, he is another collaborator in the ensemble. Perhaps he is most like the director (although not as creative) who coordinates the performance text to pluck the playwright's play from the ideality of thought to give it aesthetic completion in time and space. In a similar way, the editor helps translate the acoustical and visual world of the theater into the linguistic world of the drama to give some measure of fixed literary precision to the text. Thus, the literary text is neither prior to nor posterior to the performance text. The literary text is what Bert O. States calls "the animating current to which the actor submits his body and refines himself into an illusionary being"; the performance text is "the channel through which the poet's art can be brought out of the realm of being" (128). Whether we view these plays as being transmuted from the page to the stage or vice-versa, one text's gain is the other text's loss. What the performance text loses in malleability and representational impact, the literary text gains in objective illusion and stability of interpretation.

In editing these transcultural texts, it is often helpful to remember that an individual word often functions first as a semantic field with its own associations and then emerges with a developing life of its own within a given context. Although my only contribution to these plays was that of literary editor, I did see many of them through varying phases of development. One needs only to hear the staged reading of a play, to see it later as a finished performance, and then to edit its published version to perceive the differences among the script, the performance text, and the literary text. At a staged reading even with professional actors adept at rendering a script cold, the actor presents himself only as a kind of talking head who interprets the lines rather than acts them. He or she stands or sits there, bare of costume, no scenic context, practically no gestures, his disciplined body not quite in tune with the carefully orchestrated intentions of the playwright. However, when the actor has tuned his instrument for the finished performance, not only his voice but also his facial features, his gestures, his bodily stance, everything fall into a synthesis of expressing a complex but different world. The actor disappears into the role only to be reincarnated as a character. The actor's art thus becomes the conduit through which the playwright's script finds its artistic existence and thus becomes the theatrical or performance text. Synchronically, the actor stands outside different cultural and historical styles of acting. Whether he performs in the classical style of Japanese kabuki theater, in Stanislavski's method theater, or in Brecht's epic theater style of estrangement (*Verfremdungseffekt*), he remains the vehicle from age to age or culture to culture through which the playwright's "text" finds embodiment. With the end of the performance, any given performance text is left floating on the air until another production creates it anew. The play lapses into literature when the playwright (or, as in the case of Shakespeare, someone else) fixes it in print. Then a whole different set of political, commercial, and social conventions affect the social act of publishing. When these conditions work to frustrate or distort the playwright's intentions, the editor's job is often complicated by the negotiations between author and publisher.

When the playwright leaves the production behind for a short while and approaches the task of publication, he realizes instinctively a new kind of power in the written text. The published manuscript possesses a material richness that no effort of analysis can hope to exhaust. He or she, like the editor, knows that every time an important document is carefully preserved it has the power to break habits of thought, to penetrate new realms and to encounter the unpredictable, to examine the significations that multiply with multiple readings. What a loss to the world if John Heminges and Henry Condell had not collected the First Folio! For the profound reality of the published dramatic text lies in its productivity; it is neither exhausted nor obliterated by the weight of its possibilities.

NOTES

1. I quote Tanselle's excellent summary of the various kinds of authorial intentions and their distinctions in his article "The Problems of Final Authorial
   Intentions" without his notes.

   . . . as soon as one starts to talk about "intention," . . . various kinds of
   intention need to be distinguished, and many of the recent discussions
   of intention in literature do attempt to sub-divide the concept. Thus T.
   M. Gang differentiates between "practical intention" (intention "to
   achieve a certain result") and "literary intention" (intention to convey
   "a certain significance"); John Kemp distinguishes between "immediate
   intention" (that which a man "intends, or sets himself, to do") and
   "ulterior intention" ("that which he intends or hopes to achieve as a
   result of doing what he does"); Morse Peckham discriminates between
   "mediated intention" ("a statement or other sign") and "immediate
   intention" ("metaphorical extension of mediated intention into the area
   of 'mind'"); and Quentin Skinner, borrowing terms from J. L. Austin's
   How to Do Things with Words (1962), speaks of "illocutionary intention" (what a writer "may have been intending to do in writing what he
   wrote") and "perlocutionary intention" ("what he may have intended
   to do by writing a certain way"), as well as of "intention to do x" (a
   writer's "plan or design to create a certain type of work").

   Of such classifications of intention, one of the clearest and most useful has been set forth by Michael Hancher. In his view, "author's intentions" can be divided into three types: (1) "programmatic intention"—
   "the author's intention to make something or other"; (2) "active intention"—"the author's intention to be (understood as) acting in some way
   or other"; and (3) "final intention"—"the author's intention to cause
   something or other to happen." The first refers to the author's general
   plan to write a sonnet, say, or a realistic novel; the third refers to his
   hope that his work will change the reader's view-point, say, or bring
   wealth to himself. The second is the one which concerns the meanings
   embodied in the work: "Active intentions characterize the actions that
   the author, at the time he finishes his text, understands himself to be
   performing in that text" (p. 830). Hancher's argument is that the first
   and third kinds of intention—programmatic and final—are indeed irrelevant to the interpretation of a literary work but that the second—
   active intention—must be taken into account in the interpretation (and
   evaluation) of the work. (173–175)

WORKS CITED

Antush, John V., ed. "Introduction." *Recent Puerto Rican Theatre: Five Plays from*

New York. University of Houston: Arte Publico Press, 1991.

Bellemin-Noel, Jean. *Le texte et l'avant-texte*. Paris, 1972.

Bowers, Fredson. "Unfinished Business." *TEXT: Transactions of the Society for Textual Scholarship*. (New York: AMS Press, 1988), 4: 1–11.

Cook, Don L. "Some Considerations in the Concept of Pre-Copy-Text." *TEXT: Transactions of the Society for Textual Schlarship*. (New York: AMS Press, 1988), 4: 79–91.

Gaskell, Philip. *From Writer to Reader: Studies in Editorial Method*. Oxford: Clarendon Press, 1978.

Glavin, John. "Bulgokov's Lizard and the Problem of the Playwright's Authority." *TEXT: Transactions of the Society for Textual Scholarship*. (New York: AMS Press, 1988), 4: 385–406.

Hansberry, Lorraine. *A Raisin in the Sun*. New York: NAL, 1966.

Howard-Hill, T. H. "Playwrights' Intentions and the Editing of Plays." *TEXT: Transactions of the Society for Textual Scholarship*. (New York: AMS Press, 1988), 4: 269–78.

Shaw, George Bernard. *Pygmalion. Four Plays by Bernard Shaw*. New York: Random House, 1953.

States, Bert O. *Great Reckonings in Little Rooms: On the Phenomenology of Theater*. Berkeley: University of California Press, 1985.

Stoppard, Tom. *Jumpers*. New York: Grove, 1972.

Tanselle, G. Thomas. "The Editorial Problem of Final Authorial Intention." *Studies in Bibliography*, 29 (1976): 167–211.

Taylor, Gary. "The Rhetoric of Textual Criticism." *TEXT: Transactions of the Society for Textual Scholarship*. (New York: AMS Press, 1988), 4: 39–57.

Weiss, Samuel A., ed. *Bernard Shaw's Letters to Siegfried Trebitsch*. Stanford University Press, 1986.

Williams, Tennessee. *Memoirs*. New York: Doubleday, 1975.

Reviews

A Rationale of Textual Criticism. G. Thomas Tanselle.
Philadelphia: University of Pennsylvania Press,
1989. 104 pp. $17.95.

This volume concisely and elegantly summarizes much of its
author's thinking from the past two decades. The three lectures
brought together and published here were first delivered in the
Rosenbach Series at the University of Pennsylvania in the spring of
1987. The lectures take up many of the aesthetic and theoretical
questions that G. Thomas Tanselle has addressed from time to time
in his omnibus review articles for *Studies in Bibliography*, but here
the questions are treated as abstract matters rather than as issues
arising from the work of particular scholars. Seasoned textual critics will recognize the various theories and positions currently under
debate in the field, but the absence of specific references to this
school of thought or that group of scholars has the effect, in the
Rationale, of rendering the discussion more neutral and, I think,
more widely applicable. Those interested in attaching names to the
arguments and counter-arguments can do so by consulting Tanselle's *Textual Criticism since Greg: A Chronicle* (1987), which
brings together the three most comprehensive of the *Studies in
Bibliography* essays. The *Rationale*, in fact, can be read as a kind of
streamlined gloss on *Textual Criticism since Greg*. Soon it will also
be possible to read the *Rationale* alongside Tanselle's prefatory
essay for *Scholarly Editing: An Introductory Guide to Research*, a
volume scheduled to be published by the Modern Language Association in 1993. Both the *Rationale* and this forthcoming prefatory
essay are admirably clear and direct, and both will be helpful
guides to editors who need to think through situations involving authorial intention.

The first of Tanselle's three lectures, entitled "The Nature of Texts," focuses on aesthetics and concerns the differences between a "text" and a "work." The former, says Tanselle, is a physical artifact, the latter an abstract concept. This distinction provides an underpinning for the two subsequent lectures, "Reproducing the texts of Documents" and "Reconstructing the Texts of Works." Tanselle wishes to emphasize that reproducing documents and reconstructing texts are distinct activities. It is improper to mix the two in one's mind: the first is an act of textual transmission, with little intervention by the editor, while the second is an act of biography and literary criticism. Tanselle is insistent about the status of critical editing as the higher and more difficult of the two pursuits:

> Textual criticism is . . . basic to the critical analysis of literature (and similar arts) in a different sense from the one frequently claimed. It is often said that textual criticism is a fundamental branch of scholarship because the textual critic must provide an accurate text before the literary critic can profitably begin to analyze it. But any text that a textual critic produces is itself the product of literary criticism, reflecting a particular aesthetic position and thus a particular approach to what textual "correctness" consists of. It is true that a textual scholar can attempt to uncover, and set forth systematically, the facts constituting the textual history of a work and can stop there, without suggesting which variants might be preferred, under certain circumstances, over other variants. Such activity would indeed be preliminary to criticism (which is not to say that no judgment is involved in it), but whatever criticism followed would still have to include decisions about the makeup of the text, for those decisions are simply part of the act of reading. Anyone accepting a text uncritically—without making such decisions—is focusing not on a work but only on the text of a document. (34–35)

To help make these distinctions Tanselle introduces, in this first lecture, a discussion of the differences between restoring a work of art which exists only as a single artifact—a painting, say, or a sculpture—and reconstructing a literary or musical work, which exists in multiple texts but has no genuine corporeal reality. In the case of the painting or sculpture, writes Tanselle, "the work and the artifact are in battle for the same physical space" (29). Thus any restoration of the work will of necessity destroy the evidence of its earlier damage and corruption. Not so with the work of literature or music: here the evidence of deterioration survives and can be added to or reinterpreted in a way not possible with the evidence that was once a physical part of the painting or sculpture. The difference can be underlined by noting that a painting or sculpture will always have an owner, even hundreds of years after its creation, and the owner will have the legal authority to decide whether or not to let experts do restoration work. By contrast, a work of literature or music, once copyright has expired, cannot be owned and can therefore be restored by anyone who can persuade a publisher to print the results. The expert in musical or literary restoration, however, can only hope to approximate, in yet another text, the abstract ideal of the work. And the new text that is thus produced will itself be added to the body of evidence, which will continue to accumulate and change. Tanselle explains:

> Every verbal text, whether spoken or written down, is an attempt to convey a work. The preservation of the documents containing verbal texts, like the preservation of other artifacts, is a vital cultural activity. But the act of preserving such documents, unlike that of preserving paintings, for example, does not preserve works but only evidences of works. If, as readers, we are interested in the verbal works that their producers intended, we must constantly entertain the possibility of altering the texts we have inherited. Those texts, being reports of works, must always be suspect; and, no matter how many of them we have, we never have enough information to enable us to know with certainty what the works consist of. (68–69)

An understanding of these matters is crucial for a beginner in the field of textual criticism. Tanselle's articulation of these distinctions in the first of his lectures is quite clear and is suitable, I think, to be used in graduate seminars on scholarly editing. One can even take the distinction a step further for one's graduate students (and complicate it the more) by introducing works of architecture into the discussion. Such works are subject to the operations of time and chance, just as paintings and poems are, but typically they have grown by addition, repair, and accretion in a way that sculptures and novels have not. Thus when one sets out to save the Parthenon (for example) from damages caused by war, weather, air pollution, and tourism, one must decide how far back one wants to take the restoration. Does one wish to make an effort to recreate the Parthenon as it existed when it was originally completed? Perhaps, but can such a temporal point be located from the scanty evidence that survives? Was the Parthenon ever "complete" at any single moment in its history?

The issue is even more complex because the Parthenon has come to have immense symbolic significance in Western culture as a ruin. Will it be an act of desecration to restore it to an ersatz newness—rather like the imitation Parthenon erected in Nashville, a city which calls itself "The Athens of the South"? Should the real Parthenon therefore be restored as a ruin? If so, then the ruin of which period? The one visited by Edith Wharton in 1888, or the one that Byron knew in 1810, or the one that existed a few decades before—in 1780, say, before Lord Elgin had the statuary removed and brought to England? These questions, quite complex, are not unlike those that face textual editors as they try to decide which set of intentions, of all those that existed during the history of a given literary work, should be recovered and published in the reading text of a scholarly edition.

A related question comes up, oddly enough, when one begins to teach a restored work to one's undergraduates—a work that one has taught to them in past years in a corrupt form, simply because that form was the only text available. For example, I taught William Faulkner's eleventh novel for over twenty years in its expurgated form and under a title, *The Wild Palms*, that had been imposed on Faulkner by his publishers. Relying heavily on the work of Thomas L. McHaney, I was able to take the high moral ground from the very first lecture, operating (in the students' eyes at least) as a kind of investigative journalist, pointing out corruption in positions of responsibility. I could tell my students that Faulkner had wanted to call his book *If I Forget Thee, Jerusalem*, not *The Wild Palms*, and that this original title, with its allusion to Psalms 137, tied together the main narrative, "Wild Palms," and the secondary narrative, "Old Man," in a fashion that Faulkner had obviously intended. I could say further that Faulkner's wishes had been disregarded in the very last line of the book. He had needed to use a particular obscenity in this line to underscore the cowardice and misogyny of the character known as the "tall convict." The force of this obscenity, however, had been weakened by a trade editor's substitution of hyphens for three of the four letters in the word, so that the final line spoken by the tall convict in the first edition reads, "'Women – – –t!'" Thus (I could conclude) Faulkner's intentions for his novel had been subverted throughout, from the title page to the last line. This would usually stir up some moral indignation among my undergraduates, at least for a period or two. They were irritated that they had been reading damaged goods.

Obviously I was not teaching the first-edition text of *The Wild Palms* in the manner of the Thorpe-Peckham-McGann school. I was introducing an ethical element into the presentation that a member of that group would probably find unacceptable. So far as I can determine, a teacher of that persuasion would have to present compromised literary documents in a morally neutral way, as texts that were socialized or domesticated by their cultures before publication. Alterations that seemed to change an author's intentions for a work would be brought to the attention of students and would be commented on. The teacher, one assumes, would engage in word play and linguistic analysis, but the tone throughout would be objective and non-judgmental. My approach, with the author as hero, the publisher's editor as imperceptive villain, and the teacher as moral rectifier, would probably seem overly theatrical and accusatory by contrast.

Pedagogically, however, my approach was effective, precisely because I could appropriate a large body of free-floating virtue and, in the bargain, stage a small consciousness-raising session about the problems of textual corruption. It is therefore regrettable, in a way, to report that my intermittent run on stage as defender of Faulkner's textual rectitude is about to end. In 1990 the Library of America published a repaired text of *The Wild Palms* under its intended title and with the final obscenity restored. (And, it should be added, with a great many other errors corrected throughout the text.) This restored text is now the one that will be available as a classroom paperback. Certainly I am happy to see Faulkner's novel published in a form that would have pleased him. Of course I will order this restored text for my classes in the future. But what am I now to do for my initial lecture on *If I Forget Thee, Jerusalem*? My presentation can be adjusted, but it will lose much of its moral force. I can still recount Faulkner's problems with the first edition, and show my students xeroxes from that text, but I can no longer tell them that they have been reading a damaged product. I know from experience with another text—Dreiser's *Sister Carrie*—that when college students are told that errors in a text have been rectified and expurgated passages have been restored, their attention is not engaged in the same way as it is when they are told that their text is corrupt. Undergraduates live almost entirely in the present. Was there textual injustice in the past? Certainly that is regrettable, but so long as *they* aren't affected now, they aren't likely to be much concerned.

Is it possible, then, that novels such as *The Wild Palms* and *Sister*

Carrie carry more symbolic significance as maimed texts, in their corrupt first-edition forms, than they do in their restored forms—just as the Parthenon may have more symbolic, ethical, and environmental significance as a ruin? This thinking, applied to the Parthenon, is at least plausible. Applied to works of literature, however, it seems to me to be specious because it validates inertia and inattention toward the text. Whatever histrionic value one can extract from teaching a corrupt text in the classroom is more than outweighed by the importance of allowing students to hear an author speak, from the past, as he had intended to speak during his own time. Tanselle addresses the matter off and on throughout the second and third lectures:

> Persons not interested in taking any of the historical approaches to literature need not search for the work represented by the text, but they should realize that what they are doing is equating the text of the document before them with the text of a work—just as if the object before them were a painting. What they then say or write is further removed from works of literature than are the comments of similarly inclined art critics from paintings. Even if such art critics seem to be responding more to colors of paint than to works of painting, and even though the colors present at one moment are not exactly those present at another, the colors and the works coexist in the same objects. Nevertheless, both groups of critics are alike in taking the artifacts they encounter as the stimuli for flights of fancy and displays of intellect, for fantasias upon found objects. The results may or may not be works of interest, or of genius, in their own right; but they are not writings about works of art or of literature.(70)

Nor are they *teachings*, I might add. What Tanselle is saying, I believe, is that by reconstructing and teaching a text that has existed only in a corrupt form before, one is affirming the belief that human beings can still know about and learn from the past. Further, such attempts have value and meaning. "Of all the historical activities of textual study," writes Tanselle, "the effort to reconstruct the texts of works as intended by their creators takes us deepest into the thinking of interesting minds that preceded us. We must respect the documents that make our insights possible, but we cannot rest there if we wish to experience the works created by those minds" (92). Our recreations of past personalities and behavior will be imperfect, of course, just as the restored texts will be, but the attempts to recreate and restore will have cultural significance all the same. We will be validating the importance of what an author intended to say at some past time. If his own culture prevented him from speaking freely and fully, then ours will now allow it.

Almost any other approach proceeds from an assumption that any attempt to recreate the past is meaningless—or at least is now of marginal cultural importance. The editor, under this system of values, can only function mechanically—as a neutral presenter of documents. And the teacher who mediates between those documents and his students must do so neutrally, playing with words and interpretations but never implying that the histories of these texts might have ethical significance. All that really has value now is the commentary of academics on pre-existing textual icons, which have no importance save as detritus from the past.

This way of thinking tends, for this reviewer, toward the nihilistic and exudes the fetid breath of deconstruction. The approach must be resisted. The ethical choices faced by critical editors, finally, are the same ones addressed by Kierkegaard, Carlyle, and Camus. One must first accept the ultimate impossibility and even absurdity of the task; then one must proceed with it. The value of the past as exemplar and teacher must be reaffirmed, and the ability of human beings to communicate meaningfully with the past must be reasserted.

* * *

It is good that Tanselle has addressed these questions regularly, and in so stimulating a fashion, over the past twenty years. Most scholars in the field take up these matters only when they can or must—usually for a specific project—and do not stay actively engaged with editorial theory over the long term. We can therefore be grateful to Tanselle for functioning as a kind of adjudicator and conscience for the field. His ongoing work, of which the *Rationale* is a good example, has meant that when working editors need to re-enter the conversation about textual theory, they know whose writing first to consult.

James L. W. West III
Pennsylvania State Univ.

Devils and Angels: Textual Editing and Literary Theory, ed. Philip Cohen.
Charlottesville and London: University Press of Virginia, 1991. xviii + 212 pp. $29.50.

In a perfect world, *Devils and Angels* would be required reading in graduate or advanced undergraduate courses that survey modern literary theory or the ways that literature can be studied professionally. This lively, provocative, and varied set of essays investigates the gap between literary criticism/theory and textual criticism/theory in the hopes of closing that gap. Adapting its title form Jerome McGann's depiction of the "angels of hermeneutics" who consider textual criticism a hell best avoided, the collection presents eleven reports from the textual devils in an attempt, as Philip Cohen says, "to help editors and theorists see that heaven and hell may not be all that far apart" (xvii). The essays in different ways all attempt to theorize èditing and textual criticism from the position of imperfection and instability, so whether the wider community of literary critics and theorists will take notice remains an open question.

Devils and Angels consists of Cohen's introduction and eleven essays. The essays fall into three groups, each with two or three essays followed by a response. In the eight primary essays, Jerome J. McGann uses literary pragmatics as an approach to talking about editing Rossetti and an anthology of Romantic period verse; Peter Shillingsburg looks at Thackeray's composition of *Henry Esmond* to argue that editing according to authorial intention leads to "richness" and instability rather than to "purity" and a "correct" edition (40, 42); Paul Eggert considers whether literary works should be seen in terms of product or process and considers whether critical editions should still be produced; D. C. Greetham reads Greg-Bowers eclecticism "against the grain" by "filtering it through psychoanalytical criticism" (86); Philip Cohen and David H. Jackson look at various literary and textual theories in relation to assumptions about literary ontology; James McLaverty considers works as utterances and Joseph Grigely looks at texts as events; and Hans Walter Gabler compares Anglo-American author-based textual theories to German text-based theories. In the responses T. H. Howard-Hill responds to McGann and Shillingsburg by arguing that theories about textual matters should not lose sight of the end result of the editing process (a published edition); Steven Mailloux looks at the rhetorical strategies of Eggert, Greetham, and Cohen/ Jackson; and William E. Cain responds to McLaverty, Gabler, and Grigely rather obliquely by considering a theoretical tension between authors and editors.

The arrangement of essays and responses works nicely. The different concerns and positions within the primary essays indicate the range of possibilities and the lively debate that characterize textual studies these days, and the responses open up matters further by subjecting the essays to a critique within the book's pages. The book is also stitched together in unexpected ways, in that an issue raised as a problem in one place is frequently taken up in a later essay. Thus, Shillingsberg's question about whether a work is a product or a process (27ff) becomes the central question of Eggert's essay; Howard-Hill wonders about "the extent to which any" particular theory "can influence the production (rather than the reception) of an edition" (55), and Greetham takes this up by asking near the beginning of his essay, "how does a textual theory impinge upon the actual business of editing?" (79); Cohen and Jackson's attention to "literary ontology" (104ff) is picked up by Grigely (184). Taken as a whole, the disparate essays are united by the common purpose of discussing textual theory in light of broader issues of literary theory, even if those broader issues range from literary pragmatics (McGann) to theories of the utterance (McLaverty) and the event (Grigely) to psychoanalysis (Greetham) and New Historicism (Eggert). Cohen and Jackson speak of "a paradigm shift in editing—one that will marry bibliography with contemporary literary theory" (103), and whether the essayists support or take issue with this assumption, their essays all respond to the challenge to bring textual and literary theory together in some way.

The paradigm shift is evident both explicitly and implicitly in these essays. Besides the explicit uses of particular kinds of theory just mentioned, there are several different attempts to accommodate theoretical concepts of instability and indeterminacy within a textual framework, so that even when authorial intention is the focus, it is rethought in terms of instability (Shillingsburg, Eggert, Grigely, McLaverty). Equally important, though, is the absence of any essays speaking for the previously dominant paradigm, the eclectic text edited according to final authorial intentions. The goals and methods of eclectic editing are praised twice for their "methodological rewards" and "theoretical consistency" (119, also 156), but authorial intention is seen throughout as something to be rethought, modified, or rejected outright. Likewise, the eclectic text is rejected variously in favor of "rich editions" (42) that will foreground textual multiplicity, indeterminacy, and instability; a methodology that will highlight process as well as or instead of product (74, 119, 192); text-based rather than author-based theories (157); and an emphasis on apparatus rather than on edited text (164). Indicative of this shift in focus is the fact that W. W. Greg and Fredson Bowers are each cited in only two of the essays; G Thomas Tanselle, who is now seen as the dominant representative of the eclectic/intentional position, is cited in seven essays. Conversely, Peter Shillingsburg, whose book *Scholarly Editing in the Computer Age* and essay in *Devils and Angels* argue for textual theories and methods that will reflect the complexity and incompatibility of different theories of text, intention, etc., is also cited in seven essays, and Jerome McGann, perceived as the main theoretical alternative and challenge to eclectic/intentional editing, is cited in ten of the eleven essays and introduction that refer to other textual theorists.

To the extent that McGann, since *A Critique of Modern Textual Criticism* (1983), has been calling for a rethinking of textual criticism, *Devils and Angels* can be seen as part of a McGann paradigm. But to the extent that McGann's critique has served at least as much to open up the debate as to suggest a new paradigm, the book also reflects a discipline very much in healthy disarray. Up for grabs are responses to the questions that Cohen asks in his introduction: "What is a text and how is it constituted? What is a literary work of art? When is the literary work finished? How do we determine authorial intent and textual authority[?]" (xv). Also up for grabs is the relation between answers to these questions and textual practice. Howard-Hill distinguishes between theory's "freedom to traffic in ideas" and editing, which "aims at a product" (52, 53), but other essays see a different relationship between theory, textual or otherwise, and editing practice: Greetham considers "what might happen to our textual assumptions if we were to negotiate in terms of a particular theoretical approach (psychoanalytic criticism) and what effect such negotiation might have on our estimation of the significance of the actual appearance of 'critical' editions" (80); Mailloux warns of "the trap of thinking that theory precedes practice rather than being an extension of it" (127); Cain, without elaborating, warns that the more that theoretically-minded textual critics "delve into [recent literary and philosophical] theories, the more they will radically unsettle their own programs and practices" (203). Three of the essays consider specific actual or speculative editions (McGann on Rossetti's *The House of Life*, Shillingsburg on Thackeray's *Henry Esmond*, Eggert on Lawrence's *Lady Chatterley's Lover*), and, not surprisingly, the recent edition most often discussed either in passing or in some detail (it is mentioned in eight of the essays) is Hans Walter Gabler's edition of Joyce's *Ulysses*.

Coming at a time when, with only a few exceptions such as Gabler's *Ulysses*, textual practice has not yet caught up with textual theory and a time when the relation between textual theory and practice is still to be determined, *Devils and Angels* reflects a moment of what Cohen and Jackson call "emerging paradigms" (103). As such, it is a somewhat transitory document. But as a set of essays reflecting this particular time of textual reorientation and the implications of that shift for textual and general literary studies, the book should be read by textual theorists and, perhaps even more importantly, by literary critics and theorists who think they don't need to know about textual criticism and theory. This book should convince them that they do.

Michael Groden
University of Western Ontario

Papers from "New Directions in Textual Studies," The Harry Ransom Conference, University of Texas, 30 March-1 April, 1989, in *The Library Chronicle of the University of Texas at Austin*, ed. Dave Oliphant and Robin Bradford, intro. Larry Carver, 20.1/2 (1990), ISSN 0024-2241. 185 pp.

"Dead as a dodo"—so Jerome McGann described the copy-text school of scholarly editing at the recent (October 1991) Ann Arbor conference, "Palimpsest: Editorial theory in the Humanities." The Austin conference two years earlier, "New Directions in Textual Studies," was thus the first half of an extended wake for the once dominant school of textual and bibliographical studies inaugurated by Pollard, McKerrow, and Greg. However firmly situated in the practices of American scholarly editing by Bowers and Tanselle, it's final obsequies passed all but unnoticed at Ann Arbor. Featured speakers at Austin were textual theorists associated with the challenges to Greg-Bowers-Tanselle orthodoxy: McGann himself and D. F. McKenzie, together with textualists who have challenged the concepts of authorial intentionality fundamental to that earlier orthodoxy (Michael Warren, Randall McLeod, and Hans Walter Gabler), as well as others for whom the question whether copy-text editing is alive or dead is a non-issue: Ian Willison, former Head of the English Language Branch, and Lotte Hellinga, Head of the Incunabula Section, respectively, at the British Library, and Anne Middleton, who is annotating the Athlone text of Langland's *Piers Plowman*. At one session, when the floor was offered to an advocate—*any* advocate—of authorial intentionality as a criterion for critical editing, no one spoke up on its behalf. "The Death of the Editor," indeed. What gives this volume what coherence it has, then, is the sense of an absent center, the un-represented core of Anglo-American textual practice of an entire previous generation.

McGann's lead-off essay, "How to Read a Book," is less concerned about editing than it is to set forth a theory of reading texts that necessarily affects how we edit them. In it he expands his distinction between the lexical and the bibliographical codes of a (printed) text that he had enunciated in "What is Critical Editing?" (*TEXT* 5:15–29).[1] Using as examples Pound's macaronic and iconic pages from the Cantos and comparing Pound's *ABC of Reading* with Mortimer Adler's *How to Read a Book*, McGann proposes two alternative modes of reading, the spatial and the radial, as necessary complements to the older (Adlerian) linear and linguistic mode. The spatial he claims "is a ubiquitous function of texts," exploited by Blake exceptionally but routinely deployed by advertizing texts and by popular journalism. In post-literate textuality, it is these latter that have become the norm, the linear book the élitist fossil. Pages from Pound's "highly spatialized" *Cantos* support his point nicely. Linear copy-text editors foreground the linguistic mode of reading and as editors (though not as the bibliographers they are often trained to be as well) screen out the textually extraneous bibliographical codes imbedded in format, typography, and the other material forms of textuality. The second mode of reading is radial, which "involves decoding one or more of the contexts that interpenetrate the scripted and physical text" (28). Some texts, like Pound's *Cantos*, one does not read merely word for word, straight through, absorbed in and by the text itself; one interrupts that single focus "to look up the meaning of a word," to skip ahead or back within the volume, or pull other volumes off the shelf to conflate with the text at hand. Critical editions, because of their wealth of contextual material, stimulate such acts of "radial reading," allowing "one to imagine many possible states of text" (30). Ideally, then,

> "reading" is a reaction upon a textual field that comprises far more than the linguistic text, far more even than the linguistic and the spatial text. It is a reading which assumes that the physical texts . . . are not only linguistic and spatial, but multiple and interactive as well. It is a reading which seeks to visibilize the textual field—the scene of radial reading—by a close observation of the material, the means and the modes of textual production as they develop and interact over time. (34)

McGann's aim is to recover for readers a lost sense of empowerment, lest they be absorbed in or swallowed by the text's apparently seamless authority, lest they be read by the text rather than themselves reading it, for "Even under the best of circumstances, messages and their senders are neither innocent nor completely reliable," and readers must accordingly "be prepared to defend themselves against both the errors and the perversions of those who communicate with texts" (37). One hesitates, after such subtle and penetrating analysis of the act of reading, to say it goes without saying, but such hermeneutical wariness consorts uneasily with the assumption of authority—over the text and hence over the readers of that text—that the critical editor necessarily makes.

Michael Warren's "The Theatricalization of Text: Beckett, Jonson, Shakespeare" is more openly critical of editors but, as a theatrically-oriented critic of Shakespeare and his contemporaries, Warren acknowledges that editors and critics occupy the same lifeboat, even if thy pull on contrary oars: "The theater cannot live without editors . . . But at the same time, the edited text is so often a reading text; for all our vaunted delight in uncertainty, in unlicensed interpretation, . . . what we seem to ask of editors is certainty" (58). But such theatrically-oriented readers and actors want texts that do *not* prescribe or specify stage action, or assume a particular staging of a given scene, however useful such specificity may be to the chair-bound, non-theatrically-oriented reader. Editors' interventions in supplying modern stage directions for older texts, therefore, make "decisions about actions that are in fact not necessary decisions, and [impose] particular potential actions that become embedded in the text" (58). Even the Oxford Shakespeare, as theatrically-based as its texts are, is found wanting in this regard: "no edition in recent years has looked so canonical," so designed as a book "*for the Modern Reader*" (58).

Two solutions offer themselves. Parallel-text editions of plays that survive in distinct versions, such as J. W. Lever's parallel-text edition of Jonson's *Every Man in his Humour* (Regents Renaissance Drama Series, 1971) that do not collude with Jonson's own attempt to suppress *EMIH's* stage history, or Warren's own *The Complete "King Lear": Texts and Parallel Texts in Photographic Facsimile* (California, 1989), or, better yet, texts on disk, for "electronic devices exploit multiplicity and instability, and may just be better modes of representation of the diversity of historical process" (59). But, as with the Cornell Wordsworth cited by McGann, editions like Warren's *Complete "King Lear"* are economically feasible—be they for purchase or production—only for the most canonical of plays of our most canonical of authors, for who cares about textual instability in plays (like Beaumont and Fletcher's) that are rarely performed? Paradoxically, it is the texts of our most revered authors that our most subtle and penetrating critical intelligences are bent on destabilizing. And once instability has itself become stabilized, once formerly fixed textual landmarks are moved, or removed, or simply shifted at will, and once editors, traditionally entrusted with the care of the canon, have themselves been discredited, what texts—if any—will we have in common? Warren's response is cheerfully Beckettian:

> What more do we ask of the world? Are contingency and mutability not good enough for us? Must we retreat from the material to the ideal? We shall have texts, and documentation, the foundations of knowledge, the various manifestations of *Godot*. What will the scholar need to do? The answer may lie in the text of *Godot* itself in the first spoken line, when Estragon says: "Nothing to be done." (59)

Randall McLeod, writing under the pseudonym RANDOM CLOUD, is openly contemptuous of editors. In "from *Tranceformations in the Text of 'Orlando Furioso'*," one-third of the original talk (Carver, Intro., 10), McLeod demonstrates the bibliographical naïveté of McNulty's 1972 Oxford edition of Harington's translation, namely in his treatment of the readings of a press-corrected copy of the 1591 text of the dedicatory letter to Elizabeth as an authorial revision in the second (1607) edition. McLeod is concerned to demonstrate how modern typography invariably misrepresents a Renaissance text. Accordingly, he always uses "photoquotes"—pasted-in snippets of cited texts—instead of typographic resettings, because much of his evidence depends on visualizing the actual typography of the text in question. His more general conclusion: "Merely that photography has killed editing. Period" (72). "The simplest description of Harington's collaborations with his printer is photographic. *Someone* has to tell the editors that *critical* editions suck" (76). Lest his readers miss the point, he asks—twice: "Indeed, what rationale can there be for editing?" McLeod is given to iteration.

In effect, so hermetically sealed, so seamless is the Renaissance-text-cum-Renaissance-typography-and-bibliographic-format that no form of translation other than photographic can do text-in-type justice. "Just as the text is embodied (in the small scale) by the minutiae of its typefaces, so on the large scale it is embodied by its paperstocks and bindings, and the auras of investment and return they symbolize. At all levels, the text is mediated, and always the mediation is inseparable from the text. Because it *is* the text." (80). There is no question of the bibliographic codes' supplementing, contextualizing, or conditioning the lexical code; rather, the bibliographic text replaces the lexical text as the object of scholarly "reading"; lexical content is not only inseparable from and incarnate with physical manifestation, it is irrelevant. The medium is the *only* message. McLeod admits that he has not "read" Harington's translation itself, and his devastating criticism of McNulty's edition is confined to the prefatory letter to Elizabeth, omitting Harington's translation entirely. McLeod collates copies of the first two editions with the volume upside down to forestall the temptation to read it, and he prefaces his attack on McNulty by a serio-comic account of childhood dyslexia, his inability to read serially.

While it is difficult to ignore the sophomoric visual puns with which the piece is studded, they do make their point that visual presentation, not lexical decoding and translation, is what textuality *au nuage au hasard* is all about. But the piece is contemptuous not only of the hapless McNulty (who, being dead, is unable to defend himself) but of *all* editing, especially Bowersian "critical" editing, in which the editor presumes to understand his or her text and to translate its textual essence into more current and more available formats. That means, if I want actually to *read* Harington's *Orlando Furioso*, I must either find a copy of either the 1591 or the 1607 edition, or use McNulty's faulty edition, for Harington's translation was not one of Scolar Press's facsimile volumes. The hard-won authority and expertise of the editor, partial and contingent, subject to later amendment and correction, conditioned by the material conditions and cultural practices of his or her own era, is dismissed as fraudulent because it cannot reproduce what it never has pretended to: the specific historic form and format of a text. For those who need that sort of data, only the actual volumes will serve (or facsimiles thereof), and no critical editor, however bibliographically trained, would pretend otherwise. McGann complains that editors do too little, Warren, that editors do too much; McLeod, that they exist at all.

After bibliography for the dyslexic, it is a relief to come to D. F. McKenzie's meditation on how "Speech-Manuscript-Print" jostle one another in seventeenth-century textual practice. McKenzie is pointed in his evidence and helpful in his footnotes (which McLeod disdains), arguing that, however difficult it is "to find out how people read and what they made of their reading" (89), one can, by a patient mastery of the relevant texts, essay generalized observations on the anxieties of a people moving from one medium to another, from the—to us, paradoxical—certainty of oral "texts" to the uncertainty of written ones (92), from the limited and controlled circulation of texts by manuscript to the unlimited and uncontrolled circulation of printed texts. The law courts and the pulpit supply a number of relevant citations, and McKenzie helpfully restores what was surely the seventeenth-century perspective on these matters when he points out that manuscript was both the "normal form of personal record, and . . . a normal form of publication":

> Manuscripts were economically competitive because printing requires high initial investment in typesetting and a low unit cost . . . is achieved only by having a large number of copies. . . . Manuscript production, however, like binding, was in part a bespoke trade: one-off or several copies could be done on demand; the market was almost self-defining; there was no problem of keeping type standing; and no problem of unsold stocks. (94)

Just as the personal computer initially generated anxiety among writers used to writing (or typing) their manuscripts, so did printing provoke anxiety among writers of the seventeenth century. In response, both "writers and printers [sought] to limit the difference of print by devising ways to suggest its affinities with speaking and writing" (101), which were the older and more familiar forms of textual production. McKenzie even-handedly assesses the relative strengths and limitations of oral and print cultures:

> Printing is much inferior to speech when it comes to conveying the spatial dynamics of speaker and audience. Even word spaces are not speech pauses. Yet space is one of the strongest weapons in a printer's arsenal. The multiplication of copies, portability, and permanence are all, in some way, time-space functions. On the other hand, printing is far superior to speech in the spaced presentation of forms that cannot be read aloud (lists, tables, branching and other graphic configurations), and with those skills at their fingertips, it is only to be expected that printers would try to "set forth" in their own terms at least something of the social space of dialogue. (104)

Editors and editing are not the issues here, but what McKenzie has to say about the varieties of seventeenth-century textuality is of importance to anyone, be they editors or not, interested in how the material condition of that textuality affected its practitioners then and its students now.

Although Ian Willison's "Editorial theory and Practice and the

History of the Book" is nominally about editing, a more apt description would be: "The Rise and Fall of the Book," from its origins in medieval codices to its demise in the age of electronic and cinematic media. Granted, Willison cites Tanselle on "whether one is willing to admit the legitimacy of being interested in the artistic intentions of authors as private individuals rather than as social beings accommodating their intentions to various pressures emerging from the publishing process" (112, quoting *Textual Criticism Since Greg*, 123), but confesses that "As a historian of the book and of authorship, it seems to me I am obliged to favor the second point of view" (113). There follows an abbreviated summary of the "history of the book" in an attempt to "help at least to typify the editorial problem characteristic of a particular phase, and thereby . . . help to direct editorial practice" (113). Thus in reference to the medieval period he favors Derek Pearsall's view of the creatively collaborative scribe over Kane's view of his fundamental mediocrity, and in the period marked by the growing dominance of print he endorses McKenzie's twin axioms, that it was "the technological and entrepreneurial dynamism characteristic of print, rather than script, [that] enabled the codex to become progressively more 'ubiquitous,' socially and geopolitically," and that this same dynamic "meant that print took off in terms not so much of the book, as of what eventually expanded into newspaper publishing and reading" (117).[2]

Willison's sub-text is a Cambridge University Press project, *The History of the Book in Britain*, of which he is a founding editor and McKenzie a volume editor. Modeled on Lucien Febvre's *L'apparition du livre*, the CUP project will cover in six volumes what Willison outlines in nine text pages, so that his essay is necessarily schematic and suggestive. The closest he comes to a satisfying specificity is the discussion of Graham Greene's screen-play for *The Third Man*, which he uses to underscore the diminished status of the individually authored book in the age of film and television, inescapably collaborative media. Several of this film's most memorable features are ascribed to Greene's collaborators: Harry Lime's cuckoo clock speech, to Welles; the astringent ending, to Selznik's intervention; Alex Karas's music; Carol Reed's direction. All problematize the concept of Greene's "authorship." Despite the nominal concern with editorial practice, Willison's concerns are essentially archival and historical, not editorial, and when dealing with books, non-literary. Like McKenzie in *Bibliography and the Socio-*

logy of Texts, Willison casts his net well beyond the texts of canonical authors—i.e., those texts having a market value, cultural, commercial, or academic, that warrant sustained editorial or textual analysis. From his perspective, such "literary" texts are a tiny fraction of the whole, and it is that whole that engages Willison's intellectual commitment. The individual author and his would-be ally, the editor, are quite incidental.

Similarly incidental are the textual questions of the volumes that the incunabulist typically analyzes. Nevertheless, in "Editing Texts in the First Fifteen Years of Printing," Lotte Hellinga, likewise a volume editor for *The History of the Book in Britain*, is concerned to correct the "currently prevalent view that early printing houses were generally indifferent to the quality of the texts they printed" (149). She points out the anachronism of judging by modern standards texts printed in the infancy of printing "as specimens of textual criticism and editing," when it was precisely the phenomenon of print that itself made possible the creation of those standards. Through painstaking analysis of four examples,[3] Hellinga demonstrates the extraordinary care for textual accuracy in the editing, proofing, and printing of these early volumes. She attributes this care to the "uniquely creative" moment of the transition from manuscript to print, for it was then that "the relation of the editor, and the printing house, to the text that was produced" was being creatively reconstituted in reaction to "the new form of dissemination." At this moment in time, she sees the editor as one who, as "tirelessly inventive" as modern authors like Byron and Pound, enjoyed a "freedom to change a word, to improve fluency, to introduce some minor amendments . . . contrary to every modern principle of textual criticism" (148), as "the printing house provided the new medium (as well as its constraints)" that prompted editors "to produce texts adequate to the requirements of a new and unknown readership" (149). Like McKenzie, she is interested in the moment of transition from the dominance of one medium to that of another, and like Willison, she is interested in the relation of author (in this case, the editor acting as author) to printer. She acknowledges that she herself is not primarily interested in the history of the textual transmission of the authors and works she discusses; rather her aim—and ideally that of the textual editor as well—is "to clarify in a historical context the status of the text, by investigating the circumstances of the production of the artifact by which it is transmitted, the standards aimed at by its editor(s) and by the printing house, and by inference, the expectations of its readership" (149). With such broad aims, no one could take exception, and her essay is an exemplary model of their realization.

With even broader aims, Hans Walter Gabler's "Textual Studies and Criticism" surveys the schism between the two sub-fields in English Studies. Much of what he says about the origins and consequences of this split is familiar to anyone who has followed the developments in textual studies in the last decade. What is less familiar is Gabler's relation of his historical account to parallel developments in Germany and France. He notes the current focus on "versions" as alternatives to the critically edited, eclectic text, observing that "To define a version is essentially a critical act" (154). His examples are familiar: Quarto and Folio *King Lear*, Wordsworth's *Prelude*, James's *Roderick Hudson*. He again distinguishes between an apparatus designed to reveal transmissional corruption as demanded by Gregian copy-text editing and an apparatus designed to set forth authorial revision, as he did in TEXT 1,[4] and he notes that versioning frees the editor in his options, for he is no longer "constrained by an all-ruling respect for the author's final intentions. He is not the author's executor, but the historian of the text" (159).

The strength of the essay is its constant referencing of editorial issues to larger theoretical ones; its limitation (at least for English-speaking readers who do not read German) is that many of his references[5] are to German editions and theoretical discussions, for which Hans Zeller's 1975 *Studies in Bibliography* article, "A New Approach to the Critical Constitution of Literary Texts," and Gabler's own work on *Ulysses* must stand as proxies. As an exemplary marriage of textual and critical commentary, he applauds the Oxford Shakespeare's *Textual Companion* (1987), observing that "While commentary (as one of the sectional categories of the editorial apparatus) used to be a basic function of textual studies and editing, . . . editorial and critical commentary in editions has been drastically reduced, and the critical commentary often abandoned altogether" (164). The parallel example in German editing is supplied by Gerhard Seidel's proposal to edit "a poem by Bertolt Brecht as it went through a series of drafts and rewritings" in order to display not only the actual textual materials but also the "impulses" behind those materials as part of the *textual* commentary.

Recording the data is the editor's task; interpreting the "impulses" behind that data constitutes an act of criticism. "Thus, Seidel proposes an integral (genetic) apparatus whose formalizations modulate into discourse. Interrelating the acts and impulses of the writing, the apparatus as extended into commentary responds to the writing process as both a scribal and a mental activity" (165).

Anne Middleton's meditation on "Life in the Margins, or, What's an Annotator to Do?" is—at least for someone who has been constructing a commentary on Richard Hooker for over a decade—the most intellectually challenging essay in the volume. Like Gabler, Middleton is concerned to marry annotation to text commentary, but before the nuptials can be celebrated, an elaborate courtship must precede. The object of her annotational affections, the Athlone Edition of Langland's *Piers Plowman*, is elusive, surviving in three texts that she describes as "three blurry snapshots of something that was in some sort of motion over about twenty years" (174). In this respect it resembles "modern national scriptures."[6]

Unlike Chaucer's texts, *Piers Plowman* has no continuous reception history "of cultural importance [that is] representable as such within a regimen of annotation" (168), such as one would find in a variorum edition. Until the twentieth century it was generally regarded as more an historical than a literary document. Conventional literary annotation, she argues, assumes a stable text, with a continuous reception history, which for its contemporary readers "came into the world as an achieved unity"; its legibility in its own day is assumed as uncontested, and its legibility in our day is viewed as "an act of painstaking restoration—and thus a complement to, and logical extension of, the goals of classical scholarship" (171). The annotators of *Pier Plowman* (there are five of them) face a very different work, albeit one edited according to a "classicist model" of textual criticism, in which the aim is to reconstitute a putative lost original (or originals) from imperfect witnesses. Thus, one cannot simply attach to it a series of notes, be they textual ("crux-busting") or discursive (contextualizing individual elements of the poem). Rather, one must reconceptualize the status of the text itself, lest annotation "unwittingly lend credence to a now-largely-discredited view of the literary work," that it is a static "classic," soaring above the world's materiality, not as it is, a text-in-progress, "a work massively both *of*, and even *about*, this interesting and provisional category of 'modern scripture'" (168–169).

Rather than setting forth a Hegelian master historical narrative, "monolithically reflecting and rationalizing an implicit centrality, the sociopolitical order of the state" (171; cf. Hooker's *Polity*), *Piers Plowman*, Middleton argues, resembles more the medieval annalist's world, "in which need is everywhere present, in which scarcity is the rule of existence, and in which all of the possible agencies of satisfaction are lacking or absent or exist under imminent threat of death." (172)[7] To annotate it, therefore, as if it were "that ideally complete artifact that defines the literary text as conceived by new criticism, or a state narrative of the formation of nature or culture," or even to acknowledge it "as a text that evokes the possibility of these as lying outside itself, then to annotate it as if that were the condition to which it aspired would be . . . to misrepresent it" (172). Nor have the Athlone editors make the task of annotation any easier, supplying no discursive textual notes arguing the adoption of individual readings or solving specific textual cruces in the texts as constituted in their edition. Within the published text volumes, such examples (not elsewhere cross-referenced) are simply embedded in lengthy narrative introductions. Still, Midddleton is reconciled to her (and her colleagues') "Life in the Margins," arguing, in effect, that the Athlone editors realized that "textual evidence theorized as this has been simply did not lend itself to any of the models of annotation available for the presentation of medieval literary text—and they left it to others to propose new ones" (178), as she does here.

A necessary goal of annotation so theorized would be to engage the poem in its very incompletion (as the textual editors have the texts' various *usus scribendi*), "to allow conceptually for the continued mobile and even opportunistic development of Langland's project, while also granting the intense imaginative craftsmanship in the making at every point" (179). Because the format of the Athlone Edition is that of "a *classical* text, a text of antiquity—that is to say a text in a (socially) dead language," as distinct from a "*canonical* text, requiring an annotation regimen emphasizing reception-history," it "demands of the annotator a focus on authorial production . . . in which the author's labors as maker also situate the author himself within its reception history as reviser" (180). Comparing the Athlone texts with Skeat's parallel-text edition and with Gabler's edition of *Ulysses*, Middleton commends their distinct ways of representing "authorial process in the product," and it is this goal the Athlone annotators wish to keep firmly in sight.

One would have relished examples of just how her gang of five's notes would be different from those of her predecessors (notably Skeat)[8] or from those that Chaucerians have produced to undergird their very different texts. The strength of the essay, then, is the rigor with which she reconceptualizes the nature and status of annotation and its relation to the text to which it belongs; its limitations—apart from the density of its thought, which makes it resistant to paraphrase—are a function of its preliminary character. To someone in search of concrete guidance as to how to proceed, it is frustratingly unspecific.

In his introduction to the volume, Larry Carver states that the Conference was convened "to assess where, after a decade of question, challenge, and debate, editorial theory is going." The answer, as supplied by this volume, is "in all directions." Carver's attempt to incorporate all eight contributors under a common rubric, "a call for editor and critic to pay increasing attention to the social setting in which authors live and write their works" (9), is not very helpful. Rather, the eight essays are like puzzle pieces from different puzzles: they can hardly be expected to fit together, and they don't. The closest approach to unity lies in the joint involvement of four with *The History of the Book in Britain* (in addition to McKenzie, Willison, and Hellinga, who are volume editors, McLeod is a contributor). The other four, who *are* editors and critics, work in distinct periods and literatures. All eight may be termed "historians," and "social setting" is an obvious part of any historical narrative, but "history" is scarcely an uncontested category nowadays. Rather, what the volume witnesses—whatever its intentions—is the radical incommensurability of the critical edition as traditionally understood (as by Greg, Bowers, and Tanselle) and of critical editors (or annotators), each quintessential products of the Enlightenment ideals of rationality and order, consistency and authority, with our own post-Enlightenment experience(s) of textuality.[9]

W. Speed Hill
Lehman College and The Graduate Center
The City University of New York

NOTES

1. Both essays are reprinted in *The Textual Condition* (Princeton: Princeton UP, 1991).

2. Citing D. F. McKenzie, "Printing in England from Caxton to Milton," *The Age of Shakespeare*, in vol. 2 of *The Pelican Guide to English Literature* (Harmondsworth: Penguin Books, 1982).

3. Durandus's *Rationale Divinorum Officiorum* printed in 1459 in Mainz by Fust and Schoeffer, Boniface's *Decretals*, printed by the same house in 1465, the Mainz *Catholicon* (c. 1468–69?), and the letters of Jerome, printed by Schoeffer in 1470.

4. See "The Synchrony and Diachrony of Texts," *TEXT* 1 (1984 for 1981): 305–26.

5. The University of Michigan Press has forthcoming a collection of relevant German textual criticism, in translation, to be edited by Gabler and George Bornstein.

6. Citing McGann, *A Critique of Textual Criticism* (1983), 10, 56–59.

7. Quoting Hayden White, "The Value of Narrativity in the Representation of Reality," in *The Content of the Form* (Baltimore: Johns Hopkins UP, 1987), 11.

8. As Ralph Hanna, another Langland annotator, has done in his "Annotating *Piers Plowman*," pp. 153–63, above.

9. For a wide-raging response to the many issues raised in this volume, see D. C. Greetham's review article, "Enlarging the Text," *Review* 14 (1992): 155–87.

Editing in Australia. Ed Paul Eggert. Occasional
   Paper 17, English Department, University
   College ADFA, Canberra. Randwick: New
   South Wales University Press. 1990. ix + 199 pp.

The eleven essays and four notes which comprise this volume
are the products of a conference on editing in Australia which was
held at University College ADFA in Canberra. In the words of its
editor, the volume "reflects an opening of the boundaries of theoretical disagreement, and at precisely the time when the editing of
Australian literature is being seriously taken into hand" (x). A
group of theoretical essays participates in the ongoing scholarly discourse about versioning and the edition-as-process. In "Textual
Studies and Criticism," for example, Hans Walter Gabler affirms
the need to bridge "the gap between textual studies and literary
criticism" and to lead "textual studies out of the ghetto of their self-
inflicted specialist hermeticism" (13). Both Paul Eggert and Peter
Shillingsburg strike familiar chords when they urge recognition of
the multiplicity of forms in which literary works exist and which the
pursuit of a single, eclectic text can obscure. There is little new
here, but it is all well articulated and offers the reader a good sense
of what the status quo is in some textual critical circles today.
   The downside of this status quo is that to the uninitiated such
arguments must seem curiously motivated by the unseen, for while
the names of Greg and Bowers are often invoked in this collection—typically in tandem—their positions are never fully stated or
quoted in their own words. To a reader familiar with the development of textual criticism in this century, elliptical references to the
"Anglo-American tradition" and "single-reading-texts" present no
problem, though such readers would admittedly have little reason
to read general restatements of opposing views. To the reader unfamiliar with this development, "Greg-Bowers" must appear as the
deadly, if amorphous, shade which haunts traditional textual criti-

cism. More troubling, however, is the factual and logical imprecision which can arise in the exorcism of this specter. One writer curiously claims, for example, that the "classical theory of editing presumes that a good edition" attempts to approximate "the author's final intentions in every respect . . . perhaps even page-size and type-face and paper-stock" (169). Another contributor belittles the work of Vinton Dearing, "who devoted a very great amount of intellectual energy to discovering that gold could not, after all, be made out of sea-water" (73); since Dearing's positions are not adequately outlined, such patronizing is either gratuitous or meaningless, depending on one's familiarity with textual criticism.

In what has become almost a trope of the proscription against the work of Greg and Bowers on texts from the printed age, Harold Love observes that the "conditions of electronic transfer mimic those of scribal publication very closely" (66). For such mimicry to occur, however, one has to presume that texts are somehow autonomous semiotic objects whose creation, transmission, and significance were not contextually determined and interpreted. Ironically, the acute sense of historicity behind the work of McGann or McKenzie thus becomes the rationale to elide all historicity. Even more problematic is the exorcism of the Greg-Bower's poltergeist in Jeff Doyle's "McLeoding the Issue: The Printshop and Heywood's *Iron Age*." Doyle, following the work of Randall McLeod, warns readers against the "seamless texture which the Greg-Bowers' edition strives to provide" and wants instead to produce editions which force readers "unwilling to be waylaid" by textual knots "to read through the knots" in order to "emphasise the way in which that kind of reader assumes an authority over the text before he or she has even read it" (164–65).

First of all, there is nothing seamless about either the texts or the editions of the Greg-Bowers line of thinking; there are, in fact, seams everywhere—between text and apparatus, between variants, between substantives and accidentals. To impute a belief in seamlessness to such editions is as erroneous and self-serving as is the imputation of complete disinterest in historicity to the New Critics. Second of all, are textual critics the watchdogs of readers' cognition? It is for readers, after all, that editions are produced, and from long before "Rationale of Copy-Text"—from 1476, in fact—readers of English documents have typically confronted visually discrete texts to which supplementary material may or may not have been appended. Even before the advent of print, *texts* were clearly designed to be lucid and discursive, however much commentary material might have surrounded them. Indeed, every printed document—newspapers, hymnals, cereal boxes, whatever—aims for a physically demarcated and discursive text, even though in each of these cases the layers of composition and authorship are surely as complex as they are in the production of literary works. This is so because readers—as opposed to textual critics—want to read; and it is for readers, as both Eggert and Laurie Hergenhan (179–84) note, that editions need to be produced. If the Greg-Bowers search for the pure authorial text is the construction of the non-existent *text*, editions which force users to confront their own authority are constructed for the non-existent *reader*. I am not personally, in fact, possessed by the spirit of the "classical theory of editing," but like Shillingsburg (43) I think critics ought to try to understand the Greg-Bowers line of thinking before they condemn it, and in the current climate it has become all too easy not to do so.

Perhaps the most successful paper in this book is Stephanie Trigg's "Speaking with the Dead" (136–49), which is concerned with editorial anxiety, or "the repressed knowledge of this desire for full editorial presence and communion with the dead" (139). Carefully and thoughtfully Trigg explores the relations between editors and the ontology of the texts and authors they present. It is largely their own voice, Trigg suggests, which editors reconstruct, and this reconstruction is largely determined by the voices of previous editors of a given work.

Another group of papers relates to recent efforts to develop the editing of Australian literature. Mary Jane Edwards offers a concise, comparative account of the development of the Centre for Editing Early Canadian Texts, Wallace Kirsop reviews the ongoing project to document the history of publishing in Australia, and Laurie Hergenhan discusses the current state of editing in Australia. Harry Heseltine, Elizabeth Morrison, Chris Tiffin, and Gillian Boddy all contribute editorial case-studies; Morrison's and Boddy's essays will be of wider interest to critics working on works disseminated through newspaper publication or on the theoretical problems involved in editing journals never meant to be published.

Despite the success of individual contributions, however, the volume as a whole is not unified or cogent. On a purely practical level, as is too often the case in published conference proceedings there is no index, which becomes particularly lamentable in a volume of topics as diverse as these. While the production quality is generally good, there are some typographically garbled passages (e.g., 73, 163, 164), and notes for two of the contributions (on 167–78 and 189) are misnumbered and/or missing. It is pedantic of me to point this out, but I've always thought that such errors, as human and inevitable as we all know them to be, become particularly egregious in a work devoted to bibliography or textual criticism. The editor indicates that the contributions have been revised (vii), but several of them bear reminders of their original, oral incarnation which are so awkward as to draw attention to themselves and away from the issues being considered. One contributor, for example, observes that certain "matters are rather technical and not really suitable for an occasion such as this" (75); another refers to a book which "will be published this summer (1989)" (90)—one year before the anthology appeared; and another refers in successive sentences to "the issues of this conference" and the "papers in this volume" (163). All these qualities suggest that the book was perhaps hurriedly put together out of insufficient materials. Two of the papers, in fact, have appeared elsewhere, and another, by the author's own admission (177–78), is an oral version never meant to be published; the version which he revised for publication appeared in this journal in 1989. In the end, I have the sense that neither the contributors nor their readers are well-served by a collection as eclectic and casually produced as this. The title will draw the attention of those interested in Australian literature, about which they will find relatively little indeed—only five of fifteen contributions. But readers interested in the rhetoric of textual criticism, who would find much of value in the articles of Eggert, Shillingsburg, and Trigg, are likely to bypass the book entirely, to their loss and the contributors'.

Tim William Machan
Marquette University

Annotation and Its Texts. Ed. Stephen A. Barney.
New York and Oxford: Oxford University Press,
1991. xi + 211 pp. $35.00

Of the ten chapters in this collection, nine derive from a symposium held in April 1988 at the University of California Humanities
Research Institute at Irvine: six were major papers, three responses. The conference was organized by Stephen A. Barney, who invited participants to respond to one or more of a series of questions,
ranging from "Where does a text stop and a footnote begin?" to
"When may annotation be described as emulation, competition?"
(vii–viii). The publication of conference proceedings is perforce a
risky business, and *Annotation and Its Texts* has not escaped from
some of the common problems. To observe that "I'm in fundamental agreement with an informal exchange Steven Barney and Jim
Nohrnberg had on Saturday" (178) was doubtless telling at the time
but hardly survives its moment. More importantly, the choice of
participants is rather heavily weighted towards the earlier periods:
four of the seven major essays are on medieval or earlier materials,
and the problems in glossing such allusive twentieth-century works
as *The Waste Land* or *Ulysses* are scarcely addressed. Finally, the
very concept of "annotation" is defined very broadly indeed, so
that it covers everything from actual markings (*notare*, "to mark")
by medieval scribes to what most of us would call intertextuality.

Taken as a whole, then, the collection is not a major advance in
our understanding of an important but neglected area of critical
and editorial activity. This is not to say, however, that many of the
chapters are anything less than important contributions to particular fields. Perhaps the best of all is the opening essay by James C.
Nohrnberg, "Justifying Narrative: Commentary within Biblical
Storytelling." Theoretically sophisticated and assuming a detailed
knowledge of Biblical texts, the chapter is not easy reading, but
Nohrnberg argues persuasively that "the naturally annotative style

of the Bible precludes any strong distinction of the glosses from the discourse" (31), and he offers a provocative contrast between the glosses in the Old and New Testaments:

> The intratextual glosses in the Old Testament seem to work to recover, conserve, and appropriate received traditions. In the New Testament such glosses seem to work to mark the point at which the Gospel of the "new tradition" began . . . . (35)

In "On the Sociology of Medieval Manuscript Annotation," Stephen G. Nichols concentrates on rubrication in the *Roman de la Rose*. Providing eight black-and-white illustrations of leaves in the Pierpont Morgan Library, Nichols suggests that rubrication "seeks to channel our reading into preset rhetorical and dialectical categories" (60). His major example is the "transgressive rubric" to a passage on Empedocles and Origen, where the rubricator was engaged in "a debate of the utmost importance for medieval culture, the battle for or against thinking in images" (72). Thomas E. Toon's "Dry-Point Annotations in Early English Manuscripts: Understanding Texts and Establishing Contexts" studies annotations which have largely "gone unnoticed for centuries." Objecting to the "tyranny the modern printed page has over our conception of the book" (76), Toon emphasizes "the striking differences between studying a text in manuscript and studying the same text in the printed sources that record the manuscript's contents" (87). Traugott Lawler completes the medieval section of *Annotation and Its Texts* by comparing three commentaries on Walter Map's *Dissuasio Valerii ad Ruffinum ne ducat uxorem*, noting that their primary aim varies from straightforward explanation of individual words to the production of "a kind of rival treatise to the original" (107).

Anthony Grafton studies Garbiel Harvey's marginalia in his copy of Livy, demonstrating that the essential method of reading was not "fixed" but rather "centrifugal and mobile" (124). Moreover, "Harvey's case establishes that reading in the Renaissance was above all rhetorical enterprise": "Reading was a tool not an end" (128). In the one essay specially commissioned for this collection, Peter W. Cosgrove examines Pope's footnotes in the *Dunciad Variorum* and Gibbon's in the *Decline and Fall of Rome*. In the former, the notes "are written and appended by Pope not in order to clarify or authenticate, but in order to satirize the footnote as apparatus" (134–35). In the latter, the notes "go beyond any authenticating function to set up a variety of interactions with the text" (144). Thus:

> Both authors expose the rhetorical elements of the note, but whereas [Pope] does so as a direct attack on the note itself, [Gibbon] does so by employing it against the seduction of the narrative text. In each case the note is wrenched away from its objective aloofness and made to participate in the rhetorical process. (150)

Finally, Thomas McFarland's "Who Was Benjamin Whichcote? or, The Myth of Annotation" is largely anecdotal and autobiographical, recounting his negotiations with various publishers about the presence or absence as well as the placement of (foot)notes. Arguing that annotation is "a combination of six sources of authority and power" (159), he suggests that what "underlies the institution of annotation itself, at least in its modern currency," is nothing less than "anxiety" (165). Indeed, even "seemingly innocuous reference notes" are driven by anxiety; worse, they display two "lies against reality": that they are necessary for a reader to have access to the material being cited; and they they "connect the textual argument with other stanchions of culture, and thus allow the text to take its place in a network of cultural forms" (167). No indeed: truth be told, reference notes only allow other scholars to crib passages without consulting or even reading the original—has not McFarland seen his own translation of a long German passage so appropriated in an unidentified "book presented to me by a genial colleague" (168)? And as for the fragmentation of modern culture, did it not fall to McFarland, "having as guest at an Oxford college one of the world's chief authorities on Wordsworth," to suffer the burden of introducing him to "one of the world's most distinguished classical historians," even though for over two decades they had worked "hardly more than a hundred yards" from each other (176)? This same sad task came his way when he "gave a party for a visiting Cambridge scholar" at Princeton ("an economist of international standing," etc.). So that even though the essay concludes on a note of despair—"footnotes and other apparatus, far from being steel cables woven into a gigantic interconnection of meaning, connect to nothing" (177)—we can at least take some comfort in McFarland's continuing if doomed efforts to connect the great with the also great.

One might have looked to the three responses for some defense

of those benighted souls who, say, think it is better to inform a
reader of Yeats's "The Madness of King Goll" as to the meaning of
"tympan" than either to leave them to guess or to assume they will
not only consult the *OED* but also stumble upon the correct definition (the standard commentary on Yeats's poems has it as a kettle-
drum!); but such is not forthcoming. In "Annotation as Social
Practice," Ralph Hanna III views annotation as "necessary aggression" (183): "as annotator I am always enveloping my author,
always in the act of invading him, or delimiting his possible meaning and relevance" (182). Concentrating on the Middle Ages, especially on legal texts, Laurent Mayali's brief remarks trace the "gradual process of recognition of both the authority of the annotations
and the legitimacy of the annotator" (190).

The volume concludes with "This Is Not an Oral Footnote" by
Jacques Derrida. Barney explains that the text we are offered is "a
kind of translation from two imperfect sources": Derrida's computer prepared typescript, which "mingles two national languages";
and a "garbled transcription of the author's oral presentation,"
made by someone "who could not speak or hear [*sic*; presumably
for "understand" or "comprehend," as one is unlikely to assign
such a task to a deaf-mute] the language of the symposium, that is,
academic literary English" (xi). After further consultation with the
author—in which language and what medium is not specified—the
present chapter has issued forth. Assuredly, it would be too easy to
answer Derrida's query "I do not know if I am making myself
clear" (198) in the negative, or to agree with his assertion (two-
thirds of the way through) that "I have not yet said anything pertinent" (201). Close students of the author, at least, will be interested
in his concluding commentary on such works as *Glas* and *La Carte
postale*. But since Barney himself has declined to "presume to tell
you what Jacques Derrida means" (xi), surely a reviewer should do
no more.

Annotation and Its Texts, then, is less a coherent study of its
announced topic than a miscellany of loosely connected essays,
essays which vary not only in quality (and intelligibility) but also in
their understanding of the term "annotation" itself. Whether the
proceedings of what was doubtless an interesting conference required publication in this form remains an open question.

Richard J. Finneran
University of Tennessee, Knoxville

Representing Modernist Texts: Editing as Interpretation. Ed. George Bornstein. Ann Arbor: The University of Michigan Press, 1991. x + 288 pp. $39.50 cloth; $16.95 paper.

Which version of W. B. Yeats's "The Spur" do you prefer?

> You think it horrible that lust and rage
> ⎡Should dance attendance upon my old age;⎤
> ⎣Should dance attention upon my old age; ⎦
> They were not such a plague when I was young;
> What else have I to spur me into song?

The first version of the second line is given by Richard J. Finneran in his 1989 edition of Yeats's *Poems* and defended in his essay, "Text and Interpretation in the Poems of W. B. Yeats," in *Representing Modernist Texts*. The second version is given by A. Norman Jeffares in *his* 1989 edition of *Yeats's Poems*. The publication history of the poem authorizes both versions. Further evidence exists in the form of manuscripts and typescripts; but, as Finneran acknowledges, "one inevitably turns . . . to evaluation, to interpretation" in making editorial choices of this sort (22). Finneran prefers "attendance" on the grounds that it carries a richer range of relevant connotations. I agree; do you?

The example of "The Spur" illustrates the range of issues addressed by the contributors to this unusual and instructive collection of essays. What is the effect of interpretation upon editing, and vice versa? Are literary texts the products of authors' intentions or of historical collaborations of authors, editors, typesetters, proofreaders, audiences, et al.? How much weight should be given to manuscripts, typescripts, and proofs as opposed to published versions? Can there ever be a definitive edition (a single, incontestably authoritative text) of a written work? The aim of *Representing Modernist Texts*, according to its editor, George Bornstein (himself an experienced editor of Yeats's early poems and essays), is to remind students and scholars of modern literature that "*any* text is an edited text," that no text can be "a transparent conduit of an author's unmediated words" (8).

Students of modern literature have been slower to recognize the problematic nature of textual production and transmission than have students of Renaissance and pre-Renaissance literature, where editorial issues often impinge upon interpretation at quite an early stage. However, as the works of modern authors emerge from copyright, as alternative editions appear, and as new editions of manuscript materials swim into the canon, specialists in the twentieth century will need to become no less conscious of editorial matters. Fierce public controversies over new editions of Joyce's *Ulysses* and Yeats's poems have already occurred, and similar debates are doubtless in the offing. For modernists, too, as Finneran puts it, "the Age of Textual Innocence is lost, and we must now learn to live and to interpret in a wilderness of multiple texts, of multiple arrangements" (39).

Amidst this wilderness, Bornstein's contributors, like Wallace Stevens, place their jars. Ten of the essays focus upon individual modernist writers. Each of these pieces describes editorial problems peculiar to the *oeuvre* of the author in question, and considers their implications for interpretation, canon-formation, and/or literary theory. The contributors include Finneran on Yeats, Noel Polk on William Faulkner, Edward Mendelson on W. H. Auden, the team of A. Walton Litz and Christopher MacGowan on William Carlos Williams, Vicki Mahaffey on James Joyce, Eugene Goodheart on D. H. Lawrence, Andrew J. Kappel on Marianne Moore, Ronald Bush on Ezra Pound, Lawrence S. Rainey on H. D., and Brenda R. Silver on Virginia Woolf. Bracketing these discussions are two general accounts of recent editorial and literary theory. Bornstein's introduction, entitled "Why Editing Matters," and Michael Groden's conclusion, entitled "Contemporary Textual and Literary Theory," offer lucid summaries of complex debates.

Even though theorists such as Jerome McGann have problematized the concept of authorial intention as a criterion of editing, most of the working editors who contribute to this volume still adhere to it. In his recent edition of *Paterson*, for example, Christopher MacGowan seeks "to produce a text as close as possible to Williams's intentions" (55). This is not to say that all of the editors hold to the standard of *final* intentions; indeed, only Finneran aims to reproduce his man's texts "as they stood at the time of his death" (18). Polk, Mendelson, Litz, and MacGowan all prefer prior versions as their base-texts; they argue on various grounds that the author's earlier intentions should take precedence over changes he later introduced or approved.

Thus Polk maintains that only Faulkner's typescripts embody the syntax, punctuation, spacing, and typography that the novelist really intended. Mendelson opts for "the contents of each of [Auden's books of verse] at the time of their first publication" rather than their later, heavily revised versions (160). Litz and MacGowan follow the principles of arrangement of the 1938 *Complete Collected Poems* of Williams rather than the two-volume collected edition of 1950–51. The rationales differ from case to case, but underlying all of them is a shared commitment to a "writer-based" conception of editing (39).

Two other essays which focus upon "writer-based" approaches are contributed by scholars who identify themselves as informed spectators rather than working editors. In "Intentional Error: The Paradox of Editing Joyce's *Ulysses*," Vicki Mahaffey gives a balanced and lucid summary of the issues at stake in the controversy over Hans-Walter Gabler's *Ulysses: A Critical and Synoptic Edition* (1984). Mahaffey explains Gabler's conception of an ideal copy-text of *Ulysses* assembled from selected manuscript sources, without reference to published versions of the novel. She describes this conception as "conservative (traditional) in the premium [it] sets on authorial intention" but radical in its refusal to privilege any one manuscript as embodying that intention; Gabler sees composition "as *process* rather than product" and "define[s] authorial intention as multiple and changing" (172).

The importance of authorial intention is also affirmed by Eugene Goodheart in an essay which examines the new Cambridge University Press edition of the works of D. H. Lawrence. Noting that some of the Cambridge editors restore passages censored by Lawrence at the suggestion of his publishers, Goodheart makes a striking connection between the issue of censorship and the role of intention in editorial theory.

> The very idea of censorship brings the question of intention into the foreground, for censorship entails the counterforce of authorial desire or intentions. If there were no intention, then the alterations produced by an intentionless and consequently authorless text would not be described as censor-

ship. (225)

A social or historicist conception of texts, Goodheart argues, threatens freedom of expression by subjecting the artist's intention to "the appropriating, bowdlerizing efforts of communities of readers" and the "tyranny . . . of prevailing contemporary assumptions" (238–9).

But what if the censorship is not imposed from outside? What if it is undertaken voluntarily by the author as self-editing? This question arises in several of the essays in George Bornstein's collection, among them the late Andrew J. Kappel's "Complete with Omissions: The Text of Marianne Moore's *Complete Poems*." Moore ruthlessly pruned and suppressed many of her poems when they were republished, so that "Nine Nectarines," for example, was reduced "to approximately half its original length" (152). Kappel surveys the alterations in Moore's collections, from *Observations* (1924) to *Complete Poems* (1981), and analyzes her motives for making the changes; but he stops short of suggesting which versions should become the copy-texts of a future edition or how such an edition might register the large body of variants that Moore created.

That a writer's political profile may be affected by the editing of unpublished manuscripts and the restoration of censored material is the gist of the essays on Ezra Pound, H. D., and Virginia Woolf in *Representing Modernist Texts*. Ronald Bush adduces evidence from the manuscripts of Pound's Pisan and post-Pisan cantos to refute postmodernist characterizations of the author's politics and poetics as totalitarian. According to Bush, a careful study of the genesis of the later cantos reveals not a monolithic outlook but a dialogue of "conflicting ideologies" (88). A fascistic inclination toward closure, natural authority, patriarchy, and misogyny coexists in Pound's work with an anarchic inclination toward "programmatic openness," skepticism, antiauthoritarianism, liberation, and feminism (70). Deploying the scrupulous scholarship characteristic of all his work, Bush effectively counters recent oversimplifications of Pound's work; yet he may concede too much to his opponents by appearing to grant postmodernism an uncontested right to such terms as openness, tentativeness, and noncoerciveness.

Is Hilda Doolittle a major writer whom the patriarchy has edited to the margins of the modernist canon? The answer suggested by much recent scholarship is *yes*. In "Canon, Gender, and Text: The

Case of H. D.," Lawrence S. Rainey surveys new editions of previously unpublished manuscripts, along with many of the latest biographical and critical studies, and asks whether H. D. merits the central canonical status that her revisionist supporters have claimed for her on the basis of her "progressive politics" and her "identification with . . . Blacks, Jews, Indians, homosexuals and lesbians, women, even artists" (108). Rainey's answer, based upon a variety of considerations, is a resounding *no*. "The creation of the new 'H.D.' as the canonical figure for a poetics of political correctness is achieved largely . . . through the neglect of bibliographical, textual, and editorial considerations in assessing her work's genesis and development" (116). Rainey's eloquent rebuttal may be the boldest and most controversial piece in *Representing Modernist Texts*.

Virginia Woolf's place in the modernist canon is likewise being reassessed in the light of newly published manuscript materials. In "Textual Criticism as Feminist Practice: Or, Who's Afraid of Virginia Woolf Part II," Brenda R. Silver focuses upon "the editing and reception of manuscript versions of Woolf's novels," and the changes which those versions have made in "the way we understand her politics and art" (194). According to Silver, the manuscript versions of such novels as *The Waves, The Years*, and *The Voyage Out* express "Woolf's social and political critique, including her anger," more explicitly than do the published versions, which have undergone a process of self-censorship (209). (Since Woolf published her own novels, outside censorship does not come into play except as internalized by the writer.) If the manuscript versions are read with the published versions as a "composite text," multiple and palimpsestic rather than single and unitary, Woolf's works appear to be more radical and feminist, less apolitical and aestheticized, than criticism has traditionally allowed (206). She thus becomes more central to a feminist revision of the modernist canon.

Silver follows H. D.'s biographer, Susan Stanford Friedman, in describing manuscript drafts as a sort of "textual unconscious" which is equivalent to the "political unconscious" of the author (207). Woolf's manuscripts, then, reveal "the process of condensing, displacing, or erasing an anger that is culturally forbidden from the 'final,' public, published versions of [the] texts" (208). In other words, the manuscripts lend themselves to a "psycho-political hermeneutic" of the sort outlined by Sandra Gilbert and Susan

Gubar in *The Madwoman in the Attic* (207). As Gilbert and Gubar
adapted Harold Bloom's theory of the anxiety of influence to feminist purposes, so Silver and Friedman adapt McGann's theory of
historicized texts. As Silver puts it, "Friedman's insistence that the
composite, palimpsestic work reveals continually shifting scenes of
repression, censorship,and confrontation . . . both acknowledges
McGann's influence and helps to validate his concept of the unsta-
ble text" (216).

For Silver, then, as her title suggests, textual criticism is an excit-
ing new branch of "feminist practice." It is interesting to read her
essay on Woolf in conjunction with Eugene Goodheart's on Lawrence, because Silver's conception of feminist practice seems to
illustrate the dangers of social or historicist editing against which
Goodheart warns. By downplaying the role of the author's final
intention, feminist editors and critics are able to present a more
radical Woolf who better fits a current political agendum. The aim
of feminist editing, as Silver describes it, is to recover or generate a
text which reveals the madwoman in the attic—even if, as in the
case of Woolf, the author clearly did not wish a madwoman to
appear.

The juxtaposition of Silver's essay with Goodheart's amply illustrates the central contention of *Representing Modernist Texts*:
namely, that editorial theory and practice are inseparable from literary theory and interpretation. George Bornstein's collection
offers an instructive digest of recent editorial theory and editorial
work on modernist authors. The book could usefully be assigned in
a graduate course on twentieth-century literature to give students
an overview of a significant stratum of contemporary scholarship. It
is a pity that room could not have been made for essays on T. S.
Eliot, Wallace Stevens, Gertrude Stein, and perhaps Robert Frost.
Nevertheless, the collection is original in its conception and valuable for the wealth of thought and information it contains. The
University of Michigan Press deserves praise for putting the book
directly into paperback, thus making it affordable to individual students and scholars as well as to libraries.

Can any self-respecting review of a book on editing close without pointing out a few typographical errors? On p. 30 we are introduced to Mrs. W. B. "Years" and on p. 77 to "Sigusmundo"
Malatesta. On p. 267 an obligation is reduced to an "oligation." In
other words, not even editors being edited by another editor can

entirely safeguard their texts from the insidious corruption of the typo. If large claims are to be made for the craft of editing, one of them might well be that few other disciplines are such effective teachers of humility.

Hugh Witemeyer
University of New Mexico

Medieval Literature: Texts and Interpretation. Ed. Tim William Machan. Medieval & Renaissance Texts & Studies 79. Binghamton, N.Y.: Medieval & Renaissance Texts & Studies, 1991. vi + 202 pp. $20.00

Even though it says so at both beginning (4) and end (14), Tim William Machan's introduction, "Late Middle English Texts and the Higher and Lower Criticisms," to this collection of eight essays does not simply find "theoretical overlaps between 'textual criticism' and 'literary interpretation'": it equates the two. Likewise, in the process, his introduction wholly merges the two constituents of the volume's subtitle, "Texts and Interpretation." Indeed, after reading the introduction I cannot see that the subtitle adds anything to the title, "Medieval Literature." For as Machan points out, "the various critical approaches articulate not simply textual solutions but textual facts and problems as well; and the textual facts are what they are *because* they are being analyzed from a traditional textual critical perspective, which employs a particular definition of evidence and which recognizes the validity of particular analytical approaches" (12)—and this sentence works equally well with the words "textual" and "critical" eliminated: "the various approaches articulate not simply solutions but facts and problems as well; and the facts are what they are *because* they are being analyzed from a traditional perspective, which employs a particular definition of evidence and which recognizes the validity of particular analytical approaches." Machan quotes from Jerome McGann that "knowledge, in short, is a function of the particular lexicon, grammar, and usage in which it is pursued and framed" (6, n. 5), but has just finished saying himself that "the perspective of the linguist shapes linguistic phenomena as much as that of the historian shapes historical events or that of the literary interpreter shapes literature" (6).

In the second volume (1976) of his *Supplement to the Oxford English Dictionary*, Robert Burchfield left the *OED* entries for "**hermeneut** and related words" alone but could not resist adding, among others, the following example:

> **1967** J. MACQUARRIE *God-Talk* vii. 148 We could say that history is the hermeneutic of historical existence, or even that physics . . is the hermeneutic of nature.

Yet with the very words "historical existence" and "nature," of course, the hermeneut has already intervened. As Housman, following Aristotle, realized, however, to be alive is to want to know, [1] even if "knowing" cannot ever be anything more than mental exercise. Hence both the sanction for and (I hope) inevitability of, not only the essays in Machan's collection, but also his introduction and this review. [2]

* * *

Perhaps indicating the futility of classification, the rubrics "Authors and Editors" for the first four essays (by Hanna, Pearsall, Brewer, and Edwards) and "Manuscripts and Contexts" for the last four (by Beadle, Boffey, Keiser, and Reames) found in the table of contents do not reappear in either the body of the book or the publisher's blurb on p. [199], though Machan does allude to them at the close of his introduction (14–15).

In the first essay, "Presenting Chaucer as Author" ([17]–39), Ralph Hanna III provides a Cook's tour of modern editions' handling of the various clouds of witnesses behind—or above or below or around—several Chaucerian works before digging into *Parlement of Foules* 680–92, "the roundel sung by the birds" (29–35), convincingly, and *General Prologue* 217 with its "expletive" *eek* found in some manuscripts but not others, inconclusively (35–38).

Pace his opening remark that "none of us is going to be very ready to allow that someone else's intuitive feel [for the music of Chaucer's verse] is better than our own" ([41]), Derek Pearsall had convinced me, at least, time and again in his essay "Chaucer's Meter: The Evidence of the Manuscripts" that the earlier manuscripts of the *Canterbury Tales* scan better than either later ones or modern editions—for instance, "Than had your tale al be told in vayn" better than "Thanne haddë yourë tale be toold in veyn" or

"Thanne haddë your tale al be toold in veyn" (*Nun's Priest's Prologue* B 3989, VII.2799), both of the latter, according to Pearsall, having "a metronome-like regularity" and unable to "bear comparison with the naturalness and syntactic adequacy of the line as first quoted" (46). Trouble is, when I checked this line against the work Pearsall cites—P. G. Ruggiers, ed., *Geoffrey Chaucer, The Canterbury Tales: A Facsimile and Transcription of the Hengwrt Manuscript, with Variants from the Ellesmere Manuscript* (52, n. 16)—I found that Hengwrt and Ellesmere actually have "Thanne hadde youre tale al be toold in veyn," with a tag on "toold" in Ellesmere (Ruggiers, 390). I had already remembered that in *General Prologue* 1, Hengwrt and Ellesmere each have barred double *l*, not simply *Aueryll* or *Aprill* (45), and that Ellesmere has *hise*. These things, then (and maybe others; I have done no more checking), vitiate both of Pearsall's conclusions, that Hengwrt and Ellesmere show "what must be Chaucer's" metrical practice and that

> The freedom and generosity in the conception of the rhythmical possibilities of the pentameter, the audacity of variation and experimentation, and the subtle sense of the relation between rhetorical and syntactical impetus and rhythmical variation, are surely positive characteristics of the creative poet at work, while the mending and smoothing of lines to produce a mechanically regular syllable count or alternation of stressed and unstressed syllables, at the expense of natural speech rhythms, are surely likely to be characteristic of the improving scribe or editor. (51)

The latest in Charlotte Brewer's series of rolling criticisms of the Kane and Kane-Donaldson editions of *Piers Plowman*, "Authorial [v]s. Scribal Writing in *Piers Plowman*" ([59]–89), registers five objections: (1) the editions are hard to use, (2) "Langland may have written more than just three versions of the poem" (67), (3) Kane and Donaldson distinguish between authorial and scribal variation inconsistently and without sufficient grounds, (4) "the discrepancy between the editorial methodology of the A and the B Editions" (60), and (5) "among many of the A manuscript variants rejected by Kane are readings that . . . are also the readings of the B-Text archetype" (81–82).

The first objection applies with equal force to Brewer's own way (which I do not object to) of publishing her criticisms, in dissertation and scattered essays, and anyhow, meeting this objection fully (I do not exaggerate) would make the Kane-Donaldson edition

7,000 pages long instead of 700—which would entail new problems of accessibility. The second objection does not get down to specifics, even though Brewer has just finished explaining at length (63–66) that this is precisely what objections to Kane-Donaldson must do.

To the seemingly intractable authorial/scribal problem, I offer an observation of my own: Kane-Donaldson's pairing of manuscripts R and F—in their words, "the least speculative" and one "whose genetic character can be established to the limit of proof possible in such matters" (37, n. 47)—rests primarily on the existence of 504 examples of the variational group RF (21). Yet the variational group FH occurs 87 times before "H ceases" at Passus V, line 127 (29, n. 29). This stretch of the poem has only 65 examples of RF (25). "R is defective in Prol. 1–124 and I 141–II 40" (29, n. 29), but these two stretches have only 19 examples of FH (29). Thus in those places where both RF and FH variation *can* occur, the former does so 65 times, the latter 68. This certainly makes RF, and perhaps F as well, less maverick.

In the course of raising her fourth objection, Brewer maintains that Kane can "pronounc[e] strongly" in a single footnote in his edition of the A version (79), but that "three footnotes to the B-Text introduction" are insufficient for making a point (81). As part of her fifth objection, she claims that "Kane nowhere indicates to his readers the existence of such agreements between B and the A variants that he rejects for his text" (82). Whether Kane does or does not (in a passage from Kane, 446–47, quoted by Brewer on page 87, he certainly seems to), Kane and Donaldson do, and offer a reason for them: Langland "used a scribal copy of **A** for his revision to **B**" (Kane-Donaldson, 98, n. 2, which also cites 205 and 210f.).

Brewer mentions another possible explanation of B readings in A manuscripts: the C word, "contamination, scribes of A introducing (corrupt) archetypal B readings into their exemplars" (84). She hastens to add, however, that "this explanation . . . brings with it further problems, and was sensibly rejected," citing her dissertation. But contamination (or let's call it conflation) can also explain two other puzzles that Brewer has already noted: David Fowler's finding that "over stretches of the poem where A and B read equivalent text (2,200) lines, [Kane and Donaldson] emend one reading every sixty-two lines to restore alliteration; over stretches of text new in B (1100 lines), they emend one reading every eight lines to restore alliteration"[3] and Lee Patterson's that "Where A, B, and C read equivalent text (Patterson estimates this as some 1900 lines), once every fourteen lines (on average), B and C wrongly reproduce a reading which was correctly preserved in A. Where A and B alone read equivalent text (400 lines), once every 1.3 lines (on average), B wrongly reproduces a reading correctly preserved in A" (66, n. 16).

Though, on their own showing, the fourth through sixth essays—A. S. G. Edwards's "Middle English Romance: The Limits of Editing, the Limits of Criticism," Richard Beadle's "The York Cycle: Texts, Performances, and the Bases for Critical Enquiry," and Julia Boffey's "Middle English Lyrics: Texts and Interpretations"—deal with broadly similar materials, Edwards and Beadle come out at opposite ends: Edwards concludes that "there is little middle ground between textual and literary criticism in respect to the romances" (104), Beadle that for early drama, "at least[,] textual and literary studies are, for many important purposes, coextensive" (112). Boffey continues to speak of textual and literary criticism as different things, but does a lot with—and of—both, well. I suggest Edwards read both Beadle's and Boffey's essays, then go back and take another look at his subject. Citing G. Thomas Tanselle's seminal article, "Classical, Biblical, and Medieval Textual Criticism and Modern Editing," Beadle also points out that textual criticism "cannot be divorced from detailed codicological understanding . . . and extensive recourse to the use of external evidence;" (112 and n. 22).

In "*Ordinatio* in the Manuscripts of John Lydgate's *Lyf of Our Lady*: Its value for the Reader, Its Challenge for the Modern Editor," George R. Keiser demonstrates "the relevance of apparatus": the "*incipits, explicits,* rubrics, text-divisions, glosses, and other apparatus found in manuscripts" (140). Authors touched upon include Chaucer, Gower, Hoccleve, Malory, and Love, as well as Lydgate.

The last piece, Sherry L. Reames's "*Mouvance* and Interpretation in Late-Medieval Latin: The Legend of St. Cecilia in British Breviaries," falls little short of a monograph. Reames finds that "a remarkably large number of people—from official and semi-official compilers down to mere copyists—seem to have participated in the process" of revising breviary lessons (169, following Pierre Salmon);

in the breviaries, "The very nature of the legend [of St. Cecilia] seems to be changing . . . horizontal gaps in the narrative are carefully filled while allegorical possibilities are pruned away" (188–89); "A good deal of cultural history is preserved in these manuscripts—unnoticed until now because the scholars in the field were only looking for the original, authorial versions" (189).

General ([191]–194) and manuscript ([195]–198) indexes round off this excellent volume, which has the range and accessibility to serve as a textbook.

David Yerkes
Columbia University

NOTES

1. "'[A]ll men possess by nature a craving for knowledge'": A. E. Housman, *Introductory Lecture Delivered before the Faculties of Arts and Laws and of Science in University College London October 3, 1892* (Cambridge: Cambridge University Press, 1937), p. 32. See also, passim, Brand Blanshard, *The Nature of Thought*, 2 vols. (London: George Allen & Unwin, 1939), which opens: "Thought is that activity of mind which aims directly at truth" (§1, p. [51]).

2. Still, I cannot let one "fact" in Machan's introduction pass unchallenged: "There is some evidence that Middle English manuscripts could be corrected from one another, but such manuscripts are decide[d]ly the exception" (12, n. 26). In my experience a large proportion of Middle English manuscripts may show, physically, such "correction."

3. Brewer applies the D word, "devastating," here to Fowler's review of the Kane-Donaldson edition (65); I would reserve it for Kane's review of the Rigg-Brewer edition (cited in Machan's introduction, 8, n. 11).

Pope's "Dunciad" of 1728: A History and Facsimile. David L. Vander Meulen. Charlottesville and London: University Press of Virginia, 1991. xvii + 170 pp. $40.00

The facsimile of Pope's *Dunciad* here printed, in its original size, is one of the two copies in the Berg Collection of the New York Public Library, in which Pope's friend, the younger Jonathan Richardson, recorded his collations of earlier MS drafts of the 1728 text. The "history" of the title discusses the gestation, birth, and maturation of the first *Dunciad*; its intricate publication history; the migration of the Richardson copies from the eighteenth century to the present; Pope's relationship with Richardson and the reasons for asking him to undertake the task of collation; the complex relationship of the MS to the text; and the light that relationship casts on the evolution of the poem and thus on Pope's methods and habits of composition.

Although, as Vander Meulen correctly states, his book is a "noncritical" edition, in the sense that it reproduces rather than reconstructs the text, he nevertheless provides in five appendices "much of the textual apparatus commonly associated with a critical edition" (xiv). These print, with some peripheral exceptions (e.g., variations in printer's ornaments), a full collation of the authorized 1728 impressions; accounts of the two unauthorized editions (Dublin and, possibly, Edinburgh) with a list of the names which the Dublin reprint selects to fill Pope's blanks; a record of the varieties and states of the altar frontispiece; a facsimile of the 1728 advertisement for *The Progress of Dulness*; and the annotations in the copy of the 1728 *Dunciad* in the Huntington.

In addition to presenting the "text and typography of the earliest edition in a form as close to the original as photofacsimile will allow" (xii), the book's second purpose is to complement Maynard Mack's transcription of Richardson's marginalia in *The Last and*

Greatest Art: Some Unpublished Poetical Manuscripts of Alexander Pope (1984). Mack's transcription, scrupulously recorded and, for convenience, keyed to the Twickenham Edition, necessarily requires the reader, at times awkwardly, to juggle two volumes; the present facsimile, with the marginalia (usually) on the same page with the text, makes the comparison of earlier (modified or discarded) and printed lines not only easier but more vivid, intelligible, and instructive. Considerable value still attaches to Mack's transcription, however, for though Richardson's hand is normally quite legible, occasionally lines are crowded or blurred by show-through. In these instances Mack's eye can be trusted. I should add, in all fairness, that show-through, though usually present, becomes an impediment to reading on only a relatively few pages.

Vander Meulen's introductory pages cover the full range of problems and questions raised by the 1728 text and marginalia. But since a short review cannot allow for full details, I mention only three matters about which I found his analyses and observations especially illuminating: his examination of the role played by Swift in the genesis of the poem; his analysis of the relationship, and priority, of the printings of the two early issues (duodecimo, octavo) of the 1728 *Dunciad*; his reasons for accepting the first and second "Broglio" manuscripts as predating the 1728 publication.

In a more general way, the value of this volume extends beyond Pope and informs larger concerns—the creative process, the relationships of author, text, reader. Vander Meulen touches on a few of these concerns in his brief references to Pope's use of blanks or initials and dashes to disguise the full names of his victims: the incomplete names "encouraged the reader's participation," for to make sense of a line the reader had to supply sense and in doing so had to take the responsibility following upon that act. Moreover, by leaving the names open, the satire would gain a kind of timelessness. Who, while or after reading the *Dunciad*, cannot think of modern equivalents of Curll, Theobald, Dennis? Although Pope's later filling out the names made the satire "more determinate, and possibly weaker, . . . the identifications offered better evidence for the poem's general assertions" (24). In a literary-critical world saturated by theory, observations like these come as a refreshing reminder of the need first to become saturated in the evidence of the creative mind at work, before claiming originality for discovering the fact of textual instability and the role played by the reader in simultaneously contributing to that instability and to its partial remedy.

Such considerations aside, this handsomely printed, scrupulously reasoned book is a valuable contribution to our understanding of Pope and, not incidentally, to eighteenth-century conceptions of "correctness."

John H. Middendorf
Columbia University

The Society for
Textual Scholarship

Founded in 1979, the Society for Textual Scholarship is an organization devoted to providing a forum, in its biennial conferences and its journal *TEXT*, for the discussion of the interdisciplinary implications of current research into various aspects of contemporary textual work: the discovery, enumeration, description, bibliographical analysis, editing, and annotation of texts in disciplines such as literature (particularly European, American, and Oriental), history, musicology, classical and biblical studies, philosophy, art history, legal history, history of science and technology, computer science, library science, lexicography, epigraphy, palaeography, codicology, cinema studies, theater, linguistics, and textual and literary theory. All these, and several other fields, have been represented in conference or STS publication since the first gathering in New York in 1981, and the conference is now recognized as the most wide-ranging and most influential of meetings of textual scholars in the world. In the first seven conferences, over 600 papers have been presented by speakers representing the disciplines listed above, with a chronological range of topics from early Egyptian and Mycenean inscriptions and pre-exilic biblical texts to computer concordances of present-day authors and the examination of governmental and foundation funding for editing and textual research.

The seven presidents of the Society represent a similarly wide range of authority, from Anglo-American bibliography via Renaissance and neo-Latin scholarship to biblical studies and linguistics, philosophy, 17th-century English literature, and Italian opera: G. Thomas Tanselle (*John Simon Guggenheim Memorial Foundation*, 1981–83), Paul Oskar Kristeller (*Columbia University*, 1983–85), Fredson Bowers, (*University of Virginia*, 1985–87), Eugene A. Nida (*American Bible Society*, 1987–89), Jo Ann Boydston (*Center for Dewey Studies*, 1989–91), James Thorpe (*Huntington Library*, 1991–93), and Philip Gossett (*University of Chicago*, 1993–95). The ninety members of the Society's Advisory board, which evaluates contributions to *TEXT*, show a parallel range of interests, with a large international component.

The range of editorial work represented by members, conferees, advisors, or officers of STS is very broad, including editors of, for example, the *Anchor Bible* and the Garland James Joyce, various Old English works, Marguerite de Navarre, Chaucer, Langland, Gower, Wycliff, Hoccleve, the Polyphonic *Kyrie*, the Towneley Plays, Wyatt, Shakespeare, G. Bellini, R. Hooker, Donne, Milton, Dryden, Rochester, Pope, Jonson, Klopstock, Voltaire, Hume, Blake, Burns, Scott, Wordsworth, Coleridge, Byron, Shelley, Keats, J. F. Cooper, Rossini, Thackeray, Melville, Verdi, Flaubert, Lewis Carroll, Edison, Olmstead, Morris, Henry Adams, Conrad, D. W. Griffith, Yugoslav oral epic, Proust, Dewey, Santayana, Yeats Pound, O'Neill, Orson Welles, Spender, Pinter, and others.

The biennial conferences, held in New York City, encourage the same interdisciplinary range. While there are usually some period or author-centered sessions (e.g., on medieval, Renaissance, or modern textual studies), most sessions address a general textual problem, with contributions from speakers in various disciplines. Such sessions have included *Feminism and Editing Texts by Women, Computerizing Critical Editions, Contemporary Literary Theory and Textual Criticism, Authorial Revision, Non-Verbal Texts, Words and Music, Editorial Ethics, Editors and the Problem of Intention, The Relations of Text and Document, The Meaning of the Text, Problems in Attribution and Provenance, Stemmatics and Contamination.* A typical illustration of the cross-disciplinary aims of STS is a session at the 1987 conference called *Text as Performance, Representation, Reconstruction*, in which G. E. Bentley, Jr., spoke on Blake's verbal and visual texts as differing "performances," Stephen Orgel discussed the "representation" of a Shakespeare "score" of a play on stage, Charles E. Beveridge analyzed the relations between Olmstead's "greensward plan" for Central Park and its implementation in the park itself, and Boyd H. Davis illustrated the problems of reconstruction Saussure's *Cours* from the multilingual students' notes of lectures: four speakers from four very different disciplines, each confronted with the issue of observing the "text" in the "performance." Complementing these general sessions, STS members may also arrange their own sessions at the conferences (for example, on specific editorial projects), in which case they are responsible for confirming speakers and topics. At the conferences, a prize is awarded for a distinguished essay in textual scholarship published in the previous two years.

The editors welcome contributions for future volumes of *TEXT*. Submissions are read and evaluated by selected members of the STS Advisory Board. The Society also welcomes applications for membership. All enquiries, or submissions to *TEXT* (except requests about reviews or books for review), should be sent to:

D. C. Greetham
Executive Director
Society for Textual Scholarship
Ph.D. Program in English, Box 510
CUNY Graduate Center
33 West 42 Street
New York, NY 10036–8099
Tel: 212 642–2227 / 873–2442; Fax: 212 642–2205

Enquiries about reviews, or books for review, should be sent to:
Peter L. Shillingsburg
Book Review Editor, *TEXT*
Department of English
Mississippi State University
Starkville, MS 39762
Tel: 601 325–3644

Officers

President	Philip Gossett, University of Chicago
Executive Director	D. C. Greetham, CUNY Graduate School
Secretary-Treasurer	Adam Goldberger, CUNY Graduate School

Executive Committee

James Beck, Columbia University
Betty T. Bennett, American University
Ronald Broude, Broude Trust

Michael Carter, New York University
Mervin R. Dilts, New York University
Richard J. Finneran, University of Tennessee
W. Speed Hill, Lehman College and Graduate Center, CUNY
Reese V. Jenkins, Papers of Thomas A. Edison
Robert Penella, Fordham University
Mary B. Speer, Rutgers University
G. Thomas Tanselle, John Simon Guggenheim Memorial
    Foundation
Robert Whittaker, Lehman College, CUNY
Frederic W. Wilson, Pierpont Morgan Library

Past Presidents

James Thorpe, Huntington Library (1991–93)
Jo Ann Boydston, Center for Dewey Studies (1989–91)
Eugene A. Nida, Bible Society of America (1987–89)
Fredson Bowers, University of Virginia (1985–87)
Paul Oskar Kristeller, Columbia University (1983–85)
G. Thomas Tanselle, John Simon Guggenheim Memorial
    Foundation (1981–83)

President-Designate

Bruce M. Metzger, Princeton Theological Seminary (1995–97)

Contents of Previous Volumes

Volume 2 (1985)